Justice, Mercy, and Well-Being

Justice, Mercy, and Well-Being

Interdisciplinary Perspectives

EDITED BY PETER G. BOLT
AND JAMES R. HARRISON

☙PICKWICK *Publications* • Eugene, Oregon

JUSTICE, MERCY, AND WELL-BEING
Interdisciplinary Perspectives

Copyright © 2020 Wipf and Stock Publishers. All rights reserved. Except for brief quotations in critical publications or reviews, no part of this book may be reproduced in any manner without prior written permission from the publisher. Write: Permissions, Wipf and Stock Publishers, 199 W. 8th Ave., Suite 3, Eugene, OR 97401.

Pickwick Publications
An Imprint of Wipf and Stock Publishers
199 W. 8th Ave., Suite 3
Eugene, OR 97401

www.wipfandstock.com

PAPERBACK ISBN: 978-1-5326-7467-9
HARDCOVER ISBN: 978-1-5326-7468-6
EBOOK ISBN: 978-1-5326-7469-3

Cataloguing-in-Publication data:

Names: Bolt, Peter G., editor. | Harrison, James R., editor.

Title: Justice, mercy, and well-being : interdisciplinary perspectives / edited by Peter G. Bolt and James R. Harrison.

Description: Eugene, OR : Pickwick Publications, 2020 | Includes bibliographical references.

Identifiers: ISBN 978-1-5326-7467-9 (paperback) | ISBN 978-1-5326-7468-6 (hardcover) | ISBN 978-1-5326-7469-3 (ebook)

Subjects: LCSH: Justice. | Mercy. | Benevolence. | Christianity and Justice. | Christian ethics.

Classification: BJ1533.K5 J86 2020 (print) | BJ1533.K5 J86 (ebook)

Manufactured in the U.S.A.   MARCH 5, 2020

Contents

Contributors | ix

Introduction—Finding Well-Being in an Unjust and Unmerciful World | 1
        JAMES R. HARRISON

Part A   The Contours of Well-Being—Justice and Mercy in Panorama

    1 Jesus, the Gospels, and the Kingdom of God in Constitutional Perspective | 33
        STEPHEN C. BARTON

    2 Mercy as Divine Self-Giving—Seven Theses toward a Kenotic Ecclesiology | 56
        STEPHEN PICKARD

Part B   When Mercy Seasons Justice—Well-Being in Exegetical Perspective

    3 "I Will Walk in Your Midst"—The Implications of Leviticus 26:3–13 for Social Well-Being | 71
        G. GEOFFREY HARPER

    4 Justice, Mercy, and Predestination in Romans | 89
        ROBERT TILLEY

Part C   Encountering the Just and Merciful God—Well-Being in Theological Perspective

    5 Social Well-Being and the Humanity of God | 113
        PETER G. BOLT

    6 Asceticism, Well-Being, and Compassion in Maximus the Confessor | 134
        DORU COSTACHE

7   A Christology of Human Flourishing—Justice and Divine Participation | 148
         PETER R. LAUGHLIN

8   God Is Love, God Is Just, God Is Merciful—but Is God Tolerant?—The Relationship of Divine Love, Justice, and Mercy from a Wesleyan Perspective | 160
         DAVID B. MCEWAN

9   The Single Strife—Nurturing Wholeness in the Lives of Single Christians | 178
         KAREN M. PACK

Part D   Seeking the Welfare of the City—First-Century Perspectives on Well-Being

10   The "Clemency" of Nero and Paul's Language of "Mercy" in Romans—Paul's Reconfiguration of Imperial Values in Mid-Fifties Rome | 193
         JAMES R. HARRISON

Part E   Well-Being and Aboriginal Australians—Justice, Mercy, and Hope

11   Aboriginal Interpretations of Radical Hope—Noel Pearson's Radical Hope and Warwick Thornton's Samson and Delilah | 223
         NEIL HOLM

Part F   Healthcare, Memory Loss, and Well-Being—Ancient and Modern Perspectives

12   Late Antique Healthcare and the Early Christian Reinterpretation of Sickness and Disease | 251
         ADAM G. COOPER

13   New Every Morning—Spiritual Care in the Context of Memory Loss | 262
         STEPHEN SMITH AND CATHERINE KLEEMANN

Part G   The Moral Compass of Well-Being

14   Spiritual Care and Well-Being—Contradictions, Complexities, and Contexts | 279
         PETER CARBLIS

15 Moral Judgment—Where Christianity and Cognitive Science Intersect | 294
    ANTONIOS KALDAS

Part H   Well-Being and the Visual Arts

16 Seeing in New Ways—Justice, Mercy, and Social Well-Being through the Arts | 315
    PETER MUDGE

Contributors

STEPHEN C. BARTON

Stephen C. Barton (PhD King's College London) is a theologian with a specialism in New Testament Studies. He was Tutor in Biblical Studies at Salisbury and Wells Theological College (1984–1988), and Reader in New Testament in the Department of Theology and Religion, Durham University (1988–2010). He is an Honorary Fellow of the theology departments of both Durham and Manchester Universities. Ordained priest in the Church of England in 1994, he has assisted in parishes in Durham, Newcastle and Lichfield dioceses, often ministering alongside his wife, Helen, who is also ordained. He lives now in Lichfield, where he assists on the ministry team of St Michael's on the Greenhill. His publications include *The Spirituality of the Gospels* (SPCK, 1992), *Discipleship and Family Ties in Mark and Matthew* (CUP, 1994), *Invitation to the Bible* (SPCK, 1997), and *Life Together: Family, Sexuality and Community in the New Testament and Today* (T. & T. Clark, 2001). Currently, he is coediting a second edition of *The Cambridge Companion to the Gospels*, as well as a multi-authored volume, *One God, One People: Oneness, Unity, and Christian Origins*.

PETER G. BOLT

Associate Professor Peter G. Bolt is the Academic Director of the Sydney College of Divinity, and the Director of the SCD Centre for Gospels & Acts Research. A graduate of Moore College, Australian College of Theology, Macquarie University, and King's College London, he is a New Testament scholar with research interests in the Gospels and Acts, Biblical Theology, magic and demonology, eschatology, the earliest Christian missionary movement, and the intersection between the New Testament and the Graeco-Roman world. He has published *Jesus' Defeat of Death: Persuading Mark's Early Readers* (Cambridge, 2003, 2008); *The Cross from a Distance: Atonement in Mark's Gospel* (IVP, 2004); (with Sharon Beekmann), *Silencing Satan: A Handbook of Biblical Demonology* (Wipf & Stock, 2011); and the popular-level *Living with the Underworld* (Matthias Media, 2007); and *A Light Shining in Our Darkness: Reading Matthew Today* (Acorn Press, 2014).

CONTRIBUTORS

Peter Carblis

Peter has had a varied career in pioneering pastoral ministry and education at school, vocational, and higher educational levels. He has worked, often concurrently, in practitioner, executive, and governance roles that have included school founder, church pioneer, senior and support pastoral leader, teacher, school principal, and college principal. Recent years have seen the addition of aged-care chaplaincy. For a time in the 1990s Peter conducted a top-rated talk-back radio program called "Street Talk" on 2GO, a local radio station. He is currently a Senior Chaplain with the Churches of Christ. Following on from his PhD in Educating for Emotional Intelligence from Macquarie University, Peter is currently working toward a second PhD with the Sydney College of Divinity in which he is exploring the use of the terms of the New Covenant to provide theological validation for educational outcomes and ministry objectives.

Adam G. Cooper

Adam G. Cooper is Associate Professor of Theology at the Catholic Theological College in Melbourne. He has published numerous scholarly and popular articles in historical theology, with a focus on the theology of the body and deification. He holds a PhD from the University of Durham and an STD from the Pontifical John Paul II Institute, Rome. His books are *The Body in Saint Maximus the Confessor: Holy Flesh, Wholly Deified* (Oxford University, 2005); *Life in the Flesh: An Anti-Gnostic Spiritual Philosophy* (Oxford University, 2008); *Naturally Human, Supernaturally God: Deification in Preconciliar Catholicism* (Fortress, 2014); and *Holy Eros: A Liturgical Theology of the Body* (Angelico 2014).

Doru Costache

Protopresbyter Dr. Doru Costache is Senior Lecturer in Patristic Studies at St Cyril's Coptic Orthodox Theological College. He is a member of the International Association for Patristic Studies. Participant in Science and Orthodoxy around the World, a Templeton-funded project run by National Hellenic Research Foundation, Athens, Greece (2016–2019). He is an honorary Associate of Department of Studies in Religion, the University of Sydney (2017–2019). He was a Durham International Senior Research Fellow of Institute of Advanced Study, Durham University, United Kingdom (Epiphany Term, 2018). Author of *Humankind and the Cosmos in the Early Christian Thought* (under review) and *Reading Scripture in the Orthodox Church: The Sunday Cycle* (2018). Coauthor of *Dreams, Virtue and Divine Knowledge in Early Christian Egypt* (Cambridge University, forthcoming 2019). He has more than twenty years of ordained ministry, currently leading Saint Gregory the Theologian's Romanian Orthodox Mission in Sydney's North (2017–).

CONTRIBUTORS

G. GEOFFREY HARPER

Dr. G. Geoffrey Harper is lecturer in Hebrew and Old Testament at Sydney Missionary & Bible College (an affiliated college of the Australian College of Theology). He is a Pentateuch specialist with a particular interest in the ritual texts of the Old Testament and the book of Leviticus. Current areas of research include inner-Pentateuchal allusion, the biblical portrait of ritual impurity, and interpersonal forgiveness. He is the author of *"I Will Walk Among You": The Rhetorical Function of Allusion to Genesis 1–3 in the Book of Leviticus* (Penn State University Press, 2018) and the forthcoming "Teaching Leviticus: From Text to Message" (Christian Focus). He is also coeditor of *Finding Lost Words: The Church's Right to Lament* (Wipf & Stock, 2017) and *It's OK Not to Forgive: A Biblical, Theological, and Pastoral Defence* (forthcoming).

JAMES R. HARRISON

Professor James R. Harrison, FAHA, is Research Director of the Sydney College of Divinity and is a doctoral graduate of the Ancient History Department of Macquarie University, Australia. He is a New Testament social historian with a strong interest in the historical Jesus, the Apostle Paul, the Graeco-Roman world and Second Temple Judaism, as well as eastern Mediterranean cities as revealed in their documentary, archaeological, and iconographic context. His two Mohr Siebeck monographs are *Paul's Language of Grace in Its Graeco-Roman Context* (2003; repr. 2017 Wipf & Stock) and *Paul and the Imperial Authorities at Thessalonica and Rome: A Study in the Conflict of Ideology* (2011). With Professor L. L. Welborn, Fordham University, he is coeditor of the nine-volume SBL series *The First Urban Churches* (vols. 1–2: 2015, 2016; vols. 3–4, 2018; vol 5, forthcoming 2019) and chief editor of *New Documents Illustrating the History of Early Christianity* (Eerdmans, vols. 11–15, forthcoming). Three new monographs will appear in 2019 and 2020, respectively: *Paul and the Ancient Celebrity Circuit: The Cross and Moral Transformation* (Mohr Siebeck) and *Reading Romans with Roman Eyes* (Fortress).

NEIL HOLM

Neil Holm, DipTeach Charles Sturt University (Wagga Wagga Teachers' College), Bachelor of Arts (Honours, University of New England), Doctor of Philosophy (University of Oregon), formerly Director Coursework and Senior Lecturer in Pastoral Theology and Practice for the Sydney College of Divinity. After an early teaching career in one-teacher and Aboriginal schools NSW and the NT, he played a key role in the development of the Aboriginal Teacher Education Centre (the forerunner of Bachelor Institute for Indigenous Tertiary Education). He extended his cross-cultural education and administration skills as Director of International House at the University of

Queensland and as Administrator of St John's Anglican Church (an inner-city church working in partnership with marginalized people in the Kings Cross / Darlinghurst area of Sydney). He now lives in Inala, one of the most multicultural suburbs of Brisbane that has welcomed people from 120 different ethnicities.

Antonios Kaldas

Antonios Kaldas has served as parish priest of Archangel Michael and St. Bishoy Coptic Orthodox Church in Mount Druitt, Sydney, Australia, since 1991. He was previously a medical doctor, has been heavily involved in the spiritual education of children and youth, is currently an active researcher in the philosophy of mind and cognitive science at Macquarie University, and lectures in Philosophy and Apologetics at St. Cyril's Coptic Orthodox Theological College (formerly Pope Shenouda III Theological College) in Sydney. He is married with two children and a number of pets.

Catherine Kleemann

Catherine Kleemann commenced her career as an accountant who then decided to study theology while pregnant with her two sons. It was as part of a church-plant team, located in a low-socioeconomic area, where Cathy found her passion in caring for the vulnerable as expression of faith and Christ's love. Cathy served as senior pastor of a local church in Pendle Hill NSW for a decade, providing a wide range of ministry opportunities to the marginalized, poor, and venerable. Located on the corner of an aged-care facility, Cathy also had the opportunity to connect with aged-care residents in a pastoral capacity. Cathy is now the Dean of the Graduate School of Leadership with the Australian College of Ministries, she is currently researching for a PhD with Sydney College of Divinity, where she is looking at the impact of the restoration movement on pastoral practice today.

Peter R. Laughlin

Dr. Peter R. Laughlin (BEng, BTh [Hon], PhD [ACU]) joined the Australian College of Ministries, a member institution of SCD, as Dean of the Alliance Institute for Mission and Head of Theology in 2017. Prior to this he was the Director of the Alliance College of Australia in Canberra. His research interests include the intersection between historical Jesus studies and atonement, divine justice, theodicy, human well-being, pneumatology, and theological method. His major work, *Jesus and the Cross: Necessity, Meaning, and Atonement* [Pickwick, 2014], was published in the Princeton Theological Monograph Series and he has recently contributed to the edited work *Well-being, Personal Wholeness and the Social Fabric* [Cambridge Scholars, 2017]. A serving member of the International Commission for Theological Education for the

Alliance World Fellowship, he is also published in areas relating to the Christian and Missionary Alliance, most recently contributing to *Advancing the Gospel* (forthcoming Pickwick, 2019).

David B. McEwan

David B. McEwan (PhD, University of Queensland) is Associate Professor of Theology and Pastoral Theology and Director of Research at Nazarene Theological College Brisbane, Honorary Associate Professor at the University of Queensland, and Fellow of the Manchester Wesley Research Centre, England. He also serves as the pastor of the Logan Community Church of the Nazarene in Logan, Queensland. His area of special study is the theology of John Wesley and its practical application to ministry and social issues today. He is the author of *Wesley as a Pastoral Theologian: Theological Methodology in John Wesley's Doctrine of Christian Perfection* (Paternoster, 2011) and *The Life of God in the Soul: The Integration of Love, Holiness and Happiness in the Thought of John Wesley* (Paternoster, 2015), as well as a number of journal articles and book chapters on a range of topics from a Wesleyan perspective. In 2020 his next monograph (cowritten with James Good) on a theology of disability will be published by Pickwick Press.

Peter Mudge

Dr. Peter Mudge has recently taught face-to-face and online tertiary courses for ten years as a senior lecturer in Religious Education and Spirituality. Prior to that he was a teacher in several schools, followed by roles as a retreat team leader, an adult educator (3 years) and a secondary consultant in religious education (22 years) and then an administrator of mission (RE and spirituality) (2 years). He is an Honorary Research Associate of the Sydney College of Divinity. He teaches a range of spiritual traditions, practices, and virtues across multiple dioceses throughout Australia. His teaching and writing is currently focused on the integrated teaching of spiritual traditions, disciplines, and virtues based on the work of Nancy Ammerman and others. His recent publications include a chapter in *Religious Education in Australian Catholic Schools* (Vaughan, 2017) and articles in the journals *Australasian Catholic Record* and *Practical Theology*.

Karen M. Pack

Karen M. Pack is an ordained minister and Lecturer in Chaplaincy and Spiritual Care at Morling College. She is a doctoral candidate at Alphacrucis College, researching the lives of unmarried evangelical Christian women in Australia in the period 1890–1970. She is an experienced educator and communicator, having ministered in Australia and internationally for over twenty years, including training pastors, teachers and lay leaders throughout Africa, Asia, and the Middle East with World Outreach International. She specializes in the intersection of singleness and sexuality for unmarried Christians but has also written numerous articles on pastoral ethics and cross-cultural missions. Her papers include "The Single Saviour: How the Singleness of Jesus of Nazareth Might Impact Contemporary Discipleship of Single Christians" (*CIS/SCD*, 2017); "Mateship—a Holy Alliance: Rediscovering Covenant Friendship in the Contemporary Australian Church" (*Zadok*, 2016); and "Single and Sexual: The Challenge of Holiness for Unmarried Christians" (*Crux*, 2010).

STEPHEN PICKARD

Right Reverend Professor Stephen Pickard is Executive Director of the Australian Centre for Christianity and Culture, Canberra; Director of the Strategic Research Centre in Public and Contextual Theology and Professor of Theology, Charles Sturt University, Canberra. He is an Assistant Bishop in the Diocese of Canberra & Gouburn. He has served in a range of ministerial and academic appointments over three and a half decades in Australia and the United Kingdom, including Director of St Mark's National Theological Centre, Canberra; Assistant Bishop in the Diocese of Adelaide; chaplaincy and parish priest (UK and Australia); and for one year acting CEO of Anglicare in Canberra & Goulburn. He is deputy chair of the Archbishop of Canterbury's Standing Commission on Unity, Faith and Order; a member of the Doctrine Commission of the Anglican Church of Australia; and chair of the Public Issues Commission, Diocese of Canberra and Goulburn. In 2011 he was installed as a *Six Preacher* at Canterbury Cathedral. His teaching and writing is in the area of ecclesiology, ministry, and mission and includes *Liberating Evangelism* (Trinity Press International, 1998); *Theological Foundations for Collaborative Ministry* (Ashgate, 2009); *In-Between God: Theology, Community and Discipleship* (ATF, 2011); *Seeking the Church: An Introduction to Ecclesiology* (SCM, 2012). He is married to Jennifer and they have three adult children and three grandchildren.

STEPHEN SMITH

Associate Professor Stephen Smith holds doctorates in management (Southern Cross University) and community health (University of Sydney). He is the Principal of the Australian College of Ministries as well as the Discipline Coordinator for Christian Life and Ministry for Sydney College of Divinity. Stephen has over thirty years of "hands-on" ministry experience and serves on the board of several community-based nonprofits ministering to the disadvantaged in society. He and Edwina Blair are the editors of the forthcoming SCD Press book titled *Embracing Life and Gathering Wisdom: Theological, Pastoral, and Clinical Insights into Human Flourishing at the End of Life*.

Robert Tilley

Robert Tilley did his doctorate at the University of Sydney with a thesis entitled "Reading the Sacred Text" (awarded 2001), the goal of which was to rethink the nature of "creation as a text of God" by way of an engagement with Scripture and postmodern discussions on the nature of textuality. He currently lectures in Biblical Studies at the Catholic Institute of Sydney, as well as in the area of the arts and theology at the Aquinas Academy at Wynyard. He has also tutored in Biblical Studies at the University of Sydney and at UNDA, Sydney. He is working on a book to be titled "Mary the Temple of Scripture."

Introduction
Finding Well-Being in an Unjust and Unmerciful World

JAMES R. HARRISON

WHO cares in a world where justice and mercy seldom meet? Although the question seems at first glance a counsel of despair, it is nevertheless at the core of the social well-being of any civilization. Where justice and mercy are devalued in a society, people also are ultimately devalued. History degenerates into being only a history of the victors with no interest in the losers. Justice and mercy are at the center of the Christian tradition, but the Roman emperors also claimed them as their exclusive preserve. Augustus boasted that "clemency" and "justice" belonged to his four cardinal virtues (*Res Gestae* 32.4),[1] his personal variation upon the four Greek cardinal virtues. The philosopher Seneca, the tutor of Nero, also advised his young charge on how to exercise clemency without violating his justice (*De Clementia*).[2] The startling implications of Jesus' parables of divine mercy and Paul's declaration of believers as justified in Christ led to the establishment of beneficent communities of grace that sought to live justly and mercifully in the imperial world in a manner that challenged the status-riddled mores of the day.[3] The Western intellectual tradition still lives with the ideological tensions emanating from this cultural collision between the followers of Christ and the empire of the Caesars.[4]

A series of important questions emerge from this defining intersection of shared but vastly differently understood values. How did each tradition, Roman or Christian, contribute to shaping Western culture in this regard? How does justice and mercy, for

---

1. For the argument that Augustus's mythological ancestor, Aeneas, is presented by Virgil as unmerciful, see Poulsen, "Why No Mercy?" I am indebted to Dr. Stephen Barton, formerly Durham University, for his helpful suggestions in strengthening this essay.

2. See Braund, *Seneca: De Clementia*. For discussions of mercy in the Roman world from late republic to late antiquity, see Harris, "Idea of Mercy"; Judge, "Quest for Mercy."

3. Harrison, "Who Is the 'Lord of Grace'?"

4. See Judge, *Paul and the Conflict of Cultures*.

example, inform contemporary civic discourse and practice? What difference should each quality make to our personal, social, and political lives in a culture characterized by the decline of mercy in public life?[5] And in a world exhausted by compassion fatigue and rendered cynical by the periodic failures of the justice system, where does true justice reside?

The essays in this book, originally presented at the 2016 Sydney College of Divinity conference on well-being, address these issues from a variety of interdisciplinary and ecumenical perspectives. They comprise exegetical, theological, historical, visual arts and ethical studies of the theme. In this introductory essay to the volume, I will discuss (a) modern biblical and theological scholarship on justice and mercy, (b) the intersection of both values in the Western intellectual tradition, (c) the philosophical, cultural, and ethical context of justice and mercy, utilizing the case studies of Nietzsche, Shakespeare's treatment of Shylock in *The Merchant of Venice*, and the moral issues raised by the 1960 trial of Adolf Eichmann. From here we will be able to make a final assessment regarding how the competing demands of justice and mercy, in the face of the questions posed by the problem of theodicy in world history, might be resolved. The outworking of mercy and justice in later Christianity tradition[6] and the modern philosophical and legal debate about the intersection of justice and mercy will not be addressed in this essay.[7]

Biblical and Theological Scholarship on Justice and Mercy

Biblical studies on divine and human justice have effectively discussed the texts of the Old and New Testaments. A series of exemplary exegetical monographs have been written on δικαιοσύνη in the writings of the Apostle Paul and in the New Testament more generally, each study situating the texts in their Jewish context and progressively grappling over time with the implications of the "New Perspective" on Second Temple Judaism and the epistles of Paul that was unleashed by the 1977 magnum opus of E. P. Sanders.[8] However, a lacuna in these studies is the failure to consider the Greco-Roman usage of δικαιοσύνη and to ponder how the New Testament documents engaged its ideological and social parameters as much as the Jewish texts. Initially, the Greco-Roman context would have been the primary backdrop against which Gentile converts first assessed Paul's gospel of imputed "righteousness" in Christ. Ironically, this is confirmed by the considerable amount of LXX Scripture that Paul cites in his

---

5. See Tuckness and Parrish, *Decline of Mercy*.

6. For mercy in Augustine, Anselm and Calvin, among others, see Tuckness and Parrish, *Decline of Mercy*, 87–137.

7. Among the voluminous literature of the issue, see Brien, "Mercy"; Meyer, *Justice of Mercy*; Markosian, "Two Puzzles about Mercy."

8. Ziesler, *Meaning of Righteousness in Paul*; Reumann, *Righteousness in the New Testament*; Seifrid, *Christ, Our Righteousness*; Bird, *Saving Righteousness of God*. On "righteousness" in Second Temple Judaism, see Sanders, *Paul and Palestinian Judaism*.

letters, "backfilling," as it were, what the Gentile auditors were unaware of regarding the righteous God of Israel. In Paul's vast reconfiguration of the moral order, all virtue was now located for the believer in Christ's work on the cross. This is not to deny that Paul concedes that the Gentiles, notwithstanding the fallen state of all humanity (Rom 3:9–20, 21), were still able to act in moral ways similar to the Jews because the just requirements of the law were written upon their hearts (2:14–15). But Paul's reconfiguration of virtue stripped the great man in antiquity of his exalted status as the repository of all civic virtue,[9] and, in a remarkable case of the democratization of the merit of the local elites, transferred δικαιοσύνη to all believers because of the soteriological work of Christ (Rom 5:18–19; 2 Cor 5:21). Last, a fine study has also been written on the New Testament understanding of restorative justice and its implications for crime and punishment—a more niche approach to studies on justice.[10]

In the case of Old Testament studies on justice, we are very well served and there is little point in engaging with each work.[11] Surprisingly, however, the role of mercy in the Old Testament has been little discussed. Even Old Testament theologies touch lightly upon the topos, if at all, the older work of Edmund Jacob being a rare and conspicuous exception.[12] The main two monographs written on the topic are theological, one being the Latin American "liberation" theology of J. Sobrino, the other being the more general biblical theology of W. Kasper, with each work covering the evidence of Old and New Testaments.[13] However, no major exegetical monograph has been written on the "mercy" traditions of the Old Testament.

The intersection of justice and mercy has been occasionally addressed,[14] but there remains an important niche for further scholarly work in the area, to which, hopefully, this volume will make its own contribution. The work of Gilman notes how the intersection of justice and mercy results in a *benevolent community*, historically wrenching benefaction from the preserve of the great and virtuous man in antiquity,[15] a phenomenon noted above, and thereby highlighting what the pagan emperor Julian

---

9. In the inscriptions honoring a local benefactor, δικαιοσύνη is one of a range of virtues credited to the honorand (e.g., εὔνοια ["good will"], σπουδή ["zeal"], among many others), being mostly used as circumlocutions for the benefactions, but nevertheless accruing in a crescendo of elite merit reserved for the honorand. On δικαιοσύνη and cognates in the honorific inscriptions, see Danker, *Benefactor*, 343–48.

10. Marshall, *Beyond Retribution*.

11. Adamiak, *Justice and History*; Birch, *Let Justice Roll Down*; Weinfeld, *Social Justice in Ancient Israel*; Houston, *Contending for Justice*; Armacost and Enns, "Crying Out for Justice"; O'Brien, *Restoring the Right Relationship*.

12. Jacob, *Theology of the Old Testament*, 94–102; see also Andersen, "Yahewh, the Kind and Sensitive God."

13. Sobrino, *Principle of Mercy*; Kasper, *Mercy*. For an excellent assessment of the significance of Sobrino's seminal contribution in a Catholic context, see Walatka, "Principle of Mercy."

14. Veling, *Beatitude of Mercy*; O'Brien, *A God Merciful and Gracious*; Brien, "Mercy and Righteousness Have Met"; Gilman, *Justice, and a Politics of Mercy*.

15. Harrison, "Imitation of the Great Man."

found so socially disquieting about the Christian communities in late antiquity: that is, their communal beneficence and love feasts (Julian, *Fragment of a Letter to a Priest* 305B–C; cf. Julian, *Letter to Arsacius, High-Priest of Galatia* 429C–431B). The moral implications of this beneficent intersection of two fundamental Christian values shows how the Western intellectual tradition continues to be shaped by its Jewish roots, culminating in the redemption of the risen Christ, over against the traditions emanating from the quest for mercy in Roman antiquity:

> Christian communities who live by the courage of Eucharistic gratitude, who live in gratitude for the unmerited gratitude received through Christ's death and resurrection will practice in private and public life this self-same mercy and benevolence. They will not surrender public life to the self-interest of fallenness; they will practice the meekness they preach and not permit the positive evil and violence self-interest inflicts on the vulnerable; they will promote and practice a quality of peacemaking that distinguishes itself from the kind of peace *pax Romana* offers. Those who have so lived, like Amos, Jesus, the apostles, Ghandi, Mother Theresa, King, and the anonymous multitudes, turn the world upside down.[16]

What, then, were the ideological factors that contributed to the collision of cultures that made up the Western intellectual tradition in regards to justice and mercy? And how do we see the tensions between both traditions exemplified in the thought of Nietzsche?

Justice and Mercy in the Western Intellectual Tradition

The Ancient Near East

Before we explore justice and mercy in the Hebrew Scriptures, we need to situate the Jewish traditions within the wider context of the documentary evidence of the ancient Near East.[17] In terms of the Egyptian literature, writers can speak variously about justice, whether it is the king's judgments,[18] justice as "a wonderful gift of God,"[19] or justice having been "cast out."[20] Generally, however, justice and mercy are concentrated in the figure of the pharaoh. One particular text, which has a strong emphasis upon social justice, advises the old kingdom King Merikare about how he should behave, emphasizing how God would smite down the disaffected who might conspire to upset his reign:

---

16. Gilman, *Christian Faith*, 178. See also van Aarde, "Righteousness of God."

17. For literature on justice in the ancient Near East, see Assmann, "When Justice Fails"; Weinfeld, *Social Justice in Ancient Israel*; Berlejung, "Sin and Punishment."

18. *The Dead King Hunts and Eats the Gods*, l. 399 (Simpson, *Literature of Ancient Egypt*, 271).

19. *Instruction of Amenemope*, ch. 20 (l. 21.5) (Simpson, *Literature of Ancient Egypt*, 259).

20. *Lamentations of Khakheperre-Sonbe*, l. 11 (Simpson, *Literature of Ancient Egypt*, 232).

Do justice that you may live long upon the earth. Calm the weeper, do not oppress the widow, do not oust a man from his father's property, do not degrade magnates from their seats. Beware of punishing wrongfully; do not kill, for it will not profit you, but punish with beatings and imprisonment, for thus the land will be set in order, excepting only the rebel who has conspired, for God knows who are disaffected, and God will smite down his evil doing with blood.[21]

Conversely, two impressive examples of divine mercy appear in the Egyptian literature. First, in *The Story of Sinuhe*, the career of a royal courtier of Egypt is outlined in considerable detail from ca. 1961 BCE onward. Sinuhe is otherwise unknown to us apart from the inscription on his tomb. In the narrative about his exile from the capital, Sinuhe, who was inexplicably impelled by an inner divine force to flee from the royal court, continually returns to his experience of mercy during his flight. He finds comfort in the divine mercy and propitiation currently extended to him: "God acts in such a way to be merciful to one whom he had blamed, one whom he causes to go astray to another land. For today his heart is appeased."[22] Underscoring God's providential care mediated to him during his expulsion from the court, he prays to God thus: "O God, whoever you are, who decreed this flight, may you be merciful and may you set me in the capital. . . . Today He is merciful and He hearkens to the prayer of a man far off."[23] As a result, he feels, despite his season of exile, that "the King of Egypt is merciful to me and I live on his bounty," instancing his (previous?) friendship with the Queen and errands undertaken on behalf of the royal children.[24]

Second, in a prayer of gratitude on a memorial stela, Neb-Re, who was an outline draftsman for the Theban necropolis, renders praise to the god Amun-Re for the recovery of his son from an illness.[25] This serious threat to his son's health was apparently divinely imposed because of his impiety, though this precise misdemeanor is a speculation. In a section on the mercy of Amun-Re, the writer, while acknowledging the normality of human sin, highlights the even greater "normality" of the god in forgiving sinners. Because Amon's soul (*ka*) is eternally enduring, the god has mercifully turned around the cooling and healing northern breeze toward Neb-Re's ailing son in order to perform the cure:

---

21. *Teaching of Merikare*, section ll. 45–51 (Simpson, *Literature of Ancient Egypt*, 183). On justice in *The Tale of the Eloquent Peasant* (Simpson, *Literature of Ancient Egypt*, 31–49), see Van Blerk, *Concept of Law and Justice*.

22. *Story of Sinuhe*, section ll. 140–50 (Simpson, *Literature of Ancient Egypt*, 65).

23. *Story of Sinuhe*, section ll. 150–60 (Simpson, *Literature of Ancient Egypt*, 65–66).

24. *Story of Sinuhe*, section ll. 160–70 (Simpson, *Literature of Ancient Egypt*, 66).

25. In the *Prayer of Kantuzilis for Relief from His Sufferings*, ll. 21–24 (Pritchard, *Ancient Near Eastern Texts*, 401), we read: "Now I cry for mercy in the presence of my god. Hearken to me, my god! O my god, do not make me a man who is unwelcome at the king's court! Do not make my condition an offence to mankind!"

He says: Though it may be said that the servant is normal in doing wrong, still the Lord is normal in being merciful. The Lord of Thebes does not spend an entire day being angry. As far his anger—in the completion of a moment there is no remnant, and the wind is turned around in mercy for us, and Ammon has turned around with his breezes. As thy *ka* endures, thou wilt be merciful, and we shall not repeat what has been turned away![26]

In other ancient Near Eastern texts a similar portrait of divine receptivity to human supplication emerges. Once again the language of mercy is fundamental in describing the allocation of divine beneficence. In a Babylonian text, Marduk is regularly addressed as merciful in Akkadian texts. Mercy is invoked from Marduk, king of the gods, for Babylon and its temple ("To your city, Babylon, grant release! To Esaggil, your temple, grant mercy!"),[27] along with his faithful servants ("Grant mercy to the servant who blesses you, take his hand [when he is] in great difficulty and pain").[28] Further, in a vision of an exorcist carrying a cuneiform tablet, Marduk, whose hands are "pure," is invoked to convey prosperity to Shubshi-meshre-Shakkan. The revelatory message and its beneficent results in response to prayer are described as follows:

> [In] waking hours he sent a message
> And showed his favourable sign to my people.
> In the . . . sickness [. . .]
> My illness was quickly over and my [. . .] broken.
> After the mind of my Lord had quietened
> And the heart of merciful Marduk rejoiced,
> [After he had] received my prayers [. . .]
> To whom turning is pleasant. [. . .][29]

Elsewhere, in a Sumero-Akkadian prayer to Ishtar ("goddess of goddesses . . . queen of all people, who guides mankind aright"), the mercy of the goddess is eulogized four times in an acclamatory address:

> Thou regardest the oppressed and mistreated; daily thou
>   causest them to prosper.
> Thy mercy! O Lady of heaven and earth, shepherdess
>   of the weary people.

---

26. *Gratitude for a God's Mercy*, section *ll.* 20–25 (Pritchard, *Ancient Near Eastern Texts*, 380–81).

27. *Temple Program for New Year's Festivals at Babylon*, *ll.* 246–47 (Pritchard, *Ancient Near Eastern Texts*, 331).

28. *Temple Program for New Year's Festivals at Babylon*, *ll.* 267–68 (Pritchard, *Ancient Near Eastern Texts*, 332).

29. *Akkadian Observations on Life and the World Order*, Tablet III *ll.* 46–59 (Pritchard, *Ancient Near Eastern Texts*, 599).

Thy mercy! O Lady of holy Eanna[30] the pure storehouse.

Thy mercy! O Lady; unwearied are thy feet; swift
    are thy knees.

Thy mercy! O Lady of conflict (and)
    of all battles.[31]

Other ancient Near Eastern texts are also concerned with justice. In the prologue to the famous law code of Hammurabi, the Babylonian gods called the lawmaker to act justly for the welfare for his people:

> ... and at that time Anum and Enlil named me
>
> to promote the welfare of the people,
>
> me, Hammurabi, the devout god-fearing prince,
>
> to cause justice to prevail in the land,
>
> to destroy the wicked and the evil,
>
> that the strong might not oppress the weak,
>
> to rise like the sun over the black-headed (people),
>
> and to light up the land.[32]

In conclusion, the ancient Near Eastern texts regularly highlight the mercy and justice of the gods, among many other attributes. Lawmakers and kings are summoned, as the viceroys of the gods, to act justly and mercifully on behalf of their subjects in governing and designing legislation. However, the writers of the ancient Near Eastern texts were well aware that life had its absurdities, with the result that doubts regarding the reliability of divine justice did occasionally emerge. The routine operation of the "deed-consequence" nexus in the ancient Near East—that is, the direct connection between one's behavior and one's fate—is called into question by the apparent arbitrariness of the gods in the face of unexpected and undeserved disaster.[33] Ancient Near Eastern texts such as *A Man and His God: A Sumerian Variation of the Job Motif*[34] and the Hebrew book of Job in the Old Testament spotlight the thorny problem of theodicy in the world. Thus the foundations of divine justice and mercy

---

30. I.e., the temple of Innana-Ishtar in Urek, better known to us as biblical Erech (Gen 10:10).

31. *Prayer of Lamentation to Ishtar*, ll. 26–30 (Pritchard, *Ancient Near Eastern Texts*, 384).

32. *The Code of Hammurabi*, Prologue (i) section ll. 20–50 (Pritchard, *Ancient Near Eastern Texts*, 164). In the Epilogue (reverse xxiv) ll. 40–80, Hammurabi states that (a) he has been called by the "great gods," (b) has been appointed as "beneficent shepherd whose sceptre is righteousness," (c) has written his "precious words" on a stela "in order that the strong might not oppress the weak, that justice might be dealt the orphan (and) the widow . . . (and) to give justice to the oppressed." For further justice texts, see *King of the Road: A Self-Laudatory Shulgi Hymn*, l. 23: "I love justice" (Pritchard, *Ancient Near Eastern Texts*, 585).

33. Berlejung, "Sin and Punishment," 276–77.

34. Pritchard, *Ancient Near Eastern Texts*, 589–91.

are questioned in such texts when humans are faced with the painful results of inexplicable tragedy, but these questions are more the exception than the rule.

By contrast, how does justice and mercy intersect in the Old Testament Scriptures and in Second Temple Judaism more generally? What relationship between each divine quality emerges and how does this inform social relations?

The Hebrew Scriptures and Second Temple Judaism

The intersection between justice and mercy is set forth with the establishment of the Sinai covenant. Yahweh is a jealous God who punishes those disobedient to the covenant to the third and fourth generation, while showing steadfast love to those who keep the commandments to the thousandth generation (Exod 20:5–6). The same intersection of justice and mercy is articulated in the covenant renewal after the disobedience associated with the golden calf episode (Exod 34:6–7). Nevertheless, in the "murmuring in the wilderness" narratives in Numbers 13–14, Moses, when faced with Israel's hard-hearted ingratitude, appeals for Yahweh's mercy. Remarkably, in response, Yahweh "waives the requirement to the third and fourth generation" (Num 14:18–25).[35] In sum, as Israel had already been reminded on a previous occasion (Exod 34:6), this demonstrates the great truism: "Yahweh, Yahweh, a God merciful (*rachum*) and gracious (*henun*), slow to anger, and abounding in steadfast love (*hesed*) and faithfulness (*emet*)." Here we see how the *hesed* ("mercy") of God "is revealed in and through the covenant," functioning "less a quality or attribute of God than a proof he intends to give."[36] Yahweh, therefore, remains "faithful to himself" and his covenant promises (Gen 24:12; 1 Kgs 3:6; 2 Sam 15:20; Jer 33:11–18; Ps 100:5; 106:1; 107:1–8, 15).[37] Moreover, that *hesed* is intimately linked with mercy is further underlined by the fact that the LXX normally translates *hesed* with ἔλεος ("mercy").[38]

However, as Edmund Jacob observes,[39] with the arrival of the prophetic literature we see a deepening of the concept of *hesed*. Instead of divine *hesed* being "the bond upholding the covenant, it is the very source of the attitude which impels God to enter into relation with his people."[40] Further, in light of Israel turning away from Yahweh and experiencing exile upon the dissolution of the northern and southern kingdoms, the prophets sought to reintegrate justice and mercy in their message to the exiles. Their aim was to console the disconsolate Israelites, reconcile them to Yahweh, and empower them for renewed holy loving before Yahweh and the watching nations, either in the cities of their exile (Jer 29:7) or in their return to Jerusalem to establish the

---

35. O'Brien, *A God Merciful and Gracious*, 25.
36. Jacob, *Theology of the Old Testament*, 104.
37. Jacob, *Theology of the Old Testament*, 105.
38. See Harrison, *Paul's Language of Grace*, 106–10.
39. Jacob, *Theology of the Old Testament*, 106.
40. Jacob, *Theology of the Old Testament*, 106.

new temple.⁴¹ The prophets offer the stark choice between death in Jerusalem or living under the sentence of foreign exile (Jer 21:8–9).

Nevertheless, despite the accurate prophetic diagnosis that Israel's heart has an incurable sickness (Isa 1:5–6; Jer 6:14; 32:12–13), the prophets emphasize that healing from Yahweh is now available (cf. Exod 15:26) and that he would assemble the remnant of Israel from the nations for their return to the land of Zion in the eschatological future (Isa 11:11–12; Jer 33:33–34). Moreover, in Isaiah, there is also the promise that Yahweh would raise up a righteous Servant who will establish justice in the nations (Isa 42:1–4). Indeed, upon the fulfillment of the Isaianic new Exodus (Isa 43:16–20; 51:9–11), Yahweh will transfer righteousness to his dependents through his stricken Servant, who will make many righteous by vicariously bearing and atoning for their sins (Isa 53:8, 11–12).The New Testament takes up the prophetic motif of the "new exodus" imagery, particularly in the Gospel of Mark, the book of Acts, and the epistles of Paul.⁴² This new age of righteousness and freedom is also unveiled earlier in Isaiah through the idyllic messianic portrait of a land ruled by a Spirit-indwelt Davidic king who is just and righteous (Isa 11:29; cf. 9:7).

In light of the prophetic critique of Israel's turning from the living God to idolatry and, conversely, the promise of return from exile to a new relationship of righteousness with Yahweh, Israel is to "act justly and to love mercy and to walk humbly with your God" (Micah 6:8; cf. Isa 1:16–17; Tob 12:8). Thus injustice toward the weak and powerless was to be avoided at all costs (Pss 15:1–5; 72:4; 103:6; Isa 1:16–17; 5:23; 10:1–2; 29:21; Micah 3:11; 7:3; Amos 5:2, 7, 24; 6:12 8:4–6; Hos 2:21; 12:2; Zech 7:8–10; cf. Jas 1:27). Furthermore, in a way unknown to them at the time, Israel would become a blessing to all the nations (Isa 2:2–4; 60:1–3), a promise that would only find its full revelation in the New Testament era (Acts 13:47 [Isa 49:47]; cf. Luke 2:29–32 [cf. Isa 42:6; 49:6]; 4:18–19 [Isa 61:1–2]).

But what about the literature of Second Temple Judaism? How does it portray mercy in relation to Yahweh's covenantal choice of Abraham, Isaac, and Jacob?⁴³ Once again, there is a strong emphasis on the unilateral nature of covenantal mercy in many texts, but we do see the emergence of merit theologies in certain sectors of Judaism that throw light on the type of "works-based" spirituality against which Paul is possibly arguing in his epistles, notwithstanding their Christian configuration.⁴⁴ A few examples of the differing theological positions will establish the point. The Prayer of Azariah (early 2 cent. BCE) pleads with God for an extension of his covenantal mercy,

---

41. O'Brien, *A God Merciful and Gracious*, 25–30.

42. See Watts, *Isaiah's New Exodus*; Pao, *Acts and the Isaianic New Exodus*; Oropeza, "Echoes of Isaiah in the Rhetoric of Paul"; Sullivan, *Isaianic New Exodus in Romans 9–11*.

43. We will not discuss the later rabbinic literature. For rabbinic texts dealing with the mercy and justice of God, see Montefiore and Loewe, *Rabbinic Anthology*, 233–71.

44. This section draws upon Harrison, *Paul, Theologian of Electing Grace*, 93–94.

reminding God of his promise to Abraham (Gen 12:1–3) and its reaffirmation to his descendants:

> For your name's sake do not give us up forever, and do not annul your covenant. Do not withdraw your mercy from us, for the sake of Abraham your beloved and for the sake of your servant Isaac and Israel your holy one, to whom you promised to multiply their descendants like the stars of heaven and like the sand on the shore of the sea.[45]

The Hebrew additions to Sirach (ca. 180 BCE) highlight God's mercy throughout, discussing the three patriarchs within the framework of covenantal mercy:

> Give thanks to him who has chosen the sons of Zadok to be priests,
>   for his mercy endures forever;
> Give thanks to the shield of Abraham,
>   for his mercy endures forever;
> Give thanks to the rock of Isaac,
>   for his mercy endures forever,
> Give thanks to the mighty one of Jacob,
>   for his mercy endures forever;
> Give thanks to him who has chosen Zion,
>   for his mercy endures forever.[46]

However, as noted, there were also Torah-based traditions within Second Temple Judaism that compromised the understanding of covenantal grace underlying the Abrahamic covenant. Sirach is revealing in this regard, with its chronological reversal of the events of Genesis 12–22 and the introduction of the (then) non-existent Mosaic law:

> Abraham was the great father of a multitude of nations, and no one has been found like him in glory. He kept the law of the Most High, and entered into a covenant with him: he certified the covenant in his flesh, and when he was tested he proved faithful. Therefore the Lord assured him with an oath that the nations would be blessed through his offspring; that he would make him as numerous as the dust of the earth, and exalt his offspring like the stars.[47]

Furthermore, other traditions deny any possibility of any allocation of mercy to God's enemies, as this text from Qumran (*1QS* 2.5–8) shows:

> Be cursed in all the works of our guilty wickedness,
> May God make you an object of terror by the hands of all the avengers of vengeance . . .

---

45. PrAzar 12–13.
46. Sir 51.
47. Sir 44.19–21.

> Be cursed, without mercy, according to the darkness of your works.
>
> Be damned in the place of everlasting fire.

In sum, the unilateral and non-works-based nature of covenantal mercy is largely maintained in Second Temple Judaism, though, as we have seen from Sirach 44.19–21 cited above, there were slippages from a grace-based to a more law-based approach. However widespread was this nomistic slippage is difficult to determine, but Paul certainly detected a boasting in contemporary Judaism that was not only ethnocentric but also highly competitive in terms of its "righteous" self-promotion over against its contemporary rivals (Gal 1:14a; Josephus, *Vita* 1–9; cf. 80–83, 187–188). However, this was also the case with the highly competitive civic righteousness of the Greco-Roman world more generally. We have to allow that Paul's rejection of boasting in "works" not only has a Jewish context but also a Greco-Roman expression.

But what about the Greco-Roman world? What view of divine justice and mercy emerges in its literature and documentary evidence? What role does the ruler play in promoting these moral virtues?

The Greco-Roman World

The expression of the Roman understanding of *clementia* ("mercy") at a social level and its relation to the reign of the Julio-Claudians is set out fully in my accompanying essay in this volume.[48] Succinctly stated, according to Seneca's two treatises on *De Clementia*, the Roman ruler was to extend clemency to those in the state who showed sufficient indication of future reformation in their lives. In other words, the wisdom of allocating *clementia* must be rationally considered in advance lest clemency degenerate into *misericordia* ("pity"). In this regard, *misericordia* was an unstable emotion despised by the Stoic philosophers because it undermined the rational thinking process due to its impulsiveness.[49] If the rationality of *clementia* is upheld over the irrationality of *misericordia*, then the Roman ruler will uphold justice (*iustitia*) in his allocation of mercy to the weaker members of the state. As we will see in *The Merchant of Venice* below, Shakespeare draws upon Roman traditions within the Western intellectual tradition in suggesting that mercy is the defining characteristic of the monarch.

More generally, in terms of the divine allocation of mercy in the Greco-Roman world, David Konstan sums up the division within the Western intellectual tradition over the issue most effectively:

> Although the pagan Greek and Roman gods might feel pity on occasion, it was not their primary trait, and philosophers never endorsed it as such. In the

---

48. See also Harrison, "Who Is the 'Lord of Grace'?"
49. Konstan, *Pity Transformed*, 113.

Jewish and Christian Bibles, like the Muslim Scriptures afterwards, compassion was part of the very essence of God.[50]

Two final pieces of evidence reveal two approaches for acquiring the mercy of the gods, each human centered. First, the Cynics, in spite of their overall agnosticism, contribute incisively to the ancient debate on divine beneficence.[51] Cercidas, a Cynic from the second century BCE, typically airs the thorny issue of the impotence of divine providence, and then proposes a novel theological solution to his dilemma. In a searing critique of traditional mythology, found in a papyrus from Oxyrhynchus, Cercidas rails against the inconsistency and indifference of Zeus in meting out justice:

> For it is easy for a god to accomplish everything whenever it comes into his mind, and to empty of his swinish wealth the dirty usurer and hoarder or this outpourer and ruin of his substance, and to give the squandered means to the man who takes his bite in season and shares his cup with a neighbour. Is then the eye of Right blinded like a mole's? Does Phaethon see crookedly with a single orb, and is the vision of fair Justice dimmed? How can they who have neither hearing or inlet of sight be yet taken for deities? Nay, the august lightning-compeller sits on mid-Olympus holding even the balance and in no wise signifies his will. . . . For why does not he who controls the weights, if he is upright, incline them to me, or to Phrygia at the ends of the earth?[52]

Moreover, Zeus as the universal Father arbitrarily discriminates between his children in the disposal of his providential favor. For Cercidas, even the astrologers would be unable to divine the selection criteria that Zeus uses to determine which of his children receive beneficence:

> To what sort of lords, then, or to what children of Heaven can one go to find how he may get his deserts, when the son of Cronos, the begetter and parent of us all, is found to be a father to some and a stepfather to others? Better to leave these questions to the astrologers, for they, I expect, will have no manner of trouble.[53]

The solution for Cercidas lay in a wholesale rejection of the traditional pantheon of deities, and its replacement by a more just and beneficent alternative: "For us let *Paean* and Giving (*Metados*) be our care, for she is a goddess, with Retribution (*Nemesis*), on earth."[54] This earthly triad of *Paean* (the god Apollo as Healer), *Metados* (the hypostasis of Beneficence), and *Nemesis* (the goddess of Retribution) combines a concern for body and soul, and dispenses both grace and justice. As a result, we

---

50. Konstan, *Pity Transformed*, 124.
51. This discussion of Cercidas is borrowed from Harrison, *Paul's Language of Grace*, 198–99.
52. *P. Oxy.* VIII 1082. Col. ii. *l.* 5—Col. iii. *ll.* 1, 4–5.
53. *P. Oxy.* VIII 1082. Col. iii. *ll.* 8–14.
54. *P. Oxy.* VIII 1082. Col. iii. *ll.* 15–16.

are to honor the deity for any "favouring breeze," and cultivate a Cynic distaste for acquisitiveness and the gifts of Fortune.[55]

Second, in an inscription from Kyme (1–2 cent. CE) which recounts an autobiographical aretalogy of Isis, the goddess is depicted as just ("I made justice strong. . . . With me justice prevails") and merciful ("I legislated mercy for suppliants").[56] Here we see the unreserved extension of justice and mercy on the part of the goddess, in sharp contrast to the theodicy of Cercidas and his own "reinvention" of a just and merciful god.

Now that we have distilled the ideological context of justice and mercy in the ancient Near East, the Hebrew Scriptures, Second Temple Judaism, and the Greco-Roman world, Paul's famous passage on the intersection of divine justice and mercy in Romans 3:21–26 has to be addressed.

The Apostle Paul and the Cruciform Intersection of Justice and Mercy: Romans 3:21–26

Although Paul established that Jew and Gentile now faced the wrath of God because both ethnic groups fell short of the glory of God and his unsullied righteousness (Rom 1:18—3:20), nevertheless the apostle had already indicated that God's wrath is tempered by his kindness (2:4): "Or do you show contempt for the riches of his kindness, tolerance, and patience, not realising that God's kindness leads you to repentance?" Our pericope returns to this refrain, noting that God in his forbearance had passed over the sins previously committed (Rom 3:25b). The narrative of Yahweh's continuous extension of mercy to the disobedient and idolatrous Israel must lie behind this magnified depiction of a compassionate God impartially seeking reconciliation with humanity at large. As Walter Kasper insightfully observes,

> For this reason, mercy does not stand in opposition to the message of justice. In his mercy, God rather holds back his justified wrath; indeed, he holds himself back. He does this in order to provide people the opportunity for conversion. . . . Mercy is ultimately grace for conversion.[57]

But how can mercy be continuously offered to erring humanity without God trivializing his holy and justified reaction of wrath toward sin, without abandoning the perfect righteousness animating his universal justice, and without violating everything that makes God the one who alone dwells in inapproachable light (1 Tim 6:16)? In our pericope Paul provides several reasons why God does not violate his justice in showing mercy to disobedient mankind, opening up themes which the apostle will pursue elsewhere.

---

55. *P. Oxy.* VIII 1082, Col. iii. *l.*16—Col. iv. *l.* 4.
56. For translation, see Danker, *Benefactor*, 196–201.
57. Kasper, *Mercy*, 54.

- If we take διὰ πίστεως Ἰησοῦ Χριστοῦ (Rom 3:22a) as a subjective genitive,[58] the faithfulness of the obedient Christ is pivoted against the unfaithfulness of Israel, noted above, and of humanity more generally. But how does Christ's faithfulness make the decisive difference here? How is righteousness (δικαιοσύνη) extended to believers because of Christ's faithfulness? Humanity could not accomplish righteousness before God because of its fallen flesh (7:5), the continuous accusation of the law regarding our failure (cf. Col 2:14a), the suborning of mankind through the law to even greater sin (Rom 7:7–12), and the presence of the reign of death cutting humanity off from God (5:12–21). Christ has accomplished liberation for sinful humanity by the faithful obedience of his death (5:19), imputing his righteousness to his dependents (5:18–19; cf. 2 Cor 5:21), and, through the newness of Spirit (7:6b) and his resurrection power (6:1–14), effecting in them the righteous requirements of the law (8:3–4).

- God puts forth Christ as a ἱλαστήριον (Rom 3:25a) as a means of propitiating sin. If we take ἱλαστήριον, as some scholars have,[59] as a reference to the Levitical "mercy seat" (Lev 16), we see that the mercy opened up to human beings in Christ aligns with the mercy historically offered to erring Israel. The perfect sacrificial death of Christ, therefore, is seen to be the fulfillment of the Levitical cult. Since the "mercy seat" is the cruciform Christ, Paul spells out elsewhere in the epistle how the operations of divine mercy transform social, ethnic, and benefaction relationships within the body of Christ (ὁ ἔλεος: 9:23; 11:31; 15:9; ἐλεέω: 9:15, 16, 18; 11:30, 31, 32; 12:8; οἰκτιρμός: 12:1).

- Believers are justified by the redemption in Christ (διὰ τῆς ἀπολυτρώσεως ἐν Χριστῷ Ἰησοῦ: Rom 3:24b). Some scholars have argued[60] that we are to see here not only a metaphor which has been "borrowed from the slave market and law court" but also which carries "echoes of Israel's Exodus from Egypt."[61] The transfer from slavery to Sin and Death (Rom 5:12–21) to freedom in the Spirit (7:6b; 8:3b–17) is conveyed most effectively by such a usage. But more is to be seen here if the Exodus implications of the metaphor are present: we are reminded that the Old Testament prophetic traditions regarding a second Exodus by divine mercy (Deut 30:1–10; Isa 11:11–12, 16; 35:8–10; 43:5–7; 60:8–9; Jer 3:18; 16:1–12; 23:7–8; 31:8; Hos 11:10; Zech 2:6) have now been fulfilled in Christ (cf. 1 Cor 10:1–3). The use of δωρεάν (Rom 3:24a: "freely"), drawn from the world of Greco-Roman benefaction, points to the unconstrained generosity animating the divine Benefactor.[62]

---

58. Fitzmyer, *Romans*, 350–51.
59. Schreiner, *Romans*, 191–94.
60. Brien, "'Mercy and Righteousness Have Met,'" 190.
61. Brien, "'Mercy and Righteousness Have Met,'" 190.
62. Harrison, *Paul's Language of Grace*, 224, 333.

Thus we see how Paul has established the legitimacy of his claim that God has demonstrated that he is righteous in the present age by declaring believers righteous through the justifying death of Christ (Rom 3:26). Mercy and justice have intersected in the cruciform Christ. Mercy has overflowed and surpassed its Old Testament precedents, making plain the unlimited scope of the unconditioned divine mercy exercised toward the Gentile nations as much as the Jew, a development only partially presaged until now (cf. Jonah 4:10–11). But, intriguingly, in this process the claims of divine justice, rather than being relaxed, have been thoroughly satisfied and indeed intensified by the costliness of Christ's death (Rom 5:7–8; 8:31–32) and through the transforming effects of the newness of the Spirit within the lives of believers (7:6b; 8:3b–4).

How, then, does the Judeo-Christian understanding of divine justice and mercy, extended in Christ to unjust and unmerciful humanity, leave its indelible trace upon the Western intellectual tradition? Three case studies will enable us to see the continuing reverberations over the centuries.

Nietzsche and the Politics of Pity: A Case Study in the Collision between Roman and Christian Understandings of Mercy

A fascinating case study in the collision between Roman and Christian understandings of mercy in the Western intellectual tradition is found in the writings of the German philosopher, Friedrich Nietzsche (1844–1900). The son of a Lutheran pastor, Nietzsche considered compassion to be a weakness to be avoided as opposed to being a virtue to be cultivated. According to Nietzsche, pity represented a vice which had to be overcome because, in exercising pity toward others, one was in reality treating people with contempt. It was better for people to face up to their troubles and struggle with them rather than succumb to the religion of pity, exemplified by its demeaning central motif of a wounded and suffering deity. By contrast, the religions of ancient Greece and Rome had gods which were much more engaging because they became involved in warfare and love affairs. Nietzsche was very much aware that the Christian upending of the ancient reciprocity system and calculated self interest in giving represented "a re-evaluation of antique values."[63]

In the view of Nietzsche, pity was the preserve of the powerful, who is beyond the law and justice in allocating mercy to his dependents:

> The justice which began with, "everything is dischargeable, everything must be discharged," ends by winking and letting those incapable of discharging their debt go free: it ends, as does every good thing on earth, *by overcoming itself*. This self-overcoming of justice: one knows the beautiful name it has

---

63. Nietzsche, *Beyond Good and Evil*, 75. For a seminal essay on pity in the thought of Nietzsche, see Nussbaum, "Pity and Mercy." See also Ure, "Politics of Mercy, Forgiveness and Love."

given itself—*mercy*; it goes without saying that mercy remains the privilege of the most powerful man, or better, his—beyond the law.[64]

Furthermore, pity was also an expression of the "slave morality" where the weak redefined morality and values for the sake of utility, that is, in order to alleviate the plight of those who, like themselves, suffer:

> . . . here pity, the complaisant and obliging hand, the warm heart, patience, industry, humility, and friendliness are honoured—for here these are the most useful qualities and almost the only means for enduring the pressure of existence. Slave morality is essentially a morality of utility.[65]

Christianity, in particular, is the religion which promotes negative attitudes to life by virtue of its concentration upon pity:

> Christianity is called the religion of pity. Pity is opposed to the tonic passions which enhance the energy of the feeling of life: its action is depressing. A man loses power when he pities. By means of pity the drain on strength which suffering itself already introduces into the world is multiplied a thousandfold.[66]

In Nietzsche's view, the Christian notion of God had to be dispensed with because in subjecting those who were pitied to shame and humiliation, the danger arose that the pitied might take revenge on those who pitied them. In *Thus Spoke Zarathustra*, the "ugliest man" reveals to Zarathustra that he had murdered God out of revenge, with Nietzsche clearly aiming his polemic against traditional Christianity:

> But he had to die: he saw with eyes that saw everything; he saw man's depths and ultimate grounds, all his concealed disgrace and ugliness. His pity knew no shame: he crawled into my dirtiest nooks. This most curious, over-obtrusive, over-pitying, one had to die. He always saw me: on such a witness I wanted to have revenge or not live myself. The god who saw everything, even man—this god had to die! Man cannot bear it that such a witness should live.[67]

Last, in manner similar to Roman thinkers, Nietzsche argues that pity compromises mercy because it calls into question the legitimate social notion of the punishment of criminals because of its alleged "unfairness." But as Nietzsche caustically proceeds, we see here how "the herd morality, the morality of timidity, draws its

---

64. Nietzsche, *On the Genealogy of Morals*, second essay: "'Guilt,' 'Bad Conscience,' and Related Matters," sect. 10.

65. Nietzsche, *Beyond Good and Evil*, 260. I am indebted here to the discussion of Tuckness and Parrish, *Decline of Mercy*, 13–15.

66. Nietzsche, *Antichrist*, 7.

67. Nietzsche, "On the Pitying," 201. For discussion, see Cartwright, "Last Temptation of Zarathustra," 49–69. For a useful discussion of Nietzsche's attitude toward Christianity, see Shepard, "Sickness unto Life."

ultimate consequence."[68] This sickness of the soul reduces people to experiencing pity with their fellow citizens rather than having pity for them.[69] Thus Martha Nussbaum is correct in concluding that, as far the Western intellectual tradition is concerned, Nietzsche essentially follows the Roman Stoic tradition, no matter how complex and subtle his thought on the issue might be.[70] The collision between the Christian and Roman understandings of mercy remains at the core of our intellectual debate in the West.

The Cultural and Ethical Context of Justice and Mercy: From Shakespeare's Shylock to Adolf Eichmann

Shakespeare, Shylock and the "Quality of Mercy"

In this section we will discuss the role that Portia's "quality of mercy" speech plays in Shakespeare's *Merchant of Venice*. Is the "mercy" motif the keynote to the play?[71] Does it point—to employ a common (and unwarranted) caricature of Judaism in the Christian tradition—to the ascendancy of the freely given mercy in the New Testament over against the strictures of Mosaic law with its strong justice agenda, symbolized in the play, it might be argued, by the "merciless" Shylock? But such a theological caricature, as we have seen, misunderstands the centrality of covenantal mercy in the Old Testament, upon which, in seamless continuity, the New Testament draws in speaking about the fulfillment of Yahweh's mercy in Christ. Furthermore, it misrepresents Second Temple Judaism as hopelessly "legalistic," a presupposition challenged to the contrary by the presence of "grace" and "mercy" language in the Jewish texts. Alternatively, is the "quality of mercy" merely a cynical rhetorical ploy utilized by Portia to accomplish her ends? Are the so-called "merciful" Christians in the play merciful at all? Issues such as these pose the important question as to whether Shakespeare's portrait of Shylock is ultimately anti-Semitic, given that *The Merchant of Venice* was appropriated by the Nazis in various dramatic performances for their racist propaganda during the Third Reich. However, as Michael Connor observes, "For Shakespeare Jewishness was a matter of religion, for Goebbels Jewishness was racial difference."[72] Furthermore, considerable attention has been devoted to the treatment of Jews both

---

68. Nietzsche, *Beyond Good and Evil*, 201.

69. Nietzsche, *Beyond Good and Evil*, 225.

70. Nussbaum, "Pity and Mercy." Note the revealing extract from Nietzsche (*Daybreak*, book 1, 139): "Said to be higher!—You say that the morality of pity is higher morality than that of Stoicism? Prove it! but note that 'higher' and 'lower' morality is not to be measured by a moral yardstick: for there is no absolute morality. So take your yardstick from elsewhere and—watch out!"

71. For discussion, see Aslam, "Mercy a Virtue of Consciousness." Note the comment of Lee ("Who's Afraid of William Shakespeare?," 27): "The play suggests that, more fundamentally, we have not yet learned how to live. We do not recognize, for example, that justice and mercy must work together; they are not, as we may suspect, alternative approaches."

72. Connor, "Shylock, the Shakespearean Comic Villain."

in England and Venice, as well as possible literary precedents for Shakespeare's pay, with a view to understanding the presentation of Jews in the play. These important questions lie beyond the scope of our discussion.[73]

The plot of the play is well known. The Jew Shylock agrees to lend money to Antonio on the condition that he can cut off a pound of his flesh from his debtor should he default on the loan. Antonio borrows the money for his friend Bassanio, who requires the money in order to court the wealthy Portia. Inevitably, Antonio defaults upon the loan and, Portia, disguised as a man, defends him in court. Portia manipulates the law with hair-splitting definitions in order to overcome Shylock's relentless demands: Shylock, she argues, is entitled to a pound of Antonio's flesh, but he must not spill any blood in its acquisition. Shylock's impending murder of his debtor is now impossible. Consequently, Shylock is charged with conspiring against a Venetian citizen and his property is seized. The only escape from financial disaster in Shylock's case was for the Jew to convert to Christianity, with the result that he retained his estate.

The two most famous speeches of the play pose the question regarding the allocation of mercy. In the trial Portia argues that Shylock must exercise mercy toward Antonio by not demanding his legal right of justice upon default of payment of the loan (*Merchant of Venice*, 4.1.180–203):

> PORTIA: Then must the Jew be merciful.
>
> SHYLOCK: On what compulsion must I? tell me that.
>
> PORTIA: The quality of mercy is not strain'd,
>
> It droppeth as the gentle rain from heaven
>
> Upon the place beneath; it is twice blest,
>
> It blesseth him that gives, and him that takes,
>
> 'Tis mightiest in the mightiest, it becomes
>
> The throned monarch better than his crown.
>
> His sceptre shows the force of temporal power,
>
> The attribute to awe and majesty,
>
> Wherein doth sit the dread and fear of kings:
>
> But mercy is above this sceptred sway,
>
> It is enthroned in the hearts of kings,
>
> It is an attribute to God himself;

---

73. For discussion, see Bronstein, "Shakespeare, the Jews, and The Merchant of Venice"; Horowitz, "Shylock after Auschwitz"; Heschel, "*Merchant of Venice*"; Bonnell, "Shylock and Othello."

> And earthly power doth then show likest God's
>
> When mercy seasons justice: Therefore Jew,
>
> Though justice be thy plea, consider this,
>
> That in the course of justice, none of us
>
> Should see salvation: we do pray for mercy,
>
> And that same prayer, doth teach us all to render
>
> The deeds of mercy. I have spoke thus much
>
> To mitigate the justice of thy plea,
>
> Which if thou follow, this strict court of Venice
>
> Must needs give sentence 'gainst the merchant there.

While there is certainly an inter-textual echo of Ecclesiasticus 35:19 behind Portia's apologia for mercy, it would be a mistake to assume that Shakespeare is wanting us to conclude that unvarnished Christian sentiments are at play in this speech. First, it is worth noting that the doctrine that monarchs ought to show mercy derives from Seneca's *De Clementia*, whereas Paul, by contrast, presents the ruling authorities as divinely appointed servants dispensing justice for the social good (Rom 13:1–7).[74] In other words, Shakespeare more reflects the Roman origins of our Western intellectual tradition in this instance. Second, Shakespeare relentlessly depicts the Christians in the play as stereotyping Shylock as "devilish,"[75] a slur routinely brought against Jews because of their responsibility in the crucifixion of Christ (*The Merchant of Venice*, 4.1.221; 4.1.295), notwithstanding the deep Roman involvement in the decision. This is hardly the language of forgiveness which Christ extended to his tormentors, Jewish and Roman, on the cross (Luke 23:34a).[76] Third, the idea of a forced conversion on the part of Shylock stands at variance with the idea that "the quality of mercy is not strain'd." Surely this is a critique of the Christian morality of Portia rather than just an ironic comic flourish leading to the play's denouement?[77] Fourth, the play also confounds what one would expect of true Christian justice. As Charles Morowitz states,

---

74. See Harrison, *Paul and the Imperial Authorities*, 271–323.

75. *Merchant of Venice*, 2.2.18–26; 2.3.2; 3.1.18–19; 3.125–28; 3.1.64–65; 4.1.4–6; 4.1.72; 4.1.130–40; 4.1.210. For these references I am indebted to Sutton, "Re-examining the Merchant of Venice," 73n40.

76. Harrison, "Jesus and the Grace of the Cross." Note the comment of William Ian Miller (*An Eye for an Eye*, 83) on Portia: "Her brand of mercy to Antonio is funded by a perfect requiting and plundering of Shylock; her mercy is but revenge in sheep's clothing, and she cannot disguise her delight in exacting from Shylock everything she could exact: property, faith, dignity, and manhood."

77. However, Gorman Beauchamp ("Shylock's Conversion," 78) argues that this expects too much from the Christian characters in Shakespeare's comedies: "There are no saints in Shakespeare's comedies; no one wears hair shirts or spends much time over orisons; pleasure, not piety, is the keynote;

> One of Shakespeare's greatest virtues is that you never know where he stands on any of the issues he dramatizes, and in the case of "The Merchant," there is almost as much evil in the defending Christians as there is in the prosecuting Jew, and a verdict that relieves a moneylender of half his wealth and then forces him to convert to save his skin is not really a sterling example of Christian justice.[78]

Fifth, the exit of Shylock from the play in act 4, never mentioned again or to reappear in act 5 is telling, given that the final act has no real plot purpose other than Portia's giving away of Bassario's ring—the only issue still to be resolved. But the emotional force of Shylock's character lingers invisibly to the end of the play, despite the legal resolution of Antonio's fate and Shylock's forced conversion, defusing his threat to the lovers. What is Shakespeare intending by such a conclusion?

One approach is to suggest that the ending is cathartic, required by the conventions of a comedy, bringing the play to a harmonious conclusion after the high drama and tension of act 4. James E. Siemon, for example, suggests that act 5 represents a "ritual reiteration" of acts 1–4, repeating in the encounter between Bassiano and Portia the same pattern of threat, release, and reconciliation that the audience has already seen in the previous acts.[79] Siemon's observation is perceptive at a literary and dramatic level. But I suspect that in the vacuous speeches and scheming antics of the Venetian elites—obsessed with their rings, disguises and revelations, resulting in the contrived marriages of act 5—we are meant to hear Shakespeare's irony tolling loudly. These "beautiful" people, justified by the triumph of their version of Christian "mercy" over the "devilish" Jew of act 4, are totally blind to their own superficiality, cruelty, greed, and religious prejudice at the play's end. They celebrate together with sublime indifference to the Jew they have defeated, religiously humiliated, and economically imperilled. Neither mercy nor justice have been served in this grubby process. Ultimately, the Venetian elites demonstrate the true nature of the ruler's *clementia* prescribed by Seneca, its allocation to Shylock being dependent on his prior willingness to change by "converting" to Christianity. True *clementia* cannot be compromised by unworthy *misericordia* being extended to the Jew.

Furthermore, the famous speech of Shylock, while asserting the right to vengeance, nevertheless lifts the characterization of the merchant from the traditional comic stereotype of the sexually lustful Jew (cf. Meleager [Greek Anthology 5.160]; Tacitus, *Histories* 5.5.2; Martial, *Epigrammata* 7.30)[80] to an elevated and eloquent plea

---

but the comic world is Christian enough for the dramatist's purposes, as much so in *The Merchant of Venice* as anywhere else." However, correctly I believe, Caldwell ("Opportunistic Portia") argues in light of Renaissance iconography that Portia more represents Fortuna (Occasio), not having any affinity with mercy or justice, but rather acting as an opportunistic entrepreneur in the world of commerce and romance.

78. Morowitz, "Pinning Prejudice on Shakespeare."

79. Siemon, "Ritual Reiteration."

80. On the sexual overtones to the speech ("organs," "prick," "tickle"), as well as (what would have

for his common humanity (*Merchant of Venice*, 3.1.1285–307). The speech dominates the rest of the play and becomes a litmus test for how all people at Venice should treat each other whatever their faith might be, cutting through the glib rhetoric of justice and mercy articulated by the elites. At his ideological core, Shakespeare was essentially a humanist.[81] In the face of a choice between rival and incompatible ideological systems (Roman, Christian) in the play, Shakespeare shows himself to be a Renaissance man:

> SALARNIO: Why, I am sure, if he forfeit, thou wilt not take
>
> his flesh: what's that good for?
>
> SHYLOCK: To bait fish withal: if it will feed nothing else,
>
> it will feed my revenge. He hath disgraced me, and
>
> hindered me half a million; laughed at my losses,
>
> mocked at my gains, scorned my nation, thwarted my
>
> bargains, cooled my friends, heated mine
>
> enemies; and what's his reason? I am a Jew. Hath
>
> not a Jew eyes? hath not a Jew hands, organs,
>
> dimensions, senses, affections, passions? fed with
>
> the same food, hurt with the same weapons, subject
>
> to the same diseases, healed by the same means,
>
> warmed and cooled by the same winter and summer, as
>
> a Christian is? If you prick us, do we not bleed?
>
> if you tickle us, do we not laugh? if you poison
>
> us, do we not die? and if you wrong us, shall we not
>
> revenge? If we are like you in the rest, we will
>
> resemble you in that. If a Jew wrong a Christian,
>
> what is his humility? Revenge. If a Christian
>
> wrong a Jew, what should his sufferance be by
>
> Christian example? Why, revenge. The villany you

---

been) the accompanying hand gestures accentuating the lewd references, see Connor, "Shylock, the Shakespearean Comic Villain."

81. See Wells, *Shakespeare's Humanism*; Raspa, *Shakespeare the Renaissance Humanist*.

teach me, I will execute, and it shall go hard but I

will better the instruction.

In sum, Shakespeare plays tantalizingly with Christian and humanist traditions regarding mercy, teasing audiences to identify in a triumphal and unthinking manner with the enforced conversion of the "devilish" and "lecherous" Jew, while presenting them with the alternative of identifying with Shylock's relentlessly just demands for his pound of flesh, seemingly robbing him of any vestige of the humanity associated with his great humanist speech. Both traditions, Christian and humanist, are pushed to breaking point, with the audience called to act invisibly as judge and jury regarding the pleas of the characters representing each tradition. The collision of cultures could not be plainer.

We turn now to the famous trial of Adolf Eichmann in 1960 before an Israeli court for his role in organizing the logistics of Hitler's final solution. What potential intersections between "mercy" and "justice" occurred between the defendant and the prosecution and how did they unravel? What ethical dilemmas emerged in the process? What new challenges did they pose to the understanding of justice and mercy in the Western intellectual tradition?

The Trial of Adolf Eichmann and the Unraveling of Human Justice and Mercy: Are We Watching "Banal Evil" or "Metaphysical Revenge"?

Recently revealed documents, publicly announced by the Jewish President Reuven Rivlin on January 27, 2016, indicate that the Nazi henchman Adolf Eichmann, architect of Hitler's notorious "final solution" leading to the extermination of six million Jews, penned a hand-written letter in blue ink to the (then) Prime Minister, Yitzhak Ben-Zvi. He requests exemption from execution, claiming that he and others were "mere instruments in the hands of the leaders" who perpetrated the Holocaust. He was hanged overnight on May 31 in Ramleh prison, his body cremated hours later, and his ashes scattered in the waters of the Mediterranean.

The letter, written in German, is set out in translation below. Eichmann claims radically diminished responsibility, asserting that he was never a high placed official, neither receiving promotion for his alleged activities nor signing commands for the extermination of the Jews, deemed "outrageous human atrocities." He rejects any sense of guilt, does not accept the court's verdict, and asks for pardon from the death penalty from the President of Israel. No sense of corporate responsibility, where justice calls *all* involved in the Holocaust crimes to account no matter the level of their administrative role as low- or high-level functionaries, is accepted by Eichmann, and remarkably, he brazenly requests pardon:

To Mister President!

I join the appeal of my defense lawyer and allow myself to point out the following: The judges made a fundamental mistake in their judgment of me, because they are not able to empathize with the time and situation in which I found myself during the war years. The mistake was caused by the fact that at the time of my trial, only individual documents were presented, which, without being seen in connection with the general documents of the orders, gave an incorrect picture.

It is not true that I was personally of such a high rank as to be able to persecute, or that I myself was a persecutor in the pursuit of the Jews; in the face of such an abundant rule it is clear the judges in their ruling ignored the fact that I never served in such a high position as required to be involved independently in such decisive responsibilities. Nor did I give any order in my own name, but only ever acted "by order of." Even had I been as the judges assessed the driving, zealous force in the persecution of the Jews, such a thing would have been evident in my promotion and other awards. Yet I received no such advantages.

It is also incorrect that I never let myself be influenced by human emotions. Specifically, after having witnessed the outrageous human atrocities, I immediately asked to be transferred. Also, during the police investigation I voluntarily revealed horrors that had been unknown until then, in order to help establish the indisputable truth.

I declare once again, as I did in the presence of the court: I detest as the greatest of crimes the horrors which were perpetrated against the Jews and think it right that the initiators of these terrible deeds will stand trial before the law now and in the future.

Notwithstanding, there is a need to draw a line between the leaders responsible and the people like me forced to serve as mere instruments in the hands of the leaders. I was not a responsible leader, and as such do not feel myself guilty.

I am not able to recognize the court's ruling as just, and I ask, Your Honour Mr. President, to exercise your right to grant pardons, and order that the death penalty not be carried out.

Adolf Eichmann,
Jerusalem, 29 May 1962.

Reactions to Eichmann's execution are instructive, especially in terms of the reasons given for the rejection of his request for pardon. Two revealing examples are apposite. First, members of the nation of Israel saw in Eichmann's death an expression of the biblical "eye for an eye, tooth for a tooth" principle, though not in the original Mosaic sense of a call for measured restraint in the situation of escalating retaliation characteristic of a blood feud (Exod 21:24; Matt 5:38–42), but rather as the rightful response of retaliatory revenge in compensation for the unspeakable enormity of Jewish loss. The article of Dr. Herzl Rosenblum is representative of this viewpoint:

> Indeed, there were those who saw in it an act of metaphysical revenge. One of these was Dr. Herzl Rosenblum, editor of Yedi'otAharonot. In an article entitled, "From Ramleh Shall Go Forth Torah," he wrote that, there, gathered around the gallows in the Ramleh Prison, were "the small children who had been taken from the arms of their mothers and their heads dashed against the wall, mothers who were taken from the site of their infants' murder to the whore houses of the drunken SS vandals," and those whose "limbs were pulled out of their flesh by the dogs of the SS, whatever remained being thrown into the crematoria and the gas chambers"—all these stood and gazed at the gallows and the rope and said, "It is good, at least, that our blood shall never again be abandoned."[82]

Second, in her book on Adolf Eichmann's trial in Jerusalem,[83] Hannah Arendt wrote a detailed report and political commentary upon the trial of Adolf Eichmann, the duration of which she had attended. Segments of the book had been published in the *New Yorker* and its eventual publication caused great controversy. Arendt argued that although Eichmann was rightly considered "evil," he was "neither perverted nor sadistic . . . [but] terribly and terrifyingly normal."[84] She posited the emergence of a new type of evil in Eichmann, not the stereotypical sadistic "monster" whose overweening will to power humiliated his victims, but rather an ordinary and indistinguishable bureaucrat who embodied "the lesson of the fearsome, word-and-thought defying banality of evil"[85]—the very banality highlighted in the subtitle of her book. Moreover, it is the "thoughtlessness" of Eichmann that especially matters in this new construct of evil. The Nazi bureaucrat was unwilling to undertake the "practical reasoning" that engaged empathetically with the viewpoints of others,[86] and, lacking "imagination," "never realised what he was doing" in committing unreservedly himself to the fictional claims of National Socialism.[87]

Arendt was well aware that she was departing from the traditional paradigms of evil promoted in the Western intellectual tradition. There evil was traditionally seen in metaphysical terms as the legacy of original sin, total depravity, and the corruption

---

82. Cited by Weitz, "Holocaust on Trial," 3. Note, too, that Eichmann's wife, Vera, asked Israel's prime minister, Yitzhak Ben-Zvi, for her husband's pardon. The telegram requested that he should be spared for the sake of her "as a wife and mother of four children." Ben-Zvi attached a handwritten note to the telegram quoting 1 Samuel 15:33: "But Samuel said, 'As your sword has made women childless, so will your mother be childless among women." The same principle of retaliatory and quasi-metaphysical revenge operated in this instance as well.

83. Arendt, *Eichmann in Jerusalem*.
84. Arendt, *Eichmann in Jerusalem*, 276.
85. Arendt, *Eichmann in Jerusalem*, 252.
86. Arendt, *Eichmann in Jerusalem*, 49.
87. Arendt, *Eichmann in Jerusalem*, 287; cf. 59.

of humankind, who were held hostage to the power of Satan and the reign of death. But, as Arendt notes in her lecture notes to students at the University of Chicago in October 1963, the "banality of evil" "goes against our whole tradition where Lucifer is a fallen archangel (implying the worst were once the best), against our beliefs of the demonic nature of evil, that there is something grand in it, that it may have positive results."[88] The sentiments enunciated here find a sympathetic resonance with the outstanding poem of the Canadian poet and songwriter Leonard Cohen, "All there is to know about Adolf Eichmann."[89]

How, then, does Arendt's understanding of the "banality" of evil relate to the wider concerns of justice?[90] Here we shall conclude our discussion with a brief theological response to the lingering question posed by the unanswered demands of justice, divine and human, in the face of unspeakable evil in human history. The perspective offered is one of traditional Christian dogmatics. We do not thereby intend to imply that a commitment to these theological observations somehow diminishes the acute "rawness" of the victims' experience of impenetrable evil and their vain cries for justice in a fallen world. The agonized cry of the psalmist regarding why the wicked continue to prosper tells against such facile conclusions (Ps 73).

Notwithstanding, we must not underestimate how people can become unwitting and unthinking cogs in a bureaucratic machine with unspeakably evil results, as Arendt rightly argues. But this observation does not thereby diminish our moral accountability before God and our fellow human beings, a fundamental strut in the Christian basis of the Western intellectual tradition which Arendt challenges in her construct of the banality of evil. Human beings remain moral agents made in the image of God, albeit deeply flawed by the corrupting effects of the historical fall in Adam (Gen 3:1–19; Rom 5:12–21). But they are not thereby demonized in the process, with the result that humans are still capable by God's common grace to act mercifully and justly in civil society. All humanity will be called to moral account by a just God at the eschaton, irrespective of whether some of the guilty escape trial for their misdemeanors in the present life, as did Eichmann in Austria and Argentina from 1945 to 1960, or whether they receive a lenient judgment because of flawed and inadequate legal

---

88. Hannah Arendt, Chicago University Jewish Students Lecture Notes, 30 October 1963. The Hannah Arendt Papers, Library of Congress. Cited by Jaquiss, "Arendt on Arendt," 44.

89. The poem is found in Cohen, *Flowers for Hitler*.

90. In focusing on this narrow aperture of investigation, we are bypassing the contemporary criticism of Arendt's book, including (a) her reluctance to see anti-Semitism as the central motive of Eichmann, opting instead for the category of the unthinking "banality of evil"; (b) her ambiguous portrait of the Holocaust which emphasized Jewish as much as Nazi guilt; (c) her tarnishing of the sacred memory of Jewish victims; (d) her factual errors regarding the trial (Robinson, *And the Crooked Shall Be Made Straight*); (e) Eichmann's duplicitous reinvention of himself at the trial and the emergence of further documentation demonstrating that he was much more than a minor bureaucrat (Stangneth, *Eichmann before Jerusalem*), among other issues. For the wider details of the book's critique, see Podhoretz, "Hannah Arendt on Eichmann"; Jaquiss, "Arendt on Arendt," 33–63; Ezra, "Eichmann Politics"; Bernstein, *Hannah Arendt and the Jewish Question*.

processes. Nor must we underestimate the real potential of human legal processes to act unjustly toward the innocently accused. The trial of Jesus is a telling case in this regard. Nevertheless, the historical resurrection of Christ as Messiah and Lord verifies the surety of a just culmination of history when he returns as eschatological Judge of all. A moral reckoning will definitely take place.

The magnitude of human evil, which in the dark times of human history defies belief in its barbarity and wickedness, can never be fully accounted with sufficient retributive justice in human courts, even when savage revenge is exacted. But humans will not only have to face their human accusers but also their Creator. The full depths of human evil will be definitively accounted for on the day of judgment when God examines the secrets of all human hearts (Ps 44:21; Rom 2:16). In the meantime, because God will carry out a definitive eschatological accounting, believers are able to act mercifully toward their enemies and persecutors amid inexplicable evil (Matt 5:7, 38–48; Luke 6:32–36; 23:34), while seeking the transformation of the lives of the guilty through the application of a restorative justice paradigm. God's current restraint of the full expression of his wrath in the world (Rom 2:3–4), notwithstanding the gravity of its current expression, also becomes for believers another paradigm of mercy toward others, in addition to the mercy that they have already experienced in Christ. Ultimately, however, the questions of posed by theodicy in the world and how they can be resolved by the inadequate instruments of the human legal system, as the claims for justice and mercy intersect and press for resolution in the face of unmentionable evil, can only be permanently resolved by the arrival of eschaton and God's new creation.

Conclusion

This essay has explored the intersection between mercy and justice in the traditions of the ancient Near East, the Greco-Roman world, the Hebrew Scriptures and Second Temple Judaism, and Paul's epistle to the Romans. We have explored the ramifications of this ideological intersection in the thought of Friedrich Nietzsche, Shakespeare's *The Merchant of Venice*, and Hannah Arendt's characterization of Adolf Eichmann's trial as the "banality of evil." We see here in these case studies the legacy of the Western intellectual tradition, which is the result of this collision of cultures that began to emerge when God's mercy in Christ was first announced in the Greco-Roman world. It is hoped that the essays in this volume will contribute to helping readers understand the origins of this collision and point to helpful resolutions of some of the residual tensions for the wider well-being of our culture in the twenty-first century.

Bibliography

Adamiak, Richard. *Justice and History in the Old Testament*. Cleveland: Zubal, 1982.

Andersen, F. I. "Yahweh, the Kind and Sensitive God." In *God Who Is Rich in Mercy: Essays Presented to D. B. Knox*, edited by P. T. O'Brien and D. G. Peterson, 41–88. Homebush, Australia: Lancer, 1986.

Arendt, Hannah. *Eichmann in Jerusalem: A Report on the Banality of Evil*. New York: Viking, 1964.

Armacost, Barbara E., and Peter Enns. "Crying Out for Justice: Civil Law and the Prophets." In *Law and the Bible: Justice, Mercy and Legal Institutions*, edited by R. F. Cochran and D. VanDrunken, 121–50. Downers Grove: IVP Academic, 2013.

Aslam, Humaira. "Mercy a Virtue of Consciousness in Shakespeare's *The Merchant of Venice*." *Journal of Humanities and Social Sciences* 23 (2015) 1–8.

Assmann, Jan. "When Justice Fails: Jurisdiction and Imprecation in Ancient Egypt and the Near East." *Journal of Egyptian Archaeology* 78 (1992) 149–62.

Beauchamp, Gorman. "Shylock's Conversion." *Humanitas* 12 (2011) 55–92.

Berlejung, Angelika. "Sin and Punishment: The Ethics of Divine Justice and Retribution in Ancient Near Eastern and Old Testament Texts." *Interpretation* 69 (2015) 272–87.

Bernstein, Richard D. *Hannah Arendt and the Jewish Question*. Cambridge: Polity, 1996.

Birch, Bruce C. *Let Justice Roll Down: The Old Testament, Ethics, and Christian Life*. Louisville: Westminster John Knox, 1991.

Bird, Michael F. *The Saving Righteousness of God*. Colorado Springs: Paternoster, 2006.

Bonnell, Andrew G. "Shylock and Othello under the Nazis." *German Life and Letters* 63 (2010) 166–78.

Braund, Susanna, ed. and trans. *Seneca: De Clementia*. Oxford: Oxford University Press, 2009.

Brien, Andrew James. "Mercy: The Concept and Its Moral Standing." PhD diss., Adelaide University, 1991.

Brien, Mary T. "'Mercy and Righteousness Have Met': Literary Structure as Key to the Centrality of Mercy in Romans." PhD diss., University of Limerick, 2013.

Bronstein, Herbert. "Shakespeare, the Jews, and The Merchant of Venice." *Shakespeare Quarterly* 20 (1969) 3–10.

Caldwell, Ellen M. "Opportunistic Portia as Fortuna in Shakespeare's Merchant of Venice." *SEL Studies in English Literature 1500–1900* 54 (2014) 349–75.

Cartwright, David. E. "The Last Temptation of Zarathustra." *Journal of the History of Philosophy* 31 (1993) 49–69.

Cohen, Leonard. *Flowers for Hitler*. Toronto: McClelland and Stewart, 1964.

Connor, Michael. "Shylock, the Shakespearean Comic Villain." *Quadrant Online*, March 25, 2017. https://quadrant.org.au/magazine/2017/03/shylock-shakespearean-comic-villain/.

Danker, F. W. *Benefactor: Epigraphic Study of a Graeco-Roman and New Testament Semantic Field*. St. Louis: Clayton, 1982.

Ezra, Michael. "The Eichmann Politics: Hannah Arendt and Her Critics." *Democratiya* 9 (2007) 141–65.

Fitzmyer, J. A. *The Letter to the Romans*. New translation with introduction and commentary. New York: Doubleday, 1992.

Gilman, James E. *Christian Faith, Justice, and a Politics of Mercy: The Benevolent Community*. Lanham, MD: Lexington, 2014.

Harris, Bruce F. "The Idea of Mercy and Its Graeco-Roman Context." In *God Who Is Rich in Mercy: Essays Presented to D. B. Knox*, edited by P. T. O'Brien and D. G. Peterson, 89–105. Homebush, Australia: Lancer, 1986.

Harrison, James R. "The Imitation of the Great Man in Antiquity: Paul's Inversion of a Cultural Icon." In *Christian Origins and Classical Culture: Social and Literary Contexts for the New Testament*, edited by Stanley E. Porter and Andrew W. Pitts, 213–54. Leiden: Brill, 2013.

———. "Jesus and the Grace of the Cross: Luke 23:34a and the Politics of 'Forgiveness' in Antiquity." *Journal of Gospels and Acts Research* 1 (2017) 42–67.

———. *Paul and the Imperial Authorities at Thessalonica and Rome: A Case Study in the Conflict of Ideology*. Tübingen: Mohr Siebeck, 2011.

———. *Paul's Language of Grace in Its Graeco-Roman Context*. 2003. Reprint, Eugene: Wipf and Stock, 2017.

———. "Who Is the 'Lord of Grace'? Jesus' Parables in Imperial Context." In *Borders: Terms, Ideologies and Performances*, edited by A. Weissenrieder, 383–417. Tübingen: Mohr Siebeck, 2016.

Heschel, Susannah. "*The Merchant of Venice* and the Theological Construction of Christian Europe." In *Mediating Modernity: Challenges and Trends in the Jewish Encounter with the Modern World; Essays in Honour of Michael A. Meyer*, edited by Lauren B. Strauss and Michael Brenner, 74–92. Detroit: Wayne State University Press, 2008.

Houston, W. J. *Contending for Justice: Ideologies and Theologies of Social Justice in the Old Testament*. London: T. & T. Clark, 2006.

Horowitz, Arthur. "Shylock after Auschwitz: The Merchant of Venice on the Post-Holocaust Stage—Subversion, Confrontation, and Provocation." *Journal for Cultural and Religious Theory* 8 (2007) 7–19.

Jacob, Edmund. *Theology of the Old Testament*. London: Hodder and Stoughton, 1958.

Jaquiss, Audrey P. "Arendt on Arendt: Reflecting on the Meaning of the Eichmann Controversy." 2015 Claremont Colleges Library Undergraduate Research Award. Paper 5. http://scholarship.claremont.edu/cclura_2015/5.

Judge, E. A. *Paul and the Conflict of Cultures: The Legacy of St. Paul's Thought Today*. Edited by James R. Harrison. Eugene, OR: Cascade, 2019.

———. "The Quest for Mercy in Late Antiquity." In *God Who Is Rich in Mercy: Essays Presented to D. B. Knox*, edited by P. T. O'Brien and D. G. Peterson, 107–21. Homebush, Australia: Lancer, 1986.

Kasper, Walter. *Mercy: The Essence of the Gospel and the Key to Christian Life*. New York: Paulist, 2014.

Konstan, David. *Pity Transformed*. London: Duckworth, 2001.

Lee, Randy. "Who's Afraid of William Shakespeare? Confronting Our Concepts of Justice and Mercy in the Merchant of Venice." *University of Dayton Law Review* 32 (2006) 1–28.

Markosian, Ned. "Two Puzzles about Mercy." *Philosophical Quarterly* 63 (2013) 269–92.

Marshall, Christopher D. *Beyond Retribution: A New Testament Vision for Justice, Crime and Retribution*. Grand Rapids: Eerdmans, 2001.

Meyer, Linda Ross. *The Justice of Mercy*. Ann Arbor: University of Michigan Press, 2010.

Miller, William Ian. *Eye for an Eye*. Cambridge: Cambridge University Press, 2006.

Montefiore, C. G., and H. M. J. Loewe, eds. *A Rabbinic Anthology*. New York: Schocken, 1974.

Morowitz, Charles. "Pinning Prejudice on Shakespeare." *Los Angeles Times*, April 18, 1993. https://www.latimes.com/archives/la-xpm-1993-04-18-bk-24096-story.html.

Nietzsche, Friedrich. *The Antichrist*. In *The Complete Works of Friedrich Nietzsche*, edited by Oscar Levy, vol. 16. London: Foulis, 1911.

———. *Beyond Good and Evil: Prelude to a Philosophy of the Future*. London: Penguin, 1973.

———. *Daybreak*. Translated by R. J. Hollingdale. Cambridge: Cambridge University Press, 1982.

———. *On the Genealogy of Morality*. Edited by Keith Ansell-Pearson. Cambridge: Cambridge University Press, 1994.

———. "On the Pitying." Part 1 of *Thus Spoke Zarathustra*. In *The Portable Nietzsche*, translated by Walter Kaufmann. New York: Viking, 1968.

Nussbaum, Martha C. "Pity and Mercy: Nietzsche's Stoicism." In *Nietzsche, Genealogy, Morality: Essays on Nietzsche's* On the Genealogy of Morals, edited by Richard Schacht, 139–67. Berkeley: University of California Press, 1994.

O'Brien, Mark A. *A God Merciful and Gracious: Justice and Mercy in the Old Testament*. Alexandria, Australia: Australian Catholic Social Justice Council, 2008.

———. *Restoring the Right Relationship: The Bible on Divine Righteousness*. Hindmarsh, Australia: ATF, 2014.

Oropeza, B. J. "Echoes of Isaiah in the Rhetoric of Paul: New Exodus, Wisdom, and the Humility of the Cross in Utopian-Apocalyptic Expectations." In *The Intertexture of Apocalyptic Discourse in the New Testament*, edited by Duane Frederick Watson, 87–112. Tübingen: Mohr Siebeck, 2002.

Pao, David W. *Acts and the Isaianic New Exodus*. Grand Rapids: Baker Academic, 2002.

Podhoretz, Norman. "Hannah Arendt on Eichmann: A Study in the Perversity of Brilliance." *Commentary* 36 (1963) 201–8.

Poulsen, Aske Damtoft. "Why No Mercy? A Study of Aeneas' Missing Virtue." *Symbolae Osloensis* 87 (2013) 95–133.

Pritchard, James B., ed. *Ancient Near Eastern Texts Relating to the Old Testament*. 3rd ed., with suppl. Princeton: Princeton University Press, 1969.

Raspa, Anthony. *Shakespeare the Renaissance Humanist: Moral Philosophy and His Plays*. New York: Palgrave Mamillan, 2016.

Reumann, John. *Righteousness in the New Testament*. Philadelphia: Fortress, 1982.

Robinson, Jacob. *And the Crooked Shall Be Made Straight: The Eichmann Trial, the Jewish Catastrophe and Hannah Arendt's Narrative*. New York: Macmillan, 1965.

Sanders, E. P. *Paul and Palestinian Judaism: A Comparison of Patterns of Religion*. London: SCM, 1977.

Shepard, Frank. "Sickness unto Life: Nietzsche's Diagnosis of the Christian Condition." PhD diss., Columbia University, 2013.

Schreiner, Thomas R. *Romans*. Grand Rapids: Baker, 1998.

Seifrid, Mark A. *Christ, Our Righteousness: Paul's Theology of Justification*. Leicester, UK: Apollos, 2000.

Siemon, James E. "'The Merchant of Venice': Act V as Ritual Reiteration." *Studies in Philology* 67 (1970) 201–9.

Simpson, William Kelly. *The Literature of Ancient Egypt: An Anthology of Stories, Instructions, and Poetry*. New Haven: Yale University Press, 1973.

Sobrino, Jon. *The Principle of Mercy: Taking the Crucified People from the Cross*. Maryknoll: Orbis, 1994.

Stangneth, Bettina. *Eichmann before Jerusalem: The Unexamined Life of a Mass Murderer*. New York: Knopf, 2014.

Sullivan, Steven P. *The Isaianic New Exodus in Romans 9–11: A Biblical and Theological Study*. Silverton: Lampion, 2017.

Sutton, William. "Re-examining *The Merchant of Venice*: Politics, Religion, and Gender in Early Modern Venice." *Historia: The Alpha Rho Papers* 1 (2011) 61–86.

Tuckness, Alex, and John M. Parrish. *The Decline of Mercy in Public Life*. Cambridge: Cambridge University Press, 2014.

Ure, Michael. "The Politics of Mercy, Forgiveness and Love: A Nietzschean Appraisal." *South African Journal of Philosophy* 26 (2007) 56–69.

Van Aarde, A. G. "The Righteousness of God, Begging for the Poor and Paul's Apostolic Mission according to His Letter to the Romans." *HTS Teologiese Studies/Theological Studies* 68 (2012). Art. #1223. http://dx.doi.org/10.4102/hts.v68i1.1223.

Van Blerk, Nicolaas Johannes. "The Concept of Law and Justice in Ancient Egypt, with Specific Reference to *The Tale of the Eloquent Peasant*." MA thesis, University of South Africa, March 2006.

Veling, Terry A. *The Beatitude of Mercy: Love Watches Over Mercy*. Mulgrave, Australia: John Garrat, 2010.

Walatka, Todd. "The Principle of Mercy: Jon Sobrino and the Catholic Theological Tradition." *Theological Studies* 77 (2016) 96–117.

Watts, Ricki E. *Isaiah's New Exodus and the Gospel of Mark*. Tübingen: Mohr Siebeck, 1997.

Weinfeld, M. *Social Justice in Ancient Israel and in the Ancient Near East*. Minneapolis: Fortress, 1995.

Weitz, Yechiam. "The Holocaust on Trial: The Impact of the Kasztner and Eichmann Trials on Israeli Society." *Israel Studies* 1 (1996) 1–26.

Weinfeld, Moshe. *Social Justice in Ancient Israel and in the Ancient Near East*. Minneapolis: Fortress, 1995.

Wells, Robin Headlam. *Shakespeare's Humanism*. Cambridge: Cambridge University Press, 2016.

Ziesler, J. A. *The Meaning of Righteousness in Paul: A Linguistic and Theological Enquiry*. Cambridge: Cambridge University Press, 1972.

PART A

The Contours of Well-Being
Justice and Mercy in Panorama

1

Jesus, the Gospels, and the Kingdom of God in Constitutional Perspective[1]

Stephen C. Barton

Introduction: Keeping Our Moral Theology Theological

In reflecting as Christians on justice, mercy, and social well-being, we do well to start with two successive Beatitudes from Matthew's Sermon on the Mount:

> Blessed are those who hunger and thirst for righteousness [δικαιοσύνην],[2] for they will be filled.
>
> Blessed are the merciful [οἱ ἐλεήμονες], for they will receive mercy [ἐλεηθήσονται]. (Matt 5:6–7)

That Jesus of Nazareth was remembered as having to do with justice, mercy, and social well-being is evident from the earliest Christian testimonies. Again and again, Jesus is represented as performing healings in response to the cries for mercy of the sick, the demonized, and the disabled;[3] and one of Jesus' most powerful parables,

---

1. An expanded version of this essay has recently appeared as "Jesus on Justice and Mercy in Constitutional Perspective," *Journal for the Study of the Historical Jesus* 16 (2018) 213–42. I am very grateful to Professor James Harrison for the invitation to deliver the original version and for his encouragement with this essay.

2. Wolterstorff (*Justice: Rights and Wrongs*) argues that δικαιοσύνη should be translated "justice": but this is an unwarranted narrowing, not least, in relation to the other uses of δικαιοσύνη in the Sermon (cf. 5:10, 20; 6:1, 33). Preferable exegetically is the judgment of Davies and Allison (*Gospel according to Matthew*, 1:452) that δικαιοσύνη refers to "the right conduct which God requires"—conduct which, of course, by no means excludes the practice of justice!

3. Cf. Matt 9:27; 15:22; 17:15; 20:29–34; Mark 5:19; 10:47–48; Luke 17:13; 18:38–39.

which Matthew locates at the climax of Jesus' teaching on just community, is the Parable of the Unmerciful Servant, with the master's angry rebuke to his slave, "Should you not have had mercy [ἐλεῆσαι] on your fellow slave, as I had mercy [ἠλέησα] on you?" (Matt 18:23–35, at v. 33).

But let me say before proceeding further: given that we are engaged in an exercise in moral theology, it is crucial that we keep our moral theology *theological*.[4] Essential for understanding and appropriating the Gospel testimonies is the recognition that their subject is Jesus *interpreted eschatologically*—that is, Jesus *as Risen Lord, uniquely related to God and God's just and loving purposes in space and time*. From this point of view, therefore, anything we say as Christians about justice, mercy and social well-being will necessarily be grounded in what we believe about Christ, the Spirit, the church, and the end of all things in God.

I say this because, with a subject like ours, there is a danger of allowing an essentially liberal, universalizing, and moralizing discourse to take over, where Jesus, his teaching and practice, are reduced to moral exempla, more or less on a par with the teachings and practices of philosophers or charismatic holy men and women ancient and modern.[5] This is *not* to say that we may not have things to learn from Jesus about the moral life. Indeed, that Jesus was worthy of imitation is surely one of the reasons why the Gospels, as lives of Jesus, analogous to ancient *bioi*, were written.[6] Nevertheless, once we allow a moralizing discourse to take over, we are in danger of losing our moorings in the faith and worship which constitute us as people who, by the Spirit, live *from and into* the gift of salvation and new creation revealed in Jesus Christ.

The implication of taking this theological foundation as the point of departure is that what justice, mercy, and social well-being look like *in the light of Christ* may not cohere in any straightforward way with alternative constructions. On the contrary, they may well appear paradoxical, even counter-intuitive. Contrary to "prosperity gospels" in either their secular or sacred modes, for example, it is a serious question as to whether following Christ is good for your health. Certainly, if the lives of apostles, saints, martyrs and mystics—not to mention the life of Jesus himself—are any guide, no such simple correlation can be made. One apostle, Saint Paul, puts it memorably. Speaking allusively of a "thorn in the flesh" which he interprets eschatologically as "a messenger of Satan to torment me," he says, "Three times I appealed to the Lord about this, that it would leave me, but he said to me, 'My grace is sufficient for you, for power is made perfect in weakness'" (2 Cor 12:8–9).

What the apostle's testimony implies is that how we interpret justice, mercy, and well-being is shaped profoundly by our faith and practice—above all, by our dying and living in Christ. To put it another way, the Christian vision of the good has a

---

4. Cf. Hauerwas, "On Keeping Theological Ethics Theological."
5. Cf. McGrath, "Moral Example for Christians?"
6. Cf. Burridge, *Imitating Jesus*, 73–78.

particular *narrative shape* and a particular *form of embodiment*.[7] Its narrative shape is the story of divine grace overflowing in creation, election, redemption, and new creation. Its embodiment is "resurrection people" given over to the vocation of praise and love for the common good of church and world. This particularity is by no means a problem, even if it may place the Christian vision at a tangent with conceptions of justice, mercy and well-being grounded in other traditions. There is no gospel without the "scandal of particularity."

On Taking a Constitutional Approach

It is not at all coincidental that Christian Eucharistic liturgy (in more traditional ecclesial communions, at least) gives special place to the gospel procession, the gospel acclamation, and a reading from one of the four canonical Gospels. This is a clear expression of the conviction that the Christian's narrative identity is bound up with the story of Jesus understood eschatologically as the key to history and the cosmos. In language of parable, myth, sign, symbol, and epiphany, in stories of personal encounter, controversy, teaching and healing, in climactic narrative of trial, death, resurrection and ascension, we are *"worded" by the Spirit* into life in Christ.[8] My suggestion, therefore, is that meditation on the Gospel stories of Jesus is a sure way—and of course not the only way—of gaining Christian wisdom about justice, mercy, and social well-being.

In seeking after a heuristic framework that brings the elements of our theme into meaningful connection, I begin with the basic observation that justice, mercy, and social well-being are matters of a *relational* kind and, at the societal level, have to do with *the ordering of a people's common life for the good*. In so far as this ordering of a people's common life involves matters of authority worked out in the practices of law, governance and politics, it is (among other things) a *constitutional* matter.[9] A constitution provides a basic framework for the exercise of power and judgment for the common good. It is the expression of a people's worldview and moral vision shaped across time and space, and in the vicissitudes of history. Interpreted wisely, it bestows legitimacy, and therefore authority, on the practice of government. Such practice includes formal enactments of law, but also extends beyond the formal to all the cultural habits and practices that create and sustain order and neighborliness.

My proposal, therefore, is that an illuminating way to give an account of justice, mercy, and social well-being from a theological point of view is to attend to the Gospel portrayals of Jesus, in so doing seeking for their *potential or actual constitutional*

---

7. Valuable along these lines are the essays in Hauerwas and Wells, *Blackwell Companion to Christian Ethics*.

8. On being "worded" into life, cf. Hardy, *Wording a Radiance*.

9. Pelikan, *Interpreting the Bible and the Constitution* is suggestive in this area.

resonance. As far as I am aware, such an approach remains undeveloped.[10] In the church, at least in some circles, there is a tendency to neglect the story of Israel and to focus rather on Jesus interpreted in terms of individual spirituality and personal morality. In New Testament scholarship, the closest approximation is study of Jesus and politics, especially Jesus in the context of the Roman Empire.[11] Otherwise, there is a tendency to focus on discrete topics like the parables, the miracles, the kingdom, the law, the temple, messiahship, the crucifixion, and so on. Of course, none of this is to be gainsaid. What may yet require attention, however, are approaches that help to bring these various topics together into a more "grounded," social-historical and moral-theological whole. A constitutional approach has the potential to do precisely this—not least, with regard to matters of individual, corporate, and national existence such as justice, mercy, and well-being.[12]

That such an approach is not arbitrary, but well-grounded in historical reason, is evident from a number of considerations. First, the time of Jesus and the Gospel writers was a time of centuries-old, yet ongoing and sophisticated reflection on constitutional matters, on what forms of government, orderings of power, practices of law-making and law-enforcement, qualities of leadership, and practices of the body, were constitutive of justice and well-being for particular polities.[13] Not uncommonly—and relevant to the present study—a narrative of the life of a particular individual was made the prism through which constitutional reflection was filtered.[14] Critically also, this constitutional reflection included an account, not just of inter-human relations, but also of relations between humankind and the gods, between earth and heaven. What was important, at least in some polities, was placing earthly government in synch with heavenly, a correspondence understood as the key to peace and good order in the cosmos as a whole.

---

10. Particularly relevant are Horbury, "Constitutional Aspects of the Kingdom of God" and, most recently (and partly indebted to Horbury's essay), Bryan, "Jesus and Israel's Eschatological Constitution." Note also Holmén, *Jesus and Jewish Covenant Thinking*.

11. Representative of a massive literature is Horsley, *Jesus and Empire*.

12. Pertinent is Bryan, "Jesus and Israel's Eschatological Constitution," 2848: "We must not revert to the familiar tact [sic] that steers Jesus clear of national aspiration and into the domain of pure spirit."

13. For treatments of biblical and ancient Near Eastern traditions, see Day, *King and Messiah*. On Greco-Roman constitutional reflection, see Walbank, "Monarchies and Monarchic Ideas"; also, Rowe and Schofield, *Cambridge History of Greek and Roman Political Thought*. For an illuminating comparison of Paul and Josephus in constitutional terms, see Barclay, "Matching Theory and Practice"; and, most recently, Bitner, *Paul's Political Strategy*.

14. Cf. Kee, *Community of the New Age*, 69, where, in speaking of Second Temple Jewish traditions, says: "One of the most important literary devices of the apocalypticists is their biographical or autobiographical stance." He illustrates this, *inter alios*, with respect to Enoch in the *Book of Enoch*, Moses in *Jubilees*, the *Testaments of the Twelve Patriarchs*, and the Teacher of Righteousness in the *Damascus Document* from Qumran. He then observes (*Community of the New Age*, 70): "Apocalypticism must be seen, therefore, not only as a literary form or a pattern of history, but as a life-structure as well." The impact of traditions concerning messianic deliverers is also relevant, on which see Horbury, *Jewish Messianism and the Cult of Christ*, esp. 64–108.

Second, and related, particular to the polity of the Jews was the *Mosaic constitution*—the Torah—and its ongoing interpretation both in Galilee and Judea, and also in the Jewish diaspora.[15] Understood as divine revelation, given by God as universal Sovereign to his earthly representative Moses, on Mount Sinai,[16] the law constituted the people, within a covenantal relationship, as "a priestly kingdom and a holy nation" (Exod 19:6). That it was open to interpretation is reflected in the legal and prophetic traditions of the Bible and in post-biblical *halakhoth*.[17] It is also reflected in the "identity politics" of Jesus' day, with various parties offering different judgments about the application of Torah in changing historical circumstances. Such judgments were related to historical experience, social and geographic location, religious sensibility, cultic practice, and underlying worldview. So, among others, we know of Pharisees, Sadducees, Essenes, Qumran Covenanters, and revolutionaries, and, of course, the Jesus movement, each with its own "take" on the interpretation of the Mosaic constitution for the good ordering—in eschatological terms, the *salvation*—of the people.

Third, the Gospel portrayals of Jesus are strongly suggestive of constitutional elements in his mission. In Mark, the present and coming "kingdom" or "rule" of God is central to Jesus' teaching, whether in parables, exorcisms, healings, so-called "nature" miracles, or in symbolic action such as the entry into Jerusalem or the protest in the temple. In Matthew, Jesus is portrayed as a "new Moses,"[18] offering, in the Sermon on the Mount, a radical revision of the Mosaic constitution in a perfectionist direction (cf. Matt 5:48); offering also, in ch. 18, a little disciplinary rule for the maintenance of community solidarity. According to Luke, and consistent with Luke's overarching presentation of the fulfillment of God's plan of salvation, Jesus "confers" a kingdom upon his appointed twelve, along with the eschatological authority to judge the twelve tribes of Israel (Luke 22:29–30 par.). Luke also goes on to tell the story of how the life of the kingdom finds expression in the practices of the church. In John, Jesus is portrayed as God's royal agent, announcing the judgment of this world and the expulsion of its diabolical ruler (John 12:31), revealing a "new commandment" of love, and being "lifted up" (i.e., "exalted") on the cross as a "king."[19] In John 21, furthermore, we find clear evidence of constitution-building: Jesus the Shepherd-King passes authority on to Peter, commissioned now to be the one to feed Jesus' sheep after his departure (cf. esp. vv. 15–17). The Gospels, in brief, are shot through with constitutional motifs and their moral and political corollaries, not least to do with justice, mercy, and well-being. Indeed, the point has to be made clear: the Gospels themselves—like the

---

15. Foundational is Sanders, *Judaism: Practice and Belief*.
16. On Jewish traditions attributing kingship to Moses, see Meeks, "Moses as God and King."
17. Cf. Crawford, *Rewriting Scripture*.
18. Cf. Allison, *New Moses*.
19. Cf. Hengel, "Kingdom of Christ in John"; also, Lincoln, *Truth on Trial*.

Pentateuch before them[20]—are *constitution-shaping texts*.[21] They bear witness to the *society-forming impact* of Jesus and his prophetic mission.[22] But more on this *anon*.

Fourth, and related, warrant for taking a constitutional approach arises out of the way the traditions about Jesus and the kingdom of God, along with scriptural tradition about authority in Israel, were *received* in the early church as it spread within the Hellenized city-states of the Roman Empire. For it is certainly the case that followers of the Risen Lord in the first, second, and subsequent generations, were not reluctant to draw constitutional inferences.[23] Thus, in Paul we find the expectation of a messianic kingdom (cf. 1 Cor 15:20–28) and the redemption of the people Israel (cf. Rom 11:25–27).[24] Relations with the powers-that-be are articulated in a way that uphold God's sovereignty and Christ's lordship while allowing earthly powers their divinely-delegated role (cf. Rom 13:1–7).[25] Encouragement is given for believers to consider themselves members of an eschatological citizenship (πολίτευμα) (Phil 3:20). Christian gatherings are called ἐκκλησίαι, the standard terminology for a gathering of citizens. Considerable attention is given to the right ordering of Christian households, the basic unit of the *polis* in ancient constitutional philosophy (cf. Col 3:18—4:1). Church officeholders are appointed with such titles as ἐπίσκοπος and διάκονος, titles drawn from contemporary social groups and institutions. And so on. In other words, from the very beginning, the kingdom of God was interpreted in concrete social and constitutional terms.

I turn, then, to Jesus—the *remembered* Jesus of the gospels—in constitutional perspective.

---

20. On the Pentateuch as a constitution-shaping text, see Houston, *Pentateuch*, 11–85.

21. I owe this observation to Andrew Lincoln, in conversation. Andrew also made the important connection with recent research on the Gospels in relation to social memory theory. This theory posits *inter alia* that how the past is remembered is shaped by the social concerns of the group in the present—with the implication for Gospels interpretation that the constitutional needs of the early Christian groups shaped the ways in which the evangelists told their respective stories of Jesus. Among recent treatments are Kirk and Thatcher, *Memory, Tradition, and Text*; Barton et al., *Memory in the Bible*; and Thatcher, *Memory and Identity*.

22. Cf. Lohfink, *Jesus and Community*.

23. For what follows, see, *inter alia*, Judge, *Social Pattern*; Meeks, *First Urban Christians*.

24. Cf. Horbury, "Constitutional Aspects," 75.

25. Horbury, "Constitutional Aspects," 75, draws attention to Wisdom of Solomon 6.1–4: "Listen, therefore, O kings, and understand; learn, O judges of the ends of the earth. Give ear, you that rule over multitudes, and boast of many nations. For your dominion was given you from the Lord, and your sovereignty from the Most High; he will search out your works and inquire into your plans. Because as servants of his kingdom you did not rule rightly, or keep the law, or walk according to the purpose of God, he will come upon you terribly and swiftly."

Jesus: Eschatological Prophet of National Restoration

Accounts of the aims of Jesus are many, but I find persuasive the basic argument of E. P. Sanders and others[26] that the mission of Jesus is best understood in the light of Jewish restoration eschatology, central aspects of which are: the hope for the kingdom of God on earth; the reconstituting of the twelve tribes; a Spirit-renewed, covenant-loyal nation; and a new temple. This makes good sense of a number of factors, among which are: first, Jesus' initial association with John the Baptizer, himself an eschatological prophet, calling Israel to repentance in view of imminent judgment; second, Jesus' already-mentioned appointment of "the twelve" as judges in a restored Israel (cf. Matt 19:28); third, Jesus' intense focus on the nation of Israel as the eschatological priority, almost to the exclusion of Gentiles (cf. Matt 10:6; Mark 7:27); fourth, Jesus' move on Jerusalem, including the messianic symbolism of his entry into the city (cf. Zech 9:9), along with sayings and actions prophetic of the renewal of the temple; fifth, Jesus' crucifixion as a messianic pretender; and sixth, the evidence of Acts that, after the resurrection, Jesus' followers continued to hold restorationist views, as when the apostles ask the risen Jesus, "Lord, is this the time when you will restore the kingdom to Israel?" (Acts 1:6).

My suggestion, then, is that what we say about justice, mercy and social well-being in relation to Jesus requires a hermeneutic that takes seriously an understanding of Jesus as an eschatological prophet of national restoration. Such an understanding has several corollaries. One is that the mission of Jesus is one of *hope in God and God's providential, salvific activity in history*. It is a thoroughly theocentric vision of the nature of the authority that will underpin the people's common life. Another corollary is that the mission of Jesus has its orientation toward, and fulfillment in, *a concrete social order*. It is not other-worldly: nor is it apolitical. Rather, it looks to God to bring in a new world order—a world order free of Roman domination, and where God's kingship is acknowledged. Yet further, the new order will be *a fulfillment of God's dealings in justice and mercy with Israel*, dealings to which Israel's Scriptures bear testimony. The constitution of the new age is understood as having its roots in God's covenanting with his people Israel, and through Israel, bringing universal blessing, especially the always longed-for blessing of *peace*.

Power and Authority

To see Jesus in this way throws light on a number of aspects of Jesus' mission. First, at the heart of Jesus' teachings and actions is the announcement and celebration of

---

26. Sanders, *Jesus and Judaism*; Sanders, *Historical Figure of Jesus*; also Caird, *Jesus and the Jewish Nation*; reprinted in Dunn and McKnight, *Historical Jesus in Recent Research*, 275–87; Rowland, *Christian Origins*, part 3, section 2; Wright, *Jesus and the Victory of God*, esp. ch. 7; McKnight, *New Vision for Israel*. For an appreciative critique and modification of Sanders's position see Bryan, "Jesus and Israel's Eschatological Constitution."

the in-breaking of "the kingdom of God" (Mark 1:14–15 par.), a concept rooted in Scripture,[27] and with evident constitutional—specifically, monarchical/theocratic—overtones.[28] For Jesus, the creation and maintenance of a just and merciful society is *a response to, a participation in, and an outworking of, the power, or rule, or kingship, of God*. Justice and mercy are grounded in God, and demand orderings of life in the present, oriented toward a future when God's rule will be manifest fully on earth as it is in heaven (cf. Matt 6:10). So understood, justice and mercy are present and future eschatological realities that have to do with *salvation in historical time and space*.

This salvific aspect is crucial. In the ministry of Jesus, it helps to make sense of the outworking of his "kingdom" teaching in practices of exorcism and healing.[29] Thus, the *exorcisms* he performs display Jesus' engagement with, and judgment upon, the cosmic powers that hold people in bondage, and doing so as God's empowering agent: "But if it is by the finger of God that I cast out demons, then the kingdom of God has come upon you!" (Luke 11:20; cf. Matt 12:28).[30] For Jesus, the advent of justice on the earth requires defeat of the forces of evil in the heavens and the restoration of cosmic order. The battle is one of cosmic proportions and cosmic significance—all of which is a way of pointing to Jesus' prophetic attention to things that *really matter*, to what creates and sustains *life*.

Likewise, the *healings*. If sickness and disability are signs of demonic possession, powerlessness, social injustice, and poverty, the healings display the presence in Jesus of divine power to save and restore: and the restoration of bodies physical signals the restoration *and empowerment* of the body social.[31] Thus, when John, now in prison, inquires of Jesus via an intermediary, "Are you the one who is to come, or are we to wait for another?" Jesus replies, "Go and tell John what you hear and see: the blind receive their sight, the lame walk, the lepers are cleansed, the deaf hear, the dead are raised, and the poor have good news brought to them. And blessed is anyone who takes no offense at me" (Matt 11:2–6 par.). Here is testimony to a representative yet comprehensive healing praxis expressive of God's kingly power to save his people, exercised through his messianic agent.

Significantly, Jesus' salvific, "kingdom of God" activity does not include engaging in training or competition for formal office. In Weberian terms, Jesus' authority has

27. Cf. texts and discussion in Horbury, "Constitutional Aspects," 64–70, with particular focus on postexilic, including pentateuchal, texts; also, Wright, *New Testament and the People of God*, 303–7.

28. Cf. Rowland, "Reflections on the Politics of the Gospels," 224–41, at 238: "Yet Jesus' mission is thoroughly imbued with an understanding of polity which was rooted in a theocratic tradition derived from the Bible."

29. Cf. O'Donovan, *Desire of the Nations*, 95, commenting on Jesus' acts of exorcism and healing: "Yet that new power was directed against the forces which most immediately hindered Israel from living effectively as a community in God's service, the spiritual and natural weaknesses which drained its energies away. This was not an apolitical gesture, but a statement of true political priorities. . . . The empowerment of Israel was more important that the disempowerment of Rome."

30. Cf. Stuckenbruck, *Myth of Rebellious Angels*, esp. 161–86.

31. Cf. Theissen, "Jesus and His Followers as Healers," 45–65.

more elements of the traditional and the charismatic, than of the legal-bureaucratic.[32] Indicative is a little tradition unique to Luke. To a man who comes to him seeking a legal ruling on a matter of inheritance, Jesus says, by way of rebuke: "Friend, who set me to be a judge or arbitrator over you [κριτὴν ἢ μεριστὴν ἐφ' ὑμᾶς]?" (Luke 12:14). On the one hand, Jesus prescinds from offering advice on property law; on the other hand, he warns, prophet-style, of the danger of greed (at vv. 15–21).

Nor does Jesus' activity involve direct engagement with Roman power and authority (at least until his trial before Pilate). As Ernst Bammel has shown, Jesus was not a Zealot-style political revolutionary.[33] Rather, Jesus' understanding of the kingship of God over the nations, includes the conviction—vividly illustrated in the book of Daniel—that the kings and rulers of the earth hold power by divine permission and under the providence of God, to whom they are accountable.[34] Hence, when tested by Pharisees and Herodians over the lawfulness of paying taxes to Caesar—the trap being to repudiate either Caesar or God—Jesus offers the famous reply, "Render to Caesar the things that are Caesar's, and to God the things that are God's" (Mark 12:13–17, at 17, RSV).[35]

That said, a good case can be made in support of the claim that Jesus did indeed trouble the powers-that-be, in particular the Judean governing elite, and especially the temple authorities.[36] Notably, he begins his public ministry in the immediate wake of the imprisonment by King Herod of his trouble-making predecessor in the prophetic line, John the Baptizer (Mark 1:14a; cf. 6:17–29). Subsequently, Jesus himself attracts Herod's enmity, and is warned that the one he calls derisively, "that fox," seeks to kill him (Luke 13:31–32). Members of the Pharisaic party find him troublingly antinomian,[37] especially in respect of Sabbath observance, purity rules, and association with "sinners." He prophesies coming judgment on Israel and its leaders (cf. Matt 11:16–24; Mark 12:1–12; Luke 13:6–9; 19:41–44).[38] The high priesthood and

32. Cf. Gerth and Mills, *From Max Weber*, 324–85.

33. Bammel, "Revolution Theory from Reimarus to Brandon."

34. Telling, in this respect, are the words of the Johannine Jesus to Pilate: "You would have no power over me *unless it had been given you from above*" (John 19:11).

35. Interestingly, in relation to the temple tax, payment is made a matter of *concession*—"so that we do not give offense to them"—rather than legal or customary obligation, the reason being that "the children [of the heavenly Father] are free" (Matt 17:24–27).

36. Cf. Segal, "Jesus, the Jewish Revolutionary." Note especially Segal's observation about the typical spectrum of political action among apocalyptic groups and the authorities' response: "But regardless of the disposition of a group toward political action, either active or passive, the distinction is lost on the ruling powers. . . . The various actors within a society may interpret the movement differently, but the rulers almost always interpret the threat as a political one and deal with it accordingly" ("Jesus, the Jewish Revolutionary," 204).

37. Cf. Holmén, *Jesus and Jewish Covenant Thinking*, 340, suggesting that the opposition to Jesus arose from his failure/refusal—not least, in his role as a teacher—to make loyalty to the covenant and (what Holmén calls) covenant "path-searching" central to his ministry.

38. That Jesus is a prophet of national judgment, as well as a prophet of national restoration, is emphasized by Bryan, "Jesus and Israel's Eschatological Constitution," 2841–44.

Sanhedrin are alarmed by the threat to public order and their own authority posed by his popular reception in Jerusalem as the Davidic messiah (Mark 11:1–10 par.) and his demonstration in the temple (Mark 11:15–19 par.). And the extensive Gospel trial narratives give eloquent testimony to the challenge Jesus poses to authorities both Jewish and Roman.

If we ask after the nature of the power which the authorities find threatening, it is plausible to suggest, with the Gospels, that Jesus' power is that of *God's Spirit* received at his baptism (cf. Mark 1:9–11 par.). It is appeal to the Spirit, and evidence of Spirit-possession, however much contested by his enemies (cf. Mark 3:22–30 par.), that gives Jesus *legitimacy*—and therefore makes his power *effective*. Helpful here also is a suggestion from Gerd Theissen,[39] along more sociological lines. He argues that the power exercised by Jesus is "political" in the broad, Aristotelian sense of action for the common good of the *polis*; and that the politics of Jesus has two sides. On the negative side, is the radical refusal of politically taken-for-granted practices of coercion, along with the profoundly significant willingness to endure violence and accept victimhood, thereby opening a path to power of a different kind. On the positive side, is the practice of *proclamation and persuasion*, summoning Israel back to its core belief in the kingship of the one God who is God alone, offering a heightened moral vision with the command to love one's *enemies*, and demonstrating the reality of the in-breaking kingdom in prophetic symbolic action, and practices of humane rulership (cf. Mark 10:41–44).[40]

But Theissen's argument may be augmented by noting the pervasive sense that the kingdom of God, breaking in already in the mission of Jesus, is a μυστήριον (cf. Mark 4:11).[41] It is a reality which is hidden in heaven, its truth disclosed by divine initiative to the few able to receive it, and its articulation requiring figures of speech, metaphors, parables, and symbolic acts such as the welcome of *children* (cf. Mark

---

39. Theissen, "Political Dimension."

40. Says Theissen ("Political Dimension," 228), "Jesus was a master not only at inventing parabolic short stories, but also at performing political symbolic actions." The examples he gives (238) are: the exorcisms, symbolic of the overthrow of alien powers "latent in the demons," as in the demons named "Legion," in Mark 5:9); the appointment of the Twelve to govern Israel, "an anti-government standing over against other governmental structures"; the Triumphal Entry, when Jesus is hailed as "king" or as representative of "the kingdom of our father David"; and the Temple Cleansing, prophetically announcing the temple's destruction and depriving the temple and the ruling aristocracy of their legitimacy. In his conclusion, he says: "Jesus and his followers did not espouse political quietism. They did not remain passive. They participated in the realization of the kingdom of God by an explicit renunciation of force, by political symbolic actions, and by an in-group exercise of humane rulership" (243).

41. That this notion of the essential *hiddenness* of God and God's ways with the world is characteristic of Jewish apocalyptic is well known. It is certainly an important underlying element, in various ways, in all four canonical Gospels, not least in Mark's so-called "messianic secret." In my opinion, a good case can be made that it is an understanding of God and the rule of God shared by Jesus himself: cf. Wright, *Jesus and the Victory of God*.

9:33–37; 10:13–16).⁴² This bears on the experience of salvation, and therefore on justice, mercy and social well-being. It opens the possibility that justice, mercy and social well-being may be *inscrutable*, hidden, paradoxical, subversive, discovered in unexpected places, practiced in unexpected ways, open to unlikely recipients—and therefore also a cause of *offence* (cf. Mark 4:12).

Reflection along these lines takes us, theologically-speaking, to the heart of the gospel and the heart of the Gospels: the kingdom of God, the kingdom of justice and mercy, is revealed, not only in authoritative teaching and acts of power, but also in *the potent acceptance of the weakness and shame* attendant upon being "handed over" to crucifixion. Invoking the apocalyptic figure of the heavenly Son of Man of Daniel 7:13–14, Jesus tells the unsuspecting disciples: "the Son of man must undergo great suffering, and be rejected by the elders, the chief priests, and the scribes, and be killed, and after three days rise again" (Mark 8:31). In a word, salvation, and with it, justice, mercy and well-being, comes at a cost. It involves *sacrifice*. The man of justice is treated unjustly, the man of mercy is treated without mercy, the one who brings individual and social well-being is done to death, with "King of the Jews" the ironic *titulus* inscribed on his cross.

But the double irony is that, in the eye of faith, Jesus is *indeed* the king of the Jews, God's messiah, and that the cross is a *throne*:⁴³ for here, human judgment is judged, the power of the powers-that-be (both natural and supernatural) is rendered powerless, and God's just judgment is vindicated. Precisely here the justice and mercy of God are revealed, opening the way for a new community to come into being. There is an *incommensurability* between human justice and God's justice, between human mercy and God's mercy. It is the incommensurability of the "rightwising" grace of God whereby justice, mercy and well-being come *as unmerited gift*. The issue worth pondering at this point is *whether and how human constitutional arrangements ordered toward justice, mercy and social well-being may accommodate divine gratuity*.

Such a notion points, among a number of possibilities, to the vocation of *the church*. In ecclesiological perspective, it is the vocation of the church, as a fulfillment of the vocation of Israel, so to witness in the manner of its life and practice—its word, sacraments, and charitable works—to God's "rightwising" grace, that injustice will not have the last word, and the downtrodden of the earth will be lifted up.⁴⁴

Law and Custom

A second aspect of Jesus' mission that has constitutional resonances has to do with law and custom, often focussed on *Torah interpretation*. Given the fundamental place of Torah in the just ordering of the nation's life—where Torah is understood, with many

42. Cf. Gundry, "Children in the Gospel of Mark."
43. Cf. Marcus, "Crucifixion as Parodic Exaltation."
44. Profound on this is O'Donovan, *Desire of the* Nations, esp. 158–92.

variations, as divine revelation constituting the nation as God's own, and making possible just judgments—it is not surprising that the Gospel traditions give evidence of lively engagement between Jesus and his compatriots (especially the Pharisees) over how to interpret it. Furthermore, the Jesus movement and the Pharisaic movement are part of a history of parties in Judaism for whom Torah obedience—or, more broadly, doing the will of God—is a matter of *heightened importance*, often in the context of anxieties around discerning the meaning of current times and events.[45] The Maccabean literature (e.g., 4 Macc 8–12), for instance, bears witness to a martyr tradition articulated in terms of intense Torah loyalty, where what constitutes justice, mercy and social well-being is displayed in the total *negation* of these goods under the tyrant king Antiochus IV Epiphanes. Similarly, the texts from Qumran give evidence of a sacerdotal community[46] shaped by a distinctive constitution oriented toward the maintenance of the community as a *yahad* ("oneness").[47] Its members are given to Torah piety and Torah mysticism, and live according to an ascetical purity regime. They do so in preparation for holy war between "the sons of light" and "the sons of darkness" at the end of time. So the question of Jesus and the law, including matters bearing on justice, mercy and well-being, is bound up with the complex makeup of Judaism, and what may best be described as a *crisis of identity* in the face of perceived dangers from within and without.

But it is bound up also with *complexities inherent in the law itself*. In a valuable study,[48] Philip Alexander distinguishes no less than four interlocking circles in Jewish law: state law (either Roman law or the law devolved to a native prince like Herod Antipas); civil law, in the sense of law applied through the courts at their respective levels; religious law, divided between matters public and private; and the Pentateuch or Mosaic Torah, variously interpreted, critiqued, and augmented by appeals to custom, tradition, and even new revelation. This complexity is noteworthy. In relation to Jesus, it means that any attempt to set Jesus either "for" or "against" the law is rendered otiose, since, in such a construction, "the law" is lifted to such a high level of abstraction that it is evacuated of meaningful content. Just as serious is the way such constructions lift Jesus himself out of his historical and constitutional context as a Jew in first-century Palestinian Judaism. Only by acknowledging the rootedness of Jesus in the juridical and forensic context of his day are we able to recognize the contours

---

45. Cf. Neusner, *First Century Judaism in Crisis*.

46. The *Community Rule* offers the following: "When these things exist in Israel, the Community council shall be founded on truth, like an everlasting plantation, a holy house for Israel, and the foundation of the holy of holies for Aaron, true witnesses for the judgment and chosen by the will (of God) to atone for the earth and to render the wicked their retribution. . . . It will be the most holy dwelling for Aaron with total knowledge of the covenant of justice and in order to offer a pleasant aroma; and it will be a house of perfection and truth in Israel, . . . in order to establish a covenant in compliance with the everlasting decrees" (1QS.VIII.4–10).

47. Cf. Claussen and Davis, "Concept of Unity at Qumran."

48. Alexander, "Jewish Law in the Time of Jesus," 54–55.

of his moral and social vision. Justice, mercy, and social well-being *have a history*: and that is no less the case with Jesus, his followers and successors.

The point deserves emphasis, not least with regard to the Pharisees. Too often, in Christian imagination, the Pharisees have come to be type-cast—over against "Jesus the liberator"—as legalistic and hypocritical, to the point where the serious moral and religious concerns of *both* the Pharisees *and* Jesus get lost.[49] Those concerns are vocational, constitutional, and eschatological: with how to be holy people and a holy nation in the presence of a holy God, in anticipation of God's coming to restore Israel in justice and mercy.

Against this backdrop, the evidence of the Gospels suggests the following points pertinent to our inquiry.[50] First, Jesus gives priority to "*the weightier matters of the law*": these include justice and mercy (cf. Matt 23:23; also, 9:13; 12:7). To make a distinction bordering on the anachronistic: where a necessary *prioritizing* of forms of law-observance is required, moral considerations weigh more heavily than ritual considerations. A case in point has to do with Sabbath observance.[51] Mark 3:1–6 tells of the healing of the man with the withered hand on the Sabbath, an action defended by Jesus with the rhetorical challenge, "Is it lawful to do good or to do harm on the Sabbath, to save life or to kill?" (Mark 3:4). Here, Jesus appeals to the halakhic principle of the priority of saving a life, the implied assumption being that the physical impairment hindered the man's ability to support himself and his family. Incidentally, it is not coincidental that so many disputes between Jesus and his co-religionists concern Sabbath observance: for Sabbath involves the *ritual marking of time*, evoking the time of creation (cf. Gen 2:1–3; Exod 20:8–11), and the time of liberation from slavery (cf. Deut 5:12–15). Given that, according to Jesus, a *new time* is breaking in, it is apposite that healing and restoration to life take place on the Sabbath.

But we cannot leave the weightier matters without referring to the weightiest of all. That *love* is at the heart of life under God is displayed vividly in Mark 12:28–34 where, in response to the scribe's question, "Which commandment is first of all?" Jesus responds with the famous double commandment of love of God and love of neighbor, the first taken from the "Shema" of Deuteronomy 6:5, the second from Leviticus 19:18. Particularly emphatic is the repetition, found only in Mark's version, with the scribe echoing Jesus' words back to him, and even elaborating upon them, with the comment, "this is much more important than all whole burnt offerings and sacrifices" (12:33b). That we are in the realm of "kingdom" ethics is confirmed by Jesus' climactic response: "You are not far from the kingdom of God" (12:34). In this

---

49. Drawing the poison from traditional caricatures of the Pharisees, and of Judaism as a whole, is one of the major contributions of Sanders's *Jesus and Judaism*, as also of his earlier *Paul and Palestinian Judaism*.

50. Valuable for what follows is Bockmuehl, "Halakhah and Ethics"; also Holmén, *Jesus and Jewish Covenant Thinking*, 88–199; Sanders, *Historical Figure of Jesus*, 196–237; and Banks, *Jesus and the Law*.

51. Cf. Doering, "Sabbath Laws in the New Testament Gospels."

light, justice, mercy and social well-being are manifestations of *Jesus' radical prioritizing of the scriptural love command*.

Second, Jesus gives priority to his *prophetic vocation and eschatological message*. On some points of law or custom, this leads to a more rigorous interpretation, in line with Jesus' utopian vision that a restored Israel would, in some sense at least, represent a return to Eden—the principle of the End-time as like the Beginning-time (*Endzeit gleich Urzeit*). A case in point is his teaching on divorce (cf. Mark 10:2–9 par.), according to which the ruling by Moses in Deuteronomy 24:1 is treated as a concession, and is replaced by a prohibition based on an appeal to the Creator's original intention for the permanence of marriage (Mark 10:6–9 par.; citing Gen 1:27; 2:24). Here, Genesis is allowed to trump Deuteronomy[52]—and we are reminded of the *exegetical* character of determinations of justice, mercy and social well-being characteristic of Jesus and his times.

The Sermon on the Mount, which itself reads like a mini-constitution, offers further cases. Notably, the so-called Antitheses—even though they take the form, "You have heard that it was said. . . . But I say to you . . ."—represent, not the abolition of Torah (cf. Matt 5:17–20!), but its *intensification*, often in the direction of human interiority, of the disposition of the human heart. Such an intensification is consistent with the prophetic tradition in which Jesus stands (cf. Isa 29:13). It is consistent also with Jesus' advocacy of practices of judgment expressive of the rule of God and of God's perfection (cf. Matt 5:48).

Intriguing, however, is the fact that on other points, Jesus' prophetic vocation and eschatological message result in a *relativization* of law and custom. This is suggested in sayings which attribute to Jesus an authority greater than the temple (Matt 12:6), greater than Jonah and Solomon (Matt 12:41–42), greater even than Moses (cf. John 1:17; 5:46). It is strikingly evident also in Jesus' relativization of the responsibilities adhering to the ties that bind—family ties, in particular.[53] Notorious, for example, is the episode which hinges on the weighty custom of the burial of the dead: "Another of his disciples said to [Jesus], 'Lord, let me first go and bury my father.' But Jesus said to him, 'Follow me, and let the dead bury their own dead'" (Matt 8:21–22 par.; cf. Matt 10:34–36, 37–38).[54] In cases like this, by no means unprecedented in Jewish traditions (according to which the cause of God takes precedence over otherwise legitimate concerns), we have another hint of the eschatological urgency which dominates Jesus' words and actions.

Related to the preceding is evidence that suggests that Jesus stands in a positive—though also tangential—relation to Jewish *holy war tradition*.[55] Evocative of the

---

52. Cf. Harvey, "Genesis versus Deuteronomy?"

53. Cf. Barton, *Discipleship and Family Ties*, esp. ch. 2.

54. Foundational is Hengel, *Charismatic Leader*. For subsequent discussion, see Fletcher-Louis, "Leave the Dead to Bury Their Own Dead."

55. Cf. Hengel, *Charismatic Leader*, 18–20. For the biblical background, cf. Deut 23:10–15; 1 Sam

holy war zeal of Phineas (cf. Philo, *Vit. Mos.* I.300–304), for example, is Jesus' saying: "Do not think that I have come to bring peace to the earth; I have not come to bring peace, but a sword. For I have come to set a man against his father, and a daughter against her mother, and a daughter-in-law against her mother-in-law; and one's foes will be members of one's own household" (Matt 10:34–36 par.; cf. Luke 14:26 par.). Taken in combination with Jesus' prophetic celibacy (cf. Matt 19:12), rigorous sexual ethic, and generally ascetic lifestyle[56] (learned, no doubt, in the company of John the Baptizer), Jesus appears as one totally devoted to the cause of the kingdom of God. Spirit-empowered, Jesus is the one come to vanquish the "strong man" Satan and his minions (cf. Mark 3:22–27).

Regarding Jesus on law and custom in general, a reasonable conclusion is that, while law/Torah is neither the main symbol of Jesus' identity, nor the main focus of Jesus' mission to Israel, it is, nevertheless, a vital scriptural reference point for determinations about how to be a citizen of God's kingdom—and that, when it *does* become the point at issue, its interpretation is *re-oriented* according to Jesus' prophetic-eschatological priorities.[57] As corollaries, I would add the following. First, a re-orientation is not an abrogation; otherwise, the Jesus tradition would be innocent of halakhic concerns (which it is patently not), and the conspicuous struggles over law-observance in the early church (cf. Gal 2:11–21; Acts 15) would make no sense. Second, attention to the heart, to matters of motivation, is not a "spiritualization" of Torah: rather, it is an intensification of the demand of God for personal and societal integrity. Third, giving priority to the "weightier" matters of the law (which are essentially to do with saving life) is not a warrant for disparaging or neglecting ritual aspects. The two go in tandem—as when Jesus commands the cleansed leper: "Go, show yourself to the priest, and offer for your cleansing what Moses commanded, as a testimony to them" (Mark 1:44). Justice, mercy and social well-being, we may say, are embodied and embedded symbolically as well as pragmatically.

Once again, this invites reflection in the area of *ecclesiology*. If justice, mercy and social well-being are matters of judgment and action according to law, custom and tradition (as bearers of a community's self-understanding and hoped-for future), such

---

21:5–6; 2 Sam 11:11–13. For holy war ideology at Qumran, cf. the War Scroll (= 1QM; also 4Q491–496), cited Der Horst, "Celibacy in Early Judaism," 396.

56. Cf. Allison, *Jesus of Nazareth*, 172–216. The evidence for Jesus' asceticism is hardly affected by the slander that Jesus is "a glutton and a drunkard" (Matt 11:19 // Luke 7:34). There are, after all, different kinds and degrees of asceticism; and, in any case, the slander should not be taken literally: cf. Dunn, *Jesus Remembered*, 599–600n253.

57. Cf. Bockmuehl, "Halakhah and Ethics," 275n22: "Nevertheless, Jesus' halakhic innovations can be well understood in terms of his vision for an eschatologically revitalized Torah." Compare Holmén, *Jesus and Jewish Covenant Thinking*, 335, who argues, interestingly, that Jesus' utopian vision and distinctive approach to Torah-interpretation may have been indebted to the idea of the eschatological covenant as reflected in Jeremiah and Ezekiel (e.g., Jer 31:34; Ezek 11:19–20). Here, "no one needs to be taught how to keep the covenant, for God has 'implanted' the knowledge and wisdom of this within man [*sic*]."

matters will be sustained, negotiated, and even revitalized in the community's ritual and symbolic life. One significant place, time and people where this may happen is the church.[58]

Praxis

Christian faith is irreducibly personal, relational, and mimetic. In the Gospel traditions, this is epitomized in the command of Jesus, "Follow me!" with its implication of progression and growth—individual and social—by being in Jesus' presence and imitating him.[59] Furthermore, in the light of Jesus' crucifixion and resurrection, following Jesus is legitimized and vindicated as participation in the community of the new age. The shape of that participation is displayed in indicative action, or *praxis*. I turn, therefore, to praxis as a third aspect of Jesus' mission with constitutional resonance, not least in relation to justice, mercy and social well-being.

That Jesus gains notoriety for his apparently habitual practice of *table-fellowship with people identified as "tax collectors and sinners"* is widely attested in the tradition (cf. Matt 11:19 par.; Luke 15:2; 19:7).[60] Symptomatic is Mark 2:16–18: "When the scribes of the Pharisees saw that [Jesus] was eating with sinners and tax collectors, they said to his disciples, 'Why does he eat with tax collectors and sinners?' When Jesus heard this, he said to them, 'Those who are well have no need of a physician, but those who are sick; I have come to call not the righteous, but sinners.'"

To appreciate the Pharisaic anxieties reflected in this text, we need to step back a little. Far more than in the modern West, food and the sharing of food in traditional societies have a rich *semiotic* significance. What is consumed is, not just food, but *meaning*.[61] The meanings—carried by the complexity of food practices, food taboos, food types, and food traditions—are multiple and mutually reinforcing. Since eating is not a solitary activity but communal, these meanings have to do, above all, with *identity-conferring relationships*, their instigation, maintenance, modulation, discrimination, discipline, and cessation. The scope of such relationships is wide, for meals and meal practices display a *cosmology*. They express relations human and divine, earthly and heavenly (cf. Matt 6:11 par.!). They are therefore the stuff of life, both physical and social, with enormous material-symbolic potency, given their constant, ritualized repetition. So understood, meals and meal practices have constitutional significance. They communicate the ordering of reality (or the loss of same). In particular, they

---

58. Cf. Barton, "'Mercy and Not Sacrifice'?"

59. Interesting in this connection is Riley, "Words and Deeds"; cf. also Hengel, *Charismatic Leader*, passim.

60. Helpful for what follows is Dunn, "Jesus, Table-Fellowship, and Qumran"; Dunn, *Jesus Remembered*.

61. Foundational is Mary Douglas's essay "Deciphering a Meal"; see also her earlier work, *Purity and Danger*. Cf. also Soler, "Semiotics of Food in the Bible."

communicate a society's center and periphery, including, at multiple levels related to the distribution of power, who is in and who is out.[62]

Determining precisely the identity of the "tax-collectors and sinners" in the Markan pericope is not straightforward.[63] What is clear, however, is that, from the Pharisees' point of view, according to which the holiness of God is displayed in the extension of temple purity into the everyday rituals of bed and board, tax-collectors and sinners are on or beyond the periphery. The designations (i.e., "tax-collectors" and "sinners") are terms of discrimination and exclusion, especially in relation to spiritual and social power. By virtue of defiling occupation (so, the tax collectors) or antinomian lifestyle (so, the sinners; cf. Mark 7:21–22), they have excluded themselves from holiness groups like the Pharisees, and are themselves excluded.

Nor, among the various parties in the Judaism of Jesus' day, are the Pharisees unique in this respect. Food rules and practices of commensality play a very significant part also in the constitution of the Qumran community, where the preservation of God's holiness by observance of biblical purity laws is taken to a level of even greater intensity.[64] *Holiness as separation* is figured, not only in the movement of the sect into the desert, there to worship God in the company of the angels as a temple of men (*sic*). It is figured also in the degrees of separation or distinction which characterize the internal ordering of the sect, distinctions displayed, not least, at the meal table.

Of particular note are the purity rules, based on Lev 21:17–21, listing those denied admission to the assembly of the community in the last days:

> No man, defiled by any of the impurities of a man shall enter the assembly of these [i.e., the men previously mention]; and everyone who is defiled by them should not be established in his office amongst the congregation. And everyone who is defiled in his flesh, paralysed in his feet or in his hands, lame, blind, deaf, dumb or defiled in his flesh with a blemish visible to the eyes, or the tottering old man who cannot keep upright in the midst of the assembly, these shall not enter to take their place among the congregation of famous men, for the angels of holiness are among their congregation. (1QSa 2.3–9).[65]

Striking, by way of contrast, is the force of Jesus' table-talk, in Luke 14:12–14:

---

62. It is therefore, by no means coincidental, that one of the ways non-Jews characterize the constitution of the Jews as particular to themselves (and generally offensive to civilized cosmopolitans), is to draw attention to Jewish laws and customs prohibiting Jews from sharing board and bed with non-Jews. (Cf. Tacitus, *History*, V.5; Philostratus, *Life of Apollonius of Tyana*, V.33.) On the connection between food rules and sex rules, see Barton, "Food Rules, Sex Rules."

63. Cf. Dunn, "Pharisees, Sinners, and Jesus."

64. Cf. Davies, "Food, Drink and Sects."

65. The translation is from Martinez, *Dead Sea Scrolls Translated*. Other related texts include 1QM 7.4–6; 4QCD; 11QTemple 45.12–14, cited in Dunn, "Jesus, Table-Fellowship, and Qumran," 264. For a valuable study of the eschatological and cosmological rationale for these purity rules, see Wassen, "What Do Angels Have Against the Blind and the Deaf?"

> When you give a luncheon or a dinner, do not invite your friends or your brothers or your relatives or rich neighbours, in case they may invite you in return, and you would be repaid. But when you give a banquet, invite the poor, the crippled, the lame, and the blind. And you will be blessed, because they cannot repay you, for you will be repaid at the resurrection of the righteous.

What the contrast suggests is that Jesus' praxis of an open table and inclusive table-fellowship expresses, materially and socially, a different vision of God, God's holiness, and what it means to be the people of God. A clue to that vision comes in the account of Jesus' *last* meal where, after sharing the cup of wine, symbol of his blood to be "poured out for many," he says, "I shall not drink again of the fruit of the vine until that day when I drink it new in the kingdom of God'" (Mark 14:25).

Jesus' table-fellowship is *kingdom praxis*: it is consumption in the present which—against a rich scriptural background (cf. Isa 25:6; 54:4–8; 62:4–5; Hos 2:16–20)—looks forward to a future, glorious *consummation* in a restored Israel under the rule of God (cf. Matt 22:1–14; Luke 22:30). Jesus' alternative holiness symbolism is powerful.[66] At the risk of oversimplification, it may be characterized thus: instead of the intact body, Jesus offers the healed body and the forgiven heart; instead of holiness as separation, holiness as aggregation; instead of holiness by avoidance, contagious holiness; instead of holiness as judgment, holiness as celebration (cf. Mark 2:19); instead of holiness as a cause of division, holiness as an inalienable gift making all one.

It is not coincidental that the followers of Jesus after his death and resurrection continue practices of table-fellowship, and of hospitality more generally. Such practices have ongoing constitutional implications and resonances. As one example, the testimony of Acts to the ἅπαντα κοινά—the "all things in common"—of the early converts (cf. Acts 2:44; 4:32)[67] is indicative of a utopian society coming into being, with justice and mercy embodied in the distribution of material goods according to need, along with the practice of "breaking bread" together. It is noteworthy that the pragmatic aspects are integrally related to the symbolic and ritual aspects. The distribution of goods and the breaking of bread together are a response to, and integrated with, the apostolic preaching, baptism, prayers, "signs and wonders," temple attendance, and the praise of God (Acts 2:41–47; 4:32–37). Drawing once again an ecclesiological inference, we may say that the mission of Jesus for the restoration of Israel under the kingship of God is finding its fulfillment—its perhaps *unexpected* fulfillment—in the society of the church, and even rippling outward, its pattern of sociality generating "the goodwill of all the people [χάριν πρὸς ὅλον τὸν λαόν]" (Acts 2:47).

---

66. Cf. Segal, "Jesus, the Jewish Revolutionary," 232–33: "The presence of prostitutes and tax collectors among Jesus' supporters is probably symbolic as well as actual, vividly expressing the apocalyptic ethic of overturning the established order."

67. Valuable on this is Capper, "Earliest Christian Community of Goods."

Conclusion

Justice, mercy and social well-being are weighty, but naked, abstractions. I have tried, in the preceding, to open up various ways in which such naked abstractions are given moral-theological definition and traction by *being given a body and clothed in a narrative*. In Christian faith, that *body* is multiple. It is Israel. It is above all Jesus of Nazareth. And it is the body of Christ-followers, which is the church. The *narrative* is the one which is central to the church's liturgy and life—the story displayed in the Gospels (and, of course, in Scripture as a whole), here interpreted in broadly constitutional terms. The following four points deserve emphasis.

First, the story of Jesus situates justice, mercy, and social well-being *in the context of salvation in time and space*, from the creation of the world, and the election of Israel, onward. To put it another way, justice, mercy and well-being are relational qualities *whose fullness is eschatological*—known fully only in Christ, and experienced in the present as grace, even if only partially and in anticipatory form. As such, the quest for justice, mercy, and social well-being, as a sharing in the life of God, is the Christian's duty and joy. It is how we live *out of and into* the third petition of the Lord's Prayer, "Thy will be done, on earth as it is in heaven" (Matt 6:10b).

Second, epitomized in Jesus' call, "Follow me!" the story of Jesus offers, not philosophical definitions of justice, mercy and well-being, but *a life-structure for their discovery and practice*. Not least in its testimony to one who, in mission to Israel, healed the sick, fed the hungry, forgave "sinners," contested religiopolitical customs, and gave his life as "a ransom for many" (Mark 10:45), the story of Jesus offers a life-structure for individuals, communities, and peoples to constitute themselves in ways that open up the realization of the good in creative and transformative ways. It does so because of the *compelling authority*—the authority *of the Spirit*—manifested in Jesus. It does so also because of the compelling authority of the resurrection people whose inspired remembrance gave birth to the Gospel narratives as community-shaping testimonies.

Third, and related, interpreted through a constitutional lens, the story of Jesus does not offer a particular blueprint for the formal ordering of authority and the practices of judgment in a renewed Israel. The shape of the new temple is left undetermined—so much so that, in the light of the resurrection, the Evangelists interpret it as the very body of Jesus (cf. esp. John 2:21); and the role of the Twelve appears mainly symbolic. What is offered instead is a *vision of moral and ritual goods*, the enactment of which makes possible a *new kind of polity*, entry to which is open—grounded in the mercy of God—to the least and the lowest.

Fourth, the story of Jesus bears witness to *the element of incommensurability* which characterizes the justice, mercy, and sociality of God. For what the story of Jesus displays is *God's freedom*,[68] the freedom of divine *grace and gift*, of divine *super-*

---

68. Pertinent here is the Parable of the Workers in the Vineyard (Matt 20:1–16), as Bryan, "Jesus and Israel's Eschatological Constitution," 2851–52, notes: "Jesus tells the parable of the workers to

fluity. In this light, it may be the case that the Christian practice of justice and mercy in our day will be related in sometimes surprising, even subversive, ways to practices in society-at-large. One aspect of the vocation of the church is *to embody that surprise*—that grace, forgiveness, self-dispossession, and humility—in its own polity and practice. The fruit of so doing will be the upbuilding, not only of the church's own life, but also of the life of the world, to the glory of God.

Bibliography

Alexander, Philip S. "Jewish Law in the Time of Jesus: Towards a Clarification of the Problem." In *Law and Religion: Essays on the Place of the Law in Israel and Early Christianity*, edited by Barnabas Lindars, 44–58. Cambridge: James Clarke, 1988.

Allison, Dale C., Jr. *Jesus of Nazareth: Millenarian Prophet*. Minneapolis: Fortress, 1998.

———. *The New Moses: A Matthean Typology*. Minneapolis: Fortress, 1993.

Bammel, Ernst. "The Revolution Theory from Reimarus to Brandon." In *Jesus and the Politics of His Day*, edited by Ernst Bammel and C. F. D. Moule, 11–68. Cambridge: Cambridge University Press, 1984.

Banks, R. J. *Jesus and the Law in the Synoptic Tradition*. Cambridge: Cambridge University Press, 1975.

Barclay, John M. G. "Matching Theory and Practice: Josephus's Constitutional Ideal and Paul's Strategy in Corinth." In *Paul Beyond the Judaism/Hellenism Divide*, edited by Troels Engberg-Pedersen, 139–63. Louisville: Westminster John Knox, 2001.

Barton, Stephen C. *Discipleship and Family Ties in Mark and Matthew*. Cambridge: Cambridge University Press, 1994.

———. "Food Rules, Sex Rules and the Prohibition of Idolatry: What's the Connection?" In *Idolatry: False Worship in the Bible, Early Judaism and Christianity*, edited by Stephen Barton, 141–62. London: T. & T. Clark, 2007.

———. "'Mercy and Not Sacrifice'? Biblical Perspectives on Liturgy and Ethics." *Studies in Christian Ethics* 15 (2002) 25–39.

Barton, Stephen C., et al., eds. *Memory in the Bible and Antiquity*. Tübingen: Mohr Siebeck, 2007.

Bitner, Brad. *Paul's Political Strategy in 1 Corinthians 1–4: Constitution and Covenant*. Cambridge: Cambridge University Press, 2015.

Bockmuehl, Markus. "Halakhah and Ethics in the Jesus Tradition." In *Early Christian Thought in Its Jewish Context*, edited by John Barclay and John Sweet, 264–78. Cambridge: Cambridge University Press, 1996.

Bryan, Steven M. "Jesus and Israel's Eschatological Constitution." In *Handbook for the Study of the Historical Jesus*, vol. 3, *The Historical Jesus*, edited by Tom Holmén and Stanley E. Porter, 2835–53. Leiden: Brill, 2011.

Burridge, Richard A. *Imitating Jesus: An Inclusive Approach to New Testament Ethics*. Grand Rapids: Eerdmans, 2007.

Capper, Brian. "The Palestinian Cultural Context of Earliest Christian Community of Goods." In *The Book of Acts in Its Palestinian Setting*, edited by Richard Bauckham, 323–56. Grand Rapids: Eerdmans, 1995.

---

assert *God's absolute freedom* to determine who would participate in eschatological Israel, who would inherit the blessings of the kingdom." My emphasis.

Claussen, Carsten, and Michael Thomas Davis. "The Concept of Unity at Qumran." In *Qumran Studies: New Approaches, New Questions*, edited by Michael Thomas Davis and Brent Strawn, 232–53. Grand Rapids: Eerdmans, 2007.

Caird, G. B. *Jesus and the Jewish Nation*. London: Athlone, 1965.

Crawford, Sidnie White. *Rewriting Scripture in Second Temple Times*. Grand Rapids: Eerdmans, 2008.

Davies, Philip R. "Food, Drink and Sects: The Question of Ingestion in the Qumran Texts." *Semeia* 86 (1999) 151–63.

Davies, W. D., and Dale C. Allison, Jr. *A Critical and Exegetical Commentary on the Gospel according to Saint Matthew*. Vol. 1, *Introduction and Commentary on Matthew 1–7*. Edinburgh: T. & T. Clark, 1988.

Day, John, ed. *King and Messiah in Israel and the Ancient Near East*. Sheffield: Sheffield Academic, 1998.

Doering, Lutz. "Sabbath Laws in the New Testament Gospels." In *The New Testament and Rabbinic Literature*, edited by Reimund Bieringer et al., 207–53. Leiden: Brill, 2010.

Douglas, Mary. "Deciphering a Meal." In *Implicit Meanings: Essays in Anthropology*, 249–75. London: RKP, 1975.

———. *Purity and Danger*. London: RKP, 1966.

Dunn, J. D. G. *Jesus Remembered*. Christianity in the Making 1. Grand Rapids: Eerdmans, 2003.

———. "Jesus, Table-Fellowship, and Qumran." In *Jesus and the Dead Sea Scrolls*, edited by James H. Charlesworth, 254–72. New York: Doubleday, 1992.

———. "Pharisees, Sinners, and Jesus." In *Jesus, Paul and the Law: Studies in Mark and Galatians*, 61–88. Louisville: Westminster John Knox, 1990.

Dunn, J. D. G., and Scot McKnight, eds. *The Historical Jesus in Recent Research*. Winona Lake, IN: Eisenbrauns, 2005.

Gerth, H. H., and C. Wright Mills, eds. *From Max Weber: Essays in Sociology*. New York: Oxford University Press, 1946.

Fletcher-Louis, Crispin H. T. "'Leave the Dead to Bury Their Own Dead': Q 9.60 and the Redefinition of the People of God." *Journal for the Study of the New Testament* 26 (2003) 39–68.

Gundry, Judith M. "Children in the Gospel of Mark, with Special Attention to Jesus' Blessing of the Children (Mark 10:13–16) and the Purpose of Mark." In *The Child in the Bible*, edited by Terence E. Fretheim and Beverly Roberts Gaventa, 143–76. Grand Rapids: Eerdmans, 2008.

Hardy, Daniel W. *Wording a Radiance*. London: SCM, 2010.

Harvey, A. E. "Genesis versus Deuteronomy? Jesus on Marriage and Divorce." In *The Gospels and the Scriptures of Israel*, edited by C. A. Evans and W. R. Stegner, 55–65. Sheffield: Sheffield Academic, 1994.

Hauerwas, Stanley. "On Keeping Theological Ethics Theological." In *Against the Nations*, 23–50. Notre Dame: University of Notre Dame Press, 1992.

Hauerwas, Stanley, and Samuel Wells, eds. *The Blackwell Companion to Christian Ethics*. Oxford: Blackwell, 2006.

Hengel, Martin. *The Charismatic Leader and His Followers*. Edinburgh: T. & T. Clark, 1981.

———. "The Kingdom of Christ in John." In *Studies in Early Christology*, 333–57. Edinburgh: T. & T. Clark, 1995.

Holmén, Tom. *Jesus and Jewish Covenant Thinking*. Leiden: Brill, 2001.

Horbury, William. "Constitutional Aspects of the Kingdom of God." In *The Kingdom of God and Human Society*, edited by R. S. Barbour, 60–79. Edinburgh: T. & T. Clark, 1993.

———. *Jewish Messianism and the Cult of Christ*. London: SCM, 1998.

Horsley, Richard A. *Jesus and Empire: The Kingdom of God and the New World Disorder*. Minneapolis: Augsburg Fortress, 2003.

Houston, Walter J. *The Pentateuch*. London: SCM, 2013.

Judge, E. A. *The Social Pattern of the Christian Groups in the First Century*. London: Tyndale, 1960.

Kee, Howard C. *Community of the New Age: Studies in Mark's Gospel*. London: SCM, 1977.

Kirk, Alan, and Tom Thatcher, eds. *Memory, Tradition, and Text: Uses of the Past in Early Christianity*. Leiden: Brill, 2005.

Lincoln, Andrew T. *Truth on Trial: The Lawsuit Motif in the Fourth Gospel*. Peabody, MA: Hendrickson, 2000.

Lohfink, Gerhard. *Jesus and Community: The Social Dimension of Christian Faith*. London: SPCK, 1985.

Marcus, Joel. "Crucifixion as Parodic Exaltation." *Journal of Biblical Literature* 125 (2006) 73–87.

Martinez, Florentino García. *The Dead Sea Scrolls Translated: The Qumran Texts in English*. Leiden: Brill, 1994.

McGrath, Alister E. "In What Way Can Jesus Be a Moral Example for Christians?" *Journal of the Evangelical Theological Society* 34 (1991) 289–98.

McKnight, Scot. *A New Vision for Israel: The Teachings of Jesus in National Context*. Grand Rapids: Eerdmans, 1999.

Meeks, Wayne A. *The First Urban Christians*. New Haven: Yale University Press, 1983.

———. "Moses as God and King." In *Religions in Antiquity*, edited by Jacob Neusner, 354–71. Leiden: Brill, 1968.

Neusner, Jacob. *First Century Judaism in Crisis*. Nashville: Abingdon, 1975.

O'Donovan, Oliver. *Desire of the Nations: Rediscovering the Roots of Political Theology*. Cambridge: Cambridge University Press, 1996.

Pelikan, Jaroslav. *Interpreting the Bible and the Constitution*. New Haven: Yale University Press, 2004.

Riley, Gregory J. "Words and Deeds: Jesus as Teacher and Jesus as Pattern of Life." *Harvard Theological Review* 90 (1997) 427–36.

Rowe, Christopher, and Malcolm Schofield, eds. *The Cambridge History of Greek and Roman Political Thought*. Cambridge: Cambridge University Press, 2005.

Rowland, Christopher. *Christian Origins: An Account of the Setting and Character of the Most Important Messianic Sect of Judaism*. London: SPCK, 1985.

———. "Reflections on the Politics of the Gospels." In *The Kingdom of God and Human Society*, edited by Robin Barbour, 224–41. Edinburgh: T. & T. Clark, 1993.

Sanders, E. P. *The Historical Figure of Jesus*. London: Penguin, 1993.

———. *Jesus and Judaism*. London: SCM, 1985.

———. *Judaism: Practice and Belief, 63 BCE–66 CE*. London: SCM, 1992.

———. *Paul and Palestinian Judaism: A Comparison of Patterns of Religion*. London: SCM, 1977.

Segal, Alan F. "Jesus, the Jewish Revolutionary." In *Jesus' Jewishness: Exploring the Place of Jesus in Early Judaism*, edited by James H. Charlesworth, 199–225. New York: Crossroad, 1991.

Soler, Jean. "The Semiotics of Food in the Bible." In *Food and Drink in History: Selections from the Annales, économies, sociétés, civilisations*, vol. 5, edited by R. Forster and O. Ranum, 126–38. Translated by E. Forster and P. M. Ranum. Baltimore: Johns Hopkins University Press, 1979.

Stuckenbruck, Loren T. *The Myth of Rebellious Angels: Studies in Second Temple Judaism and New Testament Texts*. Tübingen: Mohr Siebeck, 2014.

Thatcher, Tom, ed. *Memory and Identity in Ancient Judaism and Early Christianity: A Conversation with Barry Schwartz*. Atlanta: SBL, 2014.

Theissen, Gerd. "Jesus and His Followers as Healers: Symbolic Healing in Early Christianity." In *The Problem of Ritual Efficacy*, edited by William S. Sax et al., 45–65. Oxford: Oxford University Press, 2010.

———. "The Political Dimension of Jesus' Activity." In *The Social Setting of Jesus and the Gospels*, edited by Wolfgang Stegemann et al., 225–50. Minneapolis: Fortress, 2002.

Van Der Horst, P. W. "Celibacy in Early Judaism." *Revue Biblique* 109 (2002) 390–402.

Walbank, F. W. "Monarchies and Monarchic Ideas." In *The Cambridge Ancient History*, vol. 7, pt. 1, *The Hellenistic World*, edited by F. W. Walbank et al., 62–100. 2nd ed. Cambridge: Cambridge University Press, 1984.

Wassen, Cecilia. "What Do Angels Have Against the Blind and the Deaf? Rules of Exclusion in the Dead Sea Scrolls." In *Common Judaism: Explorations in Second-Temple Judaism*, edited by Wayne O. McCready and Adele Reinhartz, 115–29. Minneapolis: Fortress, 2008.

Wolterstorff, Nicholas. *Justice: Rights and Wrongs*. Princeton: Princeton University Press, 2008.

Wright, N. T. *Jesus and the Victory of God*. London: SPCK, 1996.

———. *The New Testament and the People of God*. London: SPCK, 1992.

2

Mercy as Divine Self-Giving
Seven Theses toward a Kenotic Ecclesiology

Stephen Pickard

This chapter locates the concept of mercy within the pattern of God's self-giving love for the world and examines how this might contribute to the well-being of society. Underlying this other-directed and compassionate doctrine of the church is underlaid with what is termed a "kenotic ecclesiology." The inquiry proceeds by way of seven theses on mercy.

Thesis One
We may be living in the twilight of mercy in modern Western liberal democracies.

The theme of this volume, *Justice, Mercy and Social Well-Being*, brings together some major concerns in contemporary life at personal, institutional, national and indeed global levels. It is a complex theme and I am acutely aware of the need for genuine trans-disciplinary conversations to shed some light for our common life and practices. In particular, the theme of mercy is one of those matters that offers a window into some of our contested and complex issues both in society and church.

Generally speaking, mercy is a quality that is rarely mentioned in the everyday world, let alone in the political and economic life of our country. Competition, cut throat activity, making money, accruing as much as possible, all driven by self-interested rational autonomous agents is hardly the environment that would welcome mercy. Listening to our political leaders on matters of importance for the well-being of society makes me wonder if we are not living in the twilight of mercy. The litmus test is Government policy and action in relation to asylum seekers and refugees. Yet it is not just a people issue. The earth our home cries out for mercy. As Catholic theologian Elizabeth Johnson notes, "the tree of life now depends on one twig."[1] That twig is none other than human beings exercising responsible care of a planet that is "at our mercy." In domestic politics, environmental issues and people migration, as a society we fail the mercy test. The world can appear a merciless place at times; a world where people are cast aside on the highways of life; where inequalities grow, and more and more are denied opportunities because of gender, race and economic situation. It does appear these days that the way forward for a supposed lucky country, in order that it can remain lucky, is to make sure that we do everything in our power to keep unlucky people out; invisible, silent or ignored. We are more familiar with the voices that proclaim reward for achievement and effort, for conforming to the rules of the game for advancement (with little regard for ethics or moral responsibility). These same voices also speak of punishment for failure, for not conforming, for transgressing rules, values or criticizing sacred symbols. Reward and punishment is the natural default for human behavior. We are it seems DNA encoded for reward and punishment. It is the air we breathe; and we are easily offended, angered, indeed scandalized when this rule of life is ignored or rejected. Is this not the point of so many of the parables of Jesus?

Yet is mercy part of our DNA? In an increasingly security conscious time associated with the prevailing emotions of fear and anxiety in relation to threats real and imagined, the voices of mercy, like wisdom itself, is a muted voice at best. Perhaps this concern is a perennial one. Perhaps mercy is always in danger of being washed away in a flood of fear. Perhaps this is what led the great Bard to write:

> The quality of mercy is not strain'd.
> It droppeth as the gentle rain from heaven
> Upon the place beneath. (*Merchant of Venice*, act 4, sc. 1)

In cruel and brutal times, the gentle rain of mercy is truly heaven sent and absolutely essential for our social well-being both personally and institutionally. Cultivating mercy may indeed be a prophetic activity. The ecclesia of God may well be called to be a body of mercy for the broken body of the world.

Thesis Two

Mercy belongs to a rich and complex ecology of other-directed care.

How might we speak of mercy? How does it relate to compassion and other associated terms such as pity, sympathy and empathy? This second thesis points us in the first instance to a brief consideration of the mercy lexicon. The modern concept of

---

1. Johnson, "At Our Mercy."

mercy is informed by two different sources. One source, from the Latin, *misericordia*, suggests that one has their heart (Latin, *cor*) with those who are poor or in distress (Latin, *miseri*). This finds echoes in the biblical roots of mercy (Greek, *eleous*) which is also at times translated "compassion" or "pity." The emphasis goes beyond affective disposition and attitudes and involves physical tenderness and concrete care. In this respect Michael Angelo's Pieta in St. Peter's Basilica is probably the most powerful sculpted form of mercy we have in the Western tradition. In the biblical tradition this outward directed care for the plight of another arises from an upheaval within described as a "gut-wrenching surge of emotion" (Greek, *splangchnizomai*—Luke 10:33; Matt 18:27).[2] This powerful response arises from that part of the body thought to be the seat of the natural passions i.e., the intestines (Greek, *splangchna*). Hence the phrase "bowels of mercy" (*splangchna eleous*) could be applied to the movement of God toward the world (Luke 1:78), though rendered in the more familiar, "in the tender mercy" of our God. Importantly in this view mercy is more than a series of singular acts; rather it identifies one's habituated dealings with others. On this account mercy is a virtue embracing, in Chris Marshall's words, "a comprehensive way of life."[3]

The other source of mercy with English roots emphasizes that recompense accruing to the merciful person rather than the disposition as such. It derives from the French (*merci*) with Latin root *merces* meaning reward or fee. This becomes in post classical usage "the reward in heaven that accrues to acts of kindness to those who have no claim, and from whom no requital can be expected" (Oxford Dictionary). Hence "blessed are the merciful for mercy will be shown to them." The concept of mercy is evidently multilayered as a virtue, and as an action and entails a double benefit for recipient and giver of mercy. The dual character of mercy is formalized by the philosopher Andrew Brien who distinguishes between "mercy as an action, which in legal setting entails mitigating punishment, and mercy as a virtue, which designates a character trait involving an ongoing stance of benevolent care and concern for others that issues in merciful actions."[4] What about the relationship between mercy and compassion? Are they equivalents? Can they be distinguished? The distinguished American philosopher Martha Nussbaum in her remarkable book, *Upheavals of Thought: The Intelligence of the Emotions*, comments in her discussion of mercy and revenge in the following terms:

> Mercy does differ from compassion: for it [mercy] presupposes that the offender has done a wrong, and deserves some punishment for that wrong. . . . Nonetheless . . . it [mercy] has much in common with compassion as well—for it focuses on obstacles to flourishing that seem too great to overcome. It

---

2. Marshall, *Compassionate Justice*, 120–21.

3. Marshall, *Compassionate Justice*, 132. Marshall is drawing attention to the present continuous sense of Jesus' command to the lawyer in the parable of the Good Samaritan, "Go and do likewise" (Luke 15:37).

4. Marshall, *Compassionate Justice*, 262.

[mercy] says, yes, you did commit a deliberate wrong, but the fact that you got to that point was not altogether your fault. It [mercy] focuses on the social, the natural, and familial features of the offender's life that offer a measure of extenuation for the fault, even though the commission of the fault itself meets the law's strict standards of moral accountability. In order to do this, it takes up a narrative attitude toward the offender's history that is similar to the sympathetic perception involved in compassion.[5]

For Nussbaum it is the sympathetic narrative scrutiny of the plight of the other (in this case offender) that links mercy to compassion and in the case of mercy moves us to a more lenient penalty. This involves a merciful attitude, and like compassion it involves "the sympathetic imagining of the possibilities and obstacles that the other persons' life contains" (397). In short "the very exercise of imagination that leads to mercy seems closely linked to compassion" (397).

In Nussbaum's account mercy is essentially a cancellation of, or moderation of punishment. It has no restorative trajectory. Chris Marshall recognizes the close nexus Nussbaum draws between mercy and compassion since both involve "a sympathetic and imaginative engagement with the painful experience of others, and both seek to alleviate human distress"; the difference being that the compassionate reaction "implies innocence" whereas mercy's response to wrongdoing "confirms guilt, yet moderates punishment."[6] Though Marshall is surely right in noting that such a distinction will eventually succumb to the complexities of human behavior, "of volitional freedom and circumstantial constraint." He advocates setting aside the criterion of blameworthiness in distinguishing mercy from compassion and, "along with the New Testament writers, to understand mercy as the active expression of the underlying response of compassion, in any situation where authority or power may be exercised or withheld to another persons' detriment" (262). Marshall puts it nicely: "compassion without merciful deeds does nothing to help the needy party. Merciful action without compassion does nothing to transform the helper" (131). In such a relation, compassion as "empathetic concern" remains incomplete without concrete action. Marshall's focus is on "doing mercy"; at heart a movement toward the victim. From this perspective the Samaritan story embodies a "reckless compassion for the pressing needs of an actual human being" (132); "he feels compassion and practices mercy" (110). This suggests a basic habituated pattern of "restorative mercy" as "an essential individual requirement for entry to the age of salvation" (132). For both Nussbaum and Marshall the merciful life is a fundamental element of human self-giving in response to the needs of others. Marshall locates this within God's covenantal faithfulness, at first to Israel then extended to all through Jesus Christ. Importantly he draws attention to the cost of mercy (109) as a claim upon the giver; a theme largely ignored by Nussbaum.

---

5. Nussbaum, *Upheavals of Thought*, 396. Hereafter page references in text.
6. Marshall, *Compassionate Justice*, 262. Hereafter page references in text.

PART A—THE CONTOURS OF WELL-BEING

Thesis Three

Mercy is integral to the practice of justice and forgiveness.

More problematic in the long discussion of the tradition is the relationship between mercy and justice. In contemporary discussion the two have been often pitted against each other, with acting mercifully regarded as setting aside the requirements of justice. Leniency might on this account become a sign of injustice. On the other hand, the strict application of justice according to rules and laws is always in danger of evacuating mercy from social life leaving a cruel and heartless shell. In short justice and mercy are too often considered as contrasts, with mercy moderating justice. Yet, as John Milbank notes, such mercy always remains under suspicion as an arbitrary act on the part of the powerful that disrupts the regular, balanced interchange between people.[7] On this account mercy represents a negative cancellation and setting aside of the requirements of justice. There is no real opportunity for mercy as a positive deed that might lead to restoration and transformation of relationships. Milbank identifies the High Middle Ages as a breakthrough into a more integrated account of mercy, justice and forgiveness; a "cultural mix that did not firmly distinguish mercy from justice and thought of all giving, including forgiving, not as ideally pure, free and disinterested, but rather as situated within an economy of exchange and obligation."[8] He traces the sundering of the nexus between mercy and justice to which we are now heirs.

Following this trajectory Marshall argues for a more integrated account of mercy and justice. He notes that when justice and mercy are located within a more textured and "thicker" narrative of life mercy is no longer a substitute for justice nor an external check on retribution but rather integral to the practice of justice such that if "mercy is absent justice necessarily fails" (218). "Justice is joined at the hip with mercy in order to be truly just" (218). In this context mercy is a "way of seeing and being in the world" and the cultivation of a "stance of mercy" becomes paramount to "check the dark passions that blind policy and law enforcers" (218).

Marshall refers to a "compassionate justice" though he might just as easily have said "merciful justice" as with the father in the parable of the prodigal son (217). Mercy entails that "conscious refusal to remain indifferent" (219) such that where mercy is not cultivated we fail to produce morally acceptable outcomes and social well-being. In short for Marshall "justice encompasses mercy and mercy envisions justice" (219) as result of which he can refer to the "justice of God's forgiving mercy" which will always be restorative. Milbank draws attention to the narrative dimension this entails for both oppressor and victim. The "time of mercy" requires re-narration of failure,

---

7. Milbank, *Being Reconciled*, 48.
8. Milbank, *Being Reconciled*, 46.

time for remembering and revision en route to restoration.[9] Importantly Milbank traces the conditions for such a possibility back into the heartlands of incarnational Christianity.

Mercy belongs to a rich and integrated conceptual framework. It focuses on a dynamic concrete and practical expression of outer directed concern and care for victims, offenders and all in need, even the most unlikely and least deserving. Mercy and its cognates involve a sympathetic imagination regarding the obstacles human beings face in seeking that life of social well-being and flourishing. It sounds fairly straightforward, though the actual history of mercy in the Western tradition and its felt absence and/or denigration in our contemporary society bears closer scrutiny.

Thesis Four

In the Western philosophical tradition mercy remains more or less a transactional arrangement within unequal power relations.

Martha Nussbaum highlights two traditions in the Western philosophical tradition: the "anti-compassion" and "pro-compassion." Each has implications for the theme of mercy, and both embody visions of the ideal political community, the good citizen and notions of well-being. The Stoic anti-compassion tradition focuses on the inviolable human dignity of every person that cannot be diminished or obliterated by external circumstances. Human beings are rational agents with moral purpose. The good person needs no one and all are equal. The life of the community is best served when emotions (the passions) are not permitted to intrude into the functioning of social well-being for free responsible human beings. The purpose of the community is to assist each by judgments purified of passion. The accent is thus on internal freedom and dignity as the source of political equality. On this account acts of compassion and mercy are an implicit recognition that "external goods" and particular circumstances do in fact impact on human agency and dignity. As such they undermine human dignity and agency. In this environment mercy finds its rationale in the idea that it is hard to be good. Accordingly, it focuses on the fault but mitigates the punishment. When it is offered it is essentially a negative act, a cancellation or leniency that confirms the power of the dispenser and confirms the social status quo. It presumes that the emotions are bad guides (298); pity (mercy) must be expunged (so Kant 378) for it "is an insulting kind of benevolence." This was encapsulated crisply and coldly by Nietzsche in the phrase, "wipe your own nose" (364). Evidently there is something humiliating or demeaning in being the recipient of compassion and mercy. This is a powerful legacy that lies not far below the surface of a great deal of political rhetoric and perhaps no better exemplified than in the commendation of Australian Government's policies

---

9. Milbank, *Being Reconciled*, 54.

on asylum seekers and refugees and the associated language of "bleeding hearts" and the "misty eyed."

The "pro-compassion" tradition desires the same things as the "anti-compassion" tradition i.e., freedom and equality. However, this approach regards human beings as both rational yet subject to their passions; as aspiring, vulnerable worthy and insecure. As such freedom has to be actively fostered. The task of community is to provide for the needs of the weaker to ensure that all have equal opportunity to be free and responsible. Compassion and mercy on this account function as ethical guides and have a positive contribution to communal flourishing. Yet they are painful emotions because they involve an awareness of another's undeserved misfortune (301). Yet this requires a feeling for another's misfortune. Rousseau stated, "To see it but not feel it is not to know it" (323). Hence compassion is more than "human concern" which is simply paying "lip service" to need and insufficient "for the upheaval of compassion" (334). Both compassion and mercy involve a sympathetic imagination for the experience of others. An empathy-less environment is not amenable to acts of mercy. On the other hand, where compassion and mercy are alive other emotions may become impediments; envy, shame, disgust, confusion and scandal (300, 320). Thus Nussbaum argues for an educative approach to the development of compassion and mercy. What is desired is a culture of compassion and mercy where leaders can help to shape and guide the boundaries of compassion.

We are inheritors of two streams when it comes to the exercise of compassion and mercy. The anti-compassion tradition is at times inconsistent and opens loopholes that indicate care and empathetic concern for the plight of others against its best principles.[10] Yet the anti-compassion tradition remains the dominant voice. Mercy remains locked into a rigid framework based on unequal power relations. Mercy is that lenient, moderating reduction in punishment or response to a person's particular plight. It emanates from one who has power over another. Mercy is essentially a transactional activity that confirms existing power differentials. While it might generate a form of gratitude from the recipient it is one embedded in fear of the other's capacity to arbitrarily withdraw or modify the conditions or quality of mercy. The offer of mercy may make the giver of mercy feel good or enhance their sense of power. Critically mercy within this framework is never able to lead to a transformation of the relationship between recipient and giver in the direction of genuine mutuality. It is at best a truncated and impoverished form of mercy. This is not conducive to social well-being. As such while mercy is extended to another, an other-directed movement, it proceeds from a controlled and "calculating mercy." As a result it is never able to fully participate in the very thing that is offered. As Jon Sobrino states in a Latin American

---

10. Nussbaum, *Upheavals of Thought*, 398, observes that "compassion creeps, unnamed, into Seneca's account, due to his preoccupation with the obstacles to good actions and associated concern with 'the fact that the offender got to be immoral and blameworthy was not fully that person's own doing.'"

context: "we have awakened to the fact that a heartless humanity manages to praise works of mercy but refuses to be guided by the mercy principle."[11]

The pro-compassion tradition offers, according to Nussbaum, a better home for mercy than the anti-compassion tradition. The reason being that "compassion invites the sort of narrative scrutiny of particular lives that is likely, as well, to reveal extenuating circumstances in cases where there is culpability."[12] On this account the pro-compassion tradition is more conducive to the exercise of mercy and in producing a good society providing "an essential life and connectedness to morality, [and] without which it is dangerously empty and rootless."[13] Yet Nussbaum notes that it is only "within the limits of reason" that compassion "proves worthwhile rather than quirky and unreliable." And by extension so too mercy.

At this point the principle of mercy, even within the pro-compassion tradition, appears to be calibrated in terms of legal, economic and social criteria. Mercy evidently is not able to generate a genuinely restorative and healing power for social well-being. To this extent the philosophical tradition of compassion lacks genuine reciprocity between the giver and recipient of mercy. What results is a somewhat truncated version of mercy's true restorative dynamic in the development of the good society. Something more radical is required.

Thesis Five

The Gospels offer a scandalous account of mercy that nullifies transactional approaches to mercy based on sacrifice and opens possibilities for true praise of God.

It is difficult to overestimate the significance of the radical account of mercy that comes to sharp focus in the ministry of Jesus. In the Gospels the mercy of God enacted in the ministry of Jesus and the parables scandalizes human understanding of the ways of God with the world. Jesus' call of Matthew is a case in point:

> As Jesus was walking along, he saw a man called Matthew sitting at the tax booth; and he said to him, "Follow me." And he got up and followed him. And as he sat at dinner [a] in the house, many tax collectors and sinners came and were sitting [b] with him and his disciples. When the Pharisees saw this, they said to his disciples, "Why does your teacher eat with tax collectors and sinners?" But when he heard this, he said, "Those who are well have no need of a physician, but those who are sick. Go and learn what this means, 'I desire mercy, not sacrifice.' For I have come to call not the righteous but sinners." (Matt 9:9–13)

11. Sobrino, *Principle of Mercy*, 10.
12. Sobrino, *Principle of Mercy*, 398.
13. Sobrino, *Principle of Mercy*, 399.

The cause of the Pharisees immediate offense at Jesus' behavior is the fact that he not only associates with those considered sinners; but that he actually calls them to become disciples. However, Jesus' response to the Pharisees reveals a deeper scandal. They are unable to understand Jesus' actions because they are mistaken about who God is and what God desires. Evidently they need to re-read their own tradition and learn that God actually desires mercy being extended to sinners; that mercy is nothing less than "extending forgiving fellowship to those regarded by others as sinners."[14] In other words Jesus does not call the righteous to follow but sinners; and God does not require sacrifices and burnt offerings. This is scandalous for those who have presumed to possess the competence and power to distinguish the sinner from the righteous. And it is scandalous for those who consider themselves righteous to be told that God does not call them. Moreover, unless the Pharisees learn this they will be unable to hear Jesus' call to discipleship.

What scandalizes the Pharisees and thus blocks their path to true discipleship is precisely the same thing that, if they go and learn the truth then that which appears as a scandal to them can become the bridge into fellowship with God. The kind of mercy that God is on about contains these twin features of scandal—of both being a block and means of overcoming it (91). The Pharisees have to allow themselves to be constituted as sinners and this evidently can only occur when they hear the call of Jesus. The Giradian scholar Jeremiah Alberg states it crisply: "It is not so much that one must be an obvious sinner—a tax collector such as Matthew—to be called, but that by being called and forgiven people are fully constituted as sinners. . . . In other words Jesus doesn't call because one is a sinner and therefore has a certain claim to be called; instead, his call includes God's love and forgiveness so that the person called becomes a forgiven sinner" (76). God's mercy draws others into a new relationship with God and each other and necessarily involves forgiveness, and a response of repentance and gratitude. God's mercy is embedded in the dynamic of call and response; God's mercy is other-implicating, gracious and a scandal to be overcome. This leads to the second issue, i.e., the juxtaposition of mercy and sacrifice. In response to the scandalized Pharisees' challenge to Jesus' disciples—"Why does your teacher eat with tax collectors and sinners?"—Jesus responds in part quoting the prophet Hosea, "Go and learn what this means, 'I desire mercy not sacrifice'" (Matt 9:12–13; Hos 6:6). It is not immediately apparent how these two might be so diametrically opposed. Yet for Alberg the call of Matthew encapsulates, "the movement of the whole bible: a movement away from sacrifice toward mercy or love" (73). This relates to the deeper scandal of God's mercy; it entirely overturns received notions of what God desires. How exactly does this work? Following the argument above we note that to be constituted as a sinner is to be constituted as a sacrificer in need of forgiveness (81). To be bound by the dynamic of sacrifice is to remain trapped in an essentially cruel dialectic that splits people into insiders and outsiders, good and bad, righteous and sinner, worthy and

---

14. Alberg, *Beneath the Veil of the Strange Verses*, 76. Hereafter page references in text.

unworthy, guilty and innocent.[15] Such a sacrificial system necessitates victims who are (a) the means for the maintenance of the split and (b) provide the condition for the possibility of harmony and stasis. From this point of view the sacrificial order blocks the flourishing of people and society because it prevents the overflow of true mercy and love. The reason being that mercy, specifically God's mercy, sets aside the either/or categories; it nullifies the categories altogether and renders them of no account. Social and personal well-being is reconstituted on an altogether different basis, i.e., on the gracious call of God in Christ to all. For those who respond they discover that they are forgiven sinners. What appears as a blockage (the scandalous offer of mercy to the most unlikely by human account) becomes the bridge for a radical new appreciation and acceptance of restored life (90, 93). The consequence is that the mercy that we receive is precisely the kind of mercy that is to be the mark and pattern of our following of Jesus. In effect this is the great insight of Luther, whose phrase "we are all in the same swamp" has always echoed in my mind.

But indeed it is fundamental to the gospel. God desires not sacrifice with its attendant splitting and victims but mercy for all. This is what has to be learnt in order to be able to hear the call of God. God's mercy to sinners so brilliantly explicated in the parables of the Gospels is the antithesis of sacrifice. In the Gospels Jesus tells stories about dodgy characters, the most undeserving according to popular opinion. These unsavory types: "the unjust judge," "the cunning servants," despised tax collectors, prostitutes. Such figures repeatedly emerge in his encounters and parables. They confront us; challenge our values about who is most deserving of kindness. Indeed, the dodgy types go into the kingdom of God before the good and the great. It was offensive then and remains so. But such characters break open for us our deep need of God. Their repentance and faith show us the possibilities for new life when mercy gets a look in.

In Giradian terms the resurrection from the dead of the innocent victim Jesus (a) exposes the cruelty and repetitive necessity of sacrificial systems and (b) at the same time renders it null and void. The divine law is not sacrifice but mercy. And it is a mercy that breaks through the glass ceiling of transactional accounts of mercy.

Thesis Six

Mercy entails a dynamic movement toward another patterned after God's abundant self-giving in Christ and the Spirit.

This dynamic outer-directed movement of God has twin theological coordinates, i.e., Christology and Pneumatology. Christologically it is focused in the well-known text from Philippians regarding Christ:

---

15. This is the burden of so many of the parables of Jesus and his encounters with the religious rulers. See Alberg, *Beneath the Veil*, on the Good Samaritan (85–86).

who, though he was in the form of God, did not regard equality with God as something to be exploited, but emptied himself, taking the form of a slave, being born in human likeness. And being found in human form, he humbled himself and became obedient to the point of death—even death on a cross (2:6–8).

The movement of God for the life of the world is an eternal kenosis; a self-giving patterned according to the life of Jesus Christ. This movement of mercy to humankind in its most decisive form takes Jesus to that very place of utter lowliness, even death on a cross. As Irenaeus has rightly said, what he has not assumed he has not redeemed. This christological coordinate is cojoined with a pneumatological one. The kenosis of God in Christ is not undertaken apart from the work of the eternal Spirit of love. At every step along the incarnate God's life the Spirit is the enabling power and energy for self-giving. The humanity of Christ is empowered by the agency of the Spirit. And it is that same Spirit that is the active agent in the raising of Jesus. The divine quality of mercy is empowered by the Spirit and patterned after the way of Jesus. Henceforth mercy is discerned preeminently through Easter eyes, as James Alison has powerfully articulated.[16] It is no longer a divine transaction but a deeply personal investment of God's self for the other in which everything and everyone is changed irrevocably.

Thesis Seven

The vocation of the church is to be a body of mercy in the world.

The movement of the merciful God toward the world in Christ in the power of the Spirit is necessarily an ecclesial reality. Post Pentecost the mercy of God has to be embodied in a particular form of life that casts light on the ways of God in all life. The form of the merciful church has been powerfully and movingly articulated by Jon Sobrino in his 1994 work, *The Principle of Mercy*.[17] The subtitle is telling: *Taking the Crucified People from the Cross*. Sobrino, writing out of the Latin American context of poverty, suffering and violence, offers an uncompromising theology of the church shaped by the principle of mercy. For Sobrino it is preeminently the Samaritan church and mercy is the key. Beyond mere sentiment or "works of mercy" something more radical is envisaged. "Mercy is a basic attitude toward the suffering of another, whereby one reacts to eradicate that suffering for the sole reason that it exists, and in the conviction that, in this reaction to the ought-not-be of another's suffering one's own being, without any possibility of subterfuge, hangs in the balance" (18). The sense here that human life "hangs in the balance" is haunting to say the least. Our very humanity is endangered to the extent that we refuse to live mercifully toward the suffering of others. Taking the crucified people down from the cross is a costly and life involving

---

16. See Alison, *Joy of Being Wrong*.
17. Sobrino, *Principle of Mercy*. Hereafter page references in text.

matter. The transactional accounts of mercy—Sobrino's "calculated mercy"—so much a feature of the Western philosophical tradition are null and void on this account.

What emerges into the full light of day is Sobrino's thoroughly christological interpretation of mercy. The primordial mercy of God—the structured form of love whereby the suffering on another is interiorized—"appears concretely historicized in Jesus' practice and message" (17). It is most powerfully narrated in the parable of the Good Samaritan or might we say "merciful Samaritan." Mercy is "fundamental to the structure of the life of Jesus" (15).

What then of the church? Its vocation is to "reiterate this mercy of God's, exercising it toward others and thus rendering themselves like unto God" (17). Sobrino's theology of the church through the lens of the principle of mercy offers a powerful kenotic ecclesiology patterned after Christ. At the heart of the mercy dynamic is a going out of oneself for the other. But it is not a one-way transactional type of relation. Rather it involves genuine reciprocity mutual accountability and vulnerability. It is not simply the one to whom mercy is shown whose life "hangs in the balance" but the one who offers mercy. Their life too hangs in the balance. Such is the nature of true mercy. It generates a reciprocal relation undergirded by a theology of kenosis. A kenotic ecclesiology is the natural theological home for the vocation of the church to be a body of mercy for the world.

This of course, as thesis 6 suggests, is informed by a trinitarian dynamic of divine self-giving about which much more needs to be said than can be at present. It is, as suggested earlier, a radical move beyond the transactional frameworks in which mercy has been developed and practiced in the Western tradition. Moreover, a kenotic ecclesiology shaped by mercy is inevitably a scandalous activity of the church that generates scandal and lives in the shadow of the cross of Jesus and its attendant violence. This kind of Samaritan church offers a genuine glimmer of hope for a renewed sociality and a true praise of God.

Bibliography

Alberg, Jeremiah. *Beneath the Veil of the Strange Verses: Reading Scandalous Texts*. East Lansing: Michigan State University Press, 2013.
Alison, James. *The Joy of Being Wrong: Original Sin through Easter Eyes*. New York: Crossroad, 1998.
Johnson, Elizabeth A. "At Our Mercy: The Tree of Life Now Depends on One Twig." *Commonweal* 141 (2014) 13–16.
Marshall, Christopher D. *Compassionate Justice: An Interdisciplinary Dialogue with Two Gospel Parables on Law, Crime, and Restorative Justice*. Eugene: Cascade, 2012.
Milbank, John. *Being Reconciled: Ontology and Pardon*. London: Routledge, 2003.
Nussbaum, Martha. *Upheavals of Thought: The Intelligence of the Emotions*. New York: Cambridge University Press, 2001.
Sobrino, Jon. *The Principle of Mercy: Taking the Crucified People from the Cross*. Maryknoll: Orbis, 1994.

PART B

When Mercy Seasons Justice
Well-Being in Exegetical Perspective

3

"I Will Walk in Your Midst"
The Implications of Leviticus 26:3–13 for Social Well-Being

G. GEOFFREY HARPER

THE pressing needs of a broken world are continually brought to our attention, whether through the media or through personal experience.[1] While Christian people frequently feel compelled to respond to such patent need in both word and deed, what an appropriate response should look like remains debated. What is clear is that biblical and theological rigor is required to develop strategies that align with divine intention. Only by so doing will there be any hope of effecting lasting transformation.

Within Christian discussion of justice, mercy, and social well-being, Leviticus is frequently cited, and rightly so, for the book has much to contribute. Attention often focuses on ch. 19. There is, of course, good precedent for this. Jesus, after all, quotes Leviticus 19:18 to impress upon his listeners that love for one's neighbor is second only to love for God and must therefore be integral to the life of his followers (Matt 22:39 // Mark 12:32 // Luke 10:27; see also Paul in Gal 5:14, and James in Jas 2:8). From a literary perspective, Mary Douglas argues that Leviticus 19 forms the structural and theological heart of the book.[2] Noel Irwin even posits that Leviticus 19:18, with its injunction to love one's neighbor, is the means to understanding the content of the entire work.[3] Certainly, similar themes extend beyond ch. 19. Concern for aliens

---

1. Within the Australian context, the recent movie *Chasing Asylum* (2016) presents a visceral example of the controversial ethical and humanitarian issues which swirl around current government policy. I am grateful to Mark Brett and Janson Condren for their comments made on a previous draft of this essay.
2. Douglas, "Poetic," 251.
3. Irwin, "Wesley and Leviticus 19," 76.

and strangers permeates the so-called Holiness Code (e.g., 23:22); the humanitarian vision behind the year of Jubilee was and is revolutionary; the sacrificial system explicitly makes provision for the less well-off (e.g., 5:7, 11). Thus, Jacob Milgrom and Walter Brueggemann are correct to asset that a concern for social holiness is central to Leviticus.[4]

Yet engagement with what Leviticus says about social holiness tends to have one of two aims in mind. The first is purely historical, displaying a desire to better understand the social conditions and attitudes of the ancient Near East as an end in itself.[5] A second approach majors instead on contemporary implementation, seeking to either enact,[6] or to abrogate,[7] Levitical legislation. Much less appreciated, however, are the literary and theological underpinnings of the social justice legislation. Yet the danger of not recognizing these features of the text is to end up with abstracted principles divorced from basis, regardless of whether the concern is historical reconstruction or contemporary application. While such abstraction is not necessarily invalid, it fails to do sufficient justice to the way the issues have been presented by the author/redactor of the book.

Leviticus 26 illustrates the matter well. The pericope functions as a climax to the book, as YHWH, in first-person discourse, outlines the consequences that will accompany either obedience (vv. 1–13) or disobedience (vv. 14–39). The wording of the chapter's summary in v. 46 indicates that these divine sanctions encapsulate not only the extant text of Leviticus,[8] but arguably the entirety of the Sinai material.[9] The vision portrayed in the blessing panel (vv. 1–13) functions similarly. Terminology used here alludes to other sections of the book (e.g., v. 2; cf. 19:3) and to the Pentateuch more broadly. Of interest for this essay are allusions to Genesis 1–3 in vv. 3–13.[10] As

---

4. Milgrom, *Leviticus*, 175; Brueggemann, *Introduction*, 72–73.

5. See, e.g., Schipper and Stackert, "Blemishes."

6. E.g., Schluter and Ashcroft, *Jubilee Manifesto*.

7. See, for instance, the revisionist literature cited in Gagnon, *Bible and Homosexual Practice*, 111–46.

8. Reference in 26:46 to the "statutes" (חקים), "judgments" (משפטים), and "laws" (תורת) given by YHWH pushes beyond chs. 25–26. In Leviticus, משפט occurs most frequently in chs. 18–26 (18:4, 5, 26; 19:15, 35, 37; 20:22; 24:22; 25:18; 26:15, 43). The noun חקים appears only twice in chs. 1–16 (5:10; 9:16)—both times in the singular. In contrast, the noun חקים never appears in this form or with this meaning elsewhere in chs. 17–26; instead, the feminine form (חקה) is used (e.g., 17:7; 18:3, 4, 5, etc.). חקים does, however, appear in 10:11 as well as frequently throughout Deuteronomy (e.g., Deut 4:1, 5, 6, 8, 14, etc.). Likewise, the noun תורה is not found elsewhere in Leviticus 17–26, but occurs regularly in chs. 1–16 (e.g., 6:2 [9], 7 [14], 18 [25], etc.). Thus, 26:46 seems worded to encapsulate not only chs. 25–26, or even chs. 17–26, but Leviticus as a whole. Similarly, Marx notes the function of 26:1–2 as a "sommaire des fondamentaux de l'alliance," thereby also shifting the focus beyond the legislation of ch. 25 alone (*Lévitique 17–27*, 195).

9. The point is argued by Nihan, *Priestly*, 551. Similarly, Zenger concludes in relation to Leviticus 26:3–13, "Hier laufen die wichtigsten Texte und Linien der Urgeschichte, der Erzelternerzählungen, der Exodus- und der Sinaitheologie zusammen" ("Levitikus," 75).

10. Although beyond the scope of this essay, parallels are also evident between Lev 26:14–39 and

I hope to demonstrate, allusion to the creation narratives is not only intriguing, it is also revealing with respect to the underlying rationale of the social holiness legislation in Leviticus.

My purpose is correspondingly twofold. First, I want to demonstrate that allusion to Genesis 1–3 is, in fact, a literary device employed in Leviticus 26. Then, second, I want to tease out some of the implications that allusion has for understanding the wider literary and theological context of the book's concern with matters of social justice. In doing so, I hope to contribute to the exegetical and theological understanding of this vital part of the Old Testament and so foster a more nuanced and considered appropriation of Leviticus in relation to contemporary debate and practice.

Parallels between Leviticus 26:3–13 and Genesis 1–3

My aim in this section is to demonstrate the lexical, syntactical, and conceptual parallels that are evident between Leviticus 26:3–13 and Genesis 1–3. This is a necessary precursor to teasing out the implications these connections have for matters of justice, mercy, and social well-being.

However, to talk about evident parallels between biblical texts immediately raises questions of methodology. "Evident to whom?" seems a pertinent question to ask, especially considering that the field of biblical studies is littered with many so-called "certain" examples of intertextuality which, in the end, remain entirely unpersuasive.[11] The need for sound methodology is apparent. That said, the scope of this essay means a detailed discussion of method is not possible here. Interested readers can consult my more extended treatment elsewhere.[12] Nevertheless, the appropriateness of the criteria I will employ is widely acknowledged.[13]

There are several important markers for establishing a bone fide connection between texts. Shared words are a good starting point; shared phrases are better still. Probability of genuine connection increases further if words or phrases are rare or only appear in certain contexts. Conceptual parallels, if present, add additional weight to observed lexical semblance. The overall number of connections is also important and the presence of multiple connections to the same text indicates a high likelihood of connection. Thus, a sliding scale of probability is apparent. Parallels can, with a degree of objectivity, be understood as genuinely present.

Gen 1–3. For discussion, see Harper, *"I Will Walk among You,"* 191–216.

11. See, for example, the studies critiqued in Noble, "Criteria." Compare also the cautions voiced by Sandmel, "Parallelomania."

12. See Harper, *"I Will Walk Among You,"* 34–56.

13. Compare the criteria proposed by Nurmela, *Prophets*, 23–37; Sommer, *Prophet*, 6–31; Schultz, *Search*, 222–39; Stead, *Zechariah 1–8*, 16–39.

In relation to the pericopes at hand, Leviticus 26 shares thirty-seven lexemes with Genesis 1 and sixty-seven with Genesis 2–3.[14] While many parallels simply represent common words, several are significant due to their rarity or to their clustered use.

1. The combined use of עץ, פרי, and ארץ ("fruit," "tree," and "land") in connection with the verb נתן, "to give," occurs only four times in the Old Testament (Gen 1:29; Lev 26:4, 20; Ezek 34:27). In Genesis 1:29, God gives (נתן) all the plants of the earth (ארץ), including trees (עץ) with their fruit (פרי), as food to humanity. The next appearance of the word cluster occurs in Leviticus 26:4, where YHWH declares that obedience will result in the land giving its produce and the trees giving their fruit (ונתנה הארץ יבולה ועץ השדה יתן פריו), providing Israel with abundant food.[15]

2. The combination of אכל ("to eat") with לחם ("bread") appears approximately 135 times throughout the Old Testament. However, bread-eating as the referent of a divine pronouncement rather than narrative description occurs much less frequently. In the Pentateuch, such decrees most often appear in instructions regarding sacrificial procedure or priestly dues (Exod 29:32, 34; Lev 8:31; 21:22; 22:7, 11, 13; 23:14; Num 15:19). In three instances, however, a divine pronouncement about eating "bread" is stated more generally. In Genesis 3:17–18, the ground is cursed and YHWH declares to the man (אדם), "by the sweat of your face will you eat bread" (בזעת אפיך תאכל לחם, 3:19).[16] Henceforth, humanity would be prone to food shortages. The second pronouncement, in Leviticus 26:5, mitigates that threat. Instead, YHWH announces that, in Canaan, the people of Israel will eat bread to satisfaction (ואכלתם לחממכ לשבע). The universal danger posed by food scarcity would no longer imperil this subset of humanity.[17]

3. The syntactical combination of פרה and רבה (Gen 1:22, 28; Lev 26:9)—"to be fruitful" and "to be numerous"—is uncommon in the Old Testament.[18] In Genesis 1, imperative forms (פרו ורבו, "be fruitful and multiply") make concrete the pronouncement of divine blessing upon both creatures (v. 22) and humans (v. 28). The same combination of terms in Leviticus 26:9 highlights the potential

---

14. For convenience, I use "Genesis 1" to refer to Gen 1:1—2:3 and "Genesis 2–3" to refer to Gen 2:4—3:24 throughout.

15. Disobedience will occasion the exact reverse: "Your land will not give its increase and the trees of the land will not give their fruit" (ולא תתן ארצכם את־יבולה ועץ הארץ לא יתן פריו, 26:20).

16. Unless otherwise noted, all translations of biblical texts are my own.

17. The third general pronouncement is found in Lev 26:26, where ironic reversal of blessing is once more pictured: בשברי לכם מטה־לחם. Gerstenberger identifies here an echo of Gen 3:17–19 (*Leviticus*, 407, 416).

18. As a set phrase, the combination appears only fifteen times (Gen 1:22, 28; 8:17; 9:1, 7; 17:20; 28:3; 35:11; 47:27; 48:4; Exod 1:7; Lev 26:9; Jer 3:16; 23:3; Ezek 36:11).

blessing that awaits Israel in Canaan. Divine instrumentality will make Israel fruitful and numerous—if the people remain loyal (cf. 26:3).[19]

4. The *hithpael* of הלך with God as subject is rare, appearing only three times in the Pentateuch (Gen 3:8; Lev 26:12; Deut 23:15 [14]).[20] In Genesis 3:8, הלך (*hithpael*) is used to describe YHWH God "walking about" in the Garden (יהוה אלהים מתהלך בגן) in the context of impending judgment. In contrast, YHWH's declared intention in Leviticus 26:12, to "walk about" (הלך [*hithpael*]) among the people (והתהלכתי בתוככם), comes as the highpoint of the blessings listed in vv. 3–12 and marks the climax of a theme of increasing intimacy between YHWH and his people evident throughout the book.[21]

Evidence of lexical and syntactical parallels between Leviticus 26:3–13 and Genesis 1–3, including rare formulations, is suggestive of a deliberate connection for rhetorical aims. That premise is reinforced by several conceptual parallels. Space constraints mean I must limit discussion to the more prominent examples. These are, however, sufficient to support the case I am making.

First, in both Genesis 1 and Genesis 2–3 God is portrayed as the provider of food, a resource he can either give abundantly or withdraw completely. The same concept is central to Leviticus 26 where food and eating are dominant themes.[22] YHWH promises rain in season (v. 4) and bountiful harvests (vv. 4–5a) that will lead to eating bread to satisfaction (ואכלתם לחמכם לשבע, 26:5b). Even the increased population

---

19. Divine instrumentality is indicated by the first person *hiphil* forms used with YHWH as subject (והפריתי אתכם והרביתי אתכם).

20. The remaining Old Testament examples are found in relation to YHWH's presence in the tent (אהל) or tabernacle (משכן) (2 Sam 7:6–7 // 1 Chr 17:6). Use of הלך (*hithpael*) in connection with the tabernacle/tent raises the possibility that these structures were in some sense understood as reinstituting edenic conditions or perhaps, vice versa, that Eden was portrayed in temple-like terms. The argument has been formulated both ways in the secondary literature. For *sequential* readers of the Pentateuch the motif of temple as Eden revisited would seem to be the stronger one. However, intertextuality works both ways. Thus, for *re-readers* of the corpus, Eden would also take on temple-like qualities.

21. See Nihan, *Priestly*, 608–18. Following the narrative tension raised by the exclusion of everyone, Moses included, when the כבוד יהוה filled the tabernacle at the end of Exodus (40:34–35), Leviticus portrays a process of increasing access. In Lev 1:1, YHWH calls to Moses *from* the tabernacle. Then, in Lev 9:23, following the initiation of the cult, Moses and Aaron enter into the Tent of Meeting. In contrast to this inaugural and therefore unique entry event, the Day of Atonement enabled the high priest, representing the people, to enter before the presence of YHWH once each year (Lev 16:12–15). In 26:12, however, YHWH declares that he will "walk about" among the people. Jacob Milgrom surmises, "The clear implication is that . . . YHWH is not confined to a sanctuary but is present everywhere in the land" (*Leviticus 23–27*, 2301; so also, Rooker, *Leviticus*, 315). In other words, 26:12 pictures YHWH and the people of Israel cohabiting the same space and seems to envision a permanent (albeit contingent) state of affairs.

22. The אכל root appears seven times in Lev 26 (vv. 5, 10, 16, 26, 29[x2], 38).

promised in 26:9 will not exhaust the supply of food; in fact, the people will have so much left over they will need to clear it out to make room for the new harvest (26:10).[23]

Second, the specific mention of eating fruit from trees strengthens a connection between Genesis 1–2 and Leviticus 26. The parallel is highlighted when a comparison is made with Deuteronomy 28.[24] There too, food constitutes a key metric for projected blessing. Yet the terms employed in the Deuteronomy pericope do not include the eating of fruit from trees.[25] Use of the same phraseology in Genesis 1–2 and Leviticus 26 suggests a deliberate parallel.[26]

Third, Genesis 1 portrays a *vegetarian* diet for both humans and animals.[27] Likewise, in Leviticus 26 there is no mention of livestock or eating meat among the listed blessings, despite the book having no problem with the eating of meat and, in fact, frequently legislating its consumption (6:19 [6:26]; 7:6, 15, etc.). The absence of meat eating in ch. 26, therefore, is intriguing. Again, this is made more noticeable when compared with Deuteronomy 28 where "livestock" (בהמה), "cattle" (אלף), and the "offspring of your flock" (עשתרות צאנך) are listed, and the eating of plants *and* animals is at least implied (e.g., 28:4, 11). Accordingly, Alfred Marx suggests that the language of Leviticus 26 is intentionally worded in order to evoke Genesis 1.[28] He concludes, "Par cette discrete allusion, P renvoie à l'utopie de la paix originelle où humains et animaux vivaient en parfait harmonie."[29]

A fourth conceptual parallel concerns Sabbath rest. In Genesis 1:1—2:3, the seven-day schema climaxes with God resting (שבת). Michael Fishbane draws attention to the emphasis placed on this moment by the structure of the text: "this seventh paragraph of seven paragraphs, telling of the seventh day of the seven days of creation, is styled as a liturgical celebration of divine rest and completed creation."[30]

---

23. For details on the ideal periods for rain as well as the crops harvested in different seasons, see Noordtzij, *Leviticus*, 264. The potential drain on resources implied by an increased population (v. 9) probably explains the position of v. 10 and its resumption of the topic of abundant food (cf. 26:4–5).

24. The chronological and literary relationship between Lev 26 and Deut 28 is complex and, hence, debated. Milgrom, for example, views Lev 26 as the earlier piece (*Leviticus 23–27*, 2347–48), whereas Nihan (*Priestly*, 539) argues that Lev 26 is subsequent and was written to parallel the Deuteronomy passage.

25. The noun עץ is used thrice in Deut 28 (vv. 36, 42, 64), and ירד occurs thirteen times (vv. 4[x3], 11[x3], 18[x2], 33, 42, 51[x2], 53), but they are never used in conjunction.

26. Adding further weight to this supposition is that Leviticus has other ways of conveying the same reality. Lev 25:19, for example, describes eating fruit given by the *earth* (ונתנה הארץ פריה ואכלתם).

27. Westermann draws attention to other ANE texts that picture an original vegetarian diet (*Genesis 1–11*, 163–64).

28. "Connaissant l'attrait des Israélites pour les riches festins de viande . . . le silence de P n'en est que plus surprenant et paraît difficilement fortuit. De fait, l'accent . . . ne peut manquer d'évoquer cet autre passage sacerdotal, en Gn 1,29" (Marx, *Lévitique 17–27*, 199).

29. Marx, *Lévitique 17–27*, 200. Cf. Bonar who views Lev 26:6 as "the great proof of the land returning to something of an Eden-State, where man had full dominion over the beasts of the field" (*Leviticus*, 475).

30. Fishbane, *Text*, 11.

Sabbath rest also constitutes a major theme in Leviticus 25–26,³¹ with half of the book's use of the שבת root occurring here. Frank Gorman expands on the connection between creation ordinance and liturgical calendar. He notes, "The pattern of order established in creation is given a means of realization in the liturgical order. . . . By observing the liturgical order, Israel participates in the sustaining and maintaining of the divinely constructed order of creation."³² Thus the command in 26:2, to "keep my Sabbaths," functions as an invitation to enact and enjoy one aspect of creation order. The validity of seeing a link to creation here is supported by the following verses which outline, in terms borrowed from Genesis 1–3, the blessings that will accompany Sabbath-keeping: being fruitful and numerous, eating fruit from trees, having YHWH walk about in their midst, etc. Sabbath observance is paralleled with YHWH's rest in creation; Israel is invited to share in its accompanying blessings.

A fifth conceptual parallel relates to the presentation of Canaan and the Garden of Eden as sanctuaries. The idea that the Garden in Genesis 2–3 was understood as cultic space is not novel. The book of *Jubilees*, for example, made the association explicitly: "Eden was the holy of holies and the dwelling of the Lord" (8:19).³³ A substantial body of recent scholarship has explored this correlation more fully.³⁴ Similarly, Canaan seems to have been viewed in cultic terms. In Exodus 15:17, for instance, the destination YHWH is bringing his people to is described as the mountain of YHWH's inheritance (בהר נחלתך),³⁵ the site of his dwelling (מכון לשבתך), and the "sanctuary" (מקדש) he has established. Elsewhere in Exodus, the same destination is explicitly called "the land of the Canaanites" (ארץ הכנעני, 13:5). Thus, Christopher Wright seems correct in understanding Exodus 15:17 as a reference to the land as a whole,³⁶ implying that Canaan was conceived in terms of sacred space,³⁷ even being termed YHWH's "sanctuary" (מקדש).³⁸ Leviticus 26:12 assumes and supports a connection between land and sanctuary. The rare use of הלך (*hithpael*) with YHWH as subject connects

---

31. Willis describes Lev 23–27 as "the observance of Sabbath on multiple levels" (*Leviticus*, xxiii).

32. Gorman, *Ideology*, 219–20.

33. Text cited from Charlesworth, *Pseudepigrapha*, 2:73.

34. E.g., Wenham, "Sanctuary"; Fretheim, *Exodus*, 268–72; Beale, *Temple*, 66–80; Morales, *Tabernacle*, 245–77; Harper, "First Things." See also the collection of seminal essays reproduced in Morales, *Cult*. Correspondence between garden and temple ought not to be surprising. Temple complexes in the ancient world often contained gardens to symbolize the fertility imparted by the resident deity, thereby creating a strong conceptual link between sanctuaries and gardens. Indeed, in Mesopotamia priests were often called "gardeners" (Lundquist, "Temple Ideology," 69). Regarding the wider symbolism of gardens in ANE and Hebrew literature, see Stordalen, *Echoes*, 81–183.

35. Whether "mountain" refers to Mount Zion (so Stuart, *Exodus*, 361; Durham, *Exodus*, 209), or to the cosmic mountain (cf. Morales, *Tabernacle*, 46), the cultic resonances are evident.

36. Wright, *NIDOTTE* 1:522.

37. So Fishbane, "Sacred Center," 19, who identifies Canaan as a "*hieros topos*" on a par with Mt. Sinai.

38. For a similar conclusion, see Sailhamer, *Genesis*, 72; Joosten, *People*, 176–80; Martin, *Bound*, 78.

this verse to other occasions where YHWH's presence "walks about" in either the tabernacle or garden-temple (Gen 3:8; Deut 23:15; 2 Sam 7:6–7; 1 Chr 17:6). On this basis, it is understandable why many have suggested that the possession of Canaan is portrayed in the biblical texts as a return to Eden.[39]

A sixth parallel is evident in relation to narrative setting. Cynthia Edenburg demonstrates the presence of narrative patterning in Genesis 2–4, with Genesis 4 mirroring the sequence of events in Genesis 2–3.[40] However, the ten-point structure she identifies in the Genesis pericopes is also evident in Leviticus 26, something Edenburg herself recognizes. She concludes accordingly, "One could argue with justification that Gen 2–4 deliberately evokes Lev 26. Otherwise, the reverse is more than likely; namely that the author of Lev 26 echoed motifs and expressions in Gen 2–4."[41] Whichever way the direction is construed, Leviticus 26 and Genesis 2–3 are structured around an analogous movement from divine command through disobedience to curse and banishment.

A final parallel relates to the rhetorical progressions evident in Leviticus 26:4–12 and 26:14–33.[42] In both panels, the blessings and the threats, the escalation of eventualities climaxes on a note that derives at least some of its force from an intertextual link to Genesis: respectively, Yahweh walking about among his people as per the original creation (Lev 26:12; cf. Gen 3:8) and banishment from a land that has been portrayed as a new Eden (Lev 26:33; cf. vv. 3–12).

In summary, specific verbal and syntactical connections between Leviticus 26 and Genesis 1–3 are enhanced and supported by conceptual parallels. In multiple ways, therefore, the blessing panel in Leviticus 26:3–13 alludes to creation in its "very good" state and declares that this is something YHWH can reinstitute in Israel's lived experience. Teasing out the implications this has for our understanding of social holiness legislation is what I want to turn to next.

---

39. Eliade makes the point that settlement in a territory was an act of consecration in which place is understood to be "the replica of the paradigmatic universe created and inhabited by the gods" (*Sacred*, 299). Along these lines, Rashi understood YHWH in Lev 26:12 to be declaring, אטיל עמכם בגן עדן ("I will stroll with you in the Garden of Eden"), thus seeing an intended connection with the primeval account (*Commentary*, 3:352).

40. Edenburg, "Eden."

41. Edenburg, "Eden," 164.

42. Amit describes rhetorical progression as "a rhetorical technique, or contrivance, that organizes the data for the author in a multi-phased, hierarchical structure, wherein the elements are arranged in an ascending or descending order: from the general to the particular, or vice versa; from minor to major, or the reverse; from the expected to the unexpected; the impersonal to the personal, and so on. Often the final step in the progression is the climactic one, while each of the preceding steps plays its part in expanding or narrowing the sequence, and thereby shedding more light on the subject" ("Progression," 9).

Implications of Allusion for Justice, Mercy, and Social Well-Being in Leviticus

Parallels between Leviticus 26 and Genesis 1–3 suggest a deliberate connection between these pericopes in the final-form Pentateuch. But how is this observation helpful? More pointedly, what bearing does allusion to Genesis 1–3 in Leviticus 26:3–13 have on matters of justice, mercy, and social well-being? I want to expand briefly on three interrelated areas before drawing out some conclusions for contemporary discussion.

First, parallels between Leviticus 26 and Genesis 1–3 indicate the wider contextual framework within which the Levitical legislation is to be understood. Envisioned in Leviticus 26 is a return to edenic conditions. The land Israel was about to inherit would, dependent upon obedience, become a place of abundant food, especially abundant fruit from trees; a place where the people would multiply and become fruitful; and a domain where dangerous animals and other enemies would no longer threaten. Additionally, Canaan would become a "sanctuary" where YHWH would once again "walk about" in the midst of people. Thus, divine sanctions in Leviticus 26 offer to Israel the possibility of recapitulating creation blessing. Moreover, set against the storyline of the Pentateuch, they offer a reversal of Genesis 3 as various elements of cursed creation are undone: enmity with animals, difficulties in relation to childbirth and food production, and, most significantly, banishment from YHWH's presence. In this manner, Leviticus 26 furthers a wider intertextual strategy present across the book to frame its legislation around the restoration of creation order.[43]

While, as many have argued, the legislation in Leviticus may be idealistic, the intertextuality present is nevertheless revealing. It becomes apparent that the purview of the legal and ritual material in Leviticus is not restricted to constitutional or religious concerns; its goal is much more profound—namely, the inauguration of a transformed cosmos. YHWH's commitment to the world he made, and his resolve to see creation blessing realized (cf. Gen 1:28–31), remain unchanged. In this regard it is important to note that promised blessing was not merely an eschatological hope. It was to be inaugurated in Israel's lived experience as the people acted in obedience to the revealed will of YHWH.

Second, the picture of inaugurated creation blessing presented in Leviticus is holistic in its scope—that is, it holds together what Protestant theology tends to separate into "spiritual" and "material/physical" categories. In Leviticus 26:3–13, the necessary prerequisite for restoration of edenic conditions is obedience to YHWH's commands. This conditionality is indicated by the "if . . . then" clause of vv. 3–4: "*if* you walk in my commands . . . *then* I will give" (ונתתי . . . אם־בחקתי תלכו). Obedience underlies any hope of return to creation order. In Leviticus, therefore, the socio-economic, and even the environmental, cannot be divorced from the theological. YHWH's declaration of

---

43. I have argued this at greater length elsewhere. See Harper, *"I Will Walk Among You."*

intent ought not to be understood as a carte blanche promise of what would inevitably be; rather, it asserts what *might* be.⁴⁴

A similar logic lies behind v. 12, where YHWH declares, "I will walk in your midst and I will be your God and you will be my people." This climactic promise of Eden-like cohabitation is predicated on the transformation envisioned by the preceding chapters, a transformation that runs along both divine and human axes.

In relation to the "vertical" axis, one of the canonical functions of Leviticus 1–16 is to relieve the tension left unresolved at the end of Exodus. In Exodus 40:34–35, the glory of YHWH takes up abode in the finished tabernacle, restoring the divine presence on earth. Yet all are excluded from that glorious presence, even Moses (Exod 40:35). Accordingly, the first half of Leviticus deals primarily with issues of access: who and what may approach YHWH's tabernacle presence and, conversely, who and what must remain separated. Purity language dominates, with the terminology of "clean" and "unclean" being particularly clustered in Leviticus 11–15.⁴⁵ A similar concentration of terms is found in relation to priesthood, sacrifice, and atonement.⁴⁶ Chapter 16, arguably the central pericope of the book (*pace* Douglas),⁴⁷ brings these themes to a head. Here, uniquely in Israel's cult, blood was to be brought into the adytum to secure atonement for the sins and uncleanness of the people—whatever they may have been. As a result, the people were declared clean and fit to dwell in proximity to the divine (16:30; cf. 15:31).

Resolution of divine-human separation, however, does not exhaust the concern of the book. The second half of Leviticus shifts in emphasis toward "horizontal" relationships. Corporate holiness moves into view and is construed along social and ethical lines (thus, since Klostermann, Lev 18–26 has been termed the *Heiligkeitsgeschichte*⁴⁸). Theologically, the order is important. Even if, as critical consensus has it, Leviticus has been composed from different source materials, it remains incumbent upon interpreters to account for the logic behind the extant whole: why has the text

---

44. The conditionality inherent in the text of Leviticus is conveyed by its unusually high proportion of *weqatal* verb forms—almost three times higher than any other book. For details, see Sawyer, "Language," 16–17.

45. 132/250 occurrences (53 percent) of טמא are found in Leviticus, 96 of them in chs. 11–15. 45/98 (46 percent) and 21/96 (22 percent) occurrences of טהר and טהור appear in Leviticus, 39 and 12 times respectively in chs. 11–15.

46. 49/102 uses (48 percent) of כפר occur in Leviticus. The root occurs most frequently in chs. 1–16 (45 out of 49 occurrences), with sixteen appearances clustered in ch. 16. 196 out of 773 Old Testament uses of the noun כהן are found in Leviticus (25 percent). The relative frequencies of sacrificial terminology are as follows: עלה (63/306, 21 percent); חטאת (82/298, 28 percent); שלמים (30/87, 34 percent); אשם (27/40, 68 percent); קרבן (40/82, 49 percent). The one exception is the מנחה (36/211, 17 percent in Leviticus) which is more often referred to in Numbers (62 times, or 29 percent of total use). On how best to render the various terms in English, see Watts, *Leviticus 1–10*, 4–8; Milgrom, *Leviticus 1–16*, ad loc.

47. For discussion, see Harper, "I Will Walk Among You," 71–79.

48. See Klostermann, "Beiträge," 416.

been put together *in this manner*? The sequence of material in the received text of Leviticus makes it apparent that while restoration of relationship with YHWH may be primary, it is not, by itself, the sum total of the book's vision. That vision extends to the transformation of society in line with both creation patterns (e.g., sexuality in ch. 18)[49] and the revealed character of God (note the repeated declaration, אני יהוה, passim).

Thus, Leviticus prescribes not only the reordering of time (e.g., ch. 23) and space (e.g., 16:2) required to accommodate the divine presence, but also the (re-)creation of a transformed humanity fit to dwell before YHWH. The social holiness concern of the book needs to be set into this wider purpose. Leviticus evidences a holistic vision: "horizontal" concern for fellow humanity (and indeed the animal world; e.g., Lev 18:23; 20:16) is presented as the necessary outworking of "vertical" restoration with YHWH. Hence, issues of justice, mercy, and social well-being cannot, according to Leviticus, be separated from theological concerns. Indeed, repeatedly stated throughout the book is that *because* Israel now lives יהוה ינפל, the nation must necessarily enact interpersonal holiness at a human-human level (see 20:7–8, 22–26).[50] Living in proximity to YHWH becomes the supreme rationale for loving one's neighbor.

The intersection between who YHWH is and what Israel must do leads to a third implication stemming from parallels between Leviticus 26 and Genesis 1–3. Israel, in relation to social justice, is called to act in a manner consistent with what the nation knows of YHWH.

Leviticus 26:3–13 details potential blessings that YHWH will bestow upon Israel in the land (note the use of first person *hiphil* forms throughout). As noted earlier, the wording of these blessings frequently employs language shared with Genesis 1–3.[51] A correlation between Israel in the land and Adam in the Garden thus becomes clear. Emphasized thereby, is that YHWH's original intent to bless humanity remains; that blessing will now, potentially at least, be realized by Israel. Just as YHWH had provided abundant food for humanity in the beginning (Gen 1:29; 2:9, 16), he would provide abundant food for Israel (Lev 26:5, 10). Just as YHWH had constructed a safe environment for Adam (Gen 2:8), he would make Israel's habitation secure (Lev 26:5–8). Just as YHWH had created humans equally in the image of God (Gen 1:27), and had walked among them (Gen 3:8), he declares to a renewed people en masse: "I will walk about in your midst" (Lev 26:12).

Worth noting in this regard is that Israel's social responsibilities, at least in part, are formed along similar lines. Blessings received were to be extended to others. Hence, the Israelites were to make food available to those who had none. Regulations

---

49. I explore one example of this in Harper, "First Things," 52–55.

50. The phrase יהוה ינפל occurs with more regularity in Leviticus than elsewhere—59 times out of a total of 224 occurrences in the Old Testament (26 percent).

51. Direction of dependence could be (and has been) argued both ways. For my purposes, I do not need to decide the issue. What matters is that intertextual connections are present. It is the function performed by these connections in the final-form Pentateuch that I am interested in.

regarding gleaning and harvesting, for instance, fit within this category (e.g., 19:9–10). The land was also to be a place of safety for all. Even those classed as "aliens" and "sojourners," a precarious social status in the ancient world, were to be treated on a par with "native-born" Israelites (19:34). Thus, Israel's social obligations were to recognize a degree of equality between people, irrespective of race or culture.[52]

While more could be said, the essential point is clear: YHWH's creation blessings, offered to Israel in Canaan, were in turn to inform ethical praxis for the nation. Regarding social holiness, Israel was called to *imitatio Dei*.

Leviticus 26 and Contemporary Social-Holiness Discourse

In view of the intertextuality present in Leviticus 26, and considering the window this opens on the intent of the Levitical legislation more broadly, what implications does this pericope have for contemporary Christian discourse regarding matters of social justice?

As demonstrated, the ethical and moral vision of Leviticus is shaped, at least partly, by creation patterns. The use of allusion to Genesis 1–3 throughout the book—at lexical, syntactical, and conceptual levels—makes that connection clear for readers. The implication is that YHWH, though Israel, is engaged in an act of re-creation, righting and restoring a fractured world.[53] Yet, even if the purview of Leviticus is idealistic, it is not naïvely so; this remains a text addressed to the realities of a post-lapsarian world. The book's protracted emphasis on ritual practices for ameliorating defilement is sufficient evidence of that. However, by means of such provision, Leviticus also invites and enables transformation of the status quo. That transformation is holistic, even cosmic, in scope, incorporating reconciliation with God, a re-made humanity fit to live in the divine presence, and the very re-ordering of time and space (at least on a microcosmic level). As suggested, this is nothing less than an inaugurated new creation, and is proleptic of YHWH's intention on a global scale.

Leviticus 26 is thus in concert with a wider movement across the Scriptures that not only expects the restoration of creation but demands that God's people actively contribute toward that end. The vision of Eden restored portrayed in Leviticus 26:3–13 thus provides an insight into what God is committed to and, correspondingly, gives a broad picture of the goal to aim for.

Working out what this looks like in practice, however, is more difficult. Nevertheless, two studies—one by Steve Corbett and Brian Fikkert, and the other by Bryant

---

52. This is the case even though differences are not totally obliterated (e.g., Lev 23:42–43).

53. It is important to note that reordering acts within the Israelite cult are fundamentally different from other ANE rites of restoration. In contrast to the *akītu* festival, for instance, the cult in Israel is *not* a world-constituting event. Rather, the reordering of time and space operates at a *micro*cosmic level, not a *macro*cosmic one. Instead of ritually refashioning the entire cosmos, realignment with creation patterns in Israel's cult functions as reminder of the original state as well as being the *inauguration* of a renewed world.

Myers—provide useful examples. Both focus on cosmic transformation as the broad umbrella under which issues of social justice and well-being must be worked out. As such, proposals made by these studies resonate with the tenor of Leviticus 26:3–13 while also informing contemporary praxis.

Myers helpfully charts the broader parameters that ought to shape Christian responses to poverty and injustice. He argues for the implementation of what he calls "transformational development," that is, action that seeks to bring about "positive change in the whole of human life materially, socially, and spiritually."[54] To do so, necessarily requires the articulation of transformative aims: what people are being transformed *from*, and what they are being transformed *to*.[55] For Myers, understanding creation is crucial for shaping these aims. The opening chapters of the Bible portray the world (human and nonhuman) as it was meant to be; the subsequent storyline provides the rationale for why it is the way it is. This in turn sets appropriately broad parameters for what restoration entails.[56] All of creation—human and nonhuman—is being redeemed.

Thus, in relation to practice, transformative efforts must be comprehensive in order to deal adequately with the complexity of factors that result in the loss of well-being. For instance, while presenting needs (e.g., lack of food or water) must be addressed, at the same time work must be done to effect change at the level of ideology and values.[57] Transformation must be a holistic endeavor which eschews the physical-spiritual divide endemic to Western thinking. Thus, while reconciliation with God is certainly required, so too is reconciliation with self, with society, and with the environment.

Regarding agency, Myers helpfully holds together both human and divine action. While he acknowledges that ultimately "God brings the kingdom," Myers is clear that Christians must be committed to also work for the coming of that kingdom. This is no mere postmillennial optimism; rather, it is a case of learning to be obedient, not successful.[58] Hence, while the full realization of restoring creation order may yet lie in the future, Christian people are to act and to work with diligence toward that end, knowing that God has committed himself to it.

In *When Helping Hurts*, Corbett and Fikkert similarly argue that human beings and the conditions that contribute to the loss of social well-being are irreducibly complex. Therefore, they acknowledge that any response must be correspondingly nuanced:

---

54. Myers, *Walking with the Poor*, 3.
55. Myers, *Walking with the Poor*, 93.
56. Myers, *Walking with the Poor*, 45–46.
57. See Myers, *Walking with the Poor*, 82–83.
58. Myers, *Walking with the Poor*, 38, 110.

human beings are multifaceted, implying that poverty-alleviation efforts should be multifaceted as well. If we reduce human beings to being simply physical—as Western thought is prone to do—our poverty-alleviation efforts will tend to focus on material solutions. But if we remember that humans are spiritual, social, psychological, and physical beings, our poverty-alleviation efforts will be more holistic in their design and execution.[59]

Crucial to their argument is an expanded definition of poverty which includes spiritual, social, psychological as well as material impoverishment. It is thus a recognition, as Myers's puts it, that "poverty is the absence of shalom in all its meanings."[60] This expanded definition of poverty highlights that all are poor and needy, albeit in different ways; human experience of paucity is universal.

With that in mind, Corbett and Fikkert argue that broad-spectrum reconciliation, set against a theology of creation, must shape the goals that Christians pursue and the methods used in combatting poverty and social injustice. They suggest,

> The goal is to restore people to a full expression of humanness, to being what God created us all to be, people who glorify God by living in right relationship with God, with self, with others, and with the rest of creation.[61]

The vision of Leviticus 26:3–13 adds theological and exegetical support to the conclusions reached by Myers and by Corbett and Fikkert. The pericope portrays a picture of multiple human needs being addressed, reinforcing the requirement for holistic approaches to social justice and mercy. The promise of abundant food deals with physical privation, dwelling in safety alleviates psychological distress, being fruitful and multiplying preserves social cohesion, and having YHWH once more walk among a restored and transformed people meets deep-seated spiritual needs. The invitation extended to Israel was to experience life as it was in the beginning, to be the firstfruits of God's restoration of all things, and then to expand that blessing to others.

Moreover, Leviticus 26 also seeks to effect ideological change. This is perhaps one reason why allusion to Genesis 1–3 is used rather than explicit citation, for allusion has the ability to engage the imagination in a way that quotation does not. In relation to Leviticus 26, Gorman notes, "The blessings and curses are presented as *images* to be seen as much as heard."[62] Tacit evocation of the first humans adds poignancy and emotional force to the chapter's appeal for covenant fidelity. As Fishbane reasons, "Typological alignments have deep exegetical dimensions . . . and thereby project the

---

59. Corbett and Fikkert, *When Helping Hurts*, 57.

60. Myers, *Walking with the Poor*, 86. Wolterstorff (*Justice and Peace*, 69–72) argues that the concept of shalom is not merely the absence of strife, but incorporates relational harmony, justice, and enjoyment.

61. Corbett and Fikkert, *When Helping Hurts*, 74.

62. Gorman, *Leviticus*, 142 (emphasis his).

powerful associations of the past into future images of longing and hope."[63] Thus, allusion to Genesis 1–3 serves to reinforce the *affective* dimension of the Levitical legislation. In this way allusion also increases enjoyment of the text. As perceptive readers become aware of intertextual connections, Leviticus 26 becomes literarily more artful. Yet artistry is more than just mere adornment. Aesthetic appeal feeds into the rhetorical force of the whole and becomes another means for the text to achieve the ends for which it was written.

Conclusion

The complex and often bewildering social, economic, and environmental issues that confront contemporary Christianity are daunting. Just brief exposure can be jarring, leaving people reeling and wanting to retreat to blissful ignorance. Even when moved to act, the temptation is to pursue reductionist measures: to advocate spiritual needs as being all that Christian activity should concern itself with; or conversely, to focus on meeting material poverty, or to reform political systems, to the exclusion of other factors. Leviticus 26 roundly rejects any such approach as being woefully inadequate and indeed declares it to be out of step with what God is doing in the world. God's re-creation intentions are cosmic in scope—addressing the entirety of a broken creation and multifaceted human need. If Christians are to be imitators of God, and coworkers with him, then their horizons need to be similarly all-encompassing.

Bibliography

Amit, Yairah. "Progression as a Rhetorical Device in Biblical Literature." *Journal for the Study of the Old Testament* 28 (2003) 3–32.

Beale, Gregory K. *The Temple and the Church's Mission: A Biblical Theology of the Dwelling Place of God*. New Studies in Biblical Theology 17. Leicester: Apollos, 2004.

Bonar, Andrew A. *A Commentary on Leviticus*. 1846. Reprint, Edinburgh: Banner of Truth, 1966.

Brueggemann, Walter. *An Introduction to the Old Testament: The Canon and Christian Imagination*. Louisville: Westminster John Knox, 2003.

Charlesworth, James H., ed. *The Old Testament Pseudepigrapha*. 2 vols. New York: Doubleday, 1983–85.

Corbett, Steve, and Brian Fikkert. *When Helping Hurts: How to Alleviate Poverty without Hurting the Poor . . . and Yourself*. Chicago: Moody, 2012.

Douglas, Mary. "Poetic Structure in Leviticus." In *Pomegranates and Golden Bells: Studies in Biblical, Jewish, and Near Eastern Ritual, Law and Literature in Honor of Jacob Milgrom*, edited by David P. Wright et al., 239–56. Winona Lake: Eisenbrauns, 1995.

Durham, John I. *Exodus*. Word Biblical Commentary 3. Nashville: Nelson, 1987.

Edenburg, Cynthia. "From Eden to Babylon: Reading Genesis 2–4 as a Paradigmatic Narrative." In *Pentateuch, Hexateuch, or Enneateuch? Identifying Literary Works in*

---

63. Fishbane, *Interpretation*, 371.

Genesis through Kings, edited by T. B. Dozeman et al., 155–67. Ancient Israel and Its Literature 8. Atlanta: SBL, 2011.

Eliade, Mircea. *The Sacred and the Profane: The Nature of Religion*. Translated by W. R. Trask. 1957. Reprint, San Diego: Harcourt, 1987.

Fishbane, Michael. *Biblical Interpretation in Ancient Israel*. Oxford: Clarendon, 1988.

———. *Biblical Text and Texture: A Literary Reading of Selected Texts*. Oxford: Oneworld, 1998.

———. "The Sacred Center: The Symbolic Structure of the Bible." In *Texts and Responses: Studies Presented to Nahum N. Glatzer on the Occasion of His Seventieth Birthday by His Students*, edited by M. Fishbane and P. R. Flohr, 6–27. Leiden: Brill, 1975.

Fretheim, Terence E. *Exodus*. Interpretation. Louisville: John Knox, 1991.

Gagnon, Robert A. J. *The Bible and Homosexual Practice: Texts and Hermeneutics*. Nashville: Abingdon, 2001.

Gerstenberger, Erhard S. *Leviticus*. Translated by D. W. Stott. Old Testament Library. Louisville: Westminster John Knox, 1996.

Gorman, Frank H. *Ideology of Ritual: Space, Time and Status in the Priestly Theology*. Journal for the Study of the Old Testament Supplement Series 91. Sheffield: JSOT, 1990.

———. *Leviticus: Divine Presence and Community*. International Theological Commentary. Grand Rapids: Eerdmans, 1997.

Harper, G. Geoffrey. "First Things First: Reading Genesis 1–3 in Its Pentateuchal Context." In *The Gender Conversation: Evangelical Perspectives on Gender, Scripture and the Christian Life*, edited by E. Murphy and D. I. Starling, 45–55. Eugene: Wipf & Stock, 2016.

———. *"I Will Walk among You": The Rhetorical Function of Allusion to Genesis 1–3 in the Book of Leviticus*. Bulletin of Biblical Research Supplements Series 21. University Park: Pennsylvania State University Press / Eisenbrauns, 2018.

———. "Time for a New Diet? Allusions to Genesis 1–3 as Rhetorical Device in Leviticus 11." *Southeastern Theological Review* 4 (2013) 179–95.

Irwin, Noel. "'There Is No Holiness but Social Holiness': John Wesley and Leviticus 19." In *Leviticus in Practice*, edited by J. W. Rogerson, 69–77. Practice Interpretation. Blandford Forum, UK: Deo, 2014.

Joosten, Jan. *People and Land in the Holiness Code: An Exegetical Study of the Ideational Framework of the Law in Leviticus 17–26*. Supplements to Vetus Testamentum 67. Leiden: Brill, 1996.

Klostermann, August. "Beiträge zur Entstehungsgeschichte des Pentateuchs." *Zeitschrift für die Gesamte lutherische Theologie und Kirche* 38 (1877) 401–45.

Lundquist, John M. "The Common Temple Ideology of the Ancient Near East." In *The Temple in Antiquity: Ancient Records and Modern Perspectives*, edited by T. G. Madsen, 53–76. Provo: Brigham Young University, 1984.

Martin, Oren R. *Bound for the Promised Land: The Land Promise in God's Redemptive Plan*. New Studies in Biblical Theology 34. Downers Grove: InterVarsity, 2015.

Marx, Alfred. *Lévitique 17–27*. Commentaire de l'ancien testament 3b. Geneva: Labor et Fides, 2011.

Milgrom, Jacob. *Leviticus: A Book of Ritual and Ethics*. Continental Commentaries. Minneapolis: Fortress, 2004.

———. *Leviticus 1–16: A New Translation with Introduction and Commentary*. Anchor Bible 3. New York: Doubleday, 1991.

———. *Leviticus 23–27: A New Translation with Introduction and Commentary.* Anchor Bible 3B. New York: Doubleday, 2001.

Morales, L. Michael, ed. *Cult and Cosmos: Tilting toward a Temple-Centered Theology.* Biblical Tools and Studies 18. Leuven: Peeters, 2014.

———. *The Tabernacle Pre-figured: Cosmic Mountain Ideology in Genesis and Exodus.* Biblical Tools and Studies 15. Leuven: Peeters, 2012.

Myers, Bryant L. *Walking with the Poor: Principles and Practices of Transformational Development.* Maryknoll: Orbis, 1999.

Nihan, Christophe. *From Priestly Torah to Pentateuch: A Study in the Composition of the Book of Leviticus.* Forschungen zum Alten Testament 2/25. Tübingen: Mohr Siebeck, 2007.

Noble, Paul R. "Esau, Tamar, and Joseph: Criteria for Identifying Inner-Biblical Allusions." *Vetus Testamentum* 52 (2002) 219–52.

Noordtzij, A. *Leviticus.* Translated by R. Togtman. Bible Student's Commentary. Grand Rapids: Zondervan, 1982.

Nurmela, Risto. *Prophets in Dialogue: Inner-Biblical Allusions in Zechariah 1–8 and 9–14.* Åbo, Sweden: Åbo Akademi University Press, 1996.

Rashi. *The Torah with Rashi's Commentary Translated, Annotated, and Elucidated by Rabbi Yisrael Isser Zvi Herczeg.* Sapirstein Edition. 5 vols. Brooklyn: Mesorah, 1999.

Rooker, Mark F. *Leviticus.* New American Commentary 3A. Nashville: B&H, 2000.

Sailhamer, John H. *Genesis Unbound: A Provocative New Look at the Creation Account.* Sisters, OR: Multnomah, 1996.

Sandmel, Samuel. "Parallelomania." *Journal of Biblical Literature* 81 (1962) 1–13.

Sawyer, John F. A. "The Language of Leviticus." In *Reading Leviticus: A Conversation with Mary Douglas,* edited by J. F. A. Sawyer, 15–20. Journal for the Study of the Old Testament Supplement Series 227. Sheffield: Sheffield Academic, 1996.

Schipper, Jeremy, and Jeffrey Stackert. "Blemishes, Camouflage, and Sanctuary Service: The Priestly Deity and His Attendants." *Hebrew Bible and Ancient Israel* 2 (2013) 458–78.

Schluter, Michael, and John Ashcroft, eds. *Jubilee Manifesto: A Framework, Agenda and Strategy for Christian Social Reform.* Leicester: InterVarsity, 2005.

Schultz, Richard L. *The Search for Quotation: Verbal Parallels in the Prophets.* Journal for the Study of the Old Testament Supplement Series 180. Sheffield: Sheffield Academic, 1999.

Sommer, Benjamin D. *A Prophet Reads Scripture: Allusion in Isaiah 40–66.* Stanford: Stanford University Press, 1998.

Stead, Michael R. *The Intertextuality of Zechariah 1–8.* Library of Hebrew Bible / Old Testament Studies 506. New York: T. & T. Clark, 2009.

Stordalen, Terje. *Echoes of Eden: Genesis 2–3 and Symbolism of the Eden Garden in Biblical Hebrew Literature.* Contributions to Biblical Exegesis and Theology 25. Leuven: Peeters, 2000.

Stuart, Douglas K. *Exodus.* New American Commentary 2. Nashville: B&H, 2006.

Watts, James W. *Leviticus 1–10.* Historical Commentary on the Old Testament. Leuven: Peeters, 2013.

Wenham, Gordon J. "Sanctuary Symbolism in the Garden of Eden Story." In *"I Studied Inscriptions from before the Flood": Ancient Near Eastern, Literary and Linguistic Approaches to Genesis 1–11,* edited by R. S. Hess and D. T. Tsumura, 399–404. Sources for Biblical and Theological Study 4. Winona Lake, IN: Eisenbrauns, 1994.

Westermann, Claus. *Genesis 1–11: A Commentary.* Translated by J. J. Scullion. Continental Commentaries. Minneapolis: Augsburg, 1984.

Willis, Timothy M. *Leviticus*. Abingdon Old Testament Commentaries. Nashville: Abingdon, 2009.

Wolterstorff, Nicholas. *Until Justice and Peace Embrace*. Kuyper Lectures. Grand Rapids: Eerdmans, 1983.

Wright, Christopher J. H. "יָרֵא." In vol. 1 of *New International Dictionary of Old Testament Theology and Exegesis*, edited by W. A. VanGemeren, 518–24. Grand Rapids: Zondervan, 1997.

Zenger, Erich. "Das Buch Levitikus als Teiltext der Tora / des Pentateuch: Eine synchrone Lektüre mit kanonischer Perspektive." In *Levitikus als Buch*, edited by H.-J. Fabry and H.-W. Jüngling, 47–83. Bonner biblische Beiträge 119. Berlin: Philo, 1999.

4

Justice, Mercy, and Predestination in Romans

ROBERT TILLEY

The Problem of Justice and Mercy

ONE of the perennial problems in politics and the judiciary has to do with how justice and mercy are to fit together if the latter is not to undermine the former. This problem is writ large in the discipline of theology, often by reference to God's sovereignty and grace. This is especially so in respect of *predestining* grace, a subject that, it will be argued, forms the essence of St. Paul's Letter to the Romans.

How do justice and mercy fit together? How *can* they fit together? Arguably, the issue resolves itself into one of two positions. First, mercy is *continuous* with justice: that is, it does not annul justice but, in answering its strictures, mercy perfects justice. Second, mercy is *discontinuous* with justice: that is, it overrides justice, even annuls it, so much so that mercy can be said to be arbitrary in its expression, at least as far as the strictures of justice are concerned. The problem is that the latter position can turn mercy into a means by which injustice is not only justified but also comes to be identified with divine sovereignty and power. For, insofar as mercy can annul the claims of justice, this expresses the power of a divine will that answers to nothing else but itself. Thus, God will have mercy on whom he will have mercy and he can do so by way of simply declaring the unjust to be just. In this, theology becomes antithetical to justice for, following the lead of God, a select group, designated the "elect," can consider themselves free from those strictures that bind the rest of us. Even if they do not have a licence to sin, they consider themselves as being free from having to bear the consequences of sin.

This chapter argues that among the complex of problems confronting Paul in the church at Rome is the presence of a phenomenon similar to that which we have outlined above. Because these believers belong to the "elect" and are accordingly objects of divine grace and mercy, certain parties at Rome, under the guise of "freedom," considered themselves not bound by the law as others are, and, consequently, they behaved in ways that both Gentile and Jew considered immoral.

Justifying Injustice

In announcing the woes that will come upon Jerusalem for her many injustices, the prophet Isaiah gives us an insight into the form of her reasoning, resulting in a justification of her crimes:

> Woe to those who call evil good
> and good evil,
> who put darkness for light
> and light for darkness,
> who put bitter for sweet
> and sweet for bitter. (Isa 5:20)[1]

It is only in trite novels and bad films that perpetrators of evil boast of their evil as being evil. In the real world, however, the wicked justify their crimes as not being crimes at all. Through a strange but all too common alchemy, injustices are turned into justified actions and, through acts of Parliament and decisions of the courts, what is unjust becomes legal. For a state to get to that place where this alchemy is effected and society is morally changed, certain ideas must shape the way that the powerful think, speak, and reason.

The prophet notes that the unjust blend the identity of good and evil, darkness and light, bitter and sweet; normal oppositions no longer apply for those who exercise corrupt power. Justice and injustice often swap places in judicial decisions that appear to most people as "arbitrary." This is because the decisions are incomprehensible when examined by the normal strictures of reason, morality, justice, and the relevant law codes. Indeed, even if these law codes are not changed in this process, their interpretation can make them say the opposite of how they were originally read. The decisions express the will of the party who makes them and have no reference to an external law code or constitution that is open to all to study and apply.

In contrast, there is a general sense that justice should have an egalitarian character by its demands applying equally to all. Injustice, however, favors only a few, being the product of a will which puts into effect anything it desires. Thus, the authority to blend—or even reverse—good and evil, and to pronounce upon and authorise the

---

1. Unless otherwise stated all translations are from the Revised Standard Version (RSV).

reversal of values, is reserved only for a few—that is, for an elite, and we might even say, for *an elect*.

A just society requires an egalitarian ethos, defined by equality before the law. Such a society must therefore flow from an inclusive universalism, that is, from a metaphysics constituted by moral absolutes which relativizes all social status. A *natural moral law* must apply if there is to be a truly egalitarian and just society. Unsurprisingly, there is always the temptation for people to temper this natural moral law when they are given power. This temptation, if unleashed, will inevitably work to justify injustice: good will be made evil, and evil good. As a person rises above good and evil, they consider themselves as being justified in doing what others would consider to be unjust.

Whatever forms of reasoning Isaiah confronted, the phenomenon was certainly not unique to Judah. This side of the fall of humanity into sin, injustice finds many and varied ways to justify itself, but common to them all is the desire to legitimise arbitrary power. It is no surprise then that God—or the gods—is pressed into service, not least because he is above good and evil. And this is often done by arguing for the ultimate incomprehensibility of God. He is considered so "other" that human standards of good and evil simply do not apply. Consequently, it said is that God is sovereign and none can defy his will. By definition, what he wills is *per se* good regardless of how it measures up to our understanding of justice.

This reasoning finds its home in the language of "grace and mercy," which is applied to an "elect" exempt from the just constraints that apply to everyone else. This chapter argues that elements of this reasoning informed a problem which confronted Paul during his mission in the eastern Mediterranean basin and which came to a head in the church at Rome. The problem in Rome was not so much about the law of Moses had but more to do with grace. This grace was grounded, expressed, and reasoned within the doctrine of predestination and election. But, first, what was the place of predestination in Second Temple Judaism?

Wisdom and Predestination

We commence our discussion with a few important "predestination" passages from the Dead Sea Scrolls:

> Then the priests are to bless all those foreordained to God, who walk faultless in all of His ways, saying "May He bless you with every good thing and preserve you from every evil. May He enlighten your mind with wisdom for living, be gracious to you with the knowledge of eternal things, and lift up His gracious countenance upon you for everlasting peace." The Levites in turn shall curse all those foreordained to Belial.[2]

---

2. *Community Rule* (1QS Col. II: 1–5), using the translation by Parry and Tov, *Dead Sea Scrolls Reader*, vol. 1.

PART B—WHEN MERCY SEASONS JUSTICE

In a like manner we read in the Hymns:

> By thy wisdom [all things exist from] eternity
> And before creating them Thou knowest their works for ever and ever
> [Nothing] is done [without Thee]
> And nothing is known unless Thou desire it . . .
> In the wisdom of Thy knowledge
> Thou didst establish their destiny before they ever were.[3]

And in the "Masada Fragment":

> For from the God of knowledge (comes) all that exists for ever, [and from] his [plan]s (come) all the eternally appointed. He produces the former things in their appointed times, and the latter things in their seasons. . . . Before they came into being, (they derived) [from] His [pla]n.[4]

This passage from the *Community Rule* captures the overall tone of several documents found in the Dead Sea Scrolls (=DSS). Not a few times the DSS accent the motif of predestination and a version of the Reformed church's "double predestination": namely, that some have been predestined to be saved and others to be damned by a decree either extending to before anything was made or, at the very least, co-original with God's creation of the cosmos. Consequently, such people are depicted as pieces of clay to be modelled as the potter sees fit.[5] As Mateen Elass writes on the sectaries of Qumran: "By linking so closely the paired contrasts of 'loving/hating' and 'choosing/rejecting' with reference to God's activity toward the human race, Qumran thought emphasizes the double-sidedness of divine election which was for the most part implicit in Old Testament election thought. For Qumran, God not only chooses those to

---

3. 1QH (column 1), using the translation of Vermes, *Dead Sea Scrolls in English*, 166–67.

4. 4Q402 using the translation of Vermes, *Dead Sea Scrolls in English*, 223. For other similar and related passages, see the following texts: CD 2.7; 4.22; 1QS 1.3; 1.9; 3.26; 7.4; 1QH7.12; 4QDibHam 2.9; 4.4–5. For an extended discussion on election in the DSS, see Elass, "Paul's Understanding and Use of the Concept of Election." Available at Durham E-Theses Online: http://etheses.dur.ac.uk/5193/.

5. See the *Community Rule* 11.20–22; 1QH 1.21; 3.23; 4.29; 11.3; 12.26, 32; 18.12, 25. One of the most-cited texts in this regard is the *Treatise of the Two Spirits* (1QS). This text's relationship to the other DSS scrolls is interesting because it probably expresses a development in the doctrine of predestination. For discussion of 1QS, see Hogeterp, "Eschatology of the Two Spirits Revisited." Furthermore, other intertestamental texts (e.g., the *Wisdom of Solomon*) espouse arguments opposed to predestination. Thus, when the *Wisdom of Solomon* employs the theme of the "potter," its purpose is to denounce idolatry rather than discuss the sovereignty of God (*Wisdom of Solomon* 15:7–13). Moreover, in *Wisdom of Solomon* 1:13–16, the writer states that God did not create death, asserting instead that mortality is the result of ungodly men. Wisdom is also depicted in the same manner of Old Testament and early extrabiblical writings: that is, as a universal principle applicable to all peoples, as opposed to being confined just to Israel (*Wisdom of Solomon* 6:1–18) and her temple at Jerusalem (6:8). By contrast, in Prov 9:1–3, wisdom is not identified with the Jerusalem temple but is rather linked to all creation. Last, the statement that God does not hate anything that he has made (*Wisdom of Solomon* 11:23–24) is not easily reconcilable with the strict predestinarian teachings of the DSS.

whom He will show mercy; He also chooses those He will destroy."[6] In the *Community Rule*, this predestining decree informs and expresses the doctrine of grace and mercy, often referred to under the term "*hesed*." The blessings of the elect occur within the context of a covenant, which at the beginning of the *Community Rule* is termed the "covenant of mercy (*hesed*)."[7] It is in the Hymns (the "*hodayot*") that the themes of predestination and mercy are most referred to, with an emphasis on the inability of humanity, unaided by grace, to understand the mysterious workings of God.[8] These mysteries are synonymous with his wisdom. Human beings are but dust and clay and cannot understand God (let alone argue with him) unless God's mysterious decisions are supernaturally revealed.[9]

Similar sentiments can also be found in the intertestamental literature.[10] Thus Sirach writes about the Creator separating human beings one from the other, just as he separates the days. Some are made to be blessed and some are made to be cursed. "As clay in the hand of the potter—for all his ways are as he pleases—so men are in the hand of him who made them, to give them as he decides."[11] Other similar passages could be adduced, but perhaps the major passage from this period comes from

---

6. Elass, "Paul's Understanding," 77. Among the texts cited by Elass are 1QH 1.19–20; CD 2.7; 4.22. Drawing on the work of an earlier Boston University PhD thesis (Rogers, "Doctrine of Election," 1969), Elass expands upon the theme of predestination in the DSS by reference to what she refers to as "election" words and other concomitant themes. She also cites the work of Sohn (*Divine Election of Israel*) by way of supporting the idea that election is present in the Old Testament, albeit it is not as developed as it becomes in the Second Temple Period (Elass, "Paul's Understanding," 72). Although it cannot be addressed here, the issue as to whether or not there *was* a doctrine of predestination/fate in the Old Testament is a thorny one, not least because of the tendency to project back onto earlier texts theological matters that developed later in time. Hence one might take issue with some of the terms that Robert Rogers, Elass, and Sohn use as being indicators of election/predestination in the Old Testament. For an overview of the problems, see the review by Francesca Rochberg of Jack Lawson's work *The Concept of Fate in Ancient Mesopotamia of the First Millennium* in the *Journal of Near Eastern Studies* 58.1 (1990) 54–58. That there is a development to an unequivocal doctrine of predestination in the latter years of the Second Temple period is clear. But the issue is how and why earlier terms found in the Old Testament are made to bear meanings foreign to them, not least because they sit so uneasily with the accent on justice found in the prophets.

7. 1QS Col. 1:8.

8. See Chazon, "Prayers from Qumran." Also see Merrill, *Qumran and Predestination*; Elass, "Paul's Understanding," 67–120.

9. 1QH Col. XX: 27–34. See too 1QH Col. IV: 14–18; Col. V: 6–23; Col. VII: 12–20; Col. VIII: 20–21; Col. IX: 7–9, 24–25, 32; Col. XI: 20–22; Col. XVII: 14–15; Col. XVIII: 1–9, 14–16; Col. XIX: 9–12.

10. See the discussion in Mason, *Divine and Human Agency*. Mason's argument is that informing the use of predestination in the literature is an attempt to answer the problem that an overly pessimistic anthropology posed at the time. To wit: if humanity was so fallen that it could not see the truth concerning God and his creation, being not just passively but wilfully ignorant, then how can *any* flesh know God? It is only by means of God's predestinating work of grace that the elect can recognize and receive the truth concerning him. Indeed, it is a sign of a person's and/or community's election that they assent to and understand what is hidden from the non-elect (*Divine and Human Agency*, 108–10).

11. Sirach 33:13 RSV.

Paul himself, forming, as it does, the capstone of his argument in Romans 9–11.[12] Paul cites the several telling examples of predestination: the hardening of Pharaoh's heart; God's love for Jacob and hatred of Esau before either was born; the divine preservation of a faithful remnant; and the divine potter making pots either for honor or destruction. These arguments will be examined below, but, as a preliminary observation, few if any other texts from Second Temple Judaism argue for predestination in such a systematic manner.[13]

A salutary example of the effect that predestination has had on conceptual structures is afforded by the development of wisdom in Israel. As in the ancient Near East (ANE), the book of Proverbs depicts wisdom as a universal principle informing a natural moral law based upon natural theology. Wisdom operates in creation in a way that is accessible to all peoples. Wisdom is universal in scope and accessibility. In the latter part of the Second Temple Period (STP), in the literature under discussion, this changes. Wisdom becomes identified with the law of Moses (hereon simply the law) which was given only to Israel.[14] Concomitantly, wisdom was tied to God's electing grace. He chose Israel alone to be recipients of his mercy. Accordingly, he revealed himself exclusively to them and they became participants in divine wisdom. People, unaided by revelatory grace, could not even begin to understand the mystery of wisdom, with the result that only the elect could have access to it. What was originally conceived to apply universally, thereby being an *inclusive* principle, became an *exclusive* principle serving the elect alone.[15]

Thus divine election was understood to be the basis of God's mercy toward the elect of Israel. This mercy would be revealed to all at the eschaton when God's holy angels would purge Jerusalem of the corrupt religious authorities, overthrow Roman rule, and make the nations servants of the elect, who would then rule in Israel. God's choice of his elect was of grace and his eschatological vindication of them was testimony to his loving kindness resting upon them. In this there is no opposition between

---

12. On predestination in the period under discussion, see Lange, "Wisdom and Predestination in the Dead Sea Scrolls," and Thornhill, *Chosen People*.

13. In terms of a systematic treatment of predestination, the only text that comes close to Paul is, in my opinion, Sirach.

14. For example, see Baruch 4:1–37; Sirach 15:1; 24:1–23. In Enoch, wisdom is associated with the distinction between light and dark and, in a similar manner, with the distinction between peoples (1 Enoch 41:1–9; 42:1–2). However, there is little reference made to the law of Moses. But wisdom and mystery are tied to the "Tablets of Heaven" which pertain to the destiny of all things and which are revealed through a heavenly ascent aided by angels (1 Enoch 81:1–3; 93:1–3; 103:1–9). Since these tablets are found in the cosmic holy of Holies, a clear parallel is being drawn between them and the tablets of the law, said to have been in the earthly holy of Holies. This certainly was the implication drawn out by later rabbinic commentators. For the references, see P. Alexander's work on 3 Enoch in Charlesworth, *Old Testament Pseudepigrapha*, 1:296n45.

15. For an overview of the various positions concerning predestination and wisdom in Second Temple Judaism, see Goff, *Worldly and Heavenly Wisdom*, 1–27. Scholarly arguments have tended to revolve around wisdom being given an apocalyptic and eschatological character.

grace and law, insofar as the grace of election is tied to the reception and the keeping of the law.

From E. P. Sanders onward, the term "covenantal nomism" has been used to designate this relationship between law and grace. This term is appropriate if it is remembered that this relationship is founded upon God's electing will. In much of the literature of this period, the law is spoken of against the backdrop of *grace, as primarily expressed in election*.[16] Grace works to "theologize" and "cosmologize" an exclusive and excluding identity.[17] The term "excluding" is used here to underscore that the status of the elect necessitates a "non-elect" who are those not destined for salvation. Thus, when Paul confronts the growth of schismatic groups in the church, he is not so much confronting a problem to do with the law but rather with what lay behind the law, namely *grace*.

The Question of Antinomianism

Scholarly arguments about predestination in Second Temple Judaism and its relation to Romans revolve around whether there was a Jewish doctrine of salvation by "works" and what role, if any, free-will had to play in salvation.[18] It could be argued that this focus on salvation has obscured other issues, not least the ways in which the law could be employed. Too often "legalism" dominates the discussion, rather than antinomianism (or "anomianism"), because the latter expresses a comparatively rare phenomenon in the history of Jewish and Christian soteriology. This opinion is helped if antinomianism is regarded simply as the outright rejection of the law. But the word "rejection" obscures more than reveals in the first-century Jewish and Christian world more generally, let alone in the church in Rome.[19]

---

16. See Sanders, "Covenantal Nomism Revisited," and also his earlier magnum opus, *Paul and Palestinian Judaism*. See, however, VanLandingham (*Judgment and Justification*, 100–106), who disputes whether "covenantal nomism" is found in 1 Enoch and the DSS.

17. On the relationship between creation, election, and sectarian status, see Collins, "Sectarian Consciousness in the Dead Sea Scrolls."

18. For an overview of some of the arguments that revolve around this topic and the DSS, see Elass, "Paul's Understanding," 109–13.

19. "Antinomianism" literally means opposition to the law. But this does not necessarily involve an outright rejection of the law. For example, note what St. Epiphanius wrote in his *Against Heresies* (1:18) concerning a Jewish group that he refers to as the Nazarenes. This group rejected the law, but not Moses. They held that the law as it has come down was a forgery and did not originate with Moses at all. Hence, they are "anti" only insofar as they are opposed to the law as it had come down to Israel in the Pentateuch. But they are not anti-law per se. The other text often adduced is Philo, *Migration of Abraham* (16:89–93). But Philo here speaks of certain recluses who think of themselves as pure in soul with no body. They have a "symbolic" (i.e., "spiritual") view of the law which allows them, says Philo, to ignore the Sabbath and other exterior matters. Philo does not say they reject the law or act in an immoral way: indeed, they appear to be ascetics. They clearly do not reject the law *per se*. There is also some debate as to the derogative term "minim" used in rabbinic literature. Does it refer to antinomianism among Christians? If so, does it refer to first-century Christians or does it conflate

PART B—WHEN MERCY SEASONS JUSTICE

Although it is easy to associate antinomianism with the views held by Marcion and the Gnostics, these antinomian influences postdate the first century AD. Projecting views that, in the course of their development, became narrower and more fixed in meaning onto the earlier literature obscures the variety at which it hints. Thus, when the Gospel of Matthew is treated of in modern scholarship one of the points debated over has to do with Matthew's stance concerning Jesus' putative antinomianism. The problem is that often the question as to what exactly is meant by the term "antinomianism" is not raised, its meaning is assumed, and discussion turns on whether or not it was present in the Matthean community and what this meant for the nature of its mission.[20]

Whatever Jesus' famous logion in Matthew 5:17 might mean, when he tells the crowd, "Think not that I have come to destroy the Law and the Prophets; I have come not to abolish them but to fulfil them," it hints at the presence of a popular messianic expectation to the effect that the end of the law extends even to its destruction.[21] In contrast, such an expectation does not appear in the ascetic groups represented by the DSS.[22] Quite the reverse, from their severe view of the law, they lambast those in Jerusalem for being lax in their observance.[23] In Matthew the disciples appear to

---

Marcionism and perhaps Gnosticism with Christianity? See Vermes, "Decalogue and the Minim," and Bohak, *Ancient Jewish Magic*. Bohak notes that the etymology and origin of "*minim*" is unclear, but its use among the rabbis denotes heretics who are often associated with the use of magic. But Bohak points out that the rabbis themselves were not averse to the use of magic. Whether or not the heresies the *minim* promulgated had to do with antinomianism is not mentioned (Bohak, *Ancient Jewish Magic*, 308–405). See too Schafer, *Jesus in the Talmud*, who likewise notes that Jesus and his followers were seen to practice magic, but there is no mention if this was concomitant with antinomianism.

20. See, for example, Bauer, *Structure of Matthew's Gospel*, 356; Foster, *Community*, 211; Keener, *Gospel of Matthew*, 176. The discussions turn on the place of the law in the Matthean community's mission and how this related to this mission being universal or not. For an overview, see Brown, "Matthean Community and the Gentile Mission." By not discussing in any depth the different meanings that can attach to the term "antinomianism," most scholars persist in understanding it as denoting a simple rejection of the law. The thesis of this chapter is that, in doing this, scholars will not only end up presenting a picture that is simplistic and misleading, but also fail to recognize the subtlety of the arguments presented by Paul in Romans.

21. Although the use of later rabbinic materials to explain earlier New Testament passages is fraught with methodological problems, some scholars nevertheless cite a variety of rabbinic texts (b. Shabb. 30a, 151b; b. Sanh. 97b; Ab. Zar. 9a; Sif. Dt. 17:18; Lev. R. 9.7) to support the eschatological nullification of the law. See Davies, "Law in First-Century Judaism," esp. 25–26. However, this consensus has been challenged by Banks, "Eschatological Role of the Law," esp. 177–85. In sum, the problem with much scholarly discussion of this matter is that the meaning which much later terms have attracted is anachronistically applied to their earlier use. This is what makes Matthew 5:17 so interesting: it treats as a "commonplace" what we find, by contrast, unexpected and puzzling. For further argument on the text, see below.

22. There seems little evidence of any form of antinomianism in the DSS community and its liturgical documents. The law features little in the Enochian literature compared to the DSS: but whether or not this absence is significant is difficult to say.

23. The role of the law in the DSS is much discussed because the scrolls often impose a rigour beyond that required of the law. Discussion tends to turn on scrolls such as the *Community Discipline* (CD), the *Temple Scroll* (11QT) and 4QMMT, though these are far from being the only relevant

hold to a view of the law that sees its destruction in the coming eschaton. This necessitates Jesus correcting them. Suspecting that Jesus *does* hold to such a doctrine, the religious authorities nevertheless look for its evidence, especially in his "breaking" of the Sabbath.[24]

If the disciples thought the law was to be destroyed, on one level this might be considered antinomianism. Antinomianism can be conceived as a freedom to do anything human desires dictate, and, as will be argued below, something like this *was* becoming evident in certain quarters of the church in Rome. But although the disciples expressed what others saw as laxity in how the Sabbath was observed, there is no evidence that they condoned immoral conduct. Quite the opposite. Although it is difficult to tease out what lies behind this eschatological hope of the destruction of the law, it *quite possibly* had something to do with its association with the corrupt religious authorities in Jerusalem. When Jesus says that the Pharisees must be obeyed because they sit in the seat of Moses, and that people are to do what they say and not what they do (Matt 23:2), it is not difficult to see how the law could be damned by association with the Pharisees. The eschatological hope of the destruction of the law may have been more about the destruction of the authority of the corrupt religious rulers than of the law *per se*. This might be called a revolutionary, or even "utopian," antinomianism. Although it differed from the eschatological views concerning the law in the DSS, both shared a revulsion at the immorality and corruption of those who ruled in Jerusalem. There is a shared outrage at the injustice practiced by those who derived their authority from the law.

However, if the evidence for antinomianism among the disciples in Matthew is not of a licentious kind, something very different began to form as Christianity spread abroad, fostered by the teachings of St. Paul.

Along with Gentiles and diaspora Jews, a more licentious form of antinomianism entered into the church, even if was less politically radical because it was more individually indulgent. But again it is important to understand how this antinomianism operated. It was not so much that the law was rejected or destroyed, but that its authority no longer applied to oneself or one's group. If a person is free, then they are not *under* the law in the sense of being answerable, or subordinate to it. Quite the reverse, the law itself is subordinate and it can therefore be used in accord with one's desires. Those who are not of the superior position are still under the law and thus

---

documents. The intent appears to be to make up for the perceived "slackness" of the religious authorities in Jerusalem, including the Pharisees. See Regev, "Abominated Temple," and Harrington, "Holiness and Law."

24. So, for example, Matt 12:1–7 and Jesus' defence. See too Matt 7:23 (cf. 24:10–12) where Jesus, speaking of the eschaton, denounces those who act in a lawless ways (*anomian*). Furthermore, in Matt 23:28, Jesus excoriates the scribes and Pharisees as outwardly attractive but inwardly full of hypocrisy and lawlessness (*anomias*). On Matthew and antinomianism, see Keener, *Commentary on the Gospel of Matthew*, 176–77. Davison ("Anomia and Antinomian Polemic in Matthew") argues that in Matthew we do not see a fully-fledged doctrine of antinomianism attributable to one group, but rather, when the term is used, it merely refers to moral laxness in behavior.

must answer to the law, while those who are of the superior group, the elect, use the law but are not answerable to it in the same way as the non-elect are.

To return to Matthew, it may be that something like this operated with the *Pharisees* in Jerusalem of whom Jesus spoke, if Matthew's depiction of the Pharisees is accurate in this instance (e.g., Matt 23:3b, 16–24).[25] They applied the law rigorously to the general populace, while feeling themselves free of its strictures. If so then it was not simply a case of hypocrisy, but it was a case of *justified injustice*. By virtue of their special status, these religious authorities were not bound by the same strictures to which they bound others. They followed in the line of the corrupt authorities in Jerusalem of whom Isaiah had spoken.

Discussion on antinomianism in the early church tends to focus on Paul, and especially on his Letter to the Romans, where he refutes the charge of antinomianism and, as some argue, even casts the charge back on his "interlocutors."[26] As the argument goes, Paul's teaching on grace was so open to misinterpretation that certain people and groups employed it to justify their rejection of the law in favor of (in certain cases) a dissolute lifestyle.[27] Although the broad outlines of this position seem

---

25. The Gospels are not the only texts that espouse a low view of the Pharisees and the religious authorities located in Jerusalem. One can compare the Gospels with the DSS polemics against the contemporary religious authorities. 4QMMT is a pertinent text for it depicts the halakha of the Pharisees as not being rigorous enough. Their interpretative methods were designed, in the opinion of the sectaries, to allow for all manner of laxness in the observation of the Mosaic law. See Regev, "Abominated Temple," 249; Schwartz, "MMT, Josephus and the Pharisees." Consider, too, what Josephus says about the development of the Pharisees in his *Antiquities* (*AJ*) and the *Wars* (*BJ*). In *AJ* 13.10.5–6, Josephus writes that at the time of Hyrcanus the Pharisees were popular with the rank and file, whereas the Sadducees appealed only to the rich. However, by the time of Herod Antipater, Josephus claims that the Pharisees were a subversive sect who undermined rulers and acted mischievously (*AJ* 17.2.4,). In *BJ* 1.5.2 Josephus states that they later insinuated themselves into the court of Alexandra upon the death of Alexander Janneus and thereby controlled public affairs. What Josephus records, in my opinion, is the manner in which many successful movements devolve. Popular movements can easily be diverted from their original aims when power corrupts the leadership. To be sure, there are members who remain true to the original vision, but there are also others who exploit the movement in order co-opt power for themselves and their clients.

26. See Cottrell, *Romans*, 217; Davies, *Faith and Obedience*, 179; See also Visscher, *Romans*.

27. The New Testament evidence points to the fact that there was a problem with claims to "freedom," especially in regard to the person and teachings of Paul. In 2 Thess 2:2 Paul warns against letters purporting to be from "us." In 2 Pet 2:19 the author writes about those who promise freedom but who had become slaves to immorality and thus corruption. In 2 Pet 3:16 the author appears to tie these teachings to the misuse of Paul's letters. Even if we accept the pseudepigraphical nature of these two former texts (not necessarily a "given"), they express a tradition in which Paul's ideas about freedom were the subject of misappropriation. It can also be argued that the letter of James is written to counter just such a view of faith where the need for works (be they of charity or of the law) was being disputed (cf. Acts 21:21). An outbreak of licentiousness is also evident in the seven letters of Revelation (see Rev 2:9, 14, 20, 24; 3:9). The issue of immorality and faith is one Paul has to address in 1 and 2 Corinthians. The problems in Corinth are well known, not least in respect of sexual immorality (1 Cor 5:1–13; 6:16–20). Furthermore, this licentiousness is something about which those in the church boast (1 Cor 5:2, 6). The reason for this boasting appears to be that they feel this behavior proves that they are living out the implications of the faith, hence the repeated statement to the effect that "all things are lawful for me" (1 Cor 6:12; 10:23). In other words, their immorality is justified by a doctrine of

correct, it is too simplistic, for it obscures the way antinomianism operated in Rome, by justifying sinful conduct in the elect while judging the same conduct in others as deserving of God's wrath.

In order to make this case from Romans it is necessary first of all to raise what has become the central issue in Pauline scholarship: How exactly are we to read Paul?

Paul and Rhetoric

The problem can be put like this: To what degree does Paul's rhetoric qualify the propositional content of what he writes? This is an issue central not only to Pauline studies but to any theology that bases itself upon the biblical content. Biblical theology constantly confronts the question: How are we to convert into a systematic treatise the language of the Bible?

Given that Paul says that he strives "to become all things to all men, that I might by all means save some,"[28] and to take "every thought captive to obey Christ,"[29] to what degree ought these considerations inform how we approach his arguments? How much of what he writes ought to be qualified by reference to the possibility that he has used the arguments of others and oriented these arguments to a different end and, in so doing, effectively changed the meaning of the concepts and words used? To be succinct, this raises the problem of rhetoric. If this sounds initially obscure, the discussion of Paul's use of the doctrine of predestination will attempt to make things clearer.

First, a cautionary word on Paul and his putative use of rhetoric, which is necessary given the current enthusiasm for the topic in biblical studies. The argument of many scholars that Paul is a master of Greco-Roman rhetoric has invited an inevitable scholarly backlash.[30] Without fully entering this debate, two things can be insisted upon. First, in employing certain rhetorical forms, Paul *does* argue in such a way that, if the contents of that argument are abstracted from the context of the unfolding dynamic, the result can prove misleading. Again, this will become clearer when the example of how Paul employs the doctrine of predestination in his overall argument is investigated. Second, rather than the Greco-Roman rhetorical manuals, the source of much of Paul's argumentation is better found in Old Testament prophetic literature, and especially in its irony.[31]

---

freedom which asserts that they are not under the law and, by extension, that they are not even subject to conventional morality. Hence, in Paul's summation, to their shame, they do things that not even pagans would countenance (1 Cor 5:1).

28. 1 Cor 9:22.

29. 2 Cor 10:5.

30. On this subject, see Porter, "Ancient Literate Culture"; Reed, "Using Ancient Rhetorical Categories."

31. For further discussion, see Kern (*Rhetoric and Galatians*) who, disputing the use of the Greco-Roman rhetorical handbooks in Paul's letters, argues that other forms of Jewish rhetoric are primary

"Irony" is a difficult thing to define, existing in a number of different forms, from simple sarcasm to the more literary and sophisticated "romantic irony." In all forms of irony, however, the ostensible surface meaning is belied, deepened, or even reversed by the overarching meaning of the discourse as a whole. This overarching meaning is itself conveyed variously. While in speech it enlists tone and facial expression, writing demands a subtler approach. A text can be structured so that certain verbal cues indicate a deeper meaning that can even reverse the more immediate "surface" meaning. Even the ostensible failure of a text to make its argument can be an intentional sign of a higher meaning, one that only the "initiated" can read. However, irony can also work to deepen the surface meaning of a text and not annul it. To borrow from the words of Christ in Matthew, irony does not destroy the meaning but fulfils it. Irony is used to establish an organic continuity between levels of meanings in a text.

As with the relationship between mercy and justice something similar informs the use of irony: it can be of a *discontinuous* nature such that the higher meaning annuls the lower; or be of a *continuous* nature such that the higher elevates and perfects the lower meaning. Irony stands to a text as mercy stands to justice. Attendant upon both uses, there can be unexpected reversal when the outcome of an argument, *on reflection*, casts a very different hue on all that went before. In such a case, the basic sense of irony *is the transformation and even reversal of what, at first, ostensibly appears to be the meaning of what has been said.*

Since at least Edwin Good's work on irony in the Old Testament, scholars have become increasingly aware of the deployment of irony in both the historical and prophetic books (and, indeed, others have argued for its occurrence throughout the entire biblical corpus).[32] The prophets can use reversal to make the point about the justice and applicability of God's judgment upon Israel. Thus, the very things which the unjust boast about become the means by which they are brought undone and the trap they laid for others becomes a trap for them. Here, the rhetorical use of reversal serves to convey the justice of judgment because it signals both the responsibility of the people concerned and the appropriateness of their punishment. Best known is the case of Nathan and David where the king is brought to pass judgment upon himself, thereby showing unequivocally both his responsibility and the appropriateness of announced judgment.[33] The argument here is that this use of prophetic reversal is utilized in the writings of Paul, and especially in his treatment of predestination in

---

(i.e., the LXX texts and the synagogal sermon). Contra, for a recent convenient summary of the reasons traditionally given by scholars for Paul's intimate familiarity with the rhetorical handbooks and their conventions, along with the other New Testament writers, see Witherington, "Almost Thou Persuadest Me . . ."

32. Good, *Irony in the Old Testament*. On its use in the historical books, see Klein, *Triumph of Irony*. In narrative, see Kruschwitz, "Type Scene Connection." In the prophets, see McComiskey, "Prophetic Irony"; Holladay, "Text, Structure, and Irony." For the "maximalist" view, see Sharp, *Irony and Meaning in the Hebrew Bible*.

33. 2 Sam 12:1–9.

Romans. Paul, however, employs irony not only to pronounce judgment, but also to show how mercy answers the demands of justice. It does so, not by arbitrary decree, but by making justice *a means of grace and thus to mercy.*

Paul and Ironic Reversal

As with the prophets, so too with Paul, the problem concerns the people of God (i.e., Israel or the church) more than the world outside.[34] Paul's recapitulation of the history of fallen humanity in Romans 1:18—2:4, culminates in a second person plural address that turns the tables on his audience in the church. If Paul's audience agreed with his assessment of humanity,[35] then their mood would soon change. If it is the hypocrite who best sums up the sinfulness of humanity, then it is they, argues Paul, who best sum up hypocrisy. The sudden turn to the "you" in Paul's address mirrors the turn in Nathan's address to David: "*You* are that man!"[36] The object of Paul's condemnation turns from being about those "out there," to those who are ostensibly objects of God's mercy, those whom the letter will describe as the objects of God's electing grace.[37]

The series of reversals in the first two chapters of Romans are best expressed in the way Paul turns flattery into condemnation. He first flatters his audience by referring to their faith being spoken of (or proclaimed) throughout the world,[38] implying that their behavior and faith is famous for praiseworthy reasons. Having turned the tables upon them in respect of the sins of humanity, Paul reveals that this fame consisted in infamy. After Paul has made their hypocrisy clear, not least in their robbing

---

34. Hence 1 Cor 5:12–13.

35. Much discussion on Romans has turned upon who it is Paul is addressing: Jews, Gentiles, or even Gentiles who have become Jews, or a mixture of these and other groupings? Jews: for example, Rom 1:17–24 and 3:1–9? Or Gentiles: for example, Rom 1:6, 13, 15; 11:13; 15:14–32? Or a mixed Gentile and Jewish audience: for example, the inclusion of Jewish names in Rom 16:3–15? For a discussion on how confusing this issue can be, especially if we try to insist on clear demarcations, see Murray, *Playing a Jewish* Game, esp. 40–1 and 118–22.

36. 2 Sam 12:7.

37. One of the problems that has attended the study of Romans is the tendency of scholars to propose a "tidy" delineation of the actors and ideas being addressed. Thus all manner of assumptions are brought into play. Take, for example, what Neil Elliot asserts in what is otherwise a very informative and interesting work, *The Arrogance of Nations*. Following other scholars, Elliott argues that Romans 2–3 has the nature of a "stylized conversation with a Judean" and that it is a "rhetorical device" designed to appeal to the prejudice of a non-Jewish audience. Hence Paul's reference to the name of God being blasphemed among the nations (Rom 2:24) is not aimed at those in the church but at those outside, i.e., non-Christian Jews (*Arrogance of Nations*, 100). However, by recognizing the many ways in which an idea can operate in radically different ways among disparate groups within the same institutional body, as we are attempting to show in this chapter, we can make coherent sense of the text as it stands, without resorting to such rhetorical theories.

38. Rom 1:8.

temples, he observes that for this reason the name of God is blasphemed among the nations.[39]

As with the Pharisees in Jerusalem, it becomes clear in the course of Paul's argument that those in Rome are hypocrites, by way of an antinomian system of grace. They have misappropriated the teachings of Paul and have thereby justified their injustice such that they can commit adultery and rob temples. At the same time, they can damn others for doing what they presume licence to do. The essence of their antinomianism is not that they reject the law, but that *they* can break the law, and thereby gain an increase in grace, whereas when others break the law, they can only expect wrath. Because they are sinners who are justified, they are able to bring about the revelation of the mercy of God by way of an increase in the presence of his goodness, brought about by their freedom to sin. What provides evidence of antinomianism is the expression of a justified exemption from the law for the elect, and, for this reason, there is no equality before the law.

Paul angrily writes how some are saying, "Let us do evil so good can come," while attributing it to him, but it is not too difficult to see how this state of affairs might have come about.[40] Later in the letter Paul again has to correct a similar specious argument. So, when he writes that where sin abounds grace more abounds, a verse later he has to add the rider that explicitly opposes the saying that "we are to continue in sin that grace may abound."[41] In other words, there are those in the church in Rome who have argued that their sinning is a necessary means of God's grace becoming present in the world. Just as the antinomian libertines in Corinth "boasted" that they were free to do what they desired, there appears to be in Rome something very similar, if not the same.[42] Paul had taught that a righteousness apart from the law has been manifested[43] and that as a consequence one is not "under the law."[44] Without elaboration, such ideas were ripe for abuse. Paul then had to rein in what others inferred from his teaching on grace.[45]

39. Rom 2:24, citing Isa 52:5.

40. Rom 3:8.

41. Rom 5:20 and 6:1.

42. 1 Cor 5:2, 6 and Rom 3:27. See too 2 Pet 2:19. Hence they argue that it would be unjust for God to inflict wrath upon them because they are the means by which God is shown to be just, truthful, and good (Rom 3:5–8).

43. Rom 3:21.

44. Rom 6:14 and Gal 5:18.

45. John Barclay ("Mirror-Reading a Polemical Letter") would disagree with the approach being advocated here. For Barclay, the crucial question is how we can accurately discern what Paul's protagonists were saying, given that letters such as Galatians (and Romans) are polemical in intent. Nevertheless, there are problems with Barclay's reservations. First, he assumes in the case of Galatians that Paul's epistle was not written to address his opponents ("Mirror-Reading a Polemical Letter," 74). However, Barclay provides no substantive evidence for this assertion. One suspects that Barclay assumes a uniform Galatian audience, comprising those wavering believers whom Paul wanted to convince. Second, a more serious assumption of Barclay is that all polemics are misleading because

There is no need to assume that all who were in Rome ascribed to the same system or that all were antinomian libertines. Nevertheless, in the general contours of his argument, Paul addresses the fundamental positions of those in Rome. He does so by making *his* fundamental point, that all people, Jew and Gentile (a hendiadys that signifies all humanity), are equal in respect of God's justice as expressed through the law and/or conscience. This is the force of Paul's identifying the law with Gentile conscience. They are not the same in respect of establishing the identity of a distinct people, but they are different means by which people will be judged by the same standards. In the end, by just judgment, all will end up excluded from any claim to a righteousness associated with God.[46] Paul's point is to establish an equality in God's justice in order to counter those views that want to draw a theological and cosmological divide within humanity, expressed in terms of election. Whatever else might be said, justice is equitable and all have to answer to it. The law and conscience are based upon the same principle of universal inclusiveness. But this goes only so far, for the heart of the issue is whether mercy and grace undermine this equality, if by an arbitrary (to us) decree of God, made before the world was created, some, namely the elect, are freed from having to answer to the consequences of their crimes. Does Paul hold that mercy is continuous with justice, perfecting justice, or discontinuous because it expresses God's arbitrary decision? Is mercy as universal and inclusive as justice? This brings us to the subject of predestination.

Double Predestination

Arguably, both an antinomian libertinism or an ascetic and rigorous view of the law, are founded upon a doctrine of election entailing double predestination, in which one part of humanity is predestined to blessings and salvation, and another to dishonor, destruction, and even hell. But rather than focusing on human concerns, Paul

---

they misrepresent the arguments of those being opposed. But it is questionable to say that polemics always distort the position against which they are arguing. Quite the reverse: polemics often serve to sift and highlight the essence of an argument and thereby place its audience in a better position to assess critically its fundamental assumptions.

46. On law and conscience, see Rom 2:6–16. Paul then moves on to address the issue of whether there is anything special about being circumcised (i.e., Israel). His conclusion is that there is, insofar as circumcision is of the heart, in which the outward act is mirrored in an inward act (Rom 2:17–29). This, of course, is what the law itself says in Deut 10:16 where the Israelites are commanded to circumcise their hearts. But as with Paul, so too with Moses, for in Deuteronomy God tells Moses that the people will get even worse when he dies. God will send them into exile, and only after a suitable period of time will he bring them back. Then *he* will circumcise *their hearts* (Deut 30:6). The command becomes a promise *that only the grace of God can fulfill*. In Rom 3:1–2 Paul asks, "What advantage does the Jew have?" and answers, "Much in every way!" This we soon learn is ironic. The only advantage listed is that the Jews are entrusted with the Oracles of God, but in Rom 3:10–18 Paul then quotes from the same Oracles to demonstrate that both Jew and Greek are excluded from claims to being righteous. In other words, the only advantage to being a Jew entrusted with the Oracles of God is that the Oracles testify that the Jews are "in the same boat" as the Gentiles.

introduces his argument on predestination by way of answering the charge that his understanding of Christ and justification makes God out to be unfaithful because his promises to Israel are not being honored.[47]

A rather standard element in Paul's answer is the observation that not all who are in Israel are of Israel—it is only the remnant, the elect, who constitute the true Israel.[48] This is not a line of argument unique to Paul (as he himself demonstrates from the Scriptures) for it can be found in the DSS and other intertestamental literature, but what Paul does with this argument *is* rather unique. Employing prophetic irony, through a series of deft manoeuvres, he turns the concept of the "remnant" on its head—so that the remnant ceases to have any connection with Israel but becomes identified with the Gentiles. By using Scriptural tropes for election (the hardening of Pharaoh's heart, Jacob being loved while Esau is hated, and the example of the potter and his pots), Paul concludes that the Gentiles who were "no people" are God's people. Hence, on reflection, it is they who now occupy the place of Israel in the Exodus, of Jacob, and of the pots made for honor and good use.[49] It is the Gentiles who are found righteous. *They* are the elect and Israel becomes the non-elect—like Pharaoh, Esau, and the doomed pots. Thus, in respect of the identity of the elect everything is reversed!

However, as the argument further unfolds and the reader is forced to reconsider what has just been read, things become less clear cut and increasingly confusing, indeed, even obscure. Paul goes on to say that there *are* Israelites among the elect (and not just Gentiles), so that when Israel becomes jealous of the blessings God gives to the Gentiles he will then repent and come to the faith. Thus, will *all* Israel be saved and then will take place the eschaton for then will come the resurrection.[50] This is not the place to rehearse the endless debates as to what "all Israel" means here. Indeed, trying to find a definite and specific meaning can cut across what it is Paul wants to convey, namely that the identity of one group entails the other group but that this entailment is not one that excludes but is instead the means of universal inclusion. "Life from the dead" requires the unity of humanity. The unity of Israel entails the unity of Jew and Gentile, but this unity does not preclude a hierarchical order. Although "to the

---

47. Rom 9:1–6, 14. See too where Paul returns to this question in Rom 11:1. Of course, it may well be that the charge Paul is answering is one based upon the antinomian misrepresentation of what he actually had taught. Paul does mention predestination in Rom 8:28–30 in relation to Jesus but *not* to Israel, which may well be one reason that others charged Paul with making God out to be unfaithful to Israel.

48. Rom 9:6–7; 11:1–5.

49. Rom 9:25–31. Note how the reference to the remnant of Israel (Rom 9:27–29) is framed between the references to the Gentiles being, by grace, God's righteous people.

50. Rom 11:7–12, 15, 26.

Jew first and then to the Greek,"[51] this unity finds its proper locus in the unity of the church.[52]

As Paul uses the tropes of election, he introduces a significant obscurity about the identity of the elect. This confusion is *not* present in the DSS or in the intertestamental literature.

Paul's conclusion at the end of ch. 11 forces the reader to review the argument from the beginning of ch. 9 and to begin to see things in a very different way. The argument proceeds back and forth between Jew and Gentile (a division that is emblematic of all divisions in humanity), compromising any neat and distinct identity for the elect. Not only is Israel's assured status of being the elect of God made unsure, but so too is that of the Gentiles. After all that was said about the Gentiles becoming God's chosen people, made righteous by faith even though they did not seek righteousness, they are nevertheless soon threatened with being cut off from Israel if they become conceited.[53] Whatever else stands out from Paul's argument, election is not quite as assured for either Israel or the Gentiles, as may be imagined.

Paul concludes that Israel has been hardened (as Pharaoh had been) so that Gentiles can be brought in, as members of the elect.[54] And the Gentiles are saved in order to make Israel jealous, so that they too will turn to Christ and be saved.[55] But as Paul made clear, back in ch. 3, a necessary component of this process is that both Jew and Gentile understand that everyone is excluded from any claim to righteousness. So it is that Paul states that God has consigned all people to disobedience so that he can have mercy on all.[56] In other words, Paul has turned the doctrine of predestination and election on its head (or to borrow from Marx, on its feet) and he has used its standard tropes and arguments in order to argue that *all* are double predestined. All are destined for destruction so that all can be destined for mercy. If his argument from chs. 9 through 11 is confusing, it is in order to convey the fact that there is no predestined distinction in humanity between elect and non-elect.

Paul closes his argument with a paean of praise to the inscrutable wisdom of God and does so by reference to his mercy.[57] However, instead of a divine arbitrariness revealed in the creation and vindication of an exclusive elect, this mercy expresses an

---

51. Rom 1:16; 2:9. This pattern finds its full expression in Paul's argument concerning Israel being hardened in order for Gentiles to be brought in (Rom 11:11–12, 25, 31).

52. Thus, if one contrasts the way in which humanity is described in Rom 1:20–32, it is clear that the litany of sins comprises the love of the same, a love expressed in self-seeking and self-interest. Whereas in Paul's practical application for the church in Rom 12–16, the orientation is the reverse: first and foremost, to seek the good of the other. See, e.g., Rom 12:3–10; 13:8–10; 14:7–10, 15–19; 15:1–6, etc.

53. Rom 11:17–25.

54. Rom 11:25.

55. Rom 11:11–12.

56. Rom 11:32.

57. Rom 11:33–36.

inclusiveness that answers to the demands of justice by perfecting justice. The location of this answer to the demands of justice is the cross through the atoning blood of Christ.[58] Contrary to what some think, atonement theology *is* at the very heart of Paul's theology of the cross and of universal and inclusive mercy. It is the cross that fulfils the law because it perfectly answers to the revelation of God as One, as expressed in the Shema.[59] In ch. 3 Paul establishes the unity of human communion in a rather ironic fashion in that all are excluded from claims to righteousness. But he does not leave it at that, for he then explains how the blood of Christ is *the* principle by which all are justified. This means Jew and Gentile are one by reference both to the justice and mercy of God, hence God is revealed as one and thus "we uphold the Law."[60] The unity of human communion is an absolute necessity for the fullness of the law and the revelation of God, and it is God's mercy, perfected at the cross, that answers to the demands of the law and reveals, as Paul notes in 11:33–36, the inscrutable nature of God.

Paul, however, does more than argue for the source of God's justness and mercy, he also argues for *the means* by which this mercy is brought to apply. Just as the law (and conscience) is the means by which God's justice operates, then "faith" is the means by which mercy operates. First of all, the faith(fullness) of Jesus is perfected on the cross,[61] but this faith becomes our faith by way of a true participation in Jesus' sacrifice. It is a faith that operates to bring unity not division, especially not a division that bases itself on a doctrine of predestination. But what does the operation of this faith in Jew and Gentile look like? The answer is given in Paul's discussion on predestination.

As noted above, Paul says that Israel has been hardened so that the Gentiles can be brought in, and the Gentiles are brought in so that Israel will become jealous and so too enter in. It is a process that can be distilled into the following principle: *the very people one excludes are the very means by which one becomes a recipient of God's grace and mercy.* This is *the* unexpected reversal! This is *the* example of prophetic irony, but an irony turned from judgment to mercy and that in the most surprising of ways!

Conclusion

The arguments above should prompt us to recall the teaching of Jesus, as summed up in the Lord's prayer, which entreats God to "forgive us our sins, as we forgive those who have sinned against us." There is here a reflexive and reciprocal dynamic at work in mercy: but how does this relate to justice? The essence of the law is expressed in the *lex talionis* (Exod 21:23–27)—the law of "tooth for tooth and eye for eye." Most if not

---

58. Rom 3:25–26.
59. Deut 6:4.
60. Rom 3:27–31.
61. Hence the objective genitive in Rom 3:22.

all law is based on and informed by the need to restore a harmony and balance that has been disturbed by crime. Justice seeks to impose a just sentence that answers to the crime, thereby restoring society to its proper condition. In other words, informing the law is the principle of a social reflexivity expressed in reciprocity. It is this delicate balance that mercy can be seen to upset, especially if it is founded upon an arbitrary predestinarian decree.

However, by reference to the cross and his arguments on predestination, Paul shows that mercy does not annul the claims of reciprocity: rather it answers and elevates them. He argues that they give way to a higher divine reciprocity.[62] For, in forgiving those who have done us an injustice, we answer to the demands of justice concerning the one who has done us wrong. And, through the grace of God we are able to transform the sin done against us into an occasion for mercy, for we understand that we too need mercy. This is the meaning of Paul's statement that where sin abounds grace more abounds, referring to the means of grace which are expressed reciprocal forgiving, as opposed to being a licence to sin.

Bibliography

Banks, R. "The Eschatological Role of the Law in Pre- and Post-Christian Jewish Thought." In *Reconciliation and Hope: New Testament Essays on Atonement and Eschatology Presented to L. L. Morris on His 60th Birthday*, edited by Robert Banks, 173–85. Exeter: Paternoster, 1974.
Barclay, J. M. G. "Mirror-Reading a Polemical Letter: Galatians as a Test Case." *Journal for the Study of the New Testament* 31 (1987) 73–93.
Bauer, D. R. *The Structure of Matthew's Gospel*. London: Bloomsbury, 2015.
Bohak, G. *Ancient Jewish Magic*. Cambridge: Cambridge University Press, 2008.
Brown, S. "The Matthean Community and the Gentile Mission." *Novum Testamentum* 22 (1980) 193–221.
Buchanan, G. W. *The Gospel of Matthew*. Vol. 1. 1996. Reprint, Eugene: Wipf & Stock, 2006.
Charlesworth, J., ed. *The Old Testament Pseudepigrapha*. Vol. 1. New York: Doubleday, 1983.
Chazon, E. "Prayers from Qumran and Their Historical Implications." *Dead Sea Discoveries* 1 (1994) 265–84.
Collins, J. J. "Sectarian Consciousness in the Dead Sea Scrolls." In *Heavenly Tablets: Interpretation, Identity and Tradition in Ancient Judaism*, edited by L. LiDonnici and A. Lieber, 177–92. Leiden: Brill, 2007.
Cottrell, J. *Romans*. Joplin: Missouri College Press, 2005.
Davies, G. *Faith and Obedience in Romans*. London: Bloomsbury, 2015.
Davies, W. D. "Law in First-Century Judaism." In *Jewish and Pauline Studies*, edited by W. D. Davies, 3–26. Philadelphia: Fortress, 1984.
Davison, J. E. "Anomia and Antinomian Polemic in Matthew." *Journal of Biblical Literature* 104 (1985) 617–35.
Elass, M. A. "Paul's Understanding and Use of the Concept of Election in Romans 9–11." PhD diss., Durham University, 1996.

62. Thus Jesus' admonition in Luke 6:36 to be "merciful as your Father is merciful."

Elliott, N. *The Arrogance of Nations: Reading Romans in the Shadow of Empire*. Minneapolis: Fortress, 2008.
Foster, P. *Community, Law and Mission in Matthew's Gospel*. Tübingen: Mohr Siebeck, 2004.
Goff, M. *The Worldly and Heavenly Wisdom of 4Q Instruction*. Leiden: Brill, 2003.
Good, E. *Irony in the Old Testament*. London: SPCK, 1965.
Harrington, H. "Holiness and Law in the Dead Sea Scrolls." *Dead Sea Discoveries* 8 (2001) 124–35.
Hogeterp, A. "The Eschatology of the Two Spirits Revisited." *Revue de Qumran* 23 (2007) 247–59.
Holladay, W. "Text, Structure, and Irony in the Poem on the Fall of the Tyrant, Isaiah 14." *Catholic Biblical Quarterly* 61 (1999) 633–45.
Keener, C. S. *A Commentary on the Gospel of Matthew*. Grand Rapids: Eerdmans, 1999.
Kern, P. H. *Rhetoric and Galatians: Assessing an Approach to Paul's Epistle*. Cambridge: Cambridge University Press, 1998.
Klein, L. *The Triumph of Irony in the Book of Judges*. Sheffield: Almond, 1988.
Kruschwitz, J. "The Type Scene Connection between Genesis 38 and the Joseph Story." *Journal for the Study of the Old Testament* 36 (2012) 383–410.
Lange, A. "Wisdom and Predestination in the Dead Sea Scrolls." *Dead Sea Discoveries* 2 (1995) 340–54.
Lawson, J. N. *The Concept of Fate in Ancient Mesopotamia of the First Millennium: Toward an Understanding of šimtu*. Wiesbaden, Germany: Harrassowitz, 1994.
Mason, J. *Divine and Human Agency in Second Temple Judaism and Paul*. Tübingen: Mohr Siebeck, 2010.
McComiskey, T. "Prophetic Irony in Hosea 1:4." *Journal for the Study of the Old Testament* 58 (1993) 93–101.
Merrill, H. *Qumran and Predestination: A Theological Study of the Thanksgiving Hymns*. Leiden: Brill, 1975.
Murray, M. *Playing a Jewish Game: Gentile Christian Judaizing in the First and Second Centuries CE*. Waterloo, ON: Wilfrid Laurier University Press, 2004.
Parry, D., and E. Tov, eds. *The Dead Sea Scrolls Reader*. Vol. 1. Leiden: Brill, 2004.
Porter, S. E. "Ancient Literate Culture and Popular Rhetorical Knowledge: Implications for Studying Pauline Rhetoric." In *Paul and Ancient Rhetoric*, edited by S. E. Porter and Bryan R. Dyer, 96–115. Cambridge: Cambridge University Press, 2016.
Reed, J. "Using Ancient Rhetorical Categories to Interpret Paul's Letters." In *Rhetoric and the New Testament: Essays from the 1992 Heidelberg Conference*, edited by Stanley E. Porter and Thomas H. Olbricht, 293–324. Sheffield: JSOT, 1993.
Regev, E. "Abominated Temple and a Holy Community: The Formation of Notions of Purity and Impurity in Qumran." *Dead Sea Discoveries* 10 (2003) 243–78.
Rogers, R. G. "The Doctrine of Election in the Chronicler's Work and the Dead Sea Scrolls." PhD diss., Boston University, 1969.
Sanders, E. P. "Covenantal Nomism Revisited." *Jewish Studies Quarterly* 16 (2009) 23–55.
———. *Paul and Palestinian Judaism: A Comparison of Patterns of Religion*. London: SCM, 1977.
Schafer, P. *Jesus in the Talmud*. Princeton: Princeton University Press, 2007.
Schwartz, D. R. "MMT, Josephus and the Pharisees." In *Reading 4QMMT: New Perspectives on Qumran Law and History*, edited by J. Kampen and M. Bernstein, 74–80. Atlanta: Scholars, 1996.

Sohn, Seock-Tae. *The Divine Election of Israel*. Grand Rapids: Eerdmans, 1991.
Thornhill, A. *The Chosen People: Election, Paul and Second Temple Judaism*. Downers Grove: IVP Academic, 2015.
VanLandingham, C. *Judgment and Justification in Early Judaism and the Apostle Paul*. Peabody: Hendrickson, 2006.
Vermes, G. *The Dead Sea Scrolls in English*. London: Penguin, 1990.
———. "The Decalogue and the Minim." In *Post-Biblical Jewish Studies*, edited by Geza Vermes, 169–77. Leiden: Brill, 1975.
Visscher, G. *Romans 4 and the New Perspective on Paul*. New York: Peter Lang, 2009.
Witherington, B. "Almost Thou Persuadest Me . . . ': The Importance of Greco-Roman Rhetoric for the Understanding of the Text and Context of the NT." *Journal of the Evangelical Theological Society* 58 (2015) 63–88.

PART C

Encountering the Just and Merciful God
Well-Being in Theological Perspective

5

Social Well-Being and the Humanity of God

PETER G. BOLT

I N a world in which justice is so often absent or compromised, and mercy is so often lacking, how can Christian churches be God's instruments for social well-being?

A World of Shattered Humanity

A World on the Move

After an unprecedented 30,000 people fled their homes each day throughout 2014, by June 2015 there were 59.5 million displaced persons in the world—the population of Italy, the twenty-third-most-populated country of the 233 in the world, and 2.5 times the population of the fifty-third, Australia.[1] Or, to put it another way: "One in every 122 humans is now either a refugee, internally displaced, or seeking asylum."[2]

Australia is currently committed to the usual 13,750 immigrants on refugee and humanitarian visas, and an additional 12,000 from Syria and Iraq who began arriving Christmas 2015.[3] But even if the numbers resettled seem almost insignificant

---

1. IDMC, *Global Overview 2015*; UN Nations Population Division, "Countries in the World by Population (2016)."

2. UNHCR, "Worldwide Displacement."

3. Henderson and Uhlmann, "Asylum Seeker Intake Explained." In the last ten years, Australia has granted roughly 6,000 refugee visas and almost the same number (5,000) under the Special Humanitarian Program. The only exception was 2012–13, in which year 12,012 refugee visas were granted; Karlsen, "Refugee Resettlement to Australia." Refugee visas are given for those suffering persecution; visas under the Special Humanitarian Program (SHP), are for those "who are subject to substantial discrimination amounting to gross violation of human rights in their home country," which involves a lower threshold than for persecution (pp. 8–9).

compared to the numbers still displaced,[4] Australia now cares for people who have been driven from their homes through violent conflict, persecution, discrimination, and other atrocities perpetrated by sinful human beings upon one another. These survivors are here with us now, in our communities, and sometimes already in our congregations.

A World in Trauma

After what these people have gone through, it is really no surprise that many of them—if not most or all—will be suffering psychological trauma. Although there may well be differences,[5] to a greater or lesser degree they will be suffering the symptoms and displaying the signs of a form of complex post-traumatic stress disorder.[6]

But these recent arrivals are not the only trauma survivors who might pass by or through our congregations. In a world such as ours, there are a vast number of ways in to trauma, and they must all be acknowledged. One trauma shouldn't be played off against another, as if it is much worse on a hierarchy of suffering. Unfortunately, given the natural propensity of sinful human beings to constantly ask, "Who is the greatest?" (Mark 9:34) along any kind of scale, the same divisive game is also played when it comes to trauma survivors—and their advocates.

Sometimes this is political. As Judith Herman argued in 1992,[7] there needs to be a conducive social environment before one manifestation of trauma can even be properly recognized, let along properly dealt with. At the beginning of the twentieth century, Freud's early work on trauma ground to a halt when it threatened to expose the presence of sexual abuse among Viennese aristocratic families. It took the feminist revolution at the end of the century before there was the social environment to acknowledge this problem, and the political will to do something about it. A similar phenomenon now prevails for the decades-long men's movement struggling to alert

---

4. It is worth noting, however, that, since 1977 when Australia began participating in the UNHCR resettlement program, Australia has been consistently ranked as one of the top three resettlement countries in the world; Karlsen, "Refugee Resettlement to Australia," 6–7.

5. Ngwenya, "Healing the Wounds of *Gukurahundi*," 36, with others (48), rejects using the term PTSD for the after-effects of "ethnic-based and political violence" in favor of "extreme trauma," making the point that not everyone will end up with the "psychiatric disorder" known as PTSD (43). Ngwenya also treats PTSD as a description more appropriate to a Western focus on the individual, and fears that in non-Western contexts it would trivialize the "collective trauma" of political violence, by decoupling individual from social suffering (46). Although this is disputable, Western trauma therapists are well aware of certain features of Western individualism that inhibit healing for trauma survivors; see, for example, n59 below.

6. In what follows, the information about Complex PTSD is largely drawn from three books: Shay, *Achilles in Vietnam*; Herman, *Trauma and Recovery*; and Van der Kolk, *Body Keeps the Score*. This sampling provides access to the understanding of Complex PTSD—as well as what is needed for its recovery—that has been evolving across the decades since the Vietnam War. (Its end is marked by the capture of Saigon by the North Vietnamese Army in April 1975.)

7. Herman, *Trauma and Recovery*, ch. 1.

a community politically unwilling to listen to the cry of men who also suffer under intimate partner abuse.[8]

But it is not just politics. Trauma survivors themselves engage in the construction of "hierarchies of suffering," and Trauma Therapists speak strongly against what they see as a dangerous kind of "pissing contest" operating among their clientele:

> All who hear [trauma narratives] should understand that no person's suffering can be measured against any other person's suffering. It can be extremely damaging if anyone makes comparisons. Combat veterans frequently doubt that they are worthy of treatment, knowing other vets who are worse off now or went through worse than they did. Many survivors of appalling trauma obstruct their own healing by placing themselves in "hierarchies of suffering," usually to their own disadvantage.[9]

> One would think that severe psychological injury would give rise naturally to shared compassion and mutual respect among the many diverse groups of trauma survivors, such as have lived through genocide, political torture, domestic battering, incest, war, abusive religious cults, and coerced prostitution. Unfortunately, it has not. Veterans call it "pissing contests" when one veteran denies the validity of another veteran's war trauma. Different survivor groups eagerly start these competitions as well, each claiming that their experience is the only significant one.... These pissing contests only serve the interests of perpetrators, all perpetrators.... No person's suffering is commensurable with any other.[10]

For, despite the variety of suffering, the end-point is the same. No matter what particular kind of horrendous experience they might have endured, the resultant trauma of the survivor will be the same as the survivor of a different horrendous experience. No matter how varied the journey, when reaching the destination they share a commonality of experience as trauma survivors.

---

8. See, for example, Celi, *Breaking the Silence*, and the vast amount of literature posted as part of the "one in three" campaign, http://www.oneinthree.com.au.

9. Shay, *Achilles in Vietnam*, 192.

10. Shay, *Achilles in Vietnam*, 205–6.

\multicolumn{2}{l}{*Table 1: Complex Post-Traumatic Stress Disorder*[11]}
1.	A history of subjection to totalitarian control over a prolonged period (months to years). Examples include hostages, prisoners of war, concentration-camp survivors, and survivors of some religious cults. Examples also include those subjected to totalitarian systems in sexual and domestic life, including survivors of domestic battering, childhood physical or sexual abuse, and organized sexual exploitation.
2.	Alterations in affect regulation, including: <ul><li>persistent dysphoria</li><li>chronic suicidal preoccupation</li><li>self-injury</li><li>explosive or extremely inhibited anger (may alternate)</li><li>compulsive or extremely inhibited sexuality (may alternate)</li></ul>
3.	Alterations in consciousness, including: <ul><li>amnesia or hypermnesia for traumatic events</li><li>transient dissociative episodes</li><li>depersonalization/derealization</li><li>reliving experiences, either in the form of intrusive post-traumatic stress disorder symptoms or in the form of ruminative preoccupation</li></ul>
4.	Alterations in self-perception, including: <ul><li>Sense of helplessness or paralysis of initiative</li><li>Shame, guilt, and self-blame</li><li>Sense of defilement or stigma</li><li>Sense of complete difference form others (may include sense of specialness, utter aloneness, belief no other person can understand, or nonhuman identity)</li></ul>
5.	Alterations in perception of perpetrator, including: <ul><li>preoccupation with relationship with perpetrator (includes preoccupation with revenge)</li><li>unrealistic attribution of total power to perpetrator (caution: victim's assessment of power realities may be more realistic than clinician's)</li><li>idealization or paradoxical gratitude</li><li>sense of special or supernatural relationship</li><li>acceptance of belief system or rationalizations of perpetrator</li></ul>
6.	Alterations in relations with others, including: <ul><li>isolation and withdrawal</li><li>disruption in intimate relationships</li><li>repeated search for rescuer (may alternate with isolation and withdrawal)</li><li>persistent distrust</li><li>repeated failures of self-protection</li></ul>
7.	Alterations in systems of meaning <ul><li>loss of sustaining faith</li><li>sense of hopelessness and despair</li></ul>

11. Herman, *Trauma and Recovery*, 122.

Here is not the place for a full exposition of the experience of those suffering complex post-traumatic stress disorder (see *Table 1*), but for one brief glimpse, Judith Herman notes that

> the core experiences of psychological trauma are disempowerment and disconnection from others. . . . The psychological faculties that were damaged or deformed by the traumatic experience . . . include the basic capacities for trust, autonomy, initiative, competence, identity, and intimacy.[12]

This is the kind of deep disruption of personality with which trauma survivors live almost daily. But, without at all minimizing the situation of those who have suffered severe trauma, it is apparent that Herman's brief description in some way also applies to anyone who lives in our fallen world. By displaying what *has already* happened in this broken world, the experience of the trauma survivor shouts loudly to others about what *can still* happen to any human being—which is why it is so unsettling for others to deal with the survivors.[13] To some extent, the trauma survivor acts as a megaphone for the "more ordinary" suffering experienced by others. For, in this world which groans in its brokenness (see Rom 8:18–30), all human beings have been broken by it, and broken human beings are, at least to some degree, traumatised human beings. As the world groans, human beings groan along with it, longing for the peace and restoration which the gospel of Jesus Christ tells us will only come through resurrection. But as the world groans for this day, all human beings are far from being at peace. They are still longing for social well-being.

A World Longing for Social Well-Being

Accounts of what constitutes social well-being differ considerably depending upon the social situation in view. For the United States Institute of Peace, with an eye on societies in reconstruction after violent conflict:

> Social well-being is an end state in which basic human needs are met and people are able to coexist peacefully in communities with opportunities for advancement. This end state is characterized by equal access to and delivery of basic needs services (water, food, shelter, and health services), the provision of primary and secondary education, the return or resettlement of those displaced by violent conflict, and the restoration of social fabric and community life.[14]

Perhaps at the other end of the scale, the Centre for Well-Being within the Cambridge think tank NEF (New Economics Foundation) works within the context of Western Europe. Seeking a wholesale redefinition of wealth in terms of well-being:

---

12. Herman, *Trauma and Recovery*, 133.
13. Shay, *Achilles in Vietnam*, 193–94. See further below.
14. USIP, "10: Social Well-Being."

[NEF] has set out a radical proposal to guide the direction of modern societies and the lives of people who live in them. In contrast to the conventional narrow focus on economic indicators, it calls for governments to directly and regularly measure people's subjective well-being: their experiences, feelings and perceptions of how their lives are going, as a new way of assessing societal progress.[15]

Whether dealing with a society suffering the traumatic after-effects of violent conflict, or a society suffering the numbing effects of wealthy modernity with its own unique ways of creating trauma, social well-being is something that our world is longing for and actively working toward.

A World into which God Himself Has Come

This longing is by no means unfamiliar to the Bible reader. The contemporary concern for social well-being resonates with the OT promises of peace, shalom. This certainly meant the absence of conflict and war, but it also went further, encompassing harmonious relationships, and prosperity sufficient for every Israelite to sit under their vine and fig tree, at rest with other human beings and at rest with God, enjoying his blessing and favor. And the contemporary desire to reconfigure wealth in terms of well-being and satisfaction with life resonates with the NT picture of the kingdom of God, exemplified best, perhaps, in Jesus' call to the rich man to store up treasure in heaven (Mark 10:21; compare Matt 6:19–21), while at the same time reminding his disciples that along with eternal life in the age to come, following him brought the great riches of relational life under the blessing of God even in this present evil age (Mark 10:29–30).

By first promising peace and then by delivering it through Jesus Christ, God has entered our world to show that he is concerned for human social well-being.

Surely this means that social well-being is a goal that Christian churches already share with the wider world so desperately in need of it. Everyone involved in this common quest will bring their different definitions, perspectives, and concerns. The distinctively Christian contribution will arise from the core of our gospel, that "the Word became flesh and made his dwelling among us. We have seen his glory, the glory of the one and only Son, who came from the Father, full of grace and truth" (John 1:14).

If we take our lead from the God of the gospel, then the social well-being of humanity ultimately depends upon the humanity of God.

---

15. http://www.nationalaccountsofwellbeing.org/.

The Humanity of God and the Recovery of Shattered Humanity

The gospel proclamation that God became a man is discussed in theological circles as the doctrine of the incarnation. This is entirely apt because the gospel announces that God took on flesh, he became incarnate. But perhaps this remarkable and unique event is made more accessible to the ordinary person by the dramatic and paradoxical expression of Karl Barth: the humanity of God.[16]

The incarnation, that is, the humanity of God, is properly the central article of the Apostles' Creed, because "from it we must interpret both the first and the third."[17] According to Barth, the *glory* of God is displayed in the *humanity* of God. This has not always been taken as seriously as it requires. The gods have always been conceived of as way above human being, usually distant and often uninvolved, and Christian Theism, in a variety of its forms, has also been tainted with the same error.[18] The "glory of God" has often been the starting point for speaking about God's *exaltation*, to deliberately create the sense of distance between the majestic God and his sinful creatures. As a direct consequence, this focus upon God's Exalted Otherness has not helped Christian Theism to be well-engaged with humanity.

Barth delightfully and powerfully took this apart with a simple rhetorical progression. Because "His deity *encloses humanity in itself*," "in order to be truly God,"

> how could we see and say it otherwise when we look at Jesus Christ in whom we find man taken up into communion with God? No. God requires *no exclusion of humanity, no non-humanity, not to speak of inhumanity*.[19]

Or again, from his final series of lectures, given in the United States in 1962:[20]

> God is not the prisoner of his majesty, as though he were bound to be no more than the pertinent or impertinent Wholly Other. . . . Other theologies may be concerned with such *exalted, super-human, in-human* gods.[21]

But, according to Barth, such "inhuman gods" contrast sharply with God as revealed in Jesus Christ:

---

16. "The humanity of God! Rightly understood that is bound to mean God's relation to and turning toward man. It signifies the God who speaks with man in promise and command. It represents God's existence, intercession, and activity for man, the intercourse God holds with him, and the free grace in which He wills to be and is nothing other than the God of man" (*Humanity of God*, 37).

17. Barth, *Faith of the Church*, 45–46.

18. Barth especially targets "the god of Schleiermacher" who cannot show mercy; Barth, *Evangelical Theology*, 10.

19. Barth, *Humanity of God*, 50 (my emphasis).

20. These lectures were published (slightly modified) as *Evangelical Theology*. The lecture itself can found at https://m.youtube.com/watch?v=8y2fe2vdXqo.

21. Barth, *Evangelical Theology*, 10, 11 (my emphasis).

[They] can only be the gods of every sort of bad news, or *dysangelion*. But the God who is the object of evangelical theology is just as lowly as he is exalted. He is exalted precisely in his lowliness. And so his inevitable "No" is enclosed in his primary "Yes" to man.[22]

The glory of God does not speak of such an exalted, inhuman god, but in the gospel it is always "the glory of God *in the face of Jesus Christ*" (2 Cor 4:6). The humanity of God speaks of God coming among us; God being with us; God being for us.

> Just as his Oneness consists only of his life as Father, Son and Holy Spirit, so in relation to the reality distinct from him he is free *de jure* and *de facto* to be the God of *man*. He exists neither *next to* man nor merely *above* him, but rather *with* him, *by* him, and most important of all, *for* him.[23]

As the Apostle Paul pointed out to the Athenian Philosophers, human beings have always seriously misunderstood God as if he is distant and uninvolved with them. But, on the contrary, as our Creator and Sustainer—and so that humanity might "seek him and perhaps reach out for him and find him"—the gospel of Jesus Christ now proclaims that "he is not far from any one of us" (Acts 17:27).

The humanity of God is the climax of thousands of years of God coming close to his people (Heb 1:1–4). The presence of Jesus Christ in human history, from his conception to his resurrection from the dead, is what puts the lie to God being far from us. On the contrary, the humanity of God is the demonstration of God being with us, the Emmanuel (Matt 1:23).[24]

But the gospel of the incarnation does not stop at God being *among* us. The purpose of God becoming a man was to "bring us to God" (compare 1 Pet 3:18). God was *with us*, in order to become God *for us*. In this way, the incarnation, the humanity of God, points immediately toward the divine restoration of our humanity, which comes to us through faith.

The Life of Faith

Faith and the Fabric of Society

Faith is a word that is often misunderstood because, in English, it has two uses which, though related, should nevertheless be kept distinct. The two uses can be described

---

22. Barth, *Evangelical Theology*, 11 (original emphasis).
23. Barth, *Evangelical Theology*, 10–11 (original emphasis).
24. "Since it is 'evangelical' it can by no means be devoted to an inhuman God, for in that case it would become legalistic theology. Evangelical theology is concerned with Immanuel, God with us! Having this God for its object, it can be nothing else but the most thankful and *happy* science" (Barth, *Evangelical Theology*, 12; Barth's emphasis).

with the assistance of two separate Latin terms.[25] The first, *fides*, is an epistemological term, which speaks of *assent* and is appropriate for propositions and creeds.[26]

But *fiducia* is faith as personal trust. Although the Bible is certainly interested in faith as *fides*, belief *that*, it is overwhelmingly about faith as *fiducia*, trust between persons, whether human or divine.[27] Although when discussing *fiducia* in relation to God, some authors add the adjective "*religious* faith," this is unnecessary and actually misleading. For notwithstanding the trust is in God, this kind of divine *fiducia*, "may be compared with trust or confidence in another human person."[28] Faith (as *fiducia*) describes an ordinary and essential part of human life.[29]

Unlike *fides*, *fiducia* is not intellectual, but experiential. In fact, it does not even have to be thought about. It is a posture, an "unthinking assumption,"[30] a "sense of safety in the world,"[31] an atmosphere in which you operate, like knowing your brother is always there to play with you. It is just part of the background fabric of human life, when human life is operating as God intended.

Faith as *fiducia* is the kind of personal trust which is necessary to bring about a sense of safety and well-being for individuals, and the kind of social trust which is necessary for building society.[32] For society to operate properly, not only must people live their lives trusting others, but the others in whom they trust must be trustworthy. *Fiducia* is placed in the *fiduciary*.

In law, a *fiduciary* is a trustee, and trustees especially act for those who are vulnerable, who, in turn, act in good faith (i.e., reliance and trust in them), on the assumption that the fiduciary will act at all times for their sole benefit and interest.[33] Although the

25. For the following discussion, see Hick, *Faith and Knowledge*, 3–4. Hick's primary concern is *fides*.

26. "Faith" as *fides* also lies behind such expressions as "communities of faith," applied in the Western world even to non-Christian religions. This probably derives from all religions have a "creed" that is "believed," but whatever its origin, the use of "faith" as an alternative to religion nevertheless amounts to an imposition of Christian categories.

27. Hick, *Faith and Knowledge*, 3–4. The two conceptions can be traced in the Gospel of John, with *fides* corresponding to πιστεύω ὅτι (e.g., 20:31), and *fiducia* to πιστεύω εἰς (4:39) or ἐν (3:15), or simply πιστεύω plus the dative (5:24).

28. Hick, *Faith and Knowledge*, 3.

29. See the essays in Kelcourse, *Human Development*, which share the premise that "faith is that quality of living that makes it possible to fully live."

30. Shay, *Achilles in Vietnam*, 185.

31. Herman, *Trauma and Recovery*, 51.

32. For an analysis of the recent crisis in Australian federal politics as a loss of public trust, see Crosby, *Trust Deficit*.

33. For convenience, see *Wikipedia*, s.v. "fiduciary": "In a fiduciary relationship, one person, in a position of vulnerability, justifiably vests confidence, good faith, reliance, and trust in another whose aid, advice or protection is sought in some matter. In such a relation good conscience requires the fiduciary to act at all times for the sole benefit and interest of the one who trusts." This article refers to the judgment of Lord Millett that "a fiduciary is someone who has undertaken to act for and on behalf of another in a particular matter in circumstances which give rise to a relationship of trust and confidence."

term has now evolved to mean someone who holds someone else's money in trust, the original Roman sense was someone who held another *person* in trust.[34] Many human institutions implicitly take on a fiduciary role: the family, the class room, the boy scout troop, the boarding house, the hospital, the armed services, the church, the government, the legal profession. The various *fiduciaries* have an enormous responsibility to those who have entrusted their lives into their hands on the assumption that they are trustworthy.

The more a person owes their life and safety to an institution, the more is invested in that fiduciary and the more damage will be done when that trust is betrayed.[35]

The Betrayal of What Is Right

The "betrayal of what is right" is arguably at the core of the experience of Complex PTSD sufferers. As fiduciaries, armies, families, churches, governments—all the institutions of human life—imply a moral universe, that they have the well-being of those within them as their primary, if not sole, concern. When this moral universe is betrayed, the very fabric of society is ripped at the core. As Jonathan Shay explains of combat trauma, the betrayal of what is right is the "moral injury" that is

> an essential part of any combat trauma that leads to lifelong psychological injury. Veterans can usually recover from horror, fear, and grief once they return to civilian life, so long as "what's right" has not also been violated.[36]

The betrayal of what is right is clear in the combat trauma produced in soldiers ordered to kill civilians, or in rape, or intra-family sexual abuse, or in the corruption of justice.

But it is also there in more settled societies in much more subtle ways. In the twentieth century, writers of the New Confucianism sought to combine the ancient Confucian tradition with the benefits of Western democracy.[37] Democracy is a fiduciary community, for, in order for democracy to operate properly, it proposes a moral universe to which its citizens must entrust their lives, confident that Governments are only and primarily out for their welfare. But at the same time the New Confucianism was being attracted by democracy as a fiduciary community, Western countries were

---

34. Shay, *Achilles in Vietnam*, 15n14.

35. E.g., an army is a "moral structure, a *fiduciary*, a trustee holding the life and safety of that soldier. The need for an intact moral world increases with every added coil of a soldier's mortal dependency on others. The vulnerability of the soldier's world has vastly increased in three millennia [i.e., since Achilles]." Shay, *Achilles in Vietnam*, 15.

36. Shay, *Achilles in Vietnam*, 20–21. This betrayal of what is right creates "indignant rage" that is "the first and possibly the primary trauma that converted subsequent terror, horror, grief, and guilt into lifelong disability for Vietnam veterans"; "It is the kind of rage arising from social betrayal that impairs a person's dignity through violation of what's right"; "the rage that ruptures social attachments," in "the choking-off of the social and moral world."

37. See Berthrong, *All Under Heaven*; Chan, *Confucian Perfectionism*.

rapidly losing confidence in the ability of the democratic process to deliver Governments that took their responsibilities as fiduciaries seriously—as the string of hung parliaments in Western countries in recent years perhaps testifies.

A recent analysis of the last decade in Australian Federal politics is clear. The four components of trust are reliability, competence, openness, honesty.[38] Successive political leaders have departed from these values. This has been a massive "betrayal of what is right" and, as a result, Australian politics now has a "trust deficit."

The betrayal of what is right is present in so many ordinary areas of life that people are constantly battered into thinking it is normal, but, given the implied moral universe inherent in the *fiduciary* of democracy, the sense of betrayal cannot be erased and it continues to emerge in social outrage—or election results.

Shattered Trust

This betrayal of what is right, shatters the trauma sufferer's ability to trust.[39] The shattering of trust has devastating consequences, inhibiting or preventing human connection, the ability to love, to form intimate relationships. And this, in turn, leads to withdrawal, isolation and a secrecy that turns the trauma survivor in on themselves. This "demonic anxiety" and "inclosing reserve" (to use Kierkegaard's terms, meditating on Mark 1:24)[40] then creates further dysfunction. In addition, the betrayal of the moral universe (justice) and the shattering of trust makes it very difficult for the trauma survivor to put their trust in a loving God.[41]

The Faithful Humanity of God

But the faithful humanity of God shows God as most exalted when he is most humble,[42] as depicted by the Christological Hymn in Philippians 2:6–11, which articulates the humanity of God against the grand sweep from eternity to eternity.

It was at the point of death, when his human weakness was most apparent, that the Son of God was manifested "in the likeness of sinful flesh" (Rom 8:3). Although fully human throughout his life to that point, it was the moment of his death with which he struggled in Gethsemane, experiencing the weakness and testing of our human mortality in common with us, and yet arguably more than any other human being has had to (Heb 2:14–18; 4:14–16; 5:7–9). He endured the struggle successfully

---

38. Crosby, *Trust Deficit*, 16–19.

39. Herman, *Trauma and Recovery*, 51–53; Van der Kolk, *Body Keeps the Score*, 18, 134, 141, 150, 158, 163, 253. This, of course, makes therapy difficult.

40. See further, Bolt, "Kierkegaard."

41. E.g., Herman, *Trauma and Recovery*, 52, 94, 121 "loss of sustaining faith"; Shay, *Achilles in Vietnam*, 148.

42. Barth, *Evangelical Theology*, 11.

with his willing embrace of his destiny, "not my will, but yours be done" (Luke 22:42), so that he became "the source of eternal salvation for all who obey him" (Heb 5:9).

Rather than shying away from our suffering world, the living God entered it fully in order to bring us to himself (1 Pet 3:18). God demonstrated his justice, at the point when human justice was overturned in the death of the innocent Jesus (Rom 3:25–26). In order to save humanity, the Son of God was crushed by humanity. The sufferings of the world became the sufferings of the Son of God so that he might redeem the world from its sufferings.

With his understanding of the humanity of God, Barth easily moved from Anthropology to Christology and back again. So, for instance, as a young preacher, in a sermon on blind Bartimaeus (Mark 10:46–52), preached 4 March 1917 (as described by Willimon):

> [Barth] depicts the one who comes down the road past the beggar as also "life's victim." This one too is "about to be pushed by the world to the side of the road—and to be thrown among the dead."[43]

> "He took and bore on himself the whole terrible burden of life—godless human life, its sin, its suffering, its death." This God chose to be God "not without us, but with us."[44]

> Barth concentrates exclusively upon the one coming down the road who, though an outcast and a sufferer, is also the one who sees the blind man and builds a bridge to him, heals him, and wins him as a follower in the way. The one who comes down the road and reaches out to the blind man in his misery is more interesting than the blind man or his misery. The life and death of the one who comes down the road defines the significance of the life of the blind man.[45]

This was Christ's life of faith, to bring individuals like Bartimaeus along behind him in that life of faith, so that they might follow him on his way into the kingdom of God. Here is the humanity of God! The True God, the Son of God, reveals that true humanity is trusting the Father in the midst of human weakness and mortality, along the way to the coming kingdom of God.

But even though there is something essentially individual about faith, the humanity of God also shows faith's corporate dimension. For the church is caught up in, and is "the reflection of the humanity of God." Whereas serving an inhuman God who is "wholly Other" only breeds legalistic theology,[46] serving the God who became flesh ought to both humanize his people, and prevent them from becoming inhuman.[47]

---

43. Barth and Willimon, *Early Preaching of Karl Barth*, 10.
44. Barth and Willimon, *Early Preaching of Karl Barth*, 11.
45. Barth and Willimon, *Early Preaching of Karl Barth*, 12.
46. Barth, *Evangelical Theology*, 12.
47. Barth, *Humanity of God*, 63–64.

The Fiduciary Community: Reflecting the Humanity of God

In the incarnation, the One True God comes close to us. But at the same time, the One True God becomes the One True Man. Thus the humanity of God shows us true divinity at the same time as showing us true humanity.

The divinity and humanity of Christ are both displayed preeminently as he went to his death, the greatest demonstration of Divine love and the lowest point of human weakness. As he hung on the cross, he was mocked with the profound truth that "he trusts in God" (Matt 27:43). This was the character of life for the One True Human, faith viewed as trust (*fiducia*). But this is also the character of life for the Son of God with his Father.

Intratrinitarian relationships have long been described in terms of the indwelling of the three persons by means of mutual love.[48] But the same can be said about the mutual trust that pertains within the Godhead. The Father entrusts all things to the Son (John 3:35; compare 5:22, 26–27; Eph 1:22), the Son trusts the Father (Matt 27:43), the Spirit is the medium of both this trust and trustworthiness. God himself is a community of fiduciary relations.

And as the expression and reflection of the humanity of God, the body of Christ is likewise a fiduciary community. Christ incorporates our humanity into his. As individuals are, by faith, incorporated "in Christ," so our life is hid with Christ, where Christ is, at the right hand of the Father (Col 3:1–4). But each individual is not the only one "in Christ." By faith, Christ incorporates others drawn from the rest of humanity. This is the heavenly fiduciary community.

But then, this heavenly corporate reality finds concrete expression in the congregations of Christ's people on earth. The members first entrust themselves to God, and this trust becomes the fundamental posture of their lives. But one individual entrusting his or her life to God automatically takes place in fellowship with others who have similarly entrusted their lives to his or her God. And therefore, as a fundamental work of the Spirit who binds those "trusters" to Christ and binds them to each other, the body of Christ is characterized by mutual entrusting of one member into another. The strong are entrusted to the weak. The weak are entrusted to the strong. The more seemly members to the unseemly, the unseemly to the seemly. Yes, the greatest of all gifts may be love, but the initiatives of love are nothing without the trusting relationships it creates and works within (1 Cor 13). Like the Godhead, the body of Christ exists fundamentally as a fiduciary community.

So how can Christian congregations become the fiduciary communities Christ has liberated them to be, as the reflection of the humanity of God? And how can they be the fiduciary communities that the traumatised of our world need them to be?

---

48. This is related to the doctrine of *perichoresis*, the mutual indwelling of the persons of the trinity, which has been discussed since at least the time of John of Damascus. See Barth, *CD* I.1, 370, 396, 485.

PART C—ENCOUNTERING THE JUST AND MERCIFUL GOD

Healing through Storytelling

The Healing of Trauma

Healing from trauma is not an easy process, and never happens quickly. The question, "Is recovery from PTSD possible?" requires three answers: 1. No. Returning to normal is not possible; 2. We don't know; and, 3. Yes.[49] Some things will never be healed. There is a loss of innocence in trauma survivors that cannot be recovered. They will always see the world differently from the way the "normal" person might view it.[50] Some things might be healed, but whether or not a person might ever be completely free of PTSD, is not fully known. With increasing knowledge of the brain and its ways of recovering, the twenty-first century has opened with a much more hopeful perspective on trauma recovery than ever before. But it is still early days.[51] However, despite the "no" and "don't know" answers, there is also a "yes" answer: "Recovery is possible in many areas of life, perhaps in the most important ones for a fulfilling existence."[52]

Although it is not easy and the survivor's actual experience will inevitably be recursive,[53] recovery is usually schematised into three stages.

> The central task of the first stage is the establishment of safety. The central task of the second stage is remembrance and mourning. The central task of the third stage is reconnection with ordinary life.[54]

Whatever the length or pathway of this healing journey, it won't happen outside of a network of healing relationships.

---

49. Shay, *Achilles in Vietnam*, ch. 11.

50. Shay, *Achilles in Vietnam*, 185: "To encounter radical evil is to make one forever different from the trusting, 'normal' person who wraps the rightness of the social order around himself snugly, like a cloak of safety. Trust, which was once an unthinking assumption and granted with no awareness of possible betrayal, is now a staggering accomplishment for survivors of severe trauma. Trauma survivors grant trust only as an act of courage, after time and *tests* of trust, one after another, like trials and labors in ancient myth. Blind trust in authority, position, and credentials is a dangerous luxury of the still innocent. If recovery means return to trusting innocence, recovery is *not* possible."

51. Writing in 1994 twenty-two years after the last ground combat battalion was withdrawn from Vietnam, and when there were still 250,000 veterans who met the full DSM-III criteria for PTSD, Shay notes that "time does *not* heal all wounds" (Shay, *Achilles in Vietnam*, 184). Whereas Shay longed for new modes of healing (185–86), twenty years later, Van der Kolk, *Body Keeps the Score*, can report new and innovative therapies that have emerged alongside better understanding the effects of trauma on a human being.

52. Shay, *Achilles in Vietnam*, 186.

53. Shay, *Achilles in Vietnam*, 187.

54. Herman, *Trauma and Recovery*, 155, who adds the rider: "Like any abstract concept, these stages of recovery are a convenient fiction, not to be taken too literally. They are an attempt to impose simplicity and order upon a process that is inherently turbulent and complex. But the same basic concept of recovery stages has emerged repeatedly." She deals with these three stages in chapters 8, 9, and 10, respectively.

The essential injuries in combat PTSD are moral and social, and so the central treatment must be moral and social. The best treatment restores control to the survivor and actively encourages communalization of the trauma. Healing is done *by* survivors, not *to* survivors.[55]

But in order for the survivor to *communalize* their trauma, they will need a community in which to do it.[56] A peer group of fellow sufferers is invaluable, often providing the safe environment needed for the survivor to begin to put their story into words.[57] Establishing a relationship with the right kind of therapist is probably essential.[58] But, in fact, a wider network of supportive relationships are also necessary, and, in fact, in some senses even more important than the therapeutic relationship.[59] This is where Christian congregations can help enormously—insofar as they maintain and nurture their character as fiduciary communities.

Healing Trauma through Telling Story

A common feature of nearly all therapeutic methods dealing with trauma is that they "direct the survivor to construct a personal narrative at some time in his or her recovery, although there are powerful disagreements about the timing and venue."[60] Those in individual therapy will talk through or write their trauma narrative. Peer

---

55. Shay, *Achilles in Vietnam*, 187.

56. "The core experiences of psychological trauma are disempowerment and disconnection from others. Recovery, therefore, is based upon the empowerment of the survivor and the creation of new connections. Recovery can take place only within the context of relationships; it cannot occur in isolation. In her renewed connections with other people, the survivor re-creates the psychological faculties that were damaged or deformed by the traumatic experience. These faculties include the basic capacities for trust, autonomy, initiative, competence, identity, and intimacy. Just as these capabilities are originally formed in relationships with other people, they must be reformed in such relationships"; Herman, *Trauma and Recovery*, 133.

57. Shay, *Achilles in Vietnam*, 192. Initially such a "healing community" of victims speaks in unison, as it were, drawn together by common experience: "in this earliest form of group communication, individual experience seems to be spoken and heard as part of the discourse of mutual affirmation and recognition." Shay insists, however, that "major recovery requires that personal narrative be particular, not general.... In a fully realized personal narrative the survivor grips the herald's staff and speaks as himself."

58. Herman, *Trauma and Recovery*, ch. 7.

59. Shay, *Achilles in Vietnam*, 194. Trauma work cannot be apolitical. Professionals cannot be "affectively neutral," because "an affectively neutral position will defeat healing." This gives a special challenge to professionals and Shay admits, he "cannot escape the suspicion that what we do as mental health professionals is not as good as the healing that in other cultures has been rooted in the native soil of the returning soldier's community. Our culture has been notably deficient in providing for reception of the Furies of war into community." We need a contemporary equivalent to the Athenian tragedy, for "tragedy inclines us to prefer attachment to fragile mortals whom we love ... and to refuse promised immortality."

60. Shay, *Achilles in Vietnam*, 188. "In the telling the trauma story becomes a testimony [which is] a ritual of healing" (Herman, *Trauma and Recovery*, 181).

PART C—ENCOUNTERING THE JUST AND MERCIFUL GOD

groups share their stories. The personal "trauma narrative" has also become a feature in the many Truth (and Reconciliation) Commissions that have emerged since 1974 as part of the large-scale attempts to deal with whole societies recovering from violent conflict.[61]

At the beginning, trauma sufferers may not even be able to put their story into words. Some might act it out by intimidating their therapist or listener. This "coercive communication" might create "terror and helplessness at work, in the family, on the street, or in the clinic"[62]—or the church—forcing others to experience the fear and terror they themselves went through. But here the audience is no longer made up of listeners. They most certainly feel the emotions, but they have been made into victims. And such acting out is not ultimately productive for the survivor.

> The character damage of a trauma survivor can be understood as a reflection both of his or her radical aloneness and of the continued presence of the perpetrator in the victim's inner life. [In Acting out], aloneness is broken . . . , but the inner presence of the perpetrator has taken over. Healing does not occur.[63]

The healing journey really only begins as the survivor is enabled to put their trauma into words, to tell their story, to tell a narrative. Narrative helps the survivor with personal integration. Trauma leaves a person with scattered and shattered recollections of the past, which can then go on to intrude into life in the present, over and over again. The attempt to put it all in a narrative, organizes the mind and so the experience, and works toward turning the trauma into a memory of something now gone, rather than something that still continues to dominate.[64]

> Severe trauma explodes the cohesion of consciousness. When a survivor creates fully realized narrative that brings together the shattered knowledge of what happened, the emotions that were aroused by the meanings of the events, and the bodily sensations that the physical events created, the survivor pieces back together the fragmentation of consciousness that trauma has caused. Such narrative often results in the remission of some symptoms, particularly

---

61. Brahm, "Truth Commissions." Margaret Popkin and Naomi Roht-Arriaza describe four main goals for truth commissions. They seek to contribute to transitional peace by: "1. creating an authoritative record of what happened; 2. providing a platform for the victims to tell their stories and obtain some form of redress; 3. recommending legislative, structural or other changes to avoid a repetition of past abuses; and 4. establishing who was responsible and providing a measure of accountability for the perpetrators" (cited by Brahm [n14], from Christie, *South African Truth Commission*, 61).

62. Shay, *Achilles in Vietnam*, 192.

63. Shay, *Achilles in Vietnam*, 191–92.

64. "Narrative can transform involuntary re-experiencing of traumatic events into memory of the events, thereby re-establishing authority over memory. *Forgetting combat trauma is not a legitimate goal of treatment.* . . . The task is to remember—rather than to relive and re-enact—and to grieve" (Shay, *Achilles in Vietnam*, 192).

intrusive symptoms, dissociated bodily sensations, affects, and behaviours that inexplicably intrude into the veteran's life.[65]

Part of this integration comes from the narrative placing events into a time-frame:

> Narrative time—the idea that an event takes place in a temporal context, with other events happening before, during, and after it [. . .] severe trauma destroys the capacity to think of a future or a past. For many Vietnam combat soldiers, a cramped, eternal present, extending no further than the next C-rations, death, cigarette, or fire fight, snuffed out all other temporality. The time horizon in the future has shrunk to a few hours and to the timeless shelter of death. Narrative time is built into the very structure of the family of languages to which English belongs. This may form part of the enormous difficulty that many survivors of severe trauma have in putting their experience into words; their experience is ineffable in a language that insists on "was" and "will be." The trauma world knows only *is*.[66]

However, although this storytelling is encouraged because of its perceived therapeutic effects, it is not universally helpful, and this seems to depend, in part, on timing and venue.

In the early days of dealing with combat trauma, the folk belief that "getting it all out" was necessary led to combat debriefings, but these were catastrophic, driving many to suicide. Jonathan Shay notes that this operated on a "dangerous illusion of instant cathartic cure."[67] The victim's disturbed reality resists the "exorcism" for which both they and their therapists long.

> Before safety, self-care, and sobriety have been firmly established, active uncovering of trauma history only retraumatizes the survivor. Recovery from severe combat trauma more nearly resembles training to run a marathon than cathartic redemption in faith healing.[68]

The venue is also significant. Before a truth commission, sometimes telling the trauma narrative is beneficial, but other times it simply triggers the trauma again. The victims only get a few minutes; they are in front of a semi-legal body; there are few resources for follow-on care; and this is not the venue in which the audience can express the genuine emotional response that is required for healing to take place.[69] The evidence for the impact on the general populace is also mixed.[70]

---

65. Shay, *Achilles in Vietnam*, 188.
66. Shay, *Achilles in Vietnam*, 190, 191.
67. Shay, *Achilles in Vietnam*, 187.
68. Shay, *Achilles in Vietnam*, 187.
69. For this need for genuine emotional response, see Shay, *Achilles in Vietnam*, 191, 194.
70. Brahm, "Truth Commissions."

PART C—ENCOUNTERING THE JUST AND MERCIFUL GOD

In the end, what is significant is probably not just telling the story to get something out:

> The goal of recounting the trauma story is integration, not exorcism. . . . The fundamental premise of psychotherapeutic work is a belief in the restorative power of truth telling.[71]

After asking the question "How [does] narrative [enable] the survivor to rebuild the ruins of character," Shay then answers by saying,

> Narrative heals personality changes only if the survivor finds or creates a trustworthy community of listeners for it.[72]

Or, to put it in other words, to experience healing, the survivor needs to tell their story within a fiduciary community.

. . . in a Fiduciary Community

Several traits are required for an audience to be trustworthy in this enterprise. Listeners need to be

> strong enough to hear the story without injury; . . . strong enough to hear the story without having to deny the reality of the experience or to blame the victim.[73]

These are the two common responses from the normal population: denial and blame. Because it shatters their social construction of what is "normal life," trauma is simply too hard for ordinary people to listen to. It is easier to deny it actually happened, or to blame the victim if it did.[74] Although this is a thoroughly normal response, to respond in these ways destroys the fiduciary nature of the community, because its members no longer serve the one entrusting them with his or her story.

The fiduciary community must be "ready to experience some of the terror, grief, and rage that the victim did." This is, after all, one meaning of compassion. "Without emotion in the listener there is no communalization of the trauma."[75]

The fiduciary community must show respect of a particular kind: The "respect, embodied in this kind of listening, [with the] readiness to be changed by the narrator. The change may be small or large." Respect also means refraining from judgment,

---

71. Herman, *Trauma and Recovery*, 181.
72. Shay, *Achilles in Vietnam*, 188.
73. Shay, *Achilles in Vietnam*, 188.
74. Shay anchors his "law of forgetting and denial" in several human fragilities that are exposed when confronted by a trauma survivor. It is entirely normal that the feelings aroused by listening to a trauma narrative "are almost all unpleasant" (Shay, *Achilles in Vietnam*, 193–94).
75. Shay, *Achilles in Vietnam*, 188.

which is not easy if the victim has also been a perpetrator of their own kind of evil—as can often be the case.[76]

When the survivor tells their story in the context of a fiduciary community, something profound takes place:

> Trauma narrative imparts knowledge to the community that listens *and* responds to it emotionally. Emotion carries essential cognitive elements; it is not separable from the knowledge. Something quite profound takes place when the trauma survivor sees enlightenment take hold. The narrator now speaks as his or her free self, not as the captive of the perpetrator. The aloneness is broken in a manner that obliterates neither the narrator nor the listener in [yet another re-enactment of the trauma].[77]

Trauma-Telling and the Humanity of God

In the Christian fiduciary community, the humanity of God commits us to storytelling of two interrelated stories: God's story and our own.

First and foremost, we tell the story of the humanity of God. We proclaim and recite and sing and reenact the great deeds of God. And as we tell *God's* story, we learn that God became flesh. He came to be *with* us, in order to show that he is *for* us. So, as we hear God's story, we find that we are already part of it. We are caught up in the promises and their fulfillment. The Old Testament story of Israel and its fulfillment in Jesus Christ becomes our heritage. Our life was in his life, his death, his resurrection, his ascension, and it will be in his future kingdom. God's story gives us perspective.

And this wide-ranging story of the humanity of God therefore becomes the context in which we can tell our own stories. Standing always as the most recent examples in the long line of Christian believers who bear testimony to their transformation in Christ, we tell our story, and the story of our human brokenness becomes absorbed in the story of the humanity of God. The humanity of God has already absorbed our human brokenness, and now, through the gracious working of the Spirit of God, the humanity of God transforms us into the likeness of Christ, which is our holiness—our own divinely wrought humanity.

The Humanity of God and Social Well-Being

As we truthfully tell the story of our trauma of a greater or a lesser kind to the Christian fiduciary community, our broken humanity is being enfolded into the life of the

---

76. "Tyrants in all spheres of life, whether domestic, political, or military, have discovered that the most powerful way to break the will of another person is to coerce participation in the victimization of others. Many victims of such situations have done terrible things to survive, with devastating consequences for good character" (Shay, *Achilles in Vietnam*, 189–90).

77. Shay, *Achilles in Vietnam*, 191.

congregation, and "baptised into Christ" we become "members of one another" (1 Cor 12:13; Rom 12:4).

Incorporation into Christ and his congregation is the beginning and the means by which the humanity of God picks up people like Bartimaeus and sets them on the way to social well-being. Ultimately this will consist in the peace and blessings of the future kingdom of God. But in Christ, and—at least in part—in the fellowship of his people, this future well-being can be enjoyed even now, by faith, in hope, and worked out through love in the midst of Christ's trust-full and trust-worthy communities.

Bibliography

Barth, Karl. *Church Dogmatics*. I.1, *The Doctrine of the Word of God*. Translated by G. W. Bromiley. Edinburgh: T. & T. Clark, 1975 (German: 1936).
———. *Evangelical Theology: An Introduction*. Translated by Grover Foley. Edinburgh: T. & T. Clark, 1963.
———. *The Faith of the Church: A Commentary on the Apostles' Creed*. Translated by G. Vahanian. London: Fontana, 1967. Original French lectures: 1940–43; ET: 1958.
———. *The Humanity of God*. Translated by J. N. Thomas and T. Wieser. Richmond: John Knox, 1960. German ed., 1956.
Barth, Karl, and William H. Willimon. *The Early Preaching of Karl Barth*. Translated by J. E. Wilson. Louisville: Westminster John Knox, 2009.
Berthrong, John H. *All under Heaven: Transforming Paradigms in Confucian-Christian Dialogue*. Albany: State University of New York Press, 1994.
Bolt, Peter G. "Kierkegaard on Anxiety." In *The Consolations of Theology*, edited by B. S. Rosner, 77–108. Grand Rapids: Eerdmans, 2008.
Brahm, Eric. "Truth Commissions." June 2004. Conflict Information Consortium, University of Colorado, Boulder. http://www.beyondintractability.org/essay/truth-commissions.
Celi, Elizabeth. *Breaking the Silence: A Practical Guide for Male Victims of Domestic Abuse*. Mt. Evelyn, Australia: Global Publishing, 2011.
Chan, Joseph. *Confucian Perfectionism: A Political Philosophy for Modern Times*. Princeton: Princeton University Press, 2014.
Christie, Kenneth. *The South African Truth Commission*. New York: St. Martin's, 2000.
Crosby, Sam. *The Trust Deficit*. Melbourne: Melbourne University Press, 2016.
Henderson, Anna, and Chris Uhlmann. "Asylum Seeker Intake Explained: Who Will Come to Australia under the Government's Plan?" *ABC News*, updated September 9, 2015. http://www.abc.net.au/news/2015-09-09/refugee-intake-plan-who-will-come-to-australia/6762278.
NEF. http://www.nationalaccountsofwellbeing.org/.
Herman, Judith. *Trauma and Recovery: The Aftermath of Violence—from Domestic Abuse to Political Terror*. 2nd ed. New York: Basic, 1997.
Hick, J. *Faith and Knowledge*. 2nd ed. 1966. Reprint, London: Fontana, 1974.
IDMC. *Global Overview 2015: People Internally Displaced by Conflict and Violence*. http://www.internal-displacement.org/publications/2015/global-overview-2015-people-internally-displaced-by-conflict-and-violence.

Karlsen, Elibritt. "Refugee Resettlement to Australia: What Are the Facts?" Updated February 3, 2015. http://www.aph.gov.au/About_Parliament/Parliamentary_Departments/Parliamentary_Library/pubs/rp/rp1415/RefugeeResettlement.

Kelcourse, Felicity B., ed. *Human Development and Faith: Life-Cycle Stages of Body, Mind, and Soul.* 2nd ed. St. Louis: Chalice, 2015.

Ngwenya, Dumisani. "Healing the Wounds of *Gukurahundi*: A Participatory Action Research Project." DTech thesis, Durban University of Technology, 2014. https://ir.dut.ac.za/bitstream/10321/1300/1/NGWENYA_2014.pdf.

Shay, Jonathan. *Achilles in Vietnam: Combat Trauma and the Undoing of Character.* New York: Atheneum, 1994.

UNHCR. "Worldwide Displacement Hits All-Time High as War and Persecution Increase." June 18, 2015. http://www.unhcr.org/news/latest/2015/6/558193896/worldwide-displacement-hits-all-time-high-war-persecution-increase.html.

UN Population Division. "Countries in the World by Population (2016)." http://www.worldometers.info/world-population/population-by-country/.

USIP. "10: Social Well-Being." http://www.usip.org/guiding-principles-stabilization-and-reconstruction-the-web-version/10-social-well-being.

Van der Kolk, Bessel. *The Body Keeps the Score: Mind, Brain and Body in the Transformation of Trauma.* London: Penguin, 2014.

6

Asceticism, Well-Being, and Compassion in Maximus the Confessor

DORU COSTACHE

I N one of his better-known spiritual works, *Chapters on Love*, written before 634,[1] a writing on asceticism and compassion, Saint Maximus the Confessor (ca. 580–662) discussed a topic that was significant for the Byzantine monastic milieus of his age, to which the tract was primarily addressed, as well as the overall Christian experience. Contrary to the views, seemingly held by many ascetics of his time, that the purpose of the spiritual life was the acquisition of virtue and the attainment of dispassion or equanimity, Maximus proposed that virtue and dispassion could not have been the ultimate goal of asceticism. Granted, virtue and dispassion indicated one's healing from the wounds of sin and return to personal well-being; also, equanimity in the face of challenges. But dispassion meant more than impassivity regarding danger, pain, suffering, illness, loss, or joy, for that matter. It amounted to an ecstatic departure from one's selfish drives, an energy that was conducive to selfless love, altruism, compassion, and generosity. In other words, dispassion, and the ascetic undertakings which led to it, had social implications. Consequently, while the author agreed that sheer compassion was impossible without ascetic exertion and virtuous reformation, he emphasized that, until one became godlike by loving all people equally, virtue and dispassion remained imperfect. In maintaining this point, Maximus echoed the Lord's Sermon of the Mountain (Matthew 5:38–48) about loving the enemy and being perfect in

---

1. Jankowiak and Booth, "New Date-List," 19–83, esp. 28, 78. The earlier dating, by Sherwood, placed this writing during the Cyzicus years, namely, before 626. See Sherwood, *Annotated Date-List*, 26.

mercy.² Thus construed, Maximus' algorithm of the spiritual life in the writing under consideration—referring to ascesis, dispassion, and love—presupposed an experience of transformation, the metamorphosis of the self from one concerned with its own well-being into one capable of compassionate abnegation or altruism. The social implications of this algorithm attest to its relevance beyond the historical circumstances within which the Maximian tract was produced. It is these social implications that constitute the object of my analysis.

After sketching the Maximian views on the spiritual life within *Chapters on Love* (= *On Love*), I focus on the complex rapport of asceticism and compassion espoused therein. In so doing, I challenge the current "first world" notion of well-being, defined in selfish, acquisitive, and materialistic terms,³ by pointing out, in the light of Maximus' wisdom, that personal fullness and happiness must be associated with the transformative experience of one's reformation as a compassionate person, sensitive to the presence and needs of others. So understood, I propose, Maximus' relevant teachings are foundational for the social theory of a compassionate society.

Chapters on Love and the Spiritual Life

The conviction of Maximus was that ascesis or more generally the spiritual life aimed not at what modern, Cartesian Christians would call salvation of the soul. For him, as one discerns throughout his ranging corpus of writings, the purpose of living spiritually was to restore wholeness to the human being taken as a whole and to humankind, through healing and transformation, within the context of a fully unified reality, cosmic and heavenly, and with a view to the eschatological perfection.⁴ This holistic perspective—which illustrated the "theological, metaphysical, and existential" outlines of what Adam Cooper called the Confessor's "spiritual anthropology"⁵—was not shared by all of his contemporaries. Certain monastic milieus of that time understood ascesis as a goal in itself or, at best, as leading to a state of virtue and equanimity, namely, dispassion, lacking in existential and social resonance.⁶ In the work of interest, *On Love*, Maximus targeted this very misrepresentation of the ascetic life, which he challenged

---

2. See his references to the Sermon on the Mountain in *Chapters on Love*, 1.53, 57–62. The edition used throughout is Ceresa-Gastaldo, *Massimo Confessore*, 68, 70–72. All translations from the Greek are my own.

3. In so understanding well-being I take cue from the recent studies on the Australian landscape, typical of the "first world," by Harrison, "Introducing Well-Being," and Mayer, "Australia's Moral Compass."

4. I have addressed these matters in a series of studies: Costache, "Being, Well-Being, Being for Ever," esp. 71–85; "Mapping Reality"; "Gender, Marriage, and Holiness"; "Transdisciplinary Carats," esp. 154–57; "Living Above Gender," 261–90.

5. Cooper, "Spiritual Anthropology," esp. 360.

6. A number of scholars have addressed this situation: Cooper, "Spiritual Anthropology," 362–63; Berthold, "Christian Life and Praxis," esp. 398–400; Louth, *Maximus the Confessor*, 64–66.

indirectly by pointing out that, albeit indispensable, dispassion was merely a means, not a goal, a step on the road toward perfection. In turn, perfection, or godlikeness, had to be spelled out as altruism and compassion, embodying what Norman Russell called "the primacy of love."[7] The approach of Maximus should not be construed however as derogatory to asceticism and its significance for the spiritual life. His intention, rather, was to promote a fuller and more realistic view of the spiritual life as culminating in a state of perfect love made possible by asceticism. Maximian perfection was both dispassionate and compassionate.[8]

Dedicated to a certain Elpidius, possibly the abbot of a Palestinian monastery, *On Love* belongs to the monastic genre of κεφάλαια ("chapters" or summary formulations),[9] a fact indicated by the very title of the work. The purpose of this genre was to provide the reader with spiritual food for thought, required by the daily practice of prayerful reflection. *On Love* announces this purpose from the outset, within its prologue, by exhorting the reader to memorise, persistently ponder, and carefully consider its content by way of spiritual conferences (as signified by the noun συνεξέτασις, which means rigorous and collective examination) with other ascetics.[10] The requirement for attentive examination and communal assessment is motivated, alongside the spiritual depth of the aphorisms, by the symbolic architecture of the writing. The work, we find out in the same prologue, consists of four hundred brief yet rich aphorisms, so structured to suggest the four canonical Gospels.[11] Without an explicit declaration to that effect, one can legitimately understand the reference to the Gospels as suggesting that the tract's central topic, love,[12] corresponds to the common denominator of the Gospels and their ultimate message. The reference to the fourfold Gospel conveys furthermore that a Christian understanding of asceticism had to take it as means to an end, not a goal. In turn, the end referred to the godlike and transformative power of pure, altruistic love. Andrew Louth has captured this very message when he noted that "for Maximus, training in Christianity is training in love."[13] This message, precisely, permeates the work from beginning to end.

---

7. Russell, *Doctrine of Deification*, 265–66.

8. See Louth, *Maximus the Confessor*, 38, 39–41.

9. The adherence of Maximus to this genre and the monastic practices associated with it have long been researched by scholars. Blowers, *Maximus the Confessor*, 91–93; Harmless, *Desert Christians*, 317; Louth, *Maximus the Confessor*, 20; Louth, "Literature of the Monastic Movement," esp. 378; Sherwood, introduction to *St. Maximus the Confessor*, esp. 102.

10. *On Love*, proem. 15–21 (Ceresa-Gastaldo, 48).

11. *On Love*, 3–4 (Ceresa-Gastaldo, 48).

12. For the centrality of love in the Maximian work under consideration, see Berthold, "Christian Life and Praxis," 403–4, and Sherwood, introduction to *St. Maximus the Confessor*, 91–97.

13. Louth, *Maximus the Confessor*, 38.

Asceticism and Pure Love

According to the author, pure, altruistic love was not readily achievable. The main difficulty experienced by whomever pursued pure love derived from the winding paths of the human heart, which, largely because of misusing its capacity for free choice,[14] accommodated both evil and good thoughts, as well as virtuous and vicious drives. The heart's confusion and instability corresponded to the character of bodily life, which, in the assessment of Cooper, appeared to Maximus as "fraught with ambiguity."[15] Looking closer at this difficulty, the heart, alternatively called mind,[16] was a place of secret defilements or sinful passions. There, one's alienation from God registered as hatred toward fellow human beings and as finding delight in material goods. From a tainted heart, furthermore, and contrary to the serenity associated with pure love, upsurged thoughts that caused inner commotion.[17] A troubled heart, furthermore, though naturally disposed to treasure spiritual joy, lost this capacity when passions such as laziness or sloth overwhelmed it.[18] The reciprocal was also true. The heart of whomever made good use of the aptitude for free choice, who was spiritually vigilant and ascetically diligent, experienced unfathomable blessings. Such a heart, equanimous and free of selfish desires, was indwelled by Christ and the Holy Spirit.[19] It experienced joy and grateful contentment, which were doubled by a sense of sorrow for the failures and sufferings of fellow human beings.[20] This positive sorrow represented the other end of the spectrum—the opposite of the hatred felt by a defiled heart. Moreover, the heart that tasted the spiritual blessing of divine presence received together with it the gifts of purity, self-mastery, compassion, wisdom, and knowledge.[21] In short, given the heart's shifts from light to darkness, only the person who chose to undertake ascetic purification and attained dispassion, namely, a reorganization of the inner abysses of human consciousness, could reach pure love, compassion.

Maximus stated this up front when he pointed out that dispassion begot love.[22] By this maternal metaphor, undoubtedly borrowed from Evagrius' related image of generation,[23] the Confessor signified that one cannot become a loving person without

---

14. On free will in the work under consideration, see Berthold, "Christian Life and Praxis," 401–3.

15. Cooper, "Spiritual Anthropology," 360.

16. *On Love*, 4.73.3–4 (Ceresa-Gastaldo, 472).

17. *On Love*, 1.15.1, 3; 1.93; 2.51.1; 3.80.2–3 (Ceresa-Gastaldo, 54, 86, 118, 182).

18. *On Love*, 4.71.2 (Ceresa-Gastaldo, 224). For notes on sinful passions within this work, see Berthold, "Christian Life and Praxis," 401.

19. *On Love*, 4.70.1; 4.78.1–2 (Ceresa-Gastaldo, 224, 228).

20. *On Love*, 1.74.1, 3–4 (Ceresa-Gastaldo, 78).

21. *On Love*, 4.70.3–4; 4.72.4–5 (Ceresa-Gastaldo, 224).

22. ἀγάπην . . . τίκτει ἀπάθεια ("dispassion gives birth to love"). *On Love*, 1.2.1 (Ceresa-Gastaldo, 50).

23. See ἀπάθεια, ἧς ἔγγονον ἡ ἀγάπη ("dispassion, from which love is engendered"). Evagrius, *Praktikos*, proem. 8,49–50, in *Évagre le Pontique*, 492. Sinkewicz does not mention love as the final

the pangs of one's rebirth to a new life. The entryway to this new life was the ascetically conquered dispassion. The statement on love as an outcome of dispassion, by which Maximus put a positive spin on a negative starting point, to paraphrase Louth,[24] follows the very first aphorism of the work. The latter reads that one did not possess perfect love as long as one remained entangled through "passionate attachment" with "any of the earthly things."[25] True love possessed only someone who prioritized the knowledge of God to any part of the created world.[26] This is to say that alongside dispassion, and corresponding to the intellectual and ascetic processes that were conducive to dispassion, in order to arrive at pure, unselfish love one had to undergo a change of mentality and lifestyle.

The two initial aphorisms set the tone for the entire development of the Maximian discourse within this work. Taken together, the two sentences describe dispassion as the practical outcome of a change of mind-set, or conversion, and as a requirement for the attainment of pure love. Conversion, textually signified by faith,[27] amounted to a theocentric reorientation of life, a change of priorities manifested in the abandonment of selfishness and renunciation to all attachment to "earthly things." In turn, the outcome of one's reorientation of life made possible, alongside equanimity, pure, compassionate love. This exercise of altruism and compassion—a Maximian mirroring of Saint Isaac of Nineveh's contemporary theme of the merciful heart[28]—entailed a gradual process of inner transformation.[29] This change, furthermore, lent substance to the new cast of mind which thus acquired ontological density, becoming a state of being, a lived reality.

Maximus meant this very personal metamorphosis and embodiment of the theocentric mind-set when he pointed out that, through ascesis, human nature's energy of desire became "divine eros," whereas the energy of irascibility became "divine agape."[30] Asceticism and its fruit, dispassion, were not about annihilating human nature's energies or passions; the latter should not be confused with the sinful movements, also called passions. Instead, as George Berthold and Paul Blowers have pointed out,[31]

---

outcome of the ascetic refashioning of the human being in Evagrius; see Sinkewicz, *Evagrius of Pontus*, 249n8. For the understanding of love in Evagrius, see Ramelli, "Evagrius Ponticus," esp. 205–6, 222. Due to the connection between the two monastic authors, Maximus and Evagrius, Ramelli's observations are relevant to the understanding of love in Maximus.

24. Louth, *Maximus the Confessor*, 39.

25. See τὸν πρός τι τῶν ἐπιγείον ἔχοντα προσπάθειαν. *On Love*, 1.1.3 (Ceresa-Gastaldo, 50).

26. *On Love*, 1.1.1–2 (Ceresa-Gastaldo, 50). For brief notes on this chapter, see Sherwood, introduction to *St. Maximus the Confessor*, 92.

27. πίστις. *On Love*, 1.2.3; 1.3.1 (Ceresa-Gastaldo, 50).

28. See his famous meditation on the merciful heart in *Homily* 71, in *The Ascetical Homilies of Saint Isaac the Syrian* (Boston: Holy Transfiguration Monastery, 1984), 344–45.

29. *On Love*, 1.2–3 (Ceresa-Gastaldo, 50).

30. Verbatim, ἐπιθυμία became θεῖον ἔρωτα and θυμός became θείαν ἀγάπην. *On Love*, 2.48 (Ceresa-Gastaldo, 116).

31. Berthold, "Christian Life and Praxis," 410; Blowers, *Maximus the Confessor*, 258–71.

ascesis and dispassion were about reorienting or converting these energies. That this was so transpires through the celebrated Maximian stance on "the blessed passion of holy love,"[32] where passion and love feature together as one renewed energy. This renewal, reorientation, or transformation of energies, the Confessor argued, was at hand for whomever underwent conversion and led a life centered on God.[33] Conversion through faith meant therefore adherence to a divine model which demanded a concrete embodiment by way of personal realignment. The latter, moreover, consisted in a renewed use of the energies of desire and irascibility under the guise of love as eros and agape. This existential translation of the divine paradigm was tantamount, lastly, to attaining the "good" or normal operation of the human being suggested by the very first line of the work,[34] and thus godlikeness. Maximus returned to the latter nuance in a series of chapters on how true love required a divine way of exercising it; I look at the relevant passages in the next section.

Before moving any further, I must emphasize that for Maximus the rapport between asceticism, dispassion, and love was not only a linear progression from the first to the last mediated by dispassion. Once reached, perfect or altruistic love fed back into this chain by strengthening dispassion. The interplay of ascesis, dispassion, and love was complexly articulated. The following passage indicates that love for one's neighbor impacted dispassion as much as the latter conditioned the former. Here is the text:

> Ὁ τοῖς τοῦ κόσμου πράγμασι γνησίως ἀποταξάμενος καὶ τῷ πλησίον διὰ τῆς ἀγάπης ἀνυποκρίτως δουλεύων, παντὸς πάθους ταχέως ἐλευθεροῦται καὶ τῆς θείας ἀγάπης καὶ γνώσεως μέτοχος καθίσταται.[35]

> One who has genuinely renounced worldly things and sincerely ministers to the neighbour out of love quickly finds freedom from all passion and is made a partaker of the divine love and knowledge.

The praxis of altruism, supported by ascetic detachment from material things, led to further dispassion and facilitated the experience of divine love and knowledge. Here, again, Maximus must have drawn from Evagrius, who presented this rapport in a very similar way.[36] What matters more is that the passage offers a perfect illustration of Maximus' holistic mentality, where theology, spiritual anthropology, asceticism, and love were inextricably connected. This holistic understanding made no allowance

---

32. *On Love*, 3.67 (Ceresa-Gastaldo, 175–76). Scholars have repeatedly addressed this topic: Berthold, "Christian Life and Praxis," 401–2; Blowers, *Maximus the Confessor*, 261–62; Louth, *Maximus the Confessor*, 40–41; Neil, "Blessed Passion of Holy Love," esp. 3.

33. See οὗτινος ὁ νοῦς διαπαντός ἐστι πρὸς Θεόν ("that the mind be always turned towards God"). *On Love*, 2.48.1 (Ceresa-Gastaldo, 116).

34. Ἀγάπη μέν ἐστι διάθεσις ψυχῆς ἀγαθή ("love is the good disposition of the soul"). *On Love*, 1.1.1 (Ceresa-Gastaldo, 50).

35. *On Love*, 1.27 (Ceresa-Gastaldo, 58).

36. For the relevant views of Evagrius, see Ramelli, "Evagrius Ponticus," 222–23.

for speculative theology. As Louth observed,[37] ascetically conditioned, Maximian theology was concerned with knowing God; with experience, not speculation. But the passage under consideration has more to say about the topic at hand.

It does not simply repeat that dispassion and detachment led to love. It points to an interdependence of ascesis and compassion, which secured one's progress toward godlikeness—the latter signified by the "divine love and knowledge"[38] achieved by a selfless ascetic. Compared to the earlier ideation concerning love begotten from dispassion,[39] here Maximus did more than affirm love as a *raison d'être* of dispassion. Love was a transformative power which pushed ascetic experience forward by intensifying dispassion. Generated by ascetic detachment, compassionate love constituted a superior form of ascesis that led the spiritual experience to deeper grounds and to fulfillment. The passage sums up therefore the message of this entire tract, showing that loveless and heartless asceticism remained imperfect and far from constituting the way to perfection. As worthwhile a topic as the interplay of ascesis and love is, to which I briefly return toward the end of this study, the practice of compassion is of more immediate interest. The latter is spelled out in the above passage by the reference to one who "sincerely ministers to the neighbour out of love."[40] To this matter I now turn.

Practicing Compassion

For the Confessor, to love God meant to love *like* God who loves all people. Signified by the repeated references to prioritizing God encountered above,[41] upholding the theocentric perspective meant interest in and compassion toward one's neighbor, not neglect. Cooper's assessment of *Difficulty 7*, that the Confessor promoted as the highest Christian goal to "see, understand, and love all things as God sees, understands, and loves them,"[42] is equally valid here. Indeed, "whomever loves God cannot but love also every human being as oneself."[43] The aphorism welds together the two main axioms of the Mosaic Law (summarized by Christ in Matt 22:37–40 and Mark 12:28–31), namely, the wholehearted love for God and the corresponding love for one's neighbor, asserting their inseparability. Berthold's point that, here, "love for God and love for neighbour are the same,"[44] is justified. These lead to the conclusion that Maximus'

---

37. Louth, *Maximus the Confessor*, 33.
38. *On Love*, 1.27.3 (Ceresa-Gastaldo, 58).
39. *On Love*, 1.2.1 (Ceresa-Gastaldo, 50).
40. τῷ πλησίον διὰ τῆς ἀγάπης ἀνυποκρίτως δουλεύων. *On Love*, 1.27.1–2 (Ceresa-Gastaldo, 58).
41. *On Love*, 1.1; 2.48 (Ceresa-Gastaldo, 50, 116), etc.
42. Cooper, "Spiritual Anthropology," 367.
43. Ὁ ἀγαπῶν τὸν Θεὸν οὐ δύναται μὴ καὶ πάντα ἄνθρωπον ἀγαπῆσαι ὡς ἑαυτόν. *On Love*, 1.13.1 (Ceresa-Gastaldo, 54).
44. Berthold, "Christian Life and Praxis," 405. See also his analysis of the Maximian concept of equal love for all, in counterpoint with the views of Evagrius, at 407.

theocentric life implied a divine paradigm meant to be followed and embodied in concrete altruistic actions—the "economy" of love, as Blowers had it[45]—not a disembodied form of Christian devotion to God.

That said, Maximus went past the Lord's summary of Mosaic law, drawing from the one commandment of the New Testament, understanding "neighbor" to refer to any human being, not only the kinsfolk. More specifically, since God, who, rehearsing 1 Timothy 2:4, wills the salvation of all and desires to be known by all,[46] loves all people, righteous as well as sinners, to love in a godlike manner was to love all people without partiality. Consequently, echoing Matthew 5:45, 48 this time, Maximus affirmed that only one who was capable of "perfect love,"[47] "in imitation of God who loves all people equally," did the same, loving all people equally (ἐξ ἴσου)[48] Maximus returned to this statement several paragraphs later, when he exclaimed: "blessed is the human being who can love all people equally."[49] Both passages espouse the same theory of divine love realized on a human scale. To show how one advanced from theory to the practice of unrestricted compassion, Maximus both described the approach and offered a series of concrete examples.

It all began with the faith and prioritization of God, discussed in the foregoing. Pure, unpretentious, and compassionate love was ever theologically motivated, corresponding to the transformative process associated with the theocentric orientation earlier mentioned. "There is no doubt that the one who loves God loves his neighbour as well,"[50] stated Maximus in a paraphrase of 1 John 4:11. This theologically grounded love—or divine love, as we read above—was nevertheless irreducible to an idealistic cast of mind. It was not utopian. It took flesh in the deeds of a compassionate person who, as we found out in the previous section, ministered to the neighbor out of unpretentious love.[51] Service to the other revealed an altruistic cast of mind and was therefore the way compassion had to be applied.

Maximus gave various examples. For instance, one who attained pure love was necessarily charitable. Textually, "such a one cannot hold on to money but, handling it in a divine manner, gives to each one who is in need."[52] Mark once again the reference

---

45. Blowers, *Maximus the Confessor*, 255.
46. *On Love*, 1.61.6–7 (Ceresa-Gastaldo, 72).
47. τέλεια ἀγάπη. *On Love*, 1.61.4 (Ceresa-Gastaldo, 72).
48. *On Love*, 1.61.5–6 (Ceresa-Gastaldo, 72). For brief notes on this chapter, see Sherwood, introduction to *St. Maximus the Confessor*, 93.
49. Μακάριος ἄνθρωπος, ὁ πάντα ἀνθρώπων ἐξ ἴσου ἀγαπῆσαι δυνηθείς. *On Love*, 1.17.1 (Ceresa-Gastaldo, 56).
50. *On Love*, 1.23.1 (Ceresa-Gastaldo, 56). Berthold, "Christian Life and Praxis," 405, analyzed a reference to 1 John 4:20 in Maximus' second letter.
51. *On Love*, 1.27.1–2 (Ceresa-Gastaldo, 58).
52. Ὁ δὲ τοιοῦτος χρήματα τηρεῖν οὐ δύναται, ἀλλ' οἰκονομεῖ θεοπρεπῶς, ἑκάστῳ τῶν δεομένων παρέχων. *On Love*, 1.23.1–3 (Ceresa-Gastaldo, 56).

to the divine paradigm of love in the phrase "in a divine manner."[53] Divine exemplarity served for both the theory and the praxis of compassion. Theologically motivated, generosity proved one's detachment from "earthly things" and, divinely operating, constituted another step toward godlikeness. Maximus may have echoed here Clement the Alexandrian's view that the giver acted in a godlike manner toward—thus being a god to—the recipient of alms.[54] With or without Clement's inspiration, whom Maximus quoted elsewhere,[55] the aphorism under consideration reveals the practical sense of the Confessor's discourse on love as godlikeness. The charitable person acted like God, personally, directly, and compassionately. Theologically conditioned compassion demanded that almsgiving be subjectively effected, interpersonally, as part of a rapport between giver and receiver. Maximus' views challenge the current understanding of institutionalized aids, where the objective dimension supersedes the subjective one—against the backdrop of a lack of personal proximity between giver and receiver. For Maximus, compassion presupposed a neighborly engagement, a personal rapport, which meant that to minister to the other out of love was irreducible to almsgiving.

A couple of paragraphs later, the Confessor added: "The disposition of love is made manifest not only in the distribution of money, but much more in sharing the word of God and bodily service."[56] Compassionate love was holistic, addressing more than one dimension of human existence. It contributed to the well-being of another in various ways: materially, through distribution of money; personally, through bodily service or attending to another's material needs; and spiritually, through proclaiming the word of God for the other's salvation. These three forms of generosity presupposed personal immediacy. It would have not sufficed to send alms from a distance. True compassion corresponded to a holistic understanding of well-being, which could not have been reduced to its material aspect—and this understanding dictated an interpersonal engagement of the giver and the receiver. It was by way of interpersonal engagement that the recipient was offered, not simply money or other material goods, but human, heartfelt attention and salvific guidance. In mentioning the three forms of applied altruism, namely, material, personal, and spiritual, the sentence mirrors the three aspects of God's compassion, mentioned in *On Love*, 1.61, earlier discussed. Whereas divine compassion, salvific or restorative, was equally distributed to all people, and conducive to divine knowledge, human compassion replicated it by offering alms, support, and guidance. Divine love and human love were therefore mobilized by the same goal, namely, to serve humankind. Their symmetry suggests

---

53. *On Love*, 1.23.2 (Ceresa-Gastaldo, 56).
54. See Russell, *Doctrine of Deification*, 134–35.
55. For details, see Costache, "Being, Well-Being, Being for Ever," 72–73.
56. Οὐ μόνον διὰ μεταδόσεως χρημάτων ἡ διάθεσις τῆς ἀγάπης γνωρίζεται, ἀλλὰ πολλῷ μᾶλλον διὰ μεταδόσεως λόγου Θεοῦ καὶ σωματικῆς διακονίας. *On Love*, 1.26 (Ceresa-Gastaldo, 58).

that for Maximus, like for Clement before him,[57] godlikeness referred primarily to the disposition and practice of compassion.

Of further note the same chapter refers to love as a multifaceted manifestation of the soul's good or normal disposition, which reiterates the definition of love in the first sentence of the work.[58] Compassion envisaged more than the attainment of godlikeness in an ethical sense. It showed that godlikeness presupposed personal transformation as well, here iterated in terms of retrieving one's normal disposition, lost through selfish life. Normality for human beings was to be disposed to act divinely, to love all people in a "divine manner," by which they embodied love and became godlike.

The various expressions of love discussed above, together with the transformation they presupposed and which without a doubt was ascetically effected, suggest a social lesson—that a truly altruistic society cannot be established without drawing on theological paradigms and without practicing selflessness. To this matter I turn in the following, and last, section of this chapter.

Ascesis and the Compassionate Society

We have seen so far that Maximus believed in the interplay of theology, ascesis, and altruism on a personal and interpersonal level. Alongside adhering through faith to the theological presupposition that divine life was paradigmatic of human existence, one gradually became a compassionate person by way of ascetic transformation. The apex of this metamorphic process was the attainment of godlikeness—an experience whose best expression was a consistently altruistic cast of mind spelled out in practical terms by loving all people equally. It is at this juncture that we encounter the articulation of what one could aptly call a Maximian social theory, or rather the theory of a compassionate society, which I briefly consider in what follows.

Known to his contemporaries as a profound philosopher of unmatched theoretical acumen, Maximus was never interested, as Louth has pointed out,[59] in speculative elaborations—at least not in theorizations deprived of practical purpose. For him, theory and praxis went hand in hand,[60] converging, to limit this discussion to the topic of interest, in the complex area of spiritual anthropology.[61] Maximus' anthropological theorizations, as seen above, highlighted the transformative and social dimensions of the ascetic journey. For him, spiritual anthropology was existentially and socially

---

57. Russell, *Doctrine of Deification*, 134, 139–40.
58. *On Love*, 1.1.1 (Ceresa-Gastaldo, 50).
59. Louth, *Maximus the Confessor*, 33.
60. See for instance his formula, τὴν μὲν πρᾶξιν θεωρίαν ἐνεργουμένην, τὴν δὲ θεωρίαν πρᾶξιν μυσταγωγουμένην ("praxis is active theory, whereas theory is initiated praxis"). *To Thalassius*, 63.392–93, in Laga and Steel, *Maximi confessoris quaestiones ad Thalassium*, vol. 2. Retrieved via Thesaurus Linguae Graecae.
61. Cooper, "Spiritual Anthropology," 369–70. Louth, *Maximus the Confessor*, 33.

grounded. This understanding transpires through his conviction that, even though ascetically reformed, perfection could not be reached in isolation from the human family, and that godlikeness meant love for all people.

The same existential and social dimensions are obvious in Maximus' considerations about the impact of selfish drives. We have discovered above that the obstacles preventing one from reaching personal perfection, namely, the sinful passions, were not external, but within. One had to reconstruct oneself ascetically in order to retrieve normality. However, personal healing and the attainment of an ascetically gained wellbeing reverberated however beyond the personal sphere. Once the inner obstacles were demolished, they made room for peaceful, equanimous, and compassionate social interactions. We have seen already how hatred, which ruined interpersonal relations, was fostered by an evil heart.[62] It was there, in the inner recesses of the untamed heart, that human beings became wolves to one other, causing divisions, injustice, and violence.[63] In turn, the restoration of the heart to goodness was key to a better society, altruistic and compassionate.

Maximus' understanding of the social dimension of all human attitudes, deeds, and behaviors can be summarized in the conclusion that a society whose members do not overcome their base passions and selfish drives cannot become peaceful and compassionate. Crime stopping does not suffice to edify such a society. To reach that goal, its members must work toward healing the wounded abyss of their passionate, selfish hearts. They have to address the various causes of inequity and violence, of which one is hatred, the opposite of love. In the assessment of Maximus, to love one person while hating another, but also to love and hate the same person consecutively and for whatever reason, reveal the absence of "perfect love."[64] In the absence of love, it is selfishness, partiality, injustice, and discrimination that rule over a society. The antidote for these social tares remains, we have discovered in the foregoing, the ascetically conquered dispassion, which makes possible truly equanimous interactions and compassionate love between the members of that society.

I conclude my analysis by considering one more passage, which describes the parameters of an ideal society built from the starting point of a renewed member, a true Christian, able to love divinely:

> Ὁ τέλειος ἐν ἀγάπῃ καὶ εἰς ἄκρον ἀπαθείας ἐλθὼν οὐκ ἐπίσταται διαφορὰν ἰδίου καὶ ἀλλοτρίου ἢ ἰδίας καὶ ἀλλοτρίας ἢ πιστοῦ καὶ ἀπίστου ἢ δούλου καὶ ἐλευθέρου ἢ ὅλως ἄρσενος καὶ θηλείας· ἀλλ' ἀνώτερος τῆς τῶν παθῶν τυραννίδος γενόμενος καὶ εἰς τὴν μίαν φύσιν τῶν ἀνθρώπων ἀποβλεπόμενος, πάντας ἐξ ἴσου θεωρεῖ

---

62. *On Love*, 1.15.1 (Ceresa-Gastaldo, 54).

63. *To Thalassius*, proem. 270–72, in Laga and Steel, *Maximi confessoris quaestiones ad Thalassium*, vol. 1. Retrieved via Thesaurus Linguae Graecae. See also Louth, *Maximus the Confessor*, 38, for an analysis of the social dimension of the passions.

64. τελείαν τὴν ἀγάπην. *On Love*, 1.70 (Ceresa-Gastaldo, 76). Berthold "Christian Life and Praxis," 405–6, reviews a series of other passions, such as envy and grudge, social in nature.

καὶ πρὸς πάντας ἴσως διάκειται. Οὐκ ἔστι γὰρ ἐν αὐτῷ Ἕλλην καὶ Ἰουδαῖος οὐδὲ ἄρσεν καὶ θῆλυ οὐδὲ δοῦλος καὶ ἐλεύθερος, ἀλλὰ τὰ πάντα καὶ ἐν πᾶσι Χριστός.[65]

The one who is perfect in love and has arrived at the culmination of dispassion makes no difference between what is his own and another's or her own and another's, between believer and unbeliever, slave and free person or, ultimately, between male and female. Having indeed risen above the tyranny of the passions and focusing upon the one nature of the human beings, one regards all as equal and is equally disposed towards all. For such a one there is neither Greek nor Jew, neither male nor female, neither slave nor free person, but Christ is all and in all.

The passage returns to the topic of the changes undertaken by one through ascesis, culminating in dispassion and love. There is nothing here, not on a literal level anyway, about a compassionate society. Nevertheless, one can legitimately infer that Maximus was of the opinion that a compassionate society cannot be established through either laws and policies or by way of institutionalized almsgiving. A just and compassionate society begins with the change of one's heart, being therefore founded upon people who, corresponding to the experience described by the passage of interest, undergo the transformation made possible by the new, theocentric outlook of life. A just and compassionate society begins with the edification of just and compassionate human beings who aspire to attain the holiness of life.

The fact of the matter is that the chapter under consideration surmises its discourse from the vantage point of achieved holiness (similarly discussed in a celebrated context within the Maximian *Book of Difficulties*[66]), being no longer about the process of one's transformation. It shows how an already transformed person, dispassionate and altruistic,[67] a saint by all intents and purposes, looks at people and engages them. The phraseology of "loving all equally" is absent, but the message is the same, being signified by the notions of all people's equality and one's equal disposition toward all.[68] One who is perfect in dispassion sees clearly, namely, that all people are equal, and acts appropriately, treating all by the same, equanimous disposition. In counterpoint to the divisions and violence discussed in the prologue of *To Thalassius*, the holy person of, literally, both genders,[69] contemplates all people as being of one nature[70] and

---

65. *On Love*, 2.30 (Ceresa-Gastaldo, 106). For similar examples, see Louth, *Maximus the Confessor*, 38–39.

66. *Difficulty* 41, in *Maximos the Confessor*, 102–21. On the perspective of holy life as instrumental for the spiritual anthropology of *Difficulty* 41, see Costache, "Mapping Reality," 378, 383–84; also, Costache, "Living Above Gender," esp. 274–76, 278–80, 283–86.

67. See εἰς ἄκρον ἀπαθείας ἐλθών and τέλειος ἐν ἀγάπῃ. *On Love*, 2.30.1 (Ceresa-Gastaldo, 106).

68. See πάντας ἐξ ἴσου θεωρεῖ καὶ πρὸς πάντας ἴσως διάκειται. *On Love*, 2.30.4 (Ceresa-Gastaldo, 106).

69. See ἰδίου/ἰδίας and ἀλλοτρίου/ἀλλοτρίας. *On Love*, 2.30.2 (Ceresa-Gastaldo, 106).

70. See τὴν μίαν φύσιν τῶν ἀνθρώπων ἀποβλεπόμενος. *On Love*, 2.30.4–5 (Ceresa-Gastaldo, 106).

therefore as belonging to one human family. There is no room in the heart of a holy person for gender discrimination, racial prejudice, social injustice, or religious bias. Such a person loves all equally, recognizing the Lord's mark within all.

Perhaps not amounting to a fully-fledged social theory, nevertheless Maximus proposed in *Chapters on Love* the concrete ideal of an ascetically remade, godlike, and compassionate humanity embodied in the lives of the saints. He considered the saints, particularly their ascetic undertakings toward inner transformation, a paradigm to be observed, emulated, and replicated throughout humankind's experience, including socially. Aptly, Louth has summarized Maximus' message in the phrase "asceticism for all."[71] Above we have discovered, indeed, that ascetic endeavours represented for the Confessor the privileged way to transform and renew one's inner disposition, say, from hatred to love, and so contribute to the establishment of a peaceful, just, and compassionate society, in likeness to God and by emulating the saints who love all people equally. In the current notion, well-being is secured by way of materialistic, acquisitive, and selfish drives. At the opposite end of the spectrum, the social theory inferred from the wisdom of Maximus presupposes that, since well-being is interpersonal in nature, it is impossible without healing the self and, more so, without the self's ascetic or ecstatic exertion—compassionately, altruistically.

Bibliography

Allen, Pauline, and Bronwen Neil. *The Oxford Handbook of Maximus the Confessor*. Oxford: Oxford University Press, 2015.
Berthold, George. "Christian Life and Praxis: The *Centuries on Love*." In Allen and Neil, *Oxford Handbook of Maximus the Confessor*, 397–413.
Blowers, Paul M. *Maximus the Confessor: Jesus Christ and the Transfiguration of the World*. Christian Theology in Context. Oxford: Oxford University Press, 2016.
Ceresa-Gastaldo, Aldo, ed. *Massimo Confessore: Capitoli sulla carità*. Verba Seniorum 3. Rome: Editrice Studium, 1963.
Constas, Nicholas, ed. and trans. *Maximos the Confessor: On Difficulties in the Church Fathers—The Ambigua*. Vol. 2. Dumbarton Oaks Medieval Library 29. Cambridge: Harvard University Press, 2014.
Costache, Doru. "Being, Well-Being, Being for Ever: Creation's Existential Trajectory in Patristic Tradition." In Costache et al., *Well-Being, Personal Wholeness and the Social Fabric*, 55–87.
———. "Gender, Marriage, and Holiness in *Amb.Io.* 10 and 41." In *Men and Women in the Early Christian Centuries*, edited by Wendy Mayer and Ian J. Elmer, 351–71. Early Christian Studies 18. Strathfield, Australia: St. Paul's, 2014.
———. "Living Above Gender: Insights from Saint Maximus the Confessor." *Journal of Early Christian Studies* 21 (2013) 261–90.
———. "Mapping Reality within the Experience of Holiness." In Allen and Neil, *Oxford Handbook of Maximus the Confessor*, 378–96.

---

71. Louth, *Maximus the Confessor*, 34–35.

———. "The Transdisciplinary Carats of Patristic Byzantine Tradition." In *Transdisciplinary Education, Philosophy, and Applications*, edited by Basarab Nicolescu and Atila Ertas, 149–65. N.p.: TheAtlas, 2014.

Costache, Doru, et al., eds. *Well-Being, Personal Wholeness and the Social Fabric*. Newcastle upon Tyne: Cambridge Scholars, 2017.

Guillaumont, A., and C. Guillaumont. *Évagre le Pontique: Traité pratique ou le moine*. Vol. 2. Sources chrétiennes 171. Paris: Cerf, 1971.

Harmless, William. *Desert Christians: An Introduction to the Literature of Early Monasticism*. Oxford: Oxford University Press, 2004.

Harrison, James. R. "Introducing Well-Being, Personal Wholeness and the Australian Social Fabric: Ancient and Modern Perspectives." In Costache et al., *Well-Being, Personal Wholeness and the Social Fabric*, 2–30.

Jankowiak, Marek, and Phil Booth. "A New Date-List of the Works of Maximus the Confessor." In Allen and Neil, *Oxford Handbook of Maximus the Confessor*, 19–83.

Laga, Carla, and Carlos Steel. *Maximi confessoris quaestiones ad Thalassium*. 2 vols. Corpus Christianorum Series Graeca 7, 22. Turnhout, Belgium: Brepols, 1980–90.

Louth, Andrew. "The Literature of the Monastic Movement." In *The Cambridge History of Early Christian Literature*, edited by Frances Young et al., 373–81. Cambridge: Cambridge University Press, 2004.

———. *Maximus the Confessor*. London: Routledge, 1996.

Mayer, Wendy. "Australia's Moral Compass and Societal Well-Being." In Costache et al., *Well-Being, Personal Wholeness and the Social Fabric*, 110–31.

Neil, Bronwen. "'The Blessed Passion of Holy Love': Maximus the Confessor's Spiritual Psychology." *Australian eJournal of Theology* 2 (2004) 1–7.

Ramelli, Ilaria L. E. "Evagrius Ponticus, the Origenian Ascetic (and Not the Origenistic 'Heretic')." In *Orthodox Monasticism Past and Present*, edited by John A. McGuckin, 159–224. Piscataway, NJ: Gorgias, 2015.

Russell, Norman. *The Doctrine of Deification in the Greek Patristic Tradition*. New York: Oxford University Press, 2004.

Sherwood, Polycarp. *An Annotated Date-List of the Works of Maximus the Confessor*. Rome: Herder, 1952.

———. Introduction to *St. Maximus the Confessor: The Ascetic Life; The Four Centuries on Charity*, translated by Polycarp Sherwood, 3–102. Westminster, MD: Newman, 1955.

Sinkewicz, Robert E. *Evagrius of Pontus: The Greek Ascetic Corpus*. Oxford Early Christian Studies. Oxford: Oxford University Press, 2003.

7

A Christology of Human Flourishing
Justice and Divine Participation

PETER R. LAUGHLIN

Introduction

IN her paper presented to the 8th Nordic Patristic Conference in Sweden, Anna Marie Aagaard draws our attention to the marble font in the basilica of the Grottaferata Abbey, south of Rome.[1] The font is decorated with a human figure diving into water and just above another person is pulling a fish out of the water on a rod. A simple image but as Aagaard notes, if we know the purpose of the font within the Christian narrative, we see a person diving into the waters of baptism and being lifted out as a fish. "Set in the universe of the Christian Faith," she writes, "the font testifies to the importance of baptism: a person becomes new, is saved, is transformed—clad in the new reality of life, [that is] Christ, symbolised by the fish."[2] A simple image it may be, but nonetheless it captures the heart of a flourishing life within the Christian world-view. What it strongly suggests is that the fulfillment of life is not found in the making of one's self, the striving after self-actualization or the all too temporary achievements of leisure, comfort or prosperity. Rather it offers instead an invitation to cease wrestling with the swirling currents of the world and simply receive the gift that the font depicts: the transformative power that comes from participating in the divine life of Christ.

But how does one participate in the "divine life" of Christ? And perhaps the more obvious question is how does that lead to a sense of human flourishing? The answer is not immediately clear, particularly since Jesus' own life could hardly be described as

---

1. Aagaard, "My Eyes Have Seen," 303.
2. Aagaard, "My Eyes Have Seen," 303.

"flourishing." Nailed to a Roman cross, rejected by his nation and crying out his feelings of abandonment from the very God he served, one could be forgiven for coming to the opposite conclusion. Surely, we might ask, a flourishing life—by hope, if not by definition, is more than this? Moreover, in the Gospels Jesus seems to demand his disciples seek to emulate him. He tells them to deny themselves, to give up their possessions, and to love their enemies (Matt 19:21; cf. 5:43–48). They are to take up their own cross to follow him, to be like wheat that falls to the ground and dies and to devote themselves fully to sacrificial love and discipleship (Luke 9:23; John 12:24; 15:13). As Bonhoeffer famously said, "When Jesus calls a man he bids him come and die."[3] On the surface, it is hard to see how this leads to a flourishing life! Connect Jesus' call with the later Christian cult of martyrdom, the asceticism of the monks and the strict morality that denies the pursuit of unfettered pleasure and one could well argue that *flourishing* is not of particular interest to the Christian faith. Indeed, Jesus appears to be more concerned with his follower's *faithfulness* than he was with their flourishing.[4]

This criticism would be valid if a flourishing life is merely defined by our external circumstances, our everyday experiences and expectations of desires met. However, paradoxically, those who follow the way of Jesus—even if such a way includes experiences of suffering and hardship, nevertheless discover along that way the remarkable experience of peace, rest and joy that such a pursuit entails. For far from denying life, an encounter with Jesus is an invitation into the reign of God that is at once both transformative and life-giving. The promise of abundant life that stands as a key element of Jesus' teaching (John 10:10) is not undone by our experiences of the present life, nor is it limited to some future hope beyond this world. On the contrary, the Christian faith contends that it constitutes a very present reality, a reality that is fulfilled in the believer through union with the Spirit of the risen Christ.

Given the present interest in what constitutes true human flourishing this is a theme that is worth exploring and we will do so in two parts. The first part examines how Christ functions as the foundation of human flourishing, particularly in relation to the theme of justice; and the second asks what it means to be united with Christ and to share in his divine image.

Christ as the Foundation of Human Flourishing

An emphasis on being transformed into the image and likeness of Christ as depicted by the font invites us to consider just how the person of Jesus Christ relates to the notion of human flourishing. But to begin with we need to reflect on the underlying relationship between Christ and creation. For a Christology of human flourishing is

---

3. Bonhoeffer, *Cost of Discipleship*, 89.
4. Pope, "Jesus Christ and Human Flourishing," 1.

always going to find its grounds in the intersection between the incarnate son and the created human life.

In the New Testament it is Christ who mediates creation. Nothing comes into being apart from Christ. We see this in the prologue to the Gospel of John: "Through him all things were made; without him nothing was made that has been made" (John 1:3). And again, in the early hymn of Colossians 1, "For by him all things were created: things in heaven and on earth, visible and invisible, whether thrones or powers or rulers or authorities; all things were created by him and for him" (Col 1:16). "As the one through whom the world was made, Christ (or the Logos, or the Son) now provides the 'blueprint' for creation. . . . Indeed, Christ is the image of God, 'the exact representation' of God's very being, in which human beings are also created (Gen 1:27; 1 Cor 15:49; 2 Cor 4:4; Col 1:15; 3:10)."[5] And it is this creation of humanity in the image of God and therefore in the image of Christ that provides the necessary grounding for a flourishing life. Such a creation is, according to Genesis 1, "very good" (1:31). And despite all that might have followed in the human story—whether injustice, unrestrained violence, a lack of mercy, the palpable absence of love—that fundamental designation has never been withdrawn.[6] The human life has value, worth and the possibility of well-being precisely because God created us through Christ to live a life that reflects, however imperfectly, the divine image.

The potential value of bearing the divine image to human flourishing was made clear by the early church fathers. Writing in the second century, Tatian in his *Address to the Greeks* was bold enough to contend that bearing the divine image separates humanity out from the rest of creation because it allows us to advance "far beyond mere humanity—to God himself."[7] It is not easy to fathom how Tatian meant this to be understood—much less achieved, but it does suggest that he saw the possibility for humanity to experience a life that is not limited to its physical existence. Perhaps the last of the great Cappadocians, Gregory of Nyssa, offers us a clue to Tatian's vision when he comments that being made in the image of God is the same as to say that he made human nature participant in all good. Gregory writes, "For if the Deity is the fullness of good, and this is his image, then the image finds its resemblance to the archetype in being filled with all good."[8] The import of this lies in the fundamental ability of the image bearer to experience the Deity's "fullness of good." That is, humanity has the potential to participate in the very life of God, for the nature of God is, above all, good (Ps 107:1; Matt 19:16–17).

But however we understand it, participating in God's life in the here and now does not overcome the inevitable fact that human life is mortal and finite. The Christian tradition is overwhelmingly adamant of a future hope in which death is finally

---

5. Thompson, "Alpha and Omega," 4.
6. Tugwell, *Beatitudes*, 11.
7. Tatian, *Against the Greeks* 15:1–3; ANF 2:138.
8. *On the Making of Man* 16.10; NPNF2 5:405.

undone (Rev 20:14) but in the mean time we have to deal with the ever present reality that death comes to us all. And as such, the concept of a flourishing life must always be held in tension with the final reality of death. This tension is what makes the life of Christ so important to any Christian notion of human flourishing. For the incarnate Son reveals in his own life, suffering and even in his death, that the abundant life is not offered as an escape from the evils of the world but as a reality to be grasped *from within the midst* of life's uncertainties and challenges. Flourishing is not, in other words, the *absence* of suffering and trials but the experience of the divine life even while in their very midst.

This is why human flourishing is not lost in the face of death but becomes ever richer as our awareness of the value of life increases. Indeed, Gary Thomas reminds us that "virtually every classic [Christian] writer holds up the remembrance of death as an essential spiritual discipline."[9] Why is this the case? For when viewed through the right lens, the reality and finality of death functions to heighten our experience of life in the present. Its very unexpectedness, that it could come knocking at any time, should encourage us to take a second look at how we choose to live our lives today. Not that death becomes our sole focus but that we view it with the right perspective—as an antidote to our obsession with the trivial matters of life. As the writer to Ecclesiastes puts it, "Death is the destiny of every man; the living should take this to heart" (7:2).[10]

A flourishing life is therefore not found by denying the realities of mortal life but from experiencing the goodness of God in the midst of its shortcomings. But how is such goodness to be experienced? The first point to note is that if Christ is the agent of the old creation then Christ also mediates the new creation. "Not only were all things created *through* him, but all things were created *for* him (Col 1:16). The world's end—what it is made for, and where its true destiny lies—can be found in Christ."[11] And the New Testament understands that end primarily in terms of how the world's origins are made anew. Phrases such as new creation, new birth, new life; eternal life and renewal in the image of the creator abound (e.g., John 3:3; 17:3; 2 Cor 5:17). The imagery is clear. What was made then is now made anew, it is restored, it is a new beginning, the old has gone and the new has come. And with that new creation comes a renewed opportunity to experience the goodness of God. The image of God that was marred in humanity by the fall is restored by the fresh work of the Spirit of Christ. Ezekiel foreshadowed this when he wrote that God would "give you a new heart, and a new spirit I will put within you" (36:26) and Jesus spoke of its fulfillment to Nicodemus when he said that we must be born of the Spirit (John 3:5–6). This new birth comes about in and through Christ. There is no new life without Christ, there is,

---

9. Thomas, *Thirsting for God*, 175.

10. As the nineteenth-century Scottish evangelist Henry Drummond commented: "The man who is really concerned to live well must possess himself continually of the thought that he is not to live long." Drummond, *Greatest Thing in the World*, 250; quoted by Thomas, *Thirsting for God*, 175.

11. Thompson, "Alpha and Omega," 5.

to paraphrase the Fourth Evangelist, no possibility of flourishing fruit without deep abiding (John 15:5). Thus for the New Testament, human flourishing has both its beginning and end in Christ.

Given, then, that the location of human flourishing is found in the Christ-life, how do we participate in it? A key aspect is sharing in Christ's kingdom ministry. The human life will flourish inasmuch as we participate in Christ's ministry to bring redemption and healing to all those in need. Much could be said on this point but I have chosen by way of illustration the rubric of justice since it is a significant theme of this volume.

Flourishing through Participation in God's Goodness

The biblical concept of justice is fundamentally grounded in the character of God and is an outworking of love.[12] At its heart is the notion of equity for everyone. The poor, the fatherless and the widow are cared for, and the evil and wicked receive what is their due (Isa 10:1–2). This sense is perhaps nowhere better described than in Psalm 146 where the faithfulness of God is revealed through such compassionate acts of justice:

> He upholds the cause of the oppressed
>   and gives food to the hungry.
> The LORD sets prisoners free,
>   the LORD gives sight to the blind,
> the LORD lifts up those who are bowed down,
>   the LORD loves the righteous.
> The LORD watches over the alien and sustains the fatherless and the widow,
> but he frustrates the ways of the wicked (vv. 7–9).

The psalmist declares that God's covenant faithfulness is revealed precisely through divine acts of *restorative* justice. God acts to right what was wrong, to restore the captive, the blind and the downcast so that they can experience the fullness of life. This is who God is. It is how God chooses to make God's name known (Jer 9:23–24; 22:15–17).[13] Thus Christopher Marshall writes:

> This justice is known, not primarily through philosophical speculation, but through observing God's *actions* to liberate the oppressed, and through heeding God's *word* in the Law and the Prophets to protect and care for the weak. This means that our knowledge of justice springs ultimately from our

---

12. Keller, *Generous Justice*, 163.
13. While the Hebrew *mishpat*, which is commonly translated justice, can also mean "judgment" or "verdict" (as in the just penalty due to evil acts), it primarily has this restorative sense. See Hays, "Sell Everything You Have," 45.

knowledge of God, and that there can be no true knowledge of God without appreciation of God's own unfailing dedication to justice.[14]

What is of interest is that the prophets also confirm that participating in God's justice for others also becomes a major way in which we can experience such flourishing life for ourselves. In Isaiah we see that those who seek justice and defend the cause of the fatherless and plead the case of the widow will not only have their sins cleansed but they will also eat the best of the land (Isa 1:17–19). There is a direct connection between engaging in acts of justice and mercy and God's blessing.

The corollary, of course, is that those who do not engage in such acts stand under judgment. Consider Jeremiah 5:27–29:

> "Like cages full of birds, their houses are full of deceit;
> they have become rich and powerful and have grown fat and sleek.
> Their evil deeds have no limit; they do not plead the case of the fatherless to win it,
> they do not defend the rights of the poor.
> Should I not punish them for this?" declares the LORD.

Thus, a self-focused life, which on the outside looks like a flourishing life ("fat and sleek"), is flourishing in appearance only. Such a heart is bound and destined for judgment. But God delights in those who "love justice" as God does (Isa 61:8) and who walk humbly in its ways (Mic 6:8). Bringing justice to the other is to be in right relationship with God.

This is dramatically seen in the ministry of Jesus. Drawing on Isaiah 61 for his own vocation (Luke 4:18) the ground for Jesus' ministry is given as the ushering in of justice for those who need it most—the poor, the prisoner, the blind and the oppressed. This is why the coming of the kingdom is "good news" (Mark 1:14) for its arrival defeats evil in all its forms. Arising from that defeat is the promise of new life, well foreshadowed by the dramatic miracles that restore health, sight, mobility and the like to those who receive it. And so through the coming of the kingdom, God is working to bring wholeness, healing, justice, mercy and well-being to all of creation.

At the heart of all this activity lies, of course, love. What Jesus demonstrated was that true human flourishing lies in authentic and self-giving love.[15] Just as the Son of man came not to be served but to serve and to give his life as a ransom for many (Mark 10:45), so too our experience of the flourishing life is found in the sacrificial service of others. Not that the road is easy. While the kingdom brings life, its demands are heavy: one must renounce everything because no one can serve two masters (Matt 6:24; Luke 16:13). The rich young ruler is called to sell all that he had (Mark 10:21); family must be forsaken and those who want to follow Jesus are warned not to look back (Luke

---

14. Marshall, *Little Book of Biblical Justice*, 25; emphasis original. As quoted in Belousek, *Atonement, Justice, and Peace*, 464.

15. Pope, "Jesus Christ and Human Flourishing," 2.

9:59–62). "This is not an easy way: the gate to a flourishing life is narrow, and the way is hard because it is counter-intuitive," writes Marianne Thompson. "So much of human life, from birth to death, is about getting, attaining, building, securing: but Jesus speaks of another way of life that is about letting go, losing, about trusting and relinquishing what one has, and what one is, to God. This is what is meant by 'storing up treasure' for oneself where 'neither moth or rust consume' (Matt 6:20)."[16]

But Jesus did not refuse to walk the same road himself. Indeed, the flourishing life offered by the kingdom way is made possible precisely because of the cross:

> [The] Christian faith asserts that God is never more truly God than he is in the dying of Jesus. In the cross, as the gospel writers put it, the veil of the temple is torn in two and God stands revealed. God's *justice* also stands revealed (Rom 1:16–17; 3:20). The cross shows that God's justice is a peace-making justice (Rom 5:1), a reconciling, restoring and forgiving justice. The God who is made climactically known in the cross of Christ is a God who secures justice for both the victims and perpetrators of evil by pouring out his own life in suffering love to free them from their predicament and restore them to relationship with himself and with each other.[17]

A flourishing life is therefore secured through participating in the justice worked out on the cross. It is found in aligning oneself with God's teleological purposes, of helping to bring the world into fulfilling its good design.

All this means that an appreciation of human flourishing viewed through the lens of biblical justice finds its grounding in the restoration of creation. In particular the restoration of divine-human and inter-human relationships based in the justice of God revealed through the cross. Hence biblical justice is *comprehensively relational*, which means the desire for human flourishing must also be re-grounded in the transformation of relationships. Rightly understood then, justice is not about getting "what I deserve" as it is so often reduced to in its secular pursuit, but about the restoration of relationship between the Creator and creation and between creation and itself. Hence, to be a person who understands and experiences flourishing is to be a person who finds their "role in the building of shalom, the re-webbing of God, humanity, and all creation in justice, harmony, fulfillment, and delight."[18] This "re-webbing" is ultimately a rebuilding of creation, a return to the world as God intended it to be. When we release and empower others out of their situations of injustice, whether poverty, oppression, marginalization and the like, we enable a transformation that leads to a re-grounding of flourishing along biblical lines—both for them and for us.

But this is not all that can be said about participating in divine goodness, for when engaged in the "re-webbing" of creation people are also transformed in such

---

16. Thompson, "Alpha and Omega," 15.
17. Marshall, "Grounding Justice in Reality," 87.
18. Wytsma with Jacobsen, *Pursuing Justice*, 129.

a way as to grow accustomed to, and take part in, what Anna Marie Aagaard calls "a new Christ-formed life." This is more than a rescuing from what is wrong in the world into a newness of life, but a genuine incorporation into divine life itself. The early Christians understood what this entailed and it is to this that we must now turn.

Theosis as the Means to True Human Flourishing

To talk about participating in the divine life or being "united with Christ" is to explore what the patristics called *theosis* or deification. At its heart, *theosis* is best understood as a transformative union with Christ, made possible by God's grace and power in the life of the cooperative believer. In 2 Peter 1:4, the apostle exhorts the believer to "participate in the divine nature" in order that they might overcome the "corruption in the world." But for the creature to participate in the divine nature it must do so by way of Christ, the God-man who made possible such a participation in the first place. In *Against Heresies*, Irenaeus highlights the critical nature of the incarnation in that it is only because "God the Logos became what we are . . . that we may become what he himself is."[19] This was rephrased later by Athanasius, who said, "The Word of God Himself . . . assumed humanity that we might become God. He manifested Himself by means of a body in order that we might perceive the mind of the unseen Father. He endured shame from men that we might inherit immortality."[20] Summarizing the Patristic work on *theosis*, Bishop Alfeyev noted at the ANZATS Conference in 2004, "For Athanasius, as for all the Fathers of the age of the Ecumenical Councils, the Incarnation of the Word of God is the sole basis of man's deification."[21] Such an emphasis was maintained right through the scholastic period as well. Aquinas, for example, writes that the incarnation bestows on us "full participation of the Divinity, which is the true bliss of [humanity] and end of human life."[22] He goes on to quote one of Augustine's sermons, where he states that "God was made man, that man might be made God."[23] In other words, the kenosis of Christ was the means chosen by God to achieve the *theosis* of humanity.

To my mind this is why the criticism that *theosis* fundamentally obscures the distinction between the creator and creature fails to really drive home.[24] *Theosis* does not require the understanding that we literally "become God, or are absorbed into God, or are equal with God."[25] Rather, it is consistent with important distinctions that

---

19. *Against Heresies* 5, pref.: ANF 1:526.

20. Athanasius, *On the Incarnation of the Word*, 54, http://www.ccel.org/ccel/athanasius/incarnation.ix.html.

21. Alfeyev, "Deification of Man," 110–11.

22. Aquinas, *Summa Theologiae*, http://www.ccel.org/ccel/quinas/summa.TP_Q1_A2.html.

23. Aquinas, *Summa Theologiae*, http://www.ccel.org/ccel/quinas/summa.TP_Q1_A2.html.

24. See Pelikan, *Christian Tradition*, 1:155, 345.

25. Austin, "Doctrine of Theosis," 175.

exist between human beings and God. We are creatures, God is the Creator. We are finite, God is infinite. We cannot apprehend God on our own, we can only come to God through Christ. *Theosis* should therefore always be understood as a participation in Christ rather than an unsanctioned or unceremonious grasping of divinity by the creature itself. And importantly, it is a participation that results in a progressively transformational union in which the believer, as in the font's iconography, becomes a fish, that is, Christ-like.

In his edited book *Partakers of the Divine Nature*, Michael Christensen discusses deification in three categories: the promise, process and the problem of *theosis*.[26] The promise of *theosis* is a way of understanding the promise of salvation in its fullness. Biblical texts such as Second Peter 1:4, Romans 8:29 and Second Corinthians 3:18 all speak to the Christian hope that believers are being transformed into the image and likeness of Christ. There is then, in some sense, a work of God through the Spirit that brings the believer into ontological conformity with God. And this is the ultimate *telos* of humanity, what it means to truly "flourish." How that works, or the process of *theosis*, is the great question, and Augustine once again demonstrated his wisdom when he remarked, "That he should make men gods is to be understood in divine silence."[27] But speculation is what theologians do best, and not all church fathers were of the same mind as Augustine. According to Christensen, Origen understood the process of *theosis* as one in which the soul is educated, one's nature is transformed and the person is united with God. This only occurs, again, because of the incarnation, the prior descent of divinity so that "human and divine [can] be woven together, so that by prolonged fellowship with divinity, human nature might become divine." This is a progressive process until the soul is perfected, time becomes no more and God is found to be all in all.[28] For his part, Cyril of Alexandria emphasized how the sacraments function as the locus of participation: "Just as if someone were to entwine two pieces of wax together and melt them with a fire, so that both are made one, so too through participation in the Body of Christ and in His Precious Blood, He is united in us and we too in Him."[29]

Many other images, of course, are used in the Eastern and Western traditions to represent deification. Christensen summarizes some of them as follows: "Likeness to God as far as possible, climbing the ladder of divine ascent, crossing the chasm that divides, learning to fly, putting on the robe, interweaving threads of God and humanity, interpenetration . . . the polished human mirror reflecting its divine source, the red-hot iron receiving its heat from the divine fire, [and] fusion into a new

---

26. Christensen and Wittung, *Partakers of the Divine Nature*.
27. Keating, *Deification and Grace*, 113.
28. Christensen and Wittung, *Partakers of the Divine Nature*, 25–26.
29. *Commentary on John*, 10,2 on John 15:1. As quoted by Christensen and Wittung, *Partakers of the Divine Nature*, 27.

Divine-Humanity."[30] What this highlights for us is that whatever different nuances and images were used, there was nonetheless common agreement that "human beings are creatures called in some way, to become god."[31]

But herein lies the real problem of *theosis*. And that is, it is all well and good to describe it as a union between the believer and Christ, of divinity and humanity intertwining and of becoming what we were made to be. But if *theosis* is only a future hope, awaiting some final consummation, then it remains irrelevant to the idea of a flourishing life in the here and now. The question is, can *theosis* be understood to not only to await an eschatological fulfillment, but to invite a participation in the nature of God as part of the human experience in the here and now? I believe we *can* understand it in this way and two avenues of reflection are suggestive.

First, in the Letter to the Colossians we read that "all the fullness of God dwells" in Jesus, who is the image of the invisible God (Col 1:15). As we've seen, it is through this one that the world, in all its fullness, is created. Human beings live in this "fullness" of the world because they are created through Christ. But Colossians, like other Pauline letters, also uses the language of being "in Christ" to characterize those who, through faith and baptism into his death and resurrection, are joined to him and are thus "being renewed in knowledge according to the image of their creator" (Col 3:10). This is the fullness that Christ brings into the world in the form of restoration and recreation, and in which those in Christ participate. Hence Robert Rakestraw suggests that *theosis* can be thought of as "the restoration and reintegration of the 'image' or 'likeness' of God, seriously distorted by the fall, in the children of God."[32] This is more than the Protestant understanding of sanctification but a very real impartation of the divine life to the whole human being, which includes the potential for ontological sharing in the life of God. And most importantly, this is something that happens in the world *now*, the image is restored as the praxis of the kingdom that Jesus revealed takes shape in and through the people of God. Acts of justice and mercy, for example, function to restore, at least in part, that image to its rightful state. By no means is the process complete but it is at least on the way.

Second, participation in the divine entails what it means to live "in Christ." This strikingly Pauline term is not merely a belief about Christ, but an experience understood to be that of the risen and living Christ.[33] Somehow the abundance of life comes through participating in him, of sharing in his death and resurrection, and joining the community of all those bound to him through faith. As an experience of life there are a number of ways to describe it, not least the first three fruits of the Spirit: "love, joy and peace." Such gifts come from the fullness of God, from God's Spirit; they are embodied in practices and manifested in the way in which one lives. Thus being in

---

30. Christensen and Wittung, *Partakers of the Divine Nature*, 27.
31. Christensen and Wittung, *Partakers of the Divine Nature*, 27.
32. Rakestraw, "Becoming Like God," 261.
33. Dunn, *Theology of Paul the Apostle*, 390–412.

Christ, to participate in him, is to live empowered by the Spirit in faith, hope and love. Love, in particular, lies behind, in and ahead of the "abundant life." As we saw earlier, the way of Jesus reveals that true human flourishing lies in authentic and healthy love and his story is the definitive revelation of the love that lies at the center of every truly flourishing human life. Drawing from Maximus the Confessor, Christopher Beeley comments that "divine love alone can unify human beings beyond the motivation of mere self-love and enlightened self-interest. Divine love is the most godlike and mysterious thing we can experience; it is the power that elevates human beings to divinization."[34] One could perhaps then summarize then the source of all human flourishing in the words of the Gospel of John: "God so loved the world, that he gave his only Son" (John 3:16). The abundant life is found in receiving, participating in, and being united with, the gift of the Son.

To conclude, and to bring ourselves full circle back to the font at the Grottaferata abbey, I refer once more to Irenaeus' *Against Heresies* who notes that the experience of God's fullness begins with baptism, the bath of rebirth, whereby we receive the life-giving Spirit of God that enables us to live God's life and so to ascend to God.[35] Being thus transformed into "fish," the living presence of Christ, by the Spirit, pervades the daily lives of the people of God. And it is that presence I suggest that is both the hallmark and catalyst for human flourishing.

Bibliography

Aagaard, Anna Marie. "My Eyes Have Seen Your Salvation: On Likeness to God and Deification in Patristic Theology." *Religion & Theology* 17 (2010) 302–28.

Alfeyev, Bishop Hilarion. "The Deification of Man in Eastern Patristic Tradition (with Special Reference to Gregory Nazianzen, Symeon the New Theologian and Gregory Palamas)." *Colloquium* 36 (2004) 109–22.

Austin, Michael W. "The Doctrine of Theosis: A Transformational Union with Christ." *Journal of Spiritual Formation & Soul Care* 8 (2015) 172–86.

Beeley, Christopher A. "Christ and Human Flourishing in Patristic Theology." Christ and Human Flourishing. Yale Center for Faith & Culture, 2014. http://faith.yale.edu/sites/default/files/beeley_christ_and_human_flourishing_in_patristic_theology_-_final.pdf.

Belousek, Darrin W. Snyder. *Atonement, Justice, and Peace: The Message of the Cross and the Mission of the Church*. Grand Rapids: Eerdmans, 2012.

Bonhoeffer, Dietrich. *The Cost of Discipleship*. Translated by R. H. Fuller. New York: SCM, 1959.

Christensen, Michael J., and Jeffrey A. Wittung, eds. *Partakers of the Divine Nature: The History and Development of Deification in the Christian Traditions*. Grand Rapids: Baker Academic, 2007.

Dunn, James D. G. *The Theology of Paul the Apostle*. London: T. & T. Clark, 1998.

---

34. Ep. 2.393B. Quoted in Beeley, "Christ and Human Flourishing in Patristic Theology," 17.
35. *Against Heresies*, 3.17,1.

Hays, Daniel J. "'Sell Everything You Have and Give to the Poor': The Old Testament Prophetic Theme of Justice as the Connecting Motif of Luke 18:1—19:10." *Journal of the Evangelical Theological Society* 55 (2012) 43–63.

Keating, Daniel A. *Deification and Grace*. Naples: Sapientia, 2007.

Keller, Timothy. *Generous Justice: How God's Grace Makes Us Just*. London: Hodder & Stoughton, 2010.

Marshall, Christopher D. "Grounding Justice in Reality: Theological Reflections on Overcoming Violence in the Criminal Justice System." In *Overcoming Violence in New Zealand*, edited by J. Roberts, 81–95. Wellington: Philip Garside, 2002.

———. *The Little Book of Biblical Justice: A Fresh Approach to the Bible's Teaching on Justice*. Intercourse: Good Books, 2005.

Pope, Stephen J. "Jesus Christ and Human Flourishing: An Incarnational Perspective." Christ and Human Flourishing. Yale Center for Faith & Culture, 2014. https://faith.yale.edu/sites/default/files/pope_christ_and_flourishing.pdf.

Rakestraw, Robert V. "Becoming Like God: An Evangelical Doctrine of Theosis." *Journal for the Evangelical Theological Society* 40 (1997) 257–69.

Thomas, Gary L. *Thirsting for God: Spiritual Refreshment for the Sacred Journey*. Eugene, OR: Harvest House, 2011.

Thompson, Marianne Meye. "Alpha and Omega—and Everything in Between." Christ and Human Flourishing. Yale Center for Faith & Culture, 2014. https://faith.yale.edu/sites/default/files/thompson_alpha_and_omega.pdf.

Wytsma, Ken. *Pursuing Justice: The Call to Live & Die for Bigger Things*. With D. R. Jacobsen. Nashville: Nelson, 2013.

8

God Is Love, God Is Just, God Is Merciful—but Is God Tolerant?

The Relationship of Divine Love, Justice, and Mercy from a Wesleyan Perspective

DAVID B. MCEWAN

Introduction

In the popular media there are constant outcries against the perceived lenient sentences handed out to criminals or the benefits being given to refugees. There is also the strident demand for justice with regard to various human rights that are perceived to be denied; for example, the rejection of same-sex marriage is described as a denial of natural justice between two people who genuinely love each other.

The Christian tradition has a long heritage of dealing with the relationship of justice and mercy in terms of the God-human relationship. This paper is particularly focused on the Wesleyan theological tradition, where the essential nature of God is understood primarily as love and from this flow all other aspects of his character and actions. John Wesley maintained that divine justice provided the foundation for understanding the divine mercy, because God's holy nature means that there are consequences for words, thoughts, motives and actions that harm relationships. God has upheld justice through the death of his Son on the cross and this anticipates full justice for his creation. We are called to have confidence in both the divine justice and the divine mercy, based on the divine love and its incarnation in Jesus Christ. The church is called to participate in being merciful to those who need it and yet, at the same time, expressing this mercy in the context of God's justice demonstrated at the cross.

In much of the current debate it appears that love and mercy are intimately linked, while justice has become the "problem child." Seeing the world through the lens of love and relationships has its dangers, particularly if we value mercy over justice in the name of love. This has a particular application when considering current social issues and the promotion of "tolerance" as a supreme human virtue in and of itself. When you tie love, relationships and mercy so intimately, the danger is that you cease to value truth. This paper seeks to show that ignoring or watering down the reality of divine justice in order to exalt a particular perspective on love and mercy actually undermines these two qualities and ultimately damages all our relationships.

Tolerance, Truth, and Love

In countries like Australia, tolerance carries a wide range of meanings. At one time it simply indicated the willingness to accept that a range of views existed on many matters and that people needed to treat one another with respect and patience while discussing them. When facts and data were involved, most people accepted that some viewpoints were closer to the objective truth of the matter than others, but everyone needed to be treated with respect. William Watkins recalls that in the 1950s and 1960s

> being tolerant never meant condoning immoral behavior, letting harmful beliefs go unchallenged, or permitting a person's dangerous lifestyle to influence, much less be taught, to others. In those days we may have disagreed about what is true, but few challenged the bedrock conviction that "true" is the opposite of "false," and that truth does not tolerate untruth. We believed then that some beliefs and lifestyles promoted the common good while others undermined it.[1]

One of the major changes in recent history is the rise of the notion that all views, all beliefs, all claims are equally valid and that there is no single objective truth to be upheld—only what is true for my particular community. In such a setting, almost all truth claims are regarded as subjective and simply the product of a person's or community's perspective and history. Steve Morrison comments: "Today, we live in a vacuum of ethical thought. We live in a society where 'tolerance' trumps truth. 'Tolerance' is seen as the highest of all ethical virtues, in some cases greater even than love."[2] The greatest sin is to uphold any truth claim that excludes another. This is viewed as a violation of love and relationship, which says that nothing is more sacred than then right for all people to live in accordance with their own personal beliefs. To prevent that is a profound injustice and therefore, ironically, not to be tolerated. N. T. Wright says that

---

1. Watkins, "Is Tolerance a Virtue?"
2. Morrison, *Born This Way*, Kindle locs. 101–2.

we have become tolerant of everything except intolerance, about which we ourselves are extremely intolerant. If someone thinks through an issue and, irrespective of his or her feelings on the subject, reaches a considered judgement that doing X is right and doing Y is wrong, they no sooner come out and say so than someone else will accuse them of phobia.[3]

This raises for Christians profound questions about the nature of, and relationship between, truth and love, and what this implies for such values as tolerance and justice.

God Is Love

For John Wesley, it is love that is the essence of the life of the Triune God and it is this same quality that lies at the heart of being human—both in terms of relationship with God and with the neighbor.[4] The beginning point in understanding the genuine nature of love and relationship is the Triune God revealed to us in Christ and in Scripture. This love is not simply something that we can fill with our own meaning, but its nature is defined by God himself, particularly through the person and work of Jesus Christ.

> Loving relationships in this context are inherently transformational; you cannot remain the same if you are in genuine, loving connection with another because of an authentic desire to please them through shared conversations and interests. Loving another with integrity means you cannot do, say or think things that would damage or diminish the other and still claim to truly love. . . . To love the Lord is to be formed by that bond—which is where ethics, morality, obedience, and duty fits—they all flow from a right relationship.[5]

David Field describes how Wesley goes beyond the assertion that holiness is love to make clear the content of love.[6] In Wesley's sermon, "Of Former Things," he wrote:

> By religion I mean the love of God and man, filling the heart and governing the life. The sure effect of this is the uniform practice of justice, mercy, and truth. This is the very essence of it, the height and depth of religion.[7]

In another sermon ("On Living without God") he stated, "Indeed nothing can be more sure than that true Christianity cannot exist without both the inward experience

---

3. Wright, "Communion and Koinonia."

4. The focus on the essential nature of God as love is not unique to Wesley and several recent books emphasize its rich heritage in the theology of the church, especially the contributions of Augustine and Thomas Aquinas. See, for example: Chartier, *Analogy of Love*; Jeanrond, *Theology of Love*; Loyer, *God's Love through the Spirit*; Oord, *Nature of Love*. A recent systematic theology by Gerald Bray is organized around the declaration that God is love; see Bray, *God is Love*.

5. McEwan, *Life of God in the Soul*, 4.

6. Field, "Holiness," 180–82.

7. Outler, *Sermons*, 3:448; see also 4:172.

and outward practice of justice, mercy, and truth."[8] This triad of "justice, mercy, and truth" occurs frequently in Wesley's writings, and the vital importance of the triad arises out of Wesley's rooting it in the character of the Triune God: justice, mercy, and truth are a summary of the moral attributes of God.[9] They are the concrete expression of the love of God[10] and, as the summation of God's moral character, they are also the summation of the moral image of God in which humanity was created.[11] Holiness is the restoration of the moral image by the Spirit of God so that a person's life becomes characterized by these qualities. Wesley commented, "While thou seekest God in all things thou shalt find him in all, the fountain of all holiness, continually filling thee with his own likeness, with justice, mercy, and truth."[12]

This implies that love and truth are intimately interlinked, and it has implications for both tolerance and justice. This is especially true in connection with those who claim they have been unjustly excluded from an equal participation in society. Field records how "Wesley used the phrase 'outcasts of men' in a number of places in his writings to refer to those who are excluded from the benefits of human society and culture, and it provides a useful way of describing the socially marginalized."[13] According to Field, Wesley sees the outcasts as special objects of God's grace and so justice issues have to be seen from their perspective, not just from the perspective of the powerful.[14] It is not surprising therefore that when Wesley wrote a letter affirming the loyalty of Methodists to King George II, he could say that the Methodists "unite together for this and no other end—to promote, as far as we are capable, justice, mercy, and truth, the glory of God, and peace and goodwill among men."[15] He strongly affirmed that they are not merely personal virtues but also characteristic of a Christian engagement with society.

Justice and the God of Love

The picture of a God of grace and mercy is hard to reconcile with the picture of a God who is a righteous judge executing punishment on the offender. Clifton Black identifies the dilemma for many:

> If we convince ourselves that the Gospels' visualizations of a God of frightening judgment must be discarded because they are outmoded, ridiculous, and dangerous anthropomorphisms, on what basis can we retain the Gospels'

---

8. Outler, *Sermons*, 4:174.
9. Field, "Holiness," 179–81. See, for example, Wesley, *Sermons*, 1:452 and 2:175.
10. Wesley, *Notes*, 914, for his comment on 1 John 4:11.
11. See Wesley, *Sermons*, 2:175, 188.
12. Wesley, *Sermons*, 1:614; see also 1:307.
13. Field, "Holiness," 186. See nn41–46 for specific examples from Wesley's writings.
14. Field, "Holiness," 187.
15. Baker, *Letters*, 26:105.

pictures of a God of startling mercy: anthropomorphisms no less antiquated, over-the-top, and scandalous? If we discard the grotesque, the glorious will have to go with it, unless we verbalize, then validate, the tacit and untenable notion that Scripture reveals to us only the God who underwrites our prejudices. "God is love" (1 John 4:16b), but it is a love "hard as death" (Song 8:6) with an inbuilt passion for justice enraged by human wickedness (Rom 1:18—2:1).[16]

Raymond Schwager affirms that humans are morally responsible for their choices and for the consequences of those choices: "God's response to human rejection of the gospel is to reveal the inherent and unavoidable consequences of such a choice. Jesus' judgement sayings are not condemnation from the outside, but rather the revelation of the self-judgement or self-condemnation that human beings proclaim on themselves."[17] Within a Wesleyan understanding, the offer by God of mercy and forgiveness is made freely in and through Jesus Christ, who himself experienced the consequences of our selfish, self-centered and self-willed life. However, it must be graciously and freely received. "Human actions matter, they have consequences which must be dealt with, and human freedom must be personally engaged in the process of dealing with the consequences of previous choices. God's action for humanity is always prior to, but not separable from, a human response."[18] It is in this context that God's reconciling love, justice and mercy must be considered in the light of the Christian doctrine of hell. Brown sums it up by saying:

> In other words, hell exists not because God violently punishes but precisely because God refuses to engage in violent coercion. Inherent in the notion of creation, properly understood, is the relative autonomy of the creature, which grace does not negate but perfects. When viewed from the vantage point of God's infinite goodness, the greatest test of the coherence of justice and mercy turns out to be its greatest proof. Hell exists because God's goodness overflows into a creation that is able to stand on its own (relatively); in respecting creaturely autonomy, God shows not only immeasurable love (of which mercy is just an aspect) but also immeasurable justice (giving to creatures the respect that is their due as free creatures).[19]

Furthermore, "While the kingdom is offered freely, a certain character is nonetheless required in order to receive it. This character requires a change in human

---

16. Black, "Shouting at the Legally Deaf," 321. Black reminds us that God the righteous judge is also the God who was judged in our place.

17. Brown, "Justice and Mercy of God," 216–17.

18. Schwager, *Jesus in the Drama of Salvation*, 197.

19. Brown, "Justice and Mercy of God," 221. This essay is not focused on the question of hell as such, but Brown goes on to show how Schwager's approach, and his own development of it, is coherent with God's love, goodness, justice and mercy, by rejecting coercion and providing for even those who reject Christ.

attitude and conduct, for human beings do not yet possess it. But such a change is not easy."[20]

> God is faithful to humanity and gives it always its due, including the dignity of freedom, which must include bearing the full weight of the consequences of abusing free will. In justice, God does not rescind freedom or its effects. But God's goodness is so perfect that, when human beings are threatened by self-destruction, God does not turn away or say "I told you so," but in mercy goes to the greatest lengths possible to draw humanity back to wholeness. God does not negate but works through human freedom. This shows both a greater justice than mere punishment, and a greater mercy than mere forgiveness.[21]

A responsible moral agent must be held accountable for their choices and actions, and they merit appropriate "punishment" when they violate the moral code. From a Christian perspective, the punishment is not an end in itself, but would hopefully lead to repentance and restoration.[22] According to Jordan Ballor, a critical question is the degree to which this view of justice can include or be reconciled with coercion, punishment and sanction.[23]

> The primary rationale assumed for the administration of punishment is that it is a requisite aspect of treating criminal offenders as responsible moral agents. In this sense, punishment is deserved, and so the concept of *desert* plays an important role.... Just as the "wages of sin is death," [Rom 6:23] criminal acts earn or warrant punishment.[24]

Examining the punishment of sin in the Gospels, Black says that "in Matthew *neither grace nor judgment is an inert abstraction; both are dynamic actions among parties in relationship.*"[25] With Thorwald Lorenzen, Christianity is intrinsically relational in nature and so we all carry a responsibility for the welfare of the other person.[26] Additionally, "for Christians, 'God is love,' and love is one of those realities that increases as it loses itself in sharing. Justice is the implementation of truth and love in particular situations."[27] Merilyn Clark agrees that justice is very hard to define, "but there is consensus that, at its heart, justice is relational."[28] Justice seeks the welfare of

20. Brown, "Justice and Mercy of God," 216.
21. Brown, "Justice and Mercy of God," 222.
22. See Jones, *Embodying Forgiveness*, 270–78. See also Ballor's "Conclusion" in "To Reform or to Abolish?," 510–11.
23. Ballor, "To Reform or to Abolish?," 484.
24. Ballor, "To Reform or to Abolish?," 487.
25. Black, "Shouting at the Legally Deaf," 318 (emphasis original).
26. Lorenzen, "Justice Anchored in Truth," 290–92.
27. Lorenzen, "Justice Anchored in Truth," 298.
28. Clark, "Flood of Justice," 358. It is not just human relationships but also the God-human and the human-creation relationship; see Clark, "Flood of Justice," 369. See also Neville, "Justice and Divine Judgement"; Thomson, "Satisfying Justice," 320.

PART C—ENCOUNTERING THE JUST AND MERCIFUL GOD

other persons in order to assure the well-being of the whole community. This makes equality of the essence of justice.[29] According to Field, for Wesley

> justice refers to treating someone in accordance with who they are as a human being and in accordance with what they have done. Depriving someone of life and liberty for no reason is unjust, punishments must fit the crimes, and a person should be rewarded for their action. A society must be structured in such a way that all humans are given their full dignity and freedom as human beings.[30]

As Terry Veling says, "Justice is a debt that we owe to those who have been denied the well-being of human flourishing. Wherever we find people who lack basic human rights that are rooted in their very dignity as human persons, then justice is *owing*. Justice serves the *common good* and not simply the good of a few."[31]

At an elementary level justice is concerned with fairness but in a Christian context is tied closely to restoration grounded in the life, death and resurrection of Jesus Christ. This provides a focus on grace leading to embrace, and not exclusion for restoring justice.[32] "A common understanding of restorative justice is one that encompasses the theory and practice of justice-making in which the relationships of people and communities are integral to 'making things right.' This can be understood in terms of restitution, reparation and reconciliation."[33] This keeps the focus on relationships, and the relationship with God in Christ as absolutely central.[34] Heather Thomson points out that while justice from a Christian perspective embodies both punishment and rehabilitation, the tragedy is that it has come to focus almost exclusively on punishment. She quotes extensively from Richard Snyder to illustrate her points, especially Snyder's view that there are two critical distortions in the Christian view: an overbearing doctrine of sin with a weak doctrine of grace and creation, and a focus on theological doctrines in individualistic terms, that minimizes or denies the social and political dimensions in understanding criminal activity.[35] She draws attention to the rise of the restorative justice movement, with its focus on peace, healing and reconciliation as the counterpoint to retribution. This movement also emphasizes relationships and points out that injustice injures or breaks relationships and justice is served when they are restored.[36]

---

29. Lorenzen, "Justice Anchored in Truth," 286–87.
30. Field, "Holiness," 182.
31. Veling, "In the Name of Mercy," 220.
32. Broughton, "Restorative Justice," 301–3.
33. Broughton, "Restorative Justice," 301–3. See also Ballor, "To Reform or to Abolish?," 481.
34. Thomson, "Satisfying Justice," 320.
35. Thomson, "Satisfying Justice," 321–23. The book she references is Snyder, *Protestant Ethic*.
36. Thomson, "Satisfying Justice," 323–31.

However, there are limitations to a purely restorative model: "Punishment allows a moral order to be maintained for perpetrators, victims and societies. By punishing individual perpetrators and holding them accountable, they are accorded the dignity of being treated as rational, moral agents who have and will continue to make choices about their actions."[37] This helps to maintain society by upholding law and order. Many Christian scholars are particularly keen to show that divine justice is restorative due to the change brought about by the resurrection of Jesus Christ and the consequent gift of grace that enables a shift from one sovereignty to another. This enables God to grant forgiveness and restoration on the basis of the resurrection.[38] "What Jesus inaugurated was a new reign in which we are all redefined according to the story of divine justice and its implications for human life."[39] "For Christians, the atonement signals a change of regime that God ushers in and into which we were and are being invited."[40] According to Desmond Tutu,

> [In] restorative justice, the central concern is not retribution or punishment . . . in the spirit of *ubuntu*, the central concern is the healing of breaches, the redressing of imbalances, the restoration of broken relationships, a seeking to rehabilitate both the victim and the perpetrator, who should be given the opportunity to be reintegrated into the community he has injured by his offence.[41]

Broughton believes that "it is a theological perspective which insists that the life and teaching of Jesus demonstrate that the divine character and the nature of divine purpose in the world are restorative, not punitive. If correct, this restorative purpose of God must be equally demonstrated by the death and resurrection of Jesus, not solely by his life and teaching."[42] Therefore, "any punishment imposed by God or the community of faith nearly always has a redemptive intent. These are the theological grounds for the (limited) role of punishment within restorative justice; it is not reformative, deterrent or retributive, but deliberately restorative."[43] Neville sees this as particularly important for the vulnerable and the outsider. Such justice does have a retributive element, but in its truest and deepest sense it is restorative, rectifying or transformative, offering a sound basis for hope.[44] The critical point is whether there is

---

37. Thomson, "Satisfying Justice," 332.
38. Thomson, "Satisfying Justice," 335–37.
39. Thomson, "Satisfying Justice," 337.
40. Thomson, "Satisfying Justice," 337.
41. Desmond Tutu, *No Future without Forgiveness*, 54–55.
42. Broughton, "Restorative Justice," 311.
43. Broughton, "Restorative Justice," 315.
44. Neville, "Justice and Divine Judgement," 347–55.

an intentional and coercive infliction of pain for its own sake (retribution), or whether it is intended to lead to reconciliation and restoration.[45]

Mercy and the God of Love

This brings us to the relationship of justice to mercy and forgiveness. Henry Stob says, "Consider a judge who out of love and pity pardons and acquits a truly guilty man. Is this act of pardon really an act of love? My thesis is that he who pardons a guilty man without due cause is neither just nor loving." He views such an action as "something like romantic sentimentality."[46] Andrew Fiala, from a survey of attitudes to justice and forgiveness, notes that "justice and forgiveness cannot be easily combined. Justice appears to require that we punish wrongdoing, even if we would rather forgive and forget."[47] The relationship of justice and mercy in God has been and continues to be much debated. According to Brown, one of the root problems in the discussion is the tendency to define justice and mercy independently and then to find some degree of compatibility.[48] Louis E. Newman agrees that the definition and application of forgiveness is a much debated and complex issue.[49] He says that "forgiveness as a moral gesture is *other-regarding*. Whatever its ultimate purpose . . . it only counts as a moral act of forgiveness if it is meant to benefit the offender in some way."[50] Additionally, "There is no doubt that in many cases there are often powerful emotional benefits for one who forgives. But if forgiveness is to have any moral meaning, it must be done primarily as a response *to* and for the benefit *of* the offender."[51] Forgiveness can be given in gradations, from full reconciliation and restoration to simply treating the other with respect, but it must always involve a change of attitude and behavior toward the one who offends.[52] He shows that within a Jewish context, forgiveness is only possible if the offender acknowledges the wrongdoing and seeks to repair the damage; only then can the offended party grant it.[53]

> For the question of forgiveness poses what is really the ultimate moral problem in that it requires us to consider what is the proper moral response to immoral behavior. One possibility is that the moral response is to "undo" the immoral behavior by reasserting the demands of conventional morality and requiring the offender to restore the world to the state it was in (as much as

45. Ballor, "To Reform or to Abolish?," 493–95.
46. Stob, *Ethical Reflections*, 142.
47. Fiala, "Radical Forgiveness and Human Justice," 498.
48. Brown, "Dramatic Justice and Mercy of God," 212–28.
49. Newman, "Balancing Justice and Mercy," 435–36.
50. Newman, "Balancing Justice and Mercy," 436.
51. Newman, "Balancing Justice and Mercy," 437.
52. Newman, "Balancing Justice and Mercy," 437.
53. Newman, "Balancing Justice and Mercy," 438–41.

possible) prior to the offense. This is what we might call a "restorative" model of morality, one that sees each immoral deed as tilting the scales of the world and requiring a response that tilts them back in the opposite direction, until the world is once again in a state of moral equilibrium. On the other hand, the moral response might be to act so as to create a new moral situation, one in which the distance between the offender and the offended is overcome, in which we do not attempt to reassert the moral values on which society as we know it rests, but rather to create a new kind of society on an altogether different foundation. We might call this a "visionary" model of morality, insofar as it aims not only to transform a single offender, but to transform the world by creating a society that rests not on justice, but on mercy. Just as we treat the offender *as if* she were more deserving than she is, we act in the world *as if* it were already a place in which God's compassion flowed freely among us.[54]

Newman asks whether we want a world in which restoration is primary or one in which transformation is primary?[55] While both justice and mercy are necessary for a healthy world, neither alone is sufficient, so forgiveness must be both conditional and unconditional.[56] However, we must not mistake the nature of God's mercy:

> Mercy is an indispensable element for *shaping* mutual relationships between people.... It is impossible to establish this bond between people, if they wish to regulate their mutual relationships solely according to the measure of justice. In every sphere of interpersonal relationships justice must, so to speak, *be corrected to a considerable extent* . . . by that *merciful love* which is so much of the essence of the Gospel and Christianity.[57]

According to Veling,

> While we must necessarily attend to the social fabric of our institutional structures, political administrations and judicial systems, we must recognise that all these social institutions are not so much the *foundation* or basis of ethical relations, but the *consequences* or "guardianships" of the more ordinary ethical relation that comes to us, not from our well-constructed social theories or ethical codes, but from the fundamental relationship of the "I and the other."[58]

Veling concludes by saying that "social mercy is crucial to our society; without it we could not even claim *to be* a society—a society, that is, of any human or humane proportion, where our bonds are always ones of friendship and fraternity, forgiveness and forbearance—knowing that we are all in this boat together, and only mercy can

---

54. Newman, "Balancing Justice and Mercy," 453.
55. Newman, "Balancing Justice and Mercy," 453.
56. Newman, "Balancing Justice and Mercy," 455.
57. Pope John Paul II, *Dives in misericordia*, 76.
58. Veling, "In the Name of Mercy," 231.

sustain us."⁵⁹ It is "the practices of love and mercy [that] keep justice from becoming unjust, such that the conditions of justice are always tested against the superabundance of merciful and unconditional love?"⁶⁰ In other words, justice requires mercy if we are to avoid (or at least limit) our judgments becoming harsh and inhumane.⁶¹ Many of Jesus' parables are scandalous and irritating because they offend our human sense of justice as fairness, equality and rights.⁶²

> Justice that seeks to be true and good is always saddened by its inability to be truly just for each and every person who comes before the law, because it knows that it must necessarily weigh individual cases according to universal principles, and yet it also knows that no universal principle is ever adequate to deal with each and every human particularity that comes before it in all its special instance and circumstance.⁶³

For example, Wesley provides a detailed evaluation of the trial of a smuggler on the basis of its conformity to "justice, mercy and truth." The smuggler was clearly guilty, yet Wesley is extremely critical of the trial and the harsh sentence because the poor must not be exploited even if they are criminals. He lamented: "O England, England! Will this reproach never be rolled away from thee? Is there anything like this to be found either among Papists, Turks, or heathens? In the name of truth, justice, mercy, and common sense."⁶⁴ Field believes that for Wesley "mercy refers to active compassion for the suffering and the needy. This refers not merely to individual actions but to laws and institutions of society—they must be instruments of mercy."⁶⁵ Both Martin Luther and C. S. Lewis upheld the view that mercy is the voluntary relinquishing of the right to punish and, by an act of mercy, pardoning the offender. Mercy presupposes that the offender is actually guilty of an intentional offence, for only in this context can forgiveness have any meaning. In this way, love and justice are complementary.⁶⁶

> We tend to assume that love and mercy are different from or opposite to justice. A judge pronounces a sentence. Then as an act of mercy, she may mitigate the penalty. Biblical justice, however, grows out of love. Such justice is in fact an act of love which seeks to make things right.⁶⁷

---

59. Veling, "In the Name of Mercy," 234–35.
60. Veling, "In the Name of Mercy," 234. See also Zumdahl, "Justice Is More than a Verdict."
61. Veling, "In the Name of Mercy," 222.
62. Veling, "In the Name of Mercy," 223. See, for example, Matt 18:23–35; 20:1–16; Luke 15:11–32.
63. Veling, "In the Name of Mercy," 232.
64. Ward and Heitzenrater, *Journals*, 21:333.
65. Field, "Holiness," 182.
66. Ballor, "To Reform or to Abolish?," 496–97.
67. Zehr, *Changing Lenses*, 139.

Zehr goes on to say that "love and justice are not opposites, nor are they in conflict. Instead, love provides for a justice which seeks first to make right."[68] Love and justice are not incompatible, but the latter flows from the former: "Justice is the implementation of truth and love in particular situations."[69] Wesley writes, "Does he [God] treat us in all things according to His justice? Not so; but mercy rejoices over judgement!"[70] In particular, he notes that "for as long as we are in the body, we are liable to mistake and to speak or act according to that mistaken judgement. Therefore we cannot abide the rigor of God's strict justice, but still need mercy and forgiveness."[71] Field believes that for Wesley, "God's act of mercy to us was his suffering alongside and for us. The Christian, in Wesley's view, was to be conscientious to show mercy to those who were oppressed by the world in the same way that Christ showed mercy."[72] This point is affirmed by Veling: "To dwell mercifully in the world is to know that mercy has been shown to me, that I have received mercy, that my existence is all the time supported and upheld by mercy. We can speak of mercy only as we receive it, only as it has been revealed to us."[73]

Philip Barnes records how many Christian theologians believe that Christians are required to be like God, who loves unconditionally and therefore we must forgive others unconditionally, including our enemies.[74] On the basis of an examination of the language of the New Testament, he writes:

> In the New Testament the context of Christian forgiveness is that of personal relationships and the language is that of reconciliation and estrangement. Forgiveness is relevant to a situation where two parties are estranged from each other, typically one who is offended and the other who is the offender. The language of forgiveness presupposes that a wrong has been done. If no wrong has been committed there is no need for forgiveness; and if the offender does not admit that a wrong has been done (unlike the person offended) then there is no possibility of either repentance or forgiveness; though of course for the Christian who has been offended there is the obligation to love the offender. There can be no reconciliation in the biblical sense when one party refuses to acknowledge wrong and admit responsibility (and where there is no confession of guilt there can be no forgiveness, only the call to forgiveness).[75]

---

68. Zehr, *Changing Lenses*, 139.
69. Lorenzen, "Justice Anchored in Truth," 298.
70. Telford, *Letters*, 6:318; see also 4:13; 6:318; 8:5; Outler, *Sermons*, 1:405, 626, 653; 2:427, 434.
71. Telford, *Letters*, 4:13; see also 6:318.
72. Bara Initiative, "John Wesley on Justice and Mercy."
73. Veling, "In the Name of Mercy," 224. See also the Bara Initiative, "John Wesley on Justice and Mercy."
74. Barnes, "Talking Politics, Talking Forgiveness," 65–66.
75. Barnes, "Talking Politics, Talking Forgiveness," 69.

In other words, if there is no repentance, there can be no forgiveness and no reconciliation. Barnes notes that "forgiveness, upon repentance, initiates a new relationship with God or the restoration of a relationship which has been broken. God loves everyone, the love of the Father is unconditional, but forgiveness from the Father and reconciliation with him is conditional on repentance by the sinner."[76] This same pattern holds true for interpersonal relationships, and as a gift it goes beyond that which morality and justice require.[77] For Barnes, "Forgiveness without repentance undermines both morality and respect for persons. It is the conditional nature of forgiveness which helps to confirm the objectivity and reality of the moral law of God. At the heart of the Christian view of atonement is the view that God is right to forgive sin because he has met the requirements of the moral law in the death of Christ."[78]

> If the doctrine of forgiveness does not provide a particularly useful or appropriate basis for Christian social engagement, what Christian beliefs and convictions do provide the resources for the church to minister effectively to post-conflict situations or to communities currently in conflict with each other. The traditional answer is that the Christian notion of righteousness/justice provides the conceptual resources for positive social engagement. The advantage of the Christian doctrine of justice over that of forgiveness is that justice is multidimensional: Christian justice includes the idea of fairness, that of mercy, that of restoration and reform and so on. Giving a different weighting to these different aspects may be appropriate in different situations in which the church has to minister: the context will determine the particular form Christian justice will take. The implication of our discussion is that Christian love is expressed in two different ways, that of forgiveness upon repentance within the community of the faithful and that of justice tempered by mercy in the socio-political realm.[79]

Tolerance and the God of Love

Rivka T. Witenberg believes tolerance is a virtue defined as "a moral obligation or duty which involves respect for the individual as well as mutual respect and consideration between people. Tolerance between people makes it possible for conflicting claims of beliefs, values and ideas to coexistence [sic] as long as they fit within acceptable moral values."[80] In that light, she believes that "while different marriage practices fit in within acceptable moral values, sexual abuse of children is immoral and cannot be

---

76. Barnes, "Talking Politics, Talking Forgiveness," 70.
77. Barnes, "Talking Politics, Talking Forgiveness," 71.
78. Barnes, "Talking Politics, Talking Forgiveness," 72.
79. Barnes, "Talking Politics, Talking Forgiveness," 78–79. See also Philpott, "Justice of Forgiveness."
80. Witenberg, "Tolerance Is More than Putting Up with Things."

tolerated."[81] She believes that "moral values such as fairness, justice, empathy, tolerance and respect are shared, if not universal, values relevant to dealing with human diversity."[82] While her list of values might be shared quite broadly in Australian society, given the intensity and often polarization of debate over issues of human rights and social justice, it is highly doubtful that they are held to be universal in any simplistic manner. The virtue might be universal but the definition of it clearly is not. The critical question then becomes, what are "acceptable moral values" and who gets to define them? The modern age was generally happy to concede that science would lead into all truth, but the rise of postmodernism challenges the imperialistic view of objective observation, rationality and logic, elevating the place of our personal story to the role of arbiter of truth. Thus "my" story can be true for me but not "true" for you, and everyone's story is equally valid, worthy of respect and is to be tolerated.

However, most of society still believes some "stories" are not acceptable—racism, pedophilia, domestic violence, or murder for example. This suggests that there is in fact a standard of judgment being applied. Genuine tolerance is being patient with people whose practices or opinions you don't approve of, but it does have its limits.

Dealing with a pluralistic society is not reserved to the twenty-first century—it was a reality for the early church. Wright reminds us that a major theme in many of Paul's letters (especially those to Rome and Corinth) is the need to tolerate within the church those who have different opinions on a range of difficult issues. Yet in other passages in the same letters he shows himself to be intolerant of many things:

> When Paul appeals for "tolerance" in the church, the issues over which he is saying there should be no quarrels are precisely the issue where there were cultural boundary-markers, especially between Jewish and Gentile Christians. He is not being arbitrary in selecting some apparently "ethical" issues to go soft on, while remaining firm on others. The things about which Christians must be prepared to agree or disagree are the things which would otherwise divide the church along ethnic lines.[83]

In a later section of the paper, he says that the beliefs and practices "that were not to be tolerated were the ones that marked the difference between genuine, living, renewed humanity and false, corruptible, destructive humanity." Consequently, "When final judgement occurs, it will not be arbitrary; it is not the case that God has made up a list of rules upon some kind of whim. Final judgement will be according to genuine humanness, and genuine humanness is what truly reflects the image of God."[84] There are some things that can be tolerated because they do not impinge on holy character, and there are other things that cannot be tolerated because they do. This returns us

---

81. Witenberg, "Tolerance Is More than Putting Up with Things."
82. Witenberg, "Tolerance Is More than Putting Up with Things."
83. Wright, "Communion and Koinonia."
84. Witenberg, "Tolerance Is More than Putting Up with Things."

to the critical distinction between opinions and facts. Problems arise when we treat facts/truth as opinions, or treat opinions as facts/truth and, for Christians, this underscores the importance of Jesus' teaching on truth. For the Christian, tolerance is relevant to opinion, but not to fact/truth. One test of truth is correspondence with reality and for the Christian that is defined by God, revealed in Scripture and supremely in the person of Jesus Christ. Donald DeMarco reflects that Pilate's question about truth indicates a willingness to be tolerant of anything, whereas Christ emphasizes the importance of truth and the need to tolerate the decisions of others who are still seeking it. "This mistake leads to a radical devaluation of the importance of truth, especially truth of a moral nature. Consequently, a person may be accused of being intolerant simply because he holds to a truth." He goes on to say: "Tolerance, of itself, is not a virtue. Pseudo-tolerance that is founded on ignorance, cowardice, or apathy is actually a vice. In order for tolerance to avoid being a vice, it must be founded on a positive regard for truth and an abiding love for others."[85] The danger comes when we use power and control to force conformity in matters of opinion, or demand an open-ended tolerance for matters of truth. Genuine tolerance is being patient with people whose practices or opinions you don't approve of, but within certain limits.

That still leaves the question of defining the nature of truth and its relationship to love, justice and mercy. Timothy Cross points out that while God is revealed in Scripture as merciful, patient and forbearing, God is "intolerant" of other gods; idolatry is not tolerated by God, nor are false offers of salvation.[86] From a Christian perspective, Lorenzen reminds us that justice and truth are not the same thing, though they need each other.[87] "Truth informs and inspires justice, and the Christian understanding of truth is relational. That is, truth is not merely 'there'; it is not simply objective; its reality cannot be appreciated by an observer. Rather, truth calls for participation and praxis."[88] Truth is grounded in God and comes to us in the incarnation of Jesus Christ, so it is not the product of human beings. As Field reminds us, the commitment to truth requires that all our responses to social issues be based on a careful, critical and nuanced analysis of their causes and consequences. We must recognize the contested character of knowledge and the diverse political and economic interests that influence and, in some cases, distort information provided to the public. In keeping with Wesley's focus on the "outcasts of men," such an analysis needs to assume the perspective of the impact on the marginalized, the poor, the exploited, the powerless and the victims, rather than on the wealthy, the powerful and the influential. The analysis must be nuanced, recognizing the complexity and diversity of contexts, motivations and

---

85. DeMarco, "Is Tolerance a Virtue?"

86. Cross, "Is Tolerance a Christian Virtue?"

87. Lorenzen, "Justice Anchored in Truth," 281. He notes how the two terms are interrelated in such biblical passages as Pss 96:13; 119:142; 160; Isa 45:19; 48:1; 59:14, 15; Jer 4:2; 5:1; 9:5; Dan 4:37; Amos 5:10; Zech 8:16.

88. Lorenzen, "Justice Anchored in Truth," 282.

consequences of the issues. The commitment to truth challenges churches not only to analyze but also to propagate the truth and hence to provide the broader public with the information that they have discovered. We must affirm the dignity and value of all human beings, the right of all to due legal process, and an orientation toward the powerless and the victims. The commitment to mercy challenges churches to be the voice of the voiceless, the silenced and the victims.[89]

Conclusion

This chapter has looked at the implications of viewing God's essential nature as love for an understanding of justice and mercy in the light of the truth revealed to us in Jesus Christ. Love is not a term that we can simply fill with our own ideas. For the Christian, its nature and character are demonstrated supremely in the person of Jesus Christ and this divine love is inherently transformative, seeking to heal us and restore us to the goodness for which we were originally created. God does not leave us in the condition in which he finds us, both personally and socially. Divine love is also essentially related to justice, mercy and truth, and this has clear implications for our current preferred understanding of "tolerance." In the Wesleyan framework (and in much of the wider Christian tradition), love, truth, justice and mercy are all primarily relational qualities, both in terms of our relationship with God and with each other. It is love and truth that defines and shapes both justice and mercy, and this is supremely demonstrated in the atoning death of Christ. They are not abstract concepts, nor can they be truly defined from a human perspective alone; they are essentially revealed to us in Jesus Christ. Christians do argue with each other about their exact nature and application, but all are generally committed to there being a full and final revelation in Christ. In that sense, toleration should be exercised as we all seek to come to the fullness of the knowledge of Christ, with tolerance here referring to patience, long-suffering and forbearance as we mutually seek to know and live God's loving truth.

The implication here is that God is a God of love, truth, justice and mercy in an integrated wholeness. He exercises tolerance toward humanity in the sense of being patient with us as we allow him to transform us through our relationship with Jesus Christ in the Spirit. He treats us with the dignity that is due to us being creatures who can exercise moral choice and therefore are responsible and accountable for those choices. Justice is tied to God-honoring and healthy relationships and it is applied in that framework. The refusal to allow divine love to form us in truth carries consequences, and in that sense God is not tolerant of choices that are destructive of his creational plans and purposes. For those who are open to the process of transformation, God freely offers mercy that triumphs over strict justice on the basis of the atoning

---

89. Field, "Holiness," 192–93.

death of Christ. For those who reject the offer of transformation, God's justice will see them excluded from the benefits of that same offer of love, mercy and forgiveness.

Bibliography

Baker, Frank, ed. *Letters I–II*. Works of John Wesley: Bicentennial Edition 25–26. Nashville: Abingdon, 1980–82.

The Bara Initiative. "John Wesley on Justice and Mercy." Accessed March 4, 2017. http://thebarainitiative.com/john-wesley-on-justice-and-mercy/.

Barnes, L. Philip. "Talking Politics, Talking Forgiveness." *Scottish Journal of Theology* 64 (2011) 64–79.

Ballor, Jordan J. "To Reform or to Abolish? Christian Perspectives on Punishment, Prison, and Restorative Justice." *Ave Maria Law Review* 6 (2008) 481–511.

Black, C. Clifton. "Shouting at the Legally Deaf: Sin's Punishment in the Gospels." *Interpretation* 69 (2015) 311–22.

Bray, Gerald. *God Is Love: A Biblical and Systematic Theology*. Wheaton, IL: Crossway, 2012.

Broughton, Geoff. "Restorative Justice: Opportunities for Christian Engagement." *International Journal of Public Theology* 3 (2009) 299–318.

Brown, Benjamin. "Raymond Schwager on the Dramatic Justice and Mercy of God." *International Journal of Systematic Theology* 17 (2015) 212–28.

Chartier, Gary. *The Analogy of Love: Divine and Human Love at the Center of Christian Theology*. Exeter, UK: Imprint Academic, 2007.

Clark, Merilyn E. C. "A Flood of Justice: The Scope of Justice in the Flood Narrative (Gen. 6:5—9:19)." *International Journal of Public Theology* 3 (2009) 357–70.

Cross, Timothy. "Is Tolerance a Christian Virtue?" *Evangelical Times*, December 2015. http://www.evangelical-times.org/archive/item/7636/Comment/Is-tolerance-a-Christian-virtue-/.

DeMarco, Donald. "Is Tolerance a Virtue?" *Lay Witness*, November/December 2005, 14–15.

Fiala, Andrew. "Radical Forgiveness and Human Justice." *Heythrop Journal* 53 (2012) 494–506.

Field, David N. "Holiness, Social Justice and the Mission of the Church: John Wesley's Insights in Contemporary Context." *Holiness: The Journal of Wesley House Cambridge* 1 (2015) 177–98.

Jeanrond, Werner G. *A Theology of Love*. London: T. & T. Clark, 2010.

Jones, L. Gregory. *Embodying Forgiveness: A Theological Analysis*. Grand Rapids: Eerdmans, 1995.

Lorenzen, Thorwald. "Justice Anchored in Truth: A Theological Perspective on the Nature and Implementation of Justice." *International Journal of Public Theology* 3 (2009) 281–98.

Loyer, Kenneth M. *God's Love through the Spirit: The Holy Spirit in Thomas Aquinas and John Wesley*. Washington, DC: Catholic University of America Press, 2014.

McEwan, David B. *The Life of God in the Soul*. Milton Keynes: Paternoster, 2015.

Morrison, Steve. *Born This Way: Making Sense of Science, the Bible and Same-Sex Attraction*. Sydney: Matthias, 2015. Kindle edition.

Newman, Louis E. "Balancing Justice and Mercy: Reflections on Forgiveness in Judaism." *Journal of Religious Ethics* 41 (2013) 435–56.

Neville, David J. "Justice and Divine Judgement: Scriptural Perspectives for Public Theology." *International Journal of Public Theology* 3 (2009) 339–56.

Oord, Thomas Jay. *The Nature of Love: A Theology*. St. Louis: Chalice, 2010.

Outler, Albert, ed. *Sermons*. Works of John Wesley: Bicentennial Edition 1–4. Nashville: Abingdon, 1984–87.

Philpott, Daniel. "The Justice of Forgiveness." *Journal of Religious Ethics* 41 (2013) 400–16.

Pope John Paul II. *Dives in misericordia: Rich in Mercy*. Homebush, Australia: St. Paul's Publications, 1980.

Schwager, Raymond. *Jesus in the Drama of Salvation: Toward a Biblical Doctrine of Redemption*. New York: Crossroad, 1999.

Snyder, T. Richard. *The Protestant Ethic and the Spirit of Punishment*. Grand Rapids: Eerdmans, 2001.

Stob, Henry. *Ethical Reflections: Essays on Moral Themes*. Grand Rapids: Eerdmans, 1978.

Telford, John, ed. *The Letters of the Rev. John Wesley*. 8 vols. London: Epworth, 1931.

Thomson, Heather. "Satisfying Justice." *International Journal of Public Theology* 3 (2009) 319–38.

Veling, Terry A. "In the Name of Mercy: A Meditative Exploration." *Pacifica* 22 (2009) 215–35.

Ward, W. Reginald, and Richard P. Heitzenrater, eds. *Journals and Diaries*. Works of John Wesley: Bicentennial Edition 21. Nashville: Abingdon, 1992.

Watkins, William D. "Is Tolerance a Virtue?" Christian Research Institute, April 17, 2009. http://www.equip.org/article/is-tolerance-a-virtue/.

Wesley, John. *Explanatory Notes upon the New Testament*. London: Wesleyan Methodist Book Room, n.d.

Witenberg, Rivka T. "Tolerance Is More than Putting Up with Things—It's a Moral Virtue." *theconversation.com*, September 16, 2014. https://theconversation.com/tolerance-is-more-than-putting-up-with-things-its-a-moral-virtue-31507.

Wright, N. T. "Communion and Koinonia: Pauline Reflections on Tolerance and Boundaries." Paper given at the Future of Anglicanism Conference, Oxford, 2002. http://ntwrightpage.com/2016/07/12/communion-and-koinonia-pauline-reflections-on-tolerance-and-boundaries/.

Zehr, Howard. *Changing Lenses: A New Focus for Crime and Justice*. Harrisonburg: Herald, 1990.

Zumdahl, Laura E. "Justice Is More than a Verdict: Integrating Social Work and Legal Aid Services in the Pursuit of Justice." *Journal of the North American Association of Christians in Social Work* 38 (2011) 64–73.

9

The Single Strife

Nurturing Wholeness in the Lives of Single Christians

Karen M. Pack

Introduction

In 2009 a surprising change occurred in the traditional commitment to marriage.[1] In that year statistics showed that more than fifty percent of adult women were single in the USA. The significance of this fact needs to be fully appreciated. For the first time the number of unmarried women outnumbered married women. Moreover, in the same year the median age of first marriages was twenty-seven, a striking phenomenon given that it had been between twenty and twenty-two years old for the preceding century.[2] It could be objected, however, that this is simply an American social anomaly. So what are the current Australian statistics regarding singleness? And do they replicate the same trend?

The most recent Australian Census reveals that in 2016, 48.1 percent of all adults were in a registered marriage. But, in line with the trend of the American statistics, 51.9 percent were not.[3] Significantly, in the church the situation is not dramatically different: the proportion of those not married is 47.6 percent. Again we need to take stock of the pastoral significance of this result: 49.6 percent of women and 45.2 percent of men in the church are unmarried.[4] Given that nearly half of all adults in the

---

1. This paper is a substantial reworking of a paper originally submitted as part of my master of divinity degree at Regent College, Vancouver, Canada, in 2009.
2. See Traister, *All the Single Ladies*, 5.
3. Australian Bureau of Statistics, "2016 Census of Population and Housing."
4. Information compiled using the Australian Bureau of Statistics Census TableBuilder.

church today are unmarried, there is an increasing urgency to consider how the needs of single Christians should be addressed, rather than naively assuming that ministry within the traditionally exclusively "family" paradigm is still normative. Furthermore, the highly sexually charged culture in which we live imposes considerable pressure upon single believers in our churches.

What should our theology and pastoral practice be in a society where the dominant assumption is that unless one is sexually active, the individual in question must either be repressed or incomplete as a person? How do we honor a life of celibate singleness observed faithfully before God in a way that will strengthen the single believer in relationships? How does the church respond mercifully to single believers while still doing justice to a full-orbed understanding of biblical sexuality?

This chapter will argue that Christian discipleship is a call to live a cruciform life in community to the glory of God. The "potent particularity" of love can be found in covenantal friendship informed by a robust Trinitarian understanding of relationships. Where this vocation is pursued by single believers, they can live (what is in our society) a countercultural life, in which they are esteemed and loved members of the body of Christ contributing vitally to the mission of God.

The Contemporary Quagmire

Kate Bolick has referred to the "retrograde world" of the turn of the twenty-first century, when being single was "a choice between Carrie Bradshaw and Bridget Jones."[5] Life is either a quest for independence and self-actuation (Carrie), or a waiting game (Bridget): that is, either waiting to be complete or to be married.

> Whom to marry, and when will it happen—these two questions define every woman's existence, regardless of where she was raised or what religion she does or doesn't practice. She may grow up to love women instead of men, or to decide she simply doesn't believe in marriage. No matter. These dual contingencies govern her until they're answered, even if the answers are nobody and never.[6]

Similarly, the overwhelming message of the contemporary Protestant church in the area of sexuality and relationships is that, unless one is married (the only sanctioned context for a sexual relationship), one is incomplete, immature, selfish. Today writers such as Bolick and Traister are resisting the "prevailing matrimonial narrative" in order to pursue the "spinster wish" to be alone.[7] Sex is recognized as a biological necessity, but it is easily satisfied. How you satisfy it, and with whom (or with what), is inconsequential.

---

5. Cited in Scutts, "New York," 39.
6. Bolick, *Spinster*, 1.
7. Scutts, "New York," 39.

In the twenty-first-century Western world "sexually immoral behavior" is a diminishing category. Any sexual activity that takes place between two consenting adults is generally beyond public criticism. Contemporary sexual demeanor is determined by one's personal taste or preference, rather than an overarching moral absolute. Sex is necessary; commitment is optional.

In light of this, sexuality is one of the most divisive issues in the church today. While Western society becomes increasingly tolerant of divergent expressions of sexuality, the church seems caught in a quandary as to how it should respond. Some congregations adopt a tolerant stance, emphasizing the grace in which we stand. Other congregations become ever more vigorous in their opposition to "fornication," retreating behind a fortress of denunciation. Still others retreat into silence, leaving the impression that the community of God's people has nothing to say in this most crucial area of personhood. Those in the church who are unmarried seem to be caught in the crossfire between church and society—and sometimes between church and church.

While this debate rages unresolved, there seems little hope of presenting single Christians with a vision of joyful, cross-bearing discipleship in the area of one's sexuality.[8] Instead, there is danger of the gospel message being thoroughly enculturated, as people accept the neo-Gnostic message of our culture that sex is just a bodily act of pleasure and release, without any inherent moral value. This stands in stark contrast to the orthodox Christian understanding of humans as embodied spirits, in whom body and soul form an integrated and inextricable whole. In 2003 Philip Nesvig made the following lament:

> The classic *incurvatus in se* (curved in on self) assessment of human beings where everything is me-oriented still stands. Suddenly the ground shifts away from hetero- or homo- to ego-sexuality. Celebrate yourself! A bumper sticker in my city carried this blasphemous message: "My body is not a temple. It's an amusement park." We do not live far from Corinth![9]

The Response of the Church

If, as Nesvig suggests, we do not live far from Corinth, perhaps there is hope that the words of life addressed to the church there some two thousand years ago may provide a way forward for those seeking to give pastoral care to the sexually enmeshed in our own day. Yet a pastoral response to such a complicated issue can (and should) be drawn from the whole canon of Scripture as opposed to a truncated selection of its evidence.

---

8. "Our sexuality, our fundamental maleness or femaleness, runs deeper than the physical features that allow the procreative function" and involves all that drives us out of ourselves and toward relationship with others. Grenz, "Purpose of Sex," 29.

9. Nesvig, "Is It Lawful to Marry?," 70.

A biblical understanding of human sexuality must begin with the Genesis account. Herein we find resounding testimony that God created all human persons—male and female—in his image, and that this was "very good." Adam's exclamation on first beholding his wife (Gen 1:23) suggests that sexual intimacy was not intended merely for pragmatic procreative function, but was gifted to the human pair for their mutual delight. This reality is underscored by the inclusion of Song of Songs in the canon of Scripture. Genesis also teaches us that sexual intercourse was intended to be experienced in the context of a lifelong, indissoluble union (Gen 2:24).

Picking up on this theme, the law clearly stipulated the boundaries of the sexual relationship, locating it within the covenantal safety of marriage and insisting that sex must not involve exploitation, manipulation or abuse (cf. Lev 18:6–23; 20:10–17; Deut 22:22–30; 23:17). Proverbs gives numerous warnings about the danger (and foolishness) of engaging in sexual sin (Prov 5–7), while the prophets were also clear that sexual intercourse outside marriage was a violation of Israel's covenant with YHWH (e.g., Jer 5:7, 23, 29; Ezek 16). Joseph is lauded as a man who would not surrender his integrity in the face of sexual temptation (Gen 39:6–20), while King David does not escape censure for his abusive and self-serving sexual indulgence, culminating in its devastating consequences (2 Sam 11–12).

In the New Testament, when teaching is given on sexual conduct, appeal is made to pentateuchal law. While Paul repeatedly affirmed that Christians are free from the ceremonial requirements of the law (e.g., circumcision, celebration of feasts, or ritual washing: Gal 4:8–10; 5:2–12), suggesting that these were culturally specific to the old covenant, he is equally adamant that the traditional boundaries around sexual conduct remain (Rom 1:24–27; 1 Cor 5; 6:12–20 etc.). Similarly, when Jesus was asked to give a judgment related to the contemporary debate about "any cause" divorce, he reached back to the Genesis creation narrative to affirm God's original intention of marriage as a lifelong, exclusive union (Matt 19:4–8).[10]

Nesvig is right to affirm that "the biblical texts do not answer all our contemporary questions [about human sexuality], but their thought trajectory is clear enough."[11] Sexual intimacy is a gift from God—a good gift—but it was intended to be kept within the protective boundaries of a lifelong, monogamous, covenant relationship.

On its own, however, this is an inadequate response. Fear of the sexualization of friendship can breed suspicion of any deeply committed friendship (whether opposite sex or same sex), for fear that it may involve "benefits."[12] Fencing off marriage can inadvertently exclude single Christians from any possibility of intimacy. Katherine

---

10. For an overview of biblical teaching regarding marital fidelity, see Gill, *Doing Right*, 218–19.
11. Nesvig, "Is It Lawful to Marry?," 73.
12. I am referring to the contemporary phenomenon of "friends with benefits," where two friends have a "no strings attached" sexual relationship whenever they feel the need. Numerous other terms have also been coined to describe this phenomenon.

Wehr writes of "the idolatry of the nuclear family" within the church,[13] where marriage is often presented as normative for mature discipleship and especially for leadership. The contribution of single Christians to the life of the church community may not be fully recognized. A recent denominational publication included an article entitled, "3 Vital Signs of a Healthy Church." The first sign of a healthy church was to "lead out of a healthy marriage." The author stated, "Your clearest gospel message is your marriage. . . . Out of the primacy of that relationship, your ministry flows."[14] There was neither recognition nor conception of unmarried leaders or pastors.

Last year, the Australian Christian Churches (ACC) released a positional statement on human sexuality. While acknowledging that our sexuality entails a "God given drive for companionship," including a "need for companionship and intimacy," it stipulated that "it is to be expressed within the loving relationship of marriage between a man and a woman."[15] It continued, "Single people are not asexual and must deal with their sexual drives. . . . They should learn to accept and control their sexual feelings." Single people "should develop many relationships with others and seek emotional fulfilment through these relationships."[16] The implication is that, while God has created us all with a longing for intimacy and belonging, this can only truly be met in the context of marriage. The relationships of single people are a supplementary prize at best.

My concerns regarding such an understanding of human sexuality and intimacy are numerous. First, has the church become complicit in the lie that in order to be full and complete, one must be genitally sexually active in an exclusive partnered sexual union, with marriage painted as the ground of emotional and spiritual maturity and singleness depicted as chosen, selfish, and immature.[17]

If only there were some single people in the Bible that could show us a way of selfless love! Of course there are many, not the least of whom is Jesus. So why are their lives not speaking profoundly to our present-day singleness as a way of joyful holiness and cruciform discipleship?

Second, the language of the church is out of step with reality. Within the church, singleness tends to be defined as a "pre-marriage" state,[18] with the assumption often made that this is a *temporary* lifestyle; but in our society this is often no longer the case. As noted, there are now more single adults than married adults in most Western nations. Within the church, long-term singleness is frequently not one's preferred

13. Wehr, "Virginity, Singleness and Celibacy," 85.
14. Hunt, "3 Vital Signs," 9.
15. ACC, "Human Sexuality," 2.
16. ACC, "Human Sexuality," 3.

17. Recently I was party to a conversation with a number of Christians, most of whom were married, when one began to critique the young, tech-savvy IT guys she knows as being "so selfish and immature, they are in their thirties and still not married." In my experience, it is not unusual to hear such comments within churches.

18. Cf. Hauerwas, "Sex in Public," 503.

lifestyle, but it may be the lived reality. Grenz writes that a biblical understanding of sexuality recognizes that "the traditional Christian sex ethic rightly advocates chastity in the form of abstinence in singleness and fidelity in marriage."[19] Sadly, many unmarried Christians experience this as enforced isolation. Furthermore, is it not true that married people need at times to abstain and to exercise discipline over their desire? Don't singles need to demonstrate faithfulness in relationships?

When singleness is spoken of in church, the language used often does not reflect the actual lives of Christian singles. We speak of the "gift of celibacy," which, in evangelical Protestant circles at least, is the gift no one wants to receive and would gladly re-gift. We tell singles how lucky they are not to have the weight of family life, to be unfettered by commitments and free to "do the Lord's work." But then these words are belied by speaking of our wedding day, or the day we gave birth, as the most sacred, beautiful thing that ever happened to us. Thus Teresa Morgan concludes, "To put it crudely, involuntary singleness has no compensations: it is not a price worth paying for something, just an unfortunate fact."[20]

Third, has the church uncritically accepted the contention that marriage expresses God's particular love, and singleness his unconditional, breadth of love? This implies that single people cannot be loved *particularly*. But particular love is not only the domain of the married; every person desires and needs to be particularly loved. Yet we expect single people to forgo this and then express dismay when they sin sexually in their quest for connection and intimacy.

The church is in danger of sending mixed messages—affirming the preciousness of non-genital intimacy and friendship, while avowing that "permanence" only properly belongs to marriage.[21] Too often we have lamented the danger of deep, committed friendships "becoming ingrown and obsessively introspective,"[22] while ignoring the fact that marriage does not inoculate one against selfishness or immaturity.

However, despite the potential for marriages to become *in curvatus in se* (turned inward in exclusion of others), or for lust and selfishness in marriage to replace sacrificial, self-giving love, one does not hear contemporary sermons warning of the dangers of loving too much in marriage, or suggesting that one forgo emotional intimacy in marriage lest it become distorted or perverted. The clear implication is that marriage, and marriage alone, is the appropriate place to experience the depth of connection and intimacy for which every human longs. This double standard is neither scriptural nor helpful.

If God can express both particular and universal love without compromise, cannot we, who bear his image, seek to do the same? As David Jensen has argued,

---

19. Grenz, "Christian Sex Ethic," 133.
20. Morgan, "Bridget Jones's Theology," 33.
21. Cf. Grenz, "Christian Sex Ethic," 132, 137.
22. Hill, *Spiritual Friendship*, 109.

"Covenant teaches that we need not choose between a generalized love for the world and love for a particular beloved; rather, the two are inextricably intertwined."[23]

Pursuit of the Better

The reality of Christian discipleship is the call to a cruciform life lived to the glory of God. It is also a call into community. When we are justified in Christ, we become members of his body, the church. Thus when Peter speaks of the juxtaposition of who we once were, and who we have become, he speaks in plural nouns.

> But you are a chosen people, a royal priesthood, a holy nation, God's special possession, that you may declare the praises of him who called you out of darkness into his wonderful light. Once you were not a people, but now you are the people of God; once you had not received mercy, but now you have received mercy. (1 Pet 2:9–10)

As part of the covenant community of God's people, we are called to resist society's dominant paradigm and *incurvatus in se* mode of living.[24] This is true for *all* who call Christ "Lord," whether married or single. Holiness is inherently relational. Our sanctification is expressed in the transformation of our lives and relationships—primarily in how we treat others. Rather than being guided by an agenda of self-protection and self-satisfaction, we listen to the voice of the Spirit and take seriously the call to "look not only to [our] own interests, but also to the interests of others" (Phil 2:3–4). The goal of our lives is not self-gratification but imitation of Christ's self-emptying love (Phil 2:5–9). As Purves has said,

> Christian hope leads us to give priority to the things that make for community, to make our lives within community, and to see sin as those behaviours and structures that make for broken relationships or no possibility of relationships in the first place.[25]

For a Christian, the matter of sexual conduct is not merely an issue of societal norms. As Barth strongly asserts, we are called to live as strangers and aliens, people who live out a bold kingdom ethic that resists the pattern of this world and instead reflects the holy love of Jesus Christ.[26] But we are not called to live such a life alone.

Therefore, to view biblical sexuality for singles as an isolating list of proscriptions, would be to tell a half truth. As David Gill contends, "Christian ethics is not just about fencing off what is wrong; it is also about pursuing what is right and good."[27]

---

23. Jensen, *God, Desire, and a Theology of Human Sexuality*, 9.
24. Cf. Purves, *Pastoral Theology*, 227.
25. Purves, *Pastoral Theology*, 230.
26. Barth, *Church Dogmatics* 4/2, 727ff.
27. Gill, *Doing Right*, 219–20.

The "Potent Particularity" of Love

For Christians, singleness need not be a state of lack, defined by what one *is not*, or *does not*. Instead single Christians can walk in the way of the Master, who was himself single, and yet fully human, fully sexual, and fully alive. Jesus, though not sexually active, was engaged deeply in the lives of those around him, deliberately fostering close mutual friendships and networks of loving support.

This opens up the possibility of a pastoral theology and practice that would be genuinely incarnational and pneumatological, and an understanding of singleness was not governed by language of emptiness, lack and repression. Instead, a participatory theology could be practiced, in which the fullness of God's desire for us was experienced, and then, in turn, expressed in deeply committed covenant friendships that take seriously Jesus' words in John 13: "As I have loved you, so you must love one another. By this everyone will know that you are my disciples, if you love one another" (John 13:34–35).

The Bible is honest about the reality of sexual desire and our powerful, innate longing for intimacy. Indeed, our hunger for intimacy and community is a function of our creation in the image of a Triune God.[28]

The Bible contains the self-revelation of God, who loved us and gave himself for us. The Bible speaks of God as perfect in love, calling us to walk in holiness, not to keep us from enjoyment, but in order to fulfil his good purpose in our lives. Thus a call to sexual holiness is not merely a prohibitive, "Stop! Don't go there!" Far more than this, it is the call of Christ himself to "Come, follow me." The implication is that in doing so, we will find fullness of life.

YHWH does not create out of emptiness but out of fullness.[29] He creates not out of need, but as an overflow of the perichoretic love between the persons of the Godhead. He invites us into relationship with him in order to experience the fathomless depths of his covenant love.

> As Scripture invites us into the cadences of its narrative, it shows us how desire intensifies in its focus: God's desire for relationship with a people expresses itself in covenant; God's love for the world is expressed in particular relationship in the incarnation; God's revelation of God's very self in one human being. In each case, desire for the world gets expressed in *particularity*, in a focused intensification of God's love.[30]

---

28. Moltmann, *Trinity and the Kingdom of God*, 199. The words of Gen 2:18, "The Lord God said, 'It is not good for the man to be alone. I will make a helper suitable for him,'" should not be applied exclusively to the context of marriage, without attending sufficiently to what they say about our creation as *imago Dei*.

29. "This opening biblical account of desire proceeds from fullness to fullness." Jensen, *God, Desire and a Theology of Human Sexuality*, 8.

30. Jensen, *God, Desire and a Theology of Human Sexuality*, 15.

This potent particularity is most powerfully evident in the incarnation. Jesus did not come and simply make a declaration of universal love. This One in whom all the fullness of God dwells demonstrated his love in his specific, personal commitment to individuals. In calling the disciples to be *with* him; in seeking companionship in Gethsemane; in a transformational encounter with a Samaritan woman; in raising an adulteress from the dust; in weeping at the tomb of Lazarus; in reconciling and restoring Peter over a barbecue at the beach.

Covenant Friendship: A Way Forward for Pastoral Care of Singles

One way forward, then, is to reclaim the vast beauty of the Bible's teaching on committed, covenant friendship. The friendship between David and Jonathan is not the only example. Over and over again the Bible celebrates those who show faithful, sacrificial, bold love at cost to themselves. In the pages of Scripture, friendship matters; friendship saves lives and redeems broken people.

Moreover, the language used by the New Testament authors to describe the fledgling church is the language of friendship. Edgar points out that the NT writers adapted friendship language to describe the early Christian community.[31] The church is a community who have become friends of God and express this in countercultural friendship within the body. Fitzgerald demonstrates that within the Greco-Roman culture of the time, one of the primary meanings of "reconciliation" was "the restoration of friendship."[32] Thus, in explaining that we have been given the "ministry of reconciliation," Paul is describing the primary mission task in terms of the restoration of friendship between God and people, and consequently between previously disparate persons (2 Cor 5:18–20).

There is need for the church to speak prophetically into our culture, modeling a hope-filled way of life in which both married and single persons have the hope of deep, intimate relationships and the appropriate, fulfilling expression of their sexuality.[33] The Christian life is not about sex, or the absence of sex; it is about discipleship in which one lives a cruciform life in the context of relationship with God and membership of his body.

> As believers identify with God's story and make it their own story, they become a part of the Christian community, which nurtures and reinforces in them the virtues and values of the kingdom of God.[34]

---

31. Edgar, *God Is Friendship*, 142ff.
32. Fitzgerald, "Christian Friendship," 289.
33. Cf. Hauerwas, "Sex in Public," 495–96.
34. Trull and Carter, *Ministerial Ethics*, 61.

Pastorally, this suggests that our energy should be spent not on more events and programmes, but on nurturing genuine, intimate, relationships. It is striking that when Mark describes Jesus' appointment of the twelve, the ministry purpose is subordinated to the call first "to be with him" (Mark 3:14). Clearly, Jesus' love for his disciples was deep and genuine; their calling was not a mere utilitarian expression of the need for a ministry team.

Conclusion

From a robust, Trinitarian understanding of relationships, the call to covenant friendship is a call to participate in the ministry of reconciliation. Having been restored to friendship with the Father, we not only experience this magnanimous love for ourselves, but out of the overflow of grace, as we are indwelt by the Spirit, we offer it to others in the same way Jesus did. We nurture particular relationships, risking vulnerability, honesty and even pain.

Beginning with this understanding, Christian singles can be powerfully equipped to live from a completely different paradigm. As we experience the potent particularity of God's love we understand that we are not alone; thus we cultivate covenant friendships that incarnate the tenacious love of God and empower us to live in joyful holiness.

How should such incarnational friendships be nurtured between single Christians? A starting place is to adjust the language used to speak about singleness and sexuality, so that, rather than narrowing the lens to focus on the "can't"—the prohibition—the good is affirmed. Instead of being like Adam and Eve locking their eyes on the one thing that would kill them, while living in the Garden overflowing with good things, we need to open up the positive vision of biblical personhood and sexuality. Lauren Winner asserts that chastity is not merely about avoidance, but is an active, positive praxis in pursuit of righteousness.[35]

Within this paradigm, the focus need not be on what is being given up. Instead, we can paint a picture of life in community, of biblical covenant friendships such as those we see in Scripture. As Gill has noted,

> Sex may not be crucial to everyone, but committed relationships certainly are. Jesus and Paul had full rich lives without sex, but not without intimate friendships. Authentic human life is *koinonia* life. . . . Not just casual but intentional relationships are essential for discernment and growth, for good thoughts and actions.[36]

---

35. Lauren F. Winner, cited in Berry, *Unauthorized Guide*, 161. It is helpful to clarify that we do not conform ourselves, as if we are somehow responsible for our own transformation. Rather, we are transformed as we cooperate with the work of the Holy Spirit as he seeks to change us from glory to glory (2 Cor 3:18; Rom 8:1–11).

36. Gill, *Doing Right*, 245.

Rather than simply chanting the proscriptions—what intimacy is *not* for single Christians—we need to proclaim "a view of [singleness] that has spiritual depth and content, rather than telling us our 'time' will come and we should simply wait."[37] Such a perspective (that one's time will come) presents marriage as the final answer to one's relational longings. Life is then lived in limbo and many get tired of waiting. Hope cannot be based on the possibility of marriage (and thus sex), for such a hope may wear thin. Single Christians today need a hope that is an anchor for the soul (Heb 6:19–20). That hope is found in friendship with Christ, who teaches us to bear his image in covenant friendship with others.

We Start Loved

Despite the prevalence of thought that has come to regard sexual intercourse as a recreational act devoid of deeper emotional or spiritual meaning, many people still engage in sexual practice in a quest to be loved. The Gospel of Jesus Christ, however, brings this glorious truth: we *start* loved. John 17:23–24 teaches us that in Christ, we were loved even before the creation of the world. We do not need, therefore, to embark on a quest for love and belonging—this is the place from which we operate, the truth in which we stand, and the truth which dwells in us (Rom 5:5). Gray comments that "all human love seeks union, promises mutuality, but is lessened by the fear that love can be destroyed or can be removed."[38] The love of God, however, is not transient or finite, for Jeremiah 31:3 tells us that God has "loved you with an everlasting love; . . . drawn you with unfailing kindness."

The call to incarnate a biblical understanding of sexuality is a call to a counter-cultural life. For single Christians it is a call to take up one's cross and die to self. But it is not merely a *via negativa*. This is a call to gladly embrace life in participation with Christ. Choosing to pursue life in Christ we find the joy of friendship with the Triune God, and with the company of believers. We turn away from an introspective, self-focused way of life, to nurture robust, transparent relationships. In *participatio Christi* we find the joy of friendship with God and people.

This is the *missio dei*—to see people restored to friendship with God and each other when we love as he has loved us. We are not content to love broadly and from a distance. Instead, we imitate our Saviour in the potent particularity of our love.

In order for this to happen, the church must move from a place of fear, in which close friendships are sources of suspicion and mistrust ("How close are they *really*?"). Instead, congregations should seek to deliberately nurture and encourage covenant friendships between single Christians as places where holiness and wholeness are nurtured, and the refuge and belonging we have found in Christ is incarnated. Only then

---

37. Berry, *Unauthorized Guide*, 163.
38. Gray, "Celibacy These Days," 156.

can single Christians experience life as fully contributing members of a body in which they are esteemed, loved, and vital to the mission of God.

Bibliography

Australian Bureau of Statistics. "2016 Census of Population and Housing." https://auth.censusdata.abs.gov.au/webapi/jsf/dataCatalogueExplorer.xhtml.

———. "Census TableBuilder" https://www.censusdata.abs.gov.au/webapi/jsf/tableView/crosstabTableView.xhtml.

Australian Christian Churches. "ACC Positional Statement Human Sexuality." Released December 15, 2015.

Barth, Karl. *Church Dogmatics*. 4/2, *The Doctrine of Reconciliation*. Edited by G. W. Bromiley and T. F. Torrance. Edinburgh: T. & T. Clark, 2004.

Berry, Carmen Renee. *The Unauthorized Guide to Sex and the Church*. Nashville: Nelson, 2005.

Bolick, Kate. *Spinster: Making a Life of One's Own*. New York: Broadway, 2015.

Edgar, Brian. *God Is Friendship: A Theology of Spirituality, Community, and Society*. Wilmore: Seedbed, 2013.

Fitzgerald, John. "Christian Friendship: John, Paul, and the Philippians." *Interpretation* 61 (2007) 284–96.

Gill, David W. *Doing Right: Practicing Ethical Principles*. Downers Grove: InterVarsity, 2004.

Gray, Janette. "Celibacy These Days." In *Sex These Days: Essays on Theology, Sexuality and Society*, edited by Jon Davies and Gerard Loughlin, 141–59. Sheffield: Sheffield Academic, 1997.

Grenz, Stanley J. "Homosexuality and the Christian Sex Ethic." In *Christian Perspectives on Gender, Sexuality, and Community*, edited by Maxine Hancock, 127–50. Vancouver: Regent College Publishing, 2003.

———. "The Purpose of Sex: Toward a Theological Understanding of Human Sexuality." *Crux* 26 (1990) 27–34.

Hauerwas, Stanley. *The Hauerwas Reader*. Edited by John Berkman and Michael G. Cartwright. Durham: Duke University Press, 2001.

Hill, Wesley. *Spiritual Friendship: Finding Love in the Church as a Celibate Gay Christian*. Grand Rapids: Brazos, 2015.

Hunt, John. "3 Vital Signs of a Healthy Church." ACC eMag, June 2016, 9. http://issuu.com/accmag/docs/accemag_2/9?e=2394551/36875517.

Jensen, David H. *God, Desire, and a Theology of Human Sexuality*. Louisville: Westminster John Knox, 2013.

Moltmann, Jürgen. *The Trinity and the Kingdom of God: The Doctrine of God*. London: SCM, 1981.

Morgan, Teresa. "Bridget Jones's Theology: Reflections on Involuntary Singleness." *Theology* 108 (2005) 32–39.

Nesvig, Philip M. "Is It Lawful to Marry?" *Word & World* 23 (2003) 68–75.

Purves, Andrew. *Reconstructing Pastoral Theology: A Christological Foundation*. Louisville: Westminster John Knox, 2004.

Scutts, Joanna. "New York Still Holds Its Writers in Thrall." *Guardian Weekly*, August 14, 2015.

Traister, Rebecca. *All the Single Ladies: Unmarried Women and the Rise of an Independent Nation*. New York: Simon & Schuster, 2016.

Trull, Joe E., and James E. Carter. *Ministerial Ethics: Moral Formation for Church Leaders*. Grand Rapids: Baker Academic, 2004.

Wehr, Kathryn. "Virginity, Singleness and Celibacy: Late Fourth-Century and Recent Evangelical Visions of Unmarried Christians." *Theology & Sexuality* 17 (2011) 75–99.

PART D

Seeking the Welfare of the City
First-Century Perspectives on Well-Being

10

The "Clemency" of Nero and Paul's Language of "Mercy" in Romans

Paul's Reconfiguration of Imperial Values in Mid-Fifties Rome

JAMES R. HARRISON

Most commentators propose that Paul's Letter to the Romans was written sometime during the *Neronis quinquennium* (AD 54–59).[1] The Latin term emanates from two writers of the later Roman Empire,[2] each of whom claims that the term was coined by Trajan for the first (?) five years of Nero's reign.[3] According to Aurelius Victor (AD 320–391), this five-year period of Neronian rule was "so outstanding ... that Trajan quite often justifiably asserted that all emperors fell far short of Nero in his (first) five years."[4] Certainly the outset of Neronian rule, apart from the expedient

---

1. Dates suggested are AD 55–56, 56–57, 57, 58: Fitzmyer, *Romans*, 85–88. For the expansions of the abbreviations of the ancient literary texts used in this chapter, see Alexander, *SBL Handbook of Style*.

2. Aurelius Victor, *De Caesaribus* 5.2–4; *Epitome de Caesaribus* 5.2–5.

3. For discussion, see Syme, *Emperors and Biography*, 106–10; Levick, "Nero's Quinquennium," 211–25; Bird, *Aurelius Victor*, 65–66; Griffin, *Nero*, 244–45.

4. Aurelius Victor, *De Caesaribus* 5.3. The epithet "first" is not present in the Latin and is therefore the translator's addition and is, therefore, his historical judgment. Trajan, assuming that the late historical tradition is correction, does not specify when the *Neronis quinquennium* commenced. Aurelius, however, provides a context for Trajan's comment: "He ... nevertheless was so outstanding for five years *especially in enhancing the city*, that Trajan quite often justifiably asserted ..." On Nero's building projects, see Suetonius, *Ner.* 16.1; Tacitus, *Ann.* 15.43.1. However, as Bird (*Aurelius Victor*, 66) correctly notes, "most were, indeed, inaugurated after the great fire of Rome in July, 64." The historical context provided by Aurelius for the *Neronis quinquennium* does not coincide with the commencement of

murder of his step-brother Britannicus (AD 55), started with considerable promise in the minds of his contemporaries. Under the firm control of his advisors, Seneca and Burrus (Tacitus, *Ann.* 13.2.1), the seventeen-year-old Nero was expected to flourish under their sagacious guidance. Consequently, as Suetonius writes (*Ner.* 10.1), Nero declared "that he would rule according to the principles of Augustus,[5] and he let slip no opportunity for acts of generosity (*liberalitatis*) and mercy (*clementiae*), or even for displaying his affability."

Irrespective of whether Trajan made the *Neronis quinquennium* remark or not, and irrespective of whether the "five years" is dated from Nero's accession or not, it is intriguing that "historical writers of the fourth century thought that the best of emperors, *optimus princeps*, could find something to praise in one of the worst."[6] Despite the fact that a fearsome reputation for violence and cruelty accrued to Nero during his reign, the honorific inscriptions underscored his "god-like" status, declaring him from the outset to be "a new Apollo" (νέῳ Ἀπόλλωνι).[7] The court poets also asserted that the ruler's accession in AD 54 had inaugurated another cyclical return of the Golden Age (Calpurnius Siculus, *Eclogues*, 1.42–48; *Einsiedeln Eclogues*, 2.23–24). An Egyptian accession papyrus from Oxyrhynchus, dated 17 November, AD 54, spoke of Nero as "the expectation and hope of the world . . . the good genius of the world and the beginning of all good things."[8] In sum, if the epistle to the Romans were written in the best years of Nero's reign, perhaps that explains why Roman rule is spoken of so positively in Romans 13:1–7.[9] However, such view overlooks the subtleties of Paul's critique of the Julio-Claudian propaganda, which boasted inordinately in the exalted status of the ruler (Rom 13:4a, 4b, 6b) and his ability to wield the sword for his own purposes in rule of the Roman Empire (ἡ μάχαιρα: 8:35b; 13:4a).[10]

Of particular interest for our purposes is the emphasis upon "mercy" and "justice" that was associated with the inauguration of Nero's reign. The court poet, Calpurnius Siculus,[11] writes:

Nero's reign but rather with its *later* period. This shows us how later historians struggled to identify a precise context for Trajan's comment, given, indeed, Aurelius' own damning assessment of Nero's rule: "For Nero, in fact, spent the rest of his life so disgracefully that it is disgusting and shameful to record the existence of anyone of this kind, let alone that he was the ruler of the world." However, given the negative portrait of Nero in our ancient sources, it is very unlikely that Trajan's positive comment has been concocted by later historians. In sum, the Neronian context of Trajan's comment is irretrievable.

5. Seneca (*Clem*.1.1.6) addresses Nero thus: "No-one today talks of the deified Augustus or the early years of Tiberius Caesar, or seeks for any model he would have you copy other than yourself."

6. Champlin, *Nero*, 25.

7. Smallwood, *DocsGaius* §145.

8. P.Oxy 1021 (=*DocsGaius* §47).

9. For discussion, Burgess, "Statius' Altar of Mercy," 339–49, esp. 340–42.

10. Harrison, *Paul and the Imperial Authorities*, 271–323.

11. I accept the traditional Neronian dating of the Calpurnius Siculus' *Eclogues*, as opposed to the suggestion of a much later date the poem (e.g., the reign of Severus: AD 193–211; the reign of Carus: AD 282–283). For the Neronian date, see Wiseman, "Calpurnius Siculus," 57–67; Karakasis, *T.*

Clemency (*clementia*) has commanded every vice that wears the disguise of peace to betake itself afar: she has broken every maddened sword-blade. No more shall the funereal procession of a fettered senate weary the headsman at his task; no more will the crowded prison leave only a senator here and there for the unhappy Curia to count. Peace in her fullness shall come; knowing not the drawn sword, she shall renew once more the reign of Saturn in Latium, one more the reign of Numa who first taught the tasks of peace to armies that rejoiced in slaughter. . . . Nay, laws shall be restored; right (*ius*) will come in fullest force; a kinder god (*melior deus*) will renew the former tradition and look of the Forum and displace the age of oppression.[12]

Suetonius, too, speaks of Neronian *clementia* (*Ner.* 10.1: *liberalitatis neque clementiae*), as does Tacitus,[13] although the epitome of Cassius Dio makes no explicit reference to the ruler's clemency. Nero's general, Corbulo, is also spoken of as having earned "a reputation for mercy" (*Ann.* 14.23: *clementiae famam*). Thus clear examples of the *clementia* of Nero toward individuals during his reign can be identified terminologically, even if *clementia*, as David Shotter has argued from a Tiberian context, could be perceived as "a highly dangerous virtue."[14] Little doubt an element of caprice characterized Nero's exercise of *clementia*, although whether this was the case in Tiberius' treason trials is definitely a moot point.[15] Notwithstanding, *clementia* had acquired a long and venerable tradition as a Julio-Claudian virtue long before Nero. It was a defining characteristic, according to the imperial propaganda, of the reigns of Caesar, Augustus, Tiberius, and Claudius.[16] Furthermore, Seneca, the Stoic philosopher and tutor of Nero, has written two treatises on *clementia* for his young charge (*De clementia* ["On Mercy"]), now the subject of a major commentary.[17] Finally, in a remarkable post-Neronian text, the poet Statius presents a moving image of the Altar of Mercy

---

Calpurnius Siculus. For the later date, see Champlin, "Life and Times of Calpurnius Siculus," 95–110; Armstrong, "Stylistics and the Date of Calpurnius Siculus," 113–36.

12. Calpurnius Siculus, *Ecl.* 1.59–66, 71–73.

13. Tacitus, *Ann.* 13.11: "a display of leniency" (*lenitas*); 14.12: "evidence that his own mildness (*lenitatem*) had increased"; 15.73: "settled or cancelled by the clemency (*mansuetudine*) of the sovereign"; 14.48: "an example of public clemency (*publicae clementiae*)."

14. Shotter, *Nero Caesar Augustus*, 67; cf. 68, 181–82. See also Sutherland, "Two Virtues of Tiberius," 129–40.

15. Tacitus and Seneca wield their irony consummately to indicate that there was a "whiff of tyranny" about the so-called "clemency" of the ruler in the Julio-Claudian and Flavian periods. Note especially Burgess, "Statius' Altar of Mercy." Irrespective of the force of Tacitus' portrayal of the tyranny of Tiberius, Tacitus' jaundiced polemic is not verified by the evidence that the great historian provides for Tiberius' alleged "reign of terror." See Walker, *Annals of Tacitus*, 82–137.

16. See Harrison, "Who Is the 'Lord of Grace'?," 383–417, here 393–406.

17. For a translation and discussion of the two treatises, see Braund, *Seneca.* Additionally, see Dowling, *Clemency and Cruelty*, 194–203. Seneca appeals to the *clementia* ("mercy"), *iustitia* ("justice"), and *misericordia* ("compassion") of Claudius in his *De Consolatione ad Polybium* 13.3–4, with a view to securing his release from his exile from Rome (AD 41–49), which had been instigated by Messalina accusing Seneca of adultery with Julia Livilla.

prominently placed in the city. *Clementia* is depicted as drawing the distressed and the needy of the city into the orbit of its care (*Theb.* 12.481–496). Statius' image of the altar of Mercy provides a powerful counter narrative to the imperial version of *clementia*, implemented because of the contemporary excesses of Domitian's tyranny.[18]

Surprisingly, New Testament scholars have not examined Paul's language of "mercy" (ὁ ἔλεος: 9:23; 11:31; 15:9; ἐλεέω: 9:15, 16, 18; 11:30, 31, 32; 12:8; οἰκτιρμός: 12:1) against the backdrop of Julio-Claudian *clementia*. By contrast, significant classical investigations of clemency and pity have been undertaken. Melissa Barden Dowling has written a major study on imperial clemency;[19] David Konstan has also discussed the (unstable, from a Stoic point of view)[20] emotion of pity in antiquity.[21] To what extent might the backdrop of imperial clemency and justice have informed the worldview of Paul's auditors at Rome? What might have been their reaction when they heard for the first time Paul's gospel of justifying grace in Christ, offered by a merciful God as much as to Gentiles as to Jews? What ideological and social challenges might Paul's gospel have presented to Roman auditors in this regard? In what ways did Paul differentiate the mercy and justice of the God of Israel in Christ from the *clementia* and *iustitia* of Nero?

Moving from Neronian *clementia* to the dark underside of Nero's violence and cruelty, what alternative set of social relations did Paul construct for believers living in the capital of the empire? By contrast, what advice did Seneca give to the wise man in dealing with injury and insult in *De Constantia Sapientis* ("On the Firmness of the Wise Man")? These crucial social issues raised by Seneca—ranging from the allocation of Julio-Claudian clemency within Nero's body of the state to the private handling of provocation, injury, and insult by the Stoic sage in everyday affairs—find to some degree their counterpart in the alternative set of social relations, animated by divine mercy, that operated within the body of Christ (Rom 12:8–21). What is distinctive about Paul's social vision for Jewish and Gentile believers living in the capitol? We turn to the teaching of the Stoics on mercy in general and Seneca on *clementia* and the sage's handling of insult in particular.

18. Harrison, "Who Is the 'Lord of Grace'?," 405.

19. See Dowling, *Clemency and Cruelty*; Dowling, "Anger of Tyrants." For older works, see Adam, *Clementia Principis*, 88–101; Fears, "Nero as the Vicegerent of the Gods"; Griffin, *Seneca*, 154–62; B. Mortureux, "Les idéaux stoïciens." For general histories of *clementia*, see Griffin, "Clementia after Caesar."

20. On the Stoic view of the instability and emotional weakness of the soul as opposed to the ideal soul, see Nussbaum, *Love's Knowledge*, 390–401. Other philosophers and writers thought similarly. In the *Nichomachean Ethics* Aristotle catalogues the emotions thus: appetite, anger, fear, envy, joy, love, hatred, longing, emulation, and pity (*NE* 1105b21). Elsewhere he underscores the instability of the emotions, including, significantly, pity (*Rhet.* 2.1.8 [1378a19-21]; cf. Dionysius of Harlicarnassus, *Dem.* 22.5–10): "The emotions are all those affections which cause men to change their opinion in regard to their judgements, and are accompanied by pleasure and pain; such are anger, pity, fear, and all similar emotions and their contraries."

21. Konstan, *Pity Transformed*.

Seneca and the Stoic Understanding of Clemency at Neronian Rome

Traditional Stoic Understandings of Clemency

Before we explore Seneca's understanding of "mercy" (Latin: *clementia*; Greek: ἐπιείκεια),[22] it is important to appreciate that in orthodox Stoicism "pity" (Latin: *misericordia*; Greek: ὁ ἔλεος, ἡ ἐλεημοσύνη) was dismissed. It was founded on an unstable emotional impulse and was therefore undesirable.[23] Precisely because any exercise of *misericordia* failed to impose a just and deserved penalty upon the accused, unwisely excusing them due to the harshness of the law, the justice of its operations was held in question. A fragmentary source commenting on the Stoics (SVF 3.640) sums up the dilemma thus:

> They say that the good man is not lenient (ἐπιεικῆ), for the lenient man is critical of a punishment that is deserved; and they identify being lenient with assuming that the punishments fixed by law are too harsh for wrongdoers and with thinking that the law-giver is distributing punishments contrary to what is deserved.[24]

Diogenes Laertius (7:13 = SVF 3.641) also observes that Stoic wise men maintain the strict justice of the laws by *not* diluting their penalties through the unwise exercise of forgiveness (ἡ συγγνώμη) and mercy (ὁ ἔλεος)

> do not experience pity (συγγνώμην) or have forgiveness (τὸ εἴκειν) for anyone; they do not relax the penalties fixed by the laws, since indulgence (ὁ ἔλεος) and pity (ἐπιείκεια) and even leniency are psychological incapacity, pretending kindness in place of punishment.[25]

---

22. For the equivalence, see Nussbaum, "Equity and Mercy," 83–125, esp. 95–107.
23. See Breytenbach, "'Charis' and 'Eleos,'" 247–77, at 270–73.
24. SVF = von Arnim, *Stoicorum Veterum Fragmenta*.
25. Note Diogenes Laertius' comment (7.123) that the Stoic wise men "are not pitiful and make no allowance for anyone; they never relax the penalties fixed by the laws, since indulgence and pity (ὁ ἔλεος) and even equitable consideration are marks of a weak mind, which affects kindness in place of chastising. Nor do they deem punishments too severe." Gellius (*NA* 14.4) quotes Chrysippus' comment on Justice: "He wished it to be understood that the judge, who is the priest of Justice, should be dignified holy, austere, incorruptible, proof against flattery, pitiless and inexorable towards the wicked and guilty, upright, lofty and powerful, terrifying thanks to the force and majesty of equity and truth." Stobaeus classifies the passions under appetite, pleasure, fear and distress (2.90, 19–91, 9 = SVF 3.394, part.: trans. Long and Sedley, *Hellenistic Philosophers*, 412 §E). In the case of "pity," it is categorized under distress (cf. Diogenes Laertius 7.111). Again, Diogenes Laertius (7.115) observes: "And as in the body, there are certain predispositions [to disease], for example catarrh and diarrhoea, so too in the soul there are tendencies, such as proneness to grudging, proneness to pity (ἐλεημοσύνη), quarrelsomeness and the like." See also Seneca, *De Ira* 2.10: "That you may not be angry with individuals, you must forgive mankind at large (*universis ignoscendum est*), you must grant indulgence to the human race (*generi humano venia tribuenda est*)."

Cicero (*Tusc.* 3.20–21), too, denies that the wise man is animated by any compassion, instead maintaining in every difficult circumstance a studied impassivity:

> The wise man, however, does not come to feel envy; therefore he does not come to feel compassion either (*ergo ne misereri quidem*). But if the wise man were accustomed to feel distress he would also be accustomed to feel compassion (*miseri etiam soleret*). Therefore distress keeps way from the wise man.

Finally, Stobaeus argues that the Stoics do not extend forgiveness because the personal vices of the forgiven are inevitably whitewashed. Ultimately, forgiveness undermines moral accountability:

> They say that <the sensible man> forgives <no one; for it is characteristic of the same man to forgive> and to think that the man who has made a [moral] mistake did not do so because of himself, although [in fact] everyone who makes a [moral] mistake does so because of his own vice. And that is why it is quite proper for them to say that he does not even forgive those who make [moral] mistakes.[26]

Given this widespread depreciation of "pity" (Latin: *misericordia*; Greek: ὁ ἔλεος, ἡ ἐλεημοσύνη) in traditional Stoic thought, Seneca's approach in allowing the ruler to exercise mercy in a discerning manner (*clementia*), whereby the character of the accused is taken into account in the judgment, represents to some degree an ideological novelty in its first-century context. How can this happen without *clementia* degenerating into the despised emotion of "pity" (*misericordia*)? How is Seneca slightly different to other Stoics on the issue of clemency?

Seneca's Understanding of Clemency

Seneca's two-volume (but incomplete) work *De clementia* ("On Mercy") is datable to the year AD 55–56, given the clear allusion to the eighteenth year of Nero in Clem. 1.9.1.[27] Seneca's work is addressed to the young ruler when the *Quinquennium Neronis*, the first five golden years of Nero's rule (*pace*, n4, *supra*), were in full swing. Seneca, as Nero's tutor, intends to guide his young student toward the ideal of a being merciful ruler. The work may have been occasioned by the death of Britannicus, the son of Claudius and Messalina, who was poisoned, Tacitus alleges, by Nero's order in

---

26. Stobaeus 2.11d. Translated by Inwood and Pearson, *Hellenistic Philosophy*, 220–21.

27. This section is a reduced and adapted version of Harrison, *Paul and the Imperial Authorities*, 292–99.

the early months of his reign.[28] In Seneca's view, what determines effective rule is "not the form of the constitution, but the moral character of the emperor."[29]

Seneca (ca. 4 BC/AD 1 to AD 65) affirms the Pythagorean and Stoic emphasis that the ruler has been divinely "chosen (*electusque sum*) to serve on earth as vicar of the gods (*vice deorum*)." In a flattering aside, Seneca observes that Nero now surpassed Augustus and Tiberius as a model to be imitated (*Clem*. 1.1.6). Consequently, Seneca advises the young Nero to commune with himself in this manner so that clemency might continue to be the characteristic virtue of his reign (*Clem*. 1.1.2–4):

> I am the arbiter of life and death for the nations. . . . With me the sword is hidden, nay, is sheathed: I am sparing to the utmost of even the meanest blood; no man fails to find favour at my hands though he lacks all else but the name of man. Sternness I have kept hidden, but mercy (*clementiam*) ever ready at hand. . . . I have been moved to pity by the fresh youth of one, by the extreme old age of another; one I have pardoned for his high position, another for his humble estate; whenever I found no excuse for pity (*misericordiae*), for my own sake I have spared.

According to Seneca, mercy elevates a prince or king above the rest of humanity (*Clem*. 1.3.3) and the demonstration of mercy to his subjects represents a "godlike use of power" (*Clem*. 1.26.5; cf. 1.5.7; 1:19.9).[30] However, Nero's mercy (*clementia*) is in no way conditioned by pity: "whenever I have found no excuse for pity (*misericordia*), for my own sake I have spared."

In an interesting echo of Paul's body imagery in Romans 12:4–8, Seneca employs a "body-soul" metaphor to explain the vital role that the ruler plays in producing a healthy state (*Clem*. 1.4.1–1.5.1–2). Seneca illustrates how Nero as ruler preserves the "body" of state from social disintegration through his clemency:

> For if . . . you are the soul of the state (*animus rei publicae*) and the state your body (*illa corpus tuum*), you see, I think, how requisite is mercy (*clementia*); for you are merciful (*parcis*) to yourself when you are seemingly merciful to another (*parcere*). And so even reprobate citizens (*improbandis civibus*) should have mercy as being the weak members of the body (*membris languentibus*), and if there should ever be need to let blood, the hand must be held under control to keep it from cutting deeper than may be necessary. The quality of

---

28. Tacitus, *Ann*. 13.15–17; 14.63; 15.62 (cf. Suet., *Ner*. 33.2–3; Suet., *Tit*. 2; Cass. Dio 60.33.10; 61.7.4). See Griffin, *Seneca*, 133–35. However, A. Barrett (*Agrippina*, 171–72) argues that Britannicus was killed by an epileptic seizure. Rist ("Seneca and Stoic Orthodoxy," 2006) points to the recent "judicial abuses of Claudius' reign" as another factor why Seneca urged the young Nero to be merciful.

29. Parrott, "Paul's Political Thought," 112.

30. Note Seneca's emphasis on the prince being the author of mercy: "the more indulgent the ruler, the better he is obeyed" (*Clem*. 1.24.2). Additionally, "of all men none is better graced by mercy than a king or a prince. For great power confers grace and glory only when it is potent for benefit" (*Clem*. 1.3.2). According to Seneca, this exercise of mercy makes the ruler analogous with divinity: Nero is the bright and beneficent star (*Clem*. 1.3.1; 1.7.1–2; cf. Sen., *Apoc*. 4.1).

mercy (*clementia*), then, as I was saying, is indeed for all men in accordance with nature, but in rulers it has a special comeliness inasmuch with them it finds more to save, and exhibits itself amid ampler opportunities.³¹

Indeed, Seneca flatters Nero for never having used the sword (*Clem.* 1.11.3). Nero's restrained actions stand in contrast to Augustus, who having used the sword ruthlessly in the initial triumviral years and later at Actium (*Clem.* 1.9.1–2; 1.11.1–2), only learned to show mercy in his mature years as a ruler, as his pardon of Lucius Cinna demonstrated (*Clem.* 1.9.2–12). According to Seneca, this merciful restraint on behalf of the ruler is illustrated in nature. Just as the "king of the bees" (i.e., the queen bee) does not employ its sting in the hive because nature has "removed his weapon," so neither should the ruler intimidate by force or fear (*Clem.* 1.19.1–6).

Perhaps the most interesting observations concerning *clementia* as a royal virtue occur in *De clementia* II, a manuscript that has not come down to us intact. There the king is to demonstrate a particular type of mercy: *clementia* ("mercy") over against *misericordia* ("pity"). According to Seneca, *clementia* restrains the mind from taking vengeance in cases where retribution is deserved, or where one is tempted to be too lenient in fixing a punishment (*Clem.* 2.3.1–2). By contrast, *misericordia* is a mental defect because, according to Stoic thinking, it succumbs with sorrow at the sight of people's ills (*Clem.* 2.4.4–5.1; 2.6.4).³² As Seneca observes, "Pity (*misericordia*) regards the plight, not the cause of it; mercy (*clementia*) is combined with reason" (*Clem.* 2.5.1). By contrast, the wise man, guided by *clementia*, has a serene mind that is not clouded by the plight of others or by strong emotions such as sorrow (*Clem.* 2.5.4–5). Seneca argues that *clementia* serves the cause of justice by not succumbing to *misericordia* in pardoning crimes worthy of punishment (*Clem.* 2.7.1, 3):

> Pardon is given to a man who ought to be punished; but a wise man . . . does not remit a punishment which he ought to exact. . . . Mercy (*clementia*) has freedom in decision; it sentences not only by the letter of the law, but in accordance with what is fair and good (*aequo et bono*). . . . But to pardon is to fail to punish one whom you judge worthy of punishment; pardon is the remission of punishment that is due. Mercy (*clementia*) is superior primarily in this, that it declares that those who are let off did not deserve any treatment; it is more complete than pardon, more creditable.³³

---

31. Parrott ("Paul's Political Thought," 116) observes that in Seneca's view the ruler's extension of mercy is not altruistic: "Such mercy would in actuality be self-serving: the head or soul would be taking care of its own body (1.5.1)."

32. For sources, see n24 *supra*. Note Cicero, *Tusc.* 3.20–21: "The wise man, however, does not come to feel envy; therefore he does not come to feel compassion either (*ergo ne misereri quidem*). But if the wise man were accustomed to feel distress he would also be accustomed to feel compassion (*miseri etiam soleret*). Therefore distress keeps way from the wise man."

33. Prior to our text cited above, note how Seneca depreciates *misericordia* in *Clem* 2.6.4: "Pity (*misericordia*) is akin to wretchedness; for it is partly composed of it and partly derived from it. . . . Pity (*misericordia*) is a weakness of the mind that is much over-perturbed by suffering, and if any one

Adams argues that in Seneca's *De clementia* II, the philosopher falls back to the old Greek conception of ἐπιείκεια ("fairness," "clemency," "equity").[34] We see this emphasis appearing in Seneca's statement, cited above, that *clementia* "sentences not only by the letter of the law, but in accordance with what is fair and good (*aequo et bono*)." In Aristotle, ἐπιείκεια referred to the rectification of the law where the law is defective because of its generality (Aristotle, *Eth. nic.* 1137a–1137b). In contrast to Aristotle, however, Seneca reserves *clementia* for the ideal ruler: the ruler must not arbitrarily compromise the just and fair standards of the law through the lesser exercise of pardon.[35] Rather through the superior exercise of *clementia* the ruler expresses both the justness of his own character and of the law.

In conclusion, precisely because Seneca wanted to connect *clementia* with *iustitia* ("justice"), he made *clementia* the servant of *iustitia* in the second treatise,[36] opening up new territory in the first-century understanding of imperial *clementia*.[37] From the time of Augustus onward, *clementia* was incorporated into the Stoic teaching on the emotions as a prized feature of the Princeps, as the "römisch Tradition" of Seneca's first treatise shows.[38] But, in his second treatise, Seneca desired to form the character of Princeps more thoroughly through a new understanding of *clementia*: namely, that the Princeps will always uphold the strict demands of justice when he exercises mercy in his rule. In other words, for Seneca, the inculcation of *clementia* had become a pastoral strategy that would enable a properly counselled ruler to develop a just and merciful regime.[39]

The Impact of Seneca's Teaching on Clementia and Misericordia upon Nero

Two pieces of epigraphic evidence confirm indirectly the continuing impact of Seneca's teaching on *clementia* and *misericordia* in Nero's reign. First, the widespread Roman distaste for *misericordia*, enunciated by Seneca in several of his treatises, had made its personal impact upon Nero himself. First, in regards to *misericordia*, in a

---

requires it from a wise man, that is very much like requiring him to wail and moan at the funerals of strangers."

34. Adam, *Clementia Principis*, 90.

35. On the differences between Aristotle's understanding of ἐπιείκεια and Seneca's presentation of *clementia*, see Rist, "Seneca and Stoic Orthodoxy," 2007.

36. On the relationship between *clementia* and *iustitia*, see Braund, *De Clementia*, 40–42.

37. Griffin (*Seneca*, 169–70) and Braund (*De Clementia*, 70) also point to the originality of Seneca's position on *clementia*.

38. Adam, *Clementia Principis*, 98.

39. Seneca's understanding of *clementia* stands in contrast to the late republican concept of *clementia*. Earl (*Moral and Political Tradition of Rome*, 60) argues that *clementia* in the republic was "arbitrary mercy, bound by no law, shown by a superior to an inferior who is entirely in his power." It was for this reason that some Romans (e.g., the son of Ahenobarus) rejected Caesar's *clementia*.

famous Greek inscription, Nero proclaims his short-lived liberation of Achaia from taxation (AD 67) and recompenses the province for his providential care by the gods. Nero emphasizes, with due reference to the reciprocity system, that this recompense was not made out of "mercy" (οὐ δι' ἔλεον) but out of "good will" (ἀλλὰ δι' εὔνοιαν) to the Greeks and their gods for their care for him and land and sea.[40] Here ἔλεος is more to be understood within the framework of the Stoic deprecation of "pity" (*misericordia*). As noted, the Stoics linked pity with the unstable emotions and thus it could never acquire the status of a praiseworthy virtue or a tried and tested disposition. Nero rejects such misunderstandings by his deliberate choice of εὔνοια in explaining the motivation for his beneficence.

Second, as regards *clementia*, an inscription of the annual protocols of the priestly college of the Arval Brethren (AD 66)—outlining the public sacrifices at Rome in honor of the Roman gods, the ruler and his family—lists the following offerings: "by reason of the supplications [decreed by the senate, to Jupiter a bovine male, to Juno a cow, to Minerva] a cow, to Felicitas a cow, to Clementia [a cow - - -]."[41] It is significant that this is the only place where *Clementia* is mentioned in the thirty-nine extant inscriptions of the Arval Brethren spanning the period from Augustus to Nero. It reflects, late in Nero's reign, the continuing impact of the teaching of Seneca, his tutor, about the important role of *clementia*, at an official level at least, in the ruler's decisions and cult worship.

Having now exhausted Seneca's teaching on *clementia*, we turn to his teaching on how crises in social relations at Rome, created by personal injury and insult, were to be resolved by the Stoic sage.

Seneca and the Firmness of the Wise Man: Strategies in Dealing with Injury and Insult

According to Seneca, *clementia* is the preserve of his young charge, Nero. The ruler, as the head of the body of state, infuses the body politic with both justice and mercy when he exercises *clementia* properly in his rule. But how then does the "wise man" respond to every-day provocations—with forgiveness, or with another strategy entirely? How do the operations of *clementia* change as they move from the public arena to the private sphere of life, with its complex rituals of injury and insult in personal relations?

Seneca's answer to this question is addressed in his treatise *De Constantia Sapientis*. He argues in *De Const*. 3.2 that the wise man can receive no injury (*iniuria*) or insult (*contumelia*). This is because, as we will see, the wise man is invulnerable to injury due to his superior moral strength as opposed to the faltering endurance of normal human beings (*De Const*. 3.2–3). As Seneca elucidates, "The power of wisdom

---

40. *SIG*3 814 *ll*. 20–24. For a translation, see Danker, *Benefactor*, §44.
41. Scheid, *Commentarii Fratrum Arvalium Qui Supersunt*, §30 Col. I cd. *ll*. 17–19.

is better shown by a display of calmness in the midst of provocation." After making a distinction between *iniuria* and *contumelia* (*De Const.* 5.1), Seneca asserts that the wise man can never be robbed of his virtue (5.3–5):

> Injury has as its aim to visit evil upon a man. But wisdom leaves no room for evil, for the only evil it knows is baseness, which cannot enter where virtue and uprightness already abide. Consequently, if there can be no injury without evil, no evil without baseness, and if, moreover, baseness cannot reach a man already possessed by uprightness, then injury does not reach the wise man. . . . Virtue is free, inviolable, unmoved, unshaken, so steeled against the blows of chance that she cannot be bent, much less broken.

In this imperturbability to any injury, Seneca proposes, the wise man becomes "like a god in all save his mortality" (*De Const.* 8.2).[42] Thus the wise man casts "all injuries far from him, and by his endurance (*patientiaque*) and his greatness of soul (*magnitudine animi*) protect himself from them" (*De Const.* 9.4; cf. 15:3: *animi magnitudinem*).

In regard to the handling of insults, "magnanimity (*magnanimitatem*), the noblest of all the virtues" enables the wise man to scorn "the puffed-up attitude" of the proud and the arrogant (*De Const.* 11.1). Seneca presents Cato as the supreme exemplar (*De Const.* 14.3–4; cf. 1.3; 7.1) in handling the provocation because he does not engage in forgiving his provocateurs but instead displays sublime indifference to the world:

> "But," you ask, "if a wise man receives a blow, what shall he do?" What Cato did when he was struck in the face: he did not flare up, he did not avenge the wrong (*vindicavit iniuriam*), he did not even forgive it (*ne remisit quidem*), but he said no wrong had been done. He showed finer spirit in not acknowledging it than if he had pardoned it (*maiore animo non agnovit quam ignovisset*). . . . He does not regard what men consider base or wretched; he does not walk with the crowd, but as the planets make their way against the whirl of heaven, so he proceeds contrary to the opinion of the world.[43]

Interestingly, only in one place in *De Constantia Sapientis* (19:3) does Seneca assign a positive role to prayer. In the midst of the heated battle, it enables the warrior to move toward the truth and the imperturbability of being a wise man. But, once the

---

42. Seneca, *De Const.* 8.3: "The man who, relying on his reason, marches through mortal vicissitudes with the spirit of a god, has no vulnerable spot where he can receive an injury."

43. Note the comment of the Loeb translator (Basore, *Seneca*, 90) regarding Seneca's imagery: "It was supposed that the sphere of heaven revolved about the earth from east to west, and that while the sun, moon, and planets were swept along in this revolution, they also moved in their own courses in the opposite direction." As Seneca concludes about the wise man (*De Const.* 15.2–3), "his virtue has placed him in another region of the universe." Seneca also cites Socrates and Antisthenes (*De Const.* 18.5) as further exemplars of endurance (*quorum laudamus patientiam*).

wise man has emerged from the crucible of injury and insult, he is self-sufficient and has no further need for prayer.⁴⁴

Violence, Cruelty, and Revenge against the Enemy in Neronian Rome

We have aired earlier that we would look at the darker underside of Nero's *clementia*. The issue is important because it provides us a clue why the Apostle Paul addresses the culture of revenge toward the enemy at Rome. Notwithstanding his avowal to rule by the munificent and clement principles of Augustus, Nero ruthlessly eliminated family rivals from the beginning of his reign onward, scapegoated distinctive groups whose presence in the city, in his view, had provoked the wrath of the gods against Rome, surreptitiously satiated his own predilection for personal violence against the innocent, and upheld in his numismatic propaganda the manliness of his army in violently subjugating their foes. This ever-widening spiral of violence, cruelty, and revenge not only created apprehension for believers living at Rome under an increasingly unstable ruler, but also posed the question how they should react to violent persecution from their enemies in a godly manner (Rom 8:35–36; 12:14a, 17a; 13:4b), should it come, which the apostle prophetically foreshadowed for believers in his epistle (Rom 12:17–21).

The reign of Nero, our ancient sources assert, was characterized by bloodletting from early on from its inception and the carnage continued unabated throughout his principate. Several episodes are notorious in the popular imagination. Modern historians variously assess the ancient sources in their depiction of Nero's complicity in the deaths of his stepbrother Britannicus (AD 55),⁴⁵ his mother Agrippina (AD 59),⁴⁶ his aunt Domitia (AD 59),⁴⁷ his first wife Octavia (AD 62),⁴⁸ his new wife Poppaea (AD 65),⁴⁹ and Antonia, the daughter of Claudius.⁵⁰ While some historians legitimately argue for more nuanced approaches in grappling with the complexities of the ancient evidence in some of the deaths above, historians nevertheless accept the overall

---

44. Dio Chrysostom (*Or.* 8.15–16) states that in facing hardships the wise man does not pray for relief: "nor does he pray to draw another antagonist, but challenges them one after another, grappling with hunger and cold, withstanding thirst, and disclosing no weakness even though he must endure the lash or give his body to be cut or burned."

45. Suetonius, *Ner.* 33.2; Tacitus, *Ann.* 13.14–17; Dio Cassius 61.7.4

46. Suetonius, *Ner.* 33.1–4; Tacitus, *Ann.* 14.3–9; Dio Cassius 61.2.2; 62.13.4–62.14.4; 62.16.1–5.

47. Suetonius, *Ner.* 33.5; Dio Cassius 62.17.1.

48. Suetonius, *Ner.* 35.2; Tacitus, *Ann.* 14.63–64; Dio Cassius 62.13.1. Tacitus (*Ann.* 14.64) underscores the final humiliating indignity of Octavia's murder before Nero's new paramour Poppaea: "As a further and more hideous cruelty, the head was amputated and carried to Rome, where it was viewed by Poppaea."

49. Suetonius, *Ner.* 35.2; Tacitus, *Ann.* 15.6; Dio Cassius 62.27.4–62.28.3.

50. Suetonius, *Ner.* 35. Suetonius adds parricide to matricide (*Ner.* 33.1).

portrait of Nero's ruthless elimination of dynastic rivals, whatever qualifications might be made at the interpretative edges.[51] Nero's execution of rivals in order to consolidate power in AD 62 and 63,[52] his execution of those involved in the Pisonian conspiracy in 65,[53] and his elimination of prominent senators[54] and freedmen[55] demonstrates the calculated and unremitting violence characterizing his rule.[56]

Further, our ancient sources also depict the disguised young Nero prowling the bars and streets of Rome, looking for hapless victims to beat up on their way back home after dinner, stabbing those who fought back and dropping their bodies into the sewers (Suetonius, *Ner.* 26). There is also the savagery of Nero's persecution of the Christians at Rome.[57] Indeed, Nero's choice of the Christians as "scapegoats" for the outbreak of the fire at Rome (Tacitus, *Ann.* 15.44) has some interesting "Girardian" overtones attached to the violence.[58] The persecution of the hated sect of the *Christianoi* was designed to assuage the concerns of the Roman people and appease the wrath of the gods, restoring the *pax deorum* in the capital ("peace of the gods"). The reason for this was that Nero, as Pontifex Maximus of Rome, had already unsuccessfully tried to propitiate the gods at the outbreak of the fire by means of the consultation of the Sibylline books, public prayers, ritual banquets, and all-night vigils (*Ann.* 15.44).[59] The elimination of the Christian "scapegoats," to allude to a "Girardian" understanding, would bring peace and reconciliation back to the beleaguered city.

The evidence of the Neronian coinage is equally as revealing. The violence of Nero and his armies is depicted upon a denarius that shows the figure of *Virtus* ("manliness" or "virtue"). Normally the Neronian denarius depicts *Virtus*, helmeted and in military dress, standing with the right foot on a pile of arms, holding a *parazonium* (a long triangular dagger) on the right knee and a vertical spear in the left hand. However, in a

---

51. Griffin (*Nero*, 73, 74, 96, 98–99, 166, 169–70, 192, 193–96) accepts Nero's complicity in the deaths of all dynastic rivals, whereas more qualified appraisals of the ancient sources are found in Warmington (*Nero*, 34–51), Malitz (*Nero*, 26) and Edward Champlin (*Nero*, 104–5).

52. Suetonius, *Ner.* 37.

53. Tacitus, *Ann.* 15.47–74.

54. Suetonius, *Ner.* 37.1; Tacitus, *Ann.* 16.21; Dio Cassius 62.25.1–26.3. Note R. Mehl's cautionary comment (*Roman Historiography*, 122) regarding the so-called senatorial "Stoic opposition": "Moderns have called this opposition Stoic because the senators they class were imbued to some extent with Stoic ethics, but their 'opposition' constituted neither a unified movement in itself, nor did these senators pursue political goals, let alone real constitutional objectives. Instead, individuals who enjoyed a small following of adherents or admirers displayed their hostility and contempt for a misguided emperor in a way that condemned them to failure in advance."

55. Tacitus, *Ann.* 14.65.

56. Warmington, *Nero*, 135–41; Griffin, *Nero*, 166–70; Shotter, *Nero Caesar Augustus*, 146–50.

57. Tacitus (*Ann.* 15.44) writes: "And derision accompanied their end: they were covered with wild beasts' skins and torn to death by dogs; or they were fastened on crosses, and, when daylight failed were burned to serve as lamps by night. Nero had offered his Gardens for the spectacle."

58. Girard, *Violence and the Sacred*.

59. For discussion, see Harrison, "Persecution of the Christians," 266–300.

chilling variation on the "*Virtus*" motif, an issue of a Neronian silver denarius depicts *Virtus* as standing on the severed head of a captive instead of the traditional pile of arms and helmet.[60] A more forceful visual statement about the ability of Nero and his armies to inflict decisive violence upon the enemy is difficult to conceive.

Last, in an article on the role of dismemberment in the Neronian literature, B. Rodewyk draws attention to the Seneca's *Thyestes*, a play that depicts in Roman terms the tyrant's pathological desire for domination over his empire and subjects.[61] Written toward the last years of Nero's reign (ca. AD 62),[62] the play reflects Seneca's disquiet about Nero's cruelty and megalomania.[63] While it would be unwise to assume that Seneca's portrayal of the evil of Atreus was intended to be a critique of Nero alone,[64] the play probably functions as a warning about Rome's increasing drift toward absolutism in government and its enforcement with violence. In the play, the exiled Thyestes is deceived by the hypocritical reconciliation offered by his evil brother, Atreus (*Thy*. 491–545), with the result that Thyestes decides to return to the royal palace in the city of Argos. The consequence of Thyestes' decision is horrifically tragic. At the reconciliation banquet, Thyestes is duped into feasting upon the cooked remains of his own two dismembered sons (*Thy*. 885–1051), both of whom Atreus had slaughtered prior to the feast (683–788) in an act of revenge for Thyestes' seduction of his wife (220–244). It is little surprise that Atreus' "barbaric" slaughter of Thyestes' two sons—the nephews of Atreus—occurs at an altar in the grove at the back of the palace where spoils from conquered barbarians hang (*Thy*. 662–664).

The symbolism is potent: the royal sons of Thyestes suffer the same fate as the barbarian victims of Roman imperialism. The Roman Empire had begun to feed not only on the barbarian enemies at its borders but it was also turning upon its own ruling family in the capital. Romans, well aware of Nero's dynastic violence outlined above, could hardly have missed the point about the corruption and relentless consumption of imperial power at Rome and more widely in the empire. Indeed, the provincial iconography reinforces Seneca's depiction of Nero's brutality toward the barbarians. A relief in the Sebasteion of Aphrodisias depicts Nero hauling away a naked female barbarian figure, the personification of the defeated Armenia, in a manner

---

60. For full discussion and the image of the silver denarius, see Harrison, *Paul and the Imperial Authorities*, 112–13, "Appendix: Neronian Numismatic Evidence."

61. Rodewyk, "'Dismemberment' in Neronian Literature." See also Olberding, "A Little Throat Cutting." Lucan (*De Bello Civile*), the nephew of Seneca, presents a chilling portrait of republican society torn apart by the violence of war.

62. Nisbet, "Dating of Seneca's Tragedies"; Davis, *Seneca: Thyestes*, 16.

63. Lefèvre, "Die Philosophische Bedeutung der Seneca-Tragödie," 1279–81; Smolenaars, "Vergilian Background of Seneca's *Thyestes*"; Sideri-Tolia, "Seneca's *Thyestes*," 178–82.

64. Sideri-Tolia ("Seneca's *Thyestes*," 179) states, "The undermining of morals and values during Nero's time reinforces the concept that Atreus becomes the diabolical model of the matricidal and fratricidal tyrant, though, however, it is difficult to accept that Seneca's depiction of Atreus constituted a reproof of Nero." Cf. Harsh, *Handbook of Classical Drama*, 427.

similar to Claudius.[65] Nero's message to his provincial clients was unambiguous: he was continuing the policies of his imperial predecessor by subduing the unruly tribes on the frontiers of the Roman Empire.

Given the reign of death and violence at Rome and elsewhere in the empire toward its contumacious enemies,[66] it is worth asking how Paul addressed this violent culture of personal and political retaliation in Romans. How did Paul's countercultural theological construct of divine and human mercy address this with a new vision of grace-filled social relations in the body of Christ?

The God of Israel, the Body of Christ, and the Fate of the Gentiles: Paul's Narrative of Mercy in Comparison to Clementia in Nero's Body of State

In this section we will focus on how the LXX "mercy" texts that Paul cites in Romans 9–11 provide a different understanding of divine mercy in comparison to the way that the gods and the Julio-Claudian rulers were depicted in dispensing mercy in antiquity.[67] As far as the divine world, the ancient gods were powerful friends and dangerous enemies. Because mercy was not the essential characteristic of the gods, it could not be counted on.[68] What difference did Paul's theology of God's unsolicited mercy revealed in Christ make to Jewish and Gentile believers living at Rome, the capital of Neronian *clementia*, and to its dark underside, the cycle of imperial violence and revenge against the enemy? For the sake of brevity, our discussion below of the LXX texts cited by Paul (§§3.1–3.2) will confine ourselves to the cases where Paul retained the LXX ἔλεος/ἐλεέω terminology, as opposed to LXX Hos 2:23 (Rom 9:25) where the occurrences of ἐλεέω are replaced by different terminology.

Divine Mercy in Romans: The Basis of Covenantal Election

In Romans 9:15–18 Paul cites LXX Exod 33:19 (Rom 9:15) and LXX Exod 33:16 (Rom 9:17). Exodus 33:19 occurs in the context of YHWH's theophany before Moses during the wilderness wanderings immediately prior to the giving of the law at Mount Sinai. The "goodness" and "glory" of the Lord passes by Moses who is hidden in a cleft in a rock (Exod 33:19a, 21–23), proclaiming the divine name to the patriarch (33:19a), though the divine face remains hidden from him (33:20, 23b). The theophanic event is occasioned by Moses' request to YHWH to confirm his continuing presence with him

---

65. Smith, *Marble Reliefs*, C8 (fig. 90), 141–43; Plates 61–62, 96.

66. See Harrison, "Paul and the Social Relations of Death at Rome"; Harrison, "Apostle Paul and the Spiral of Roman Violence."

67. On divine ἔλεος (*hesed*) in the Old Testament, see Jacob, *Theology of the Old Testament*, 103–7. More widely in Second Temple Judaism, see Victor, "Giving, Leading, Caring," 141–46.

68. See the full discussion of Konstan, *Pity Transformed*, 105–24.

as leader of Israel by showing him his glory (Exod 33:12–18), especially in view of the spiritual debacle of the golden calf episode immediately prior to this (32:1–33:6).[69]

In Romans 9:15, LXX Exod 33:19 is prefaced by Paul's question as to whether God is just in electing Isaac and Jacob (Rom 9:6–13) on the basis of his unilateral grace (Rom 15:14a)—the answer to which the apostle positively affirms.[70] The LXX text, as cited by Paul, says: "I will have mercy (Ἐλεήσω) on whom I have mercy (ἐλεῶ), and I will have compassion (οἰκτιρήσω) on whom I will have compassion (οἰκτίρω)." As we have seen, in its LXX context Exod 33:19 underscores God's sovereign freedom in deciding to continue to show mercy and compassion to the idolatrous covenantal nation of Israel, chosen by grace, and to its beleaguered but divinely appointed leader, Moses. In its Pauline context, LXX Exod 33:19 demonstrates, as Thomas R. Schreiner has correctly observed, that "God is righteous because he is committed to proclaiming his name and advertising his glory by showing his goodness, grace, and mercy to people as he freely chooses."[71] This means that he chooses Isaac over Ishmael and Jacob over Esau (Rom 9:6–13; cf. 9:18a: "God has mercy on whom he wants to have mercy"),[72] whereas, conversely, he sovereignly hardens Pharaoh (LXX Exod 3:19 [Rom 9:17; 18b]) for his own salvation-historical purposes regarding Israel's exodus from Egypt. Thus covenantal election depends on God's unilateral mercy (τοῦ ἐλεῶντος θεοῦ) over against human will or effort (Rom 9:16): it provides the only possible basis for God's revelation of the riches of his glory to his predestined "objects of mercy" (9:23: ἐπὶ σκεύη ἐλέους), which Paul identifies as the elect church consisting of Jew and Gentile (Rom 9:24). The theme of "predetermined election," enacted in the present, is reinforced by the repetition of ἐκάλεσεν throughout Romans 9 ("he called": Rom 9:7, 12, 24–26).[73]

Roman auditors hearing Paul's papyrus being read out aloud the first time would have been puzzled by several features of Paul's exegesis here. As noted, the concept of the God of Israel choosing to exercise unsolicited mercy to those he had determined to bless from ages past (Rom 16:25–27; cf. Eph 1:4), independently of their will or effort, wrenched the religious initiative entirely from human hands. It made the cult, indigenous and imperial, irrelevant as far as securing divine favor or divine appeasement. At best, imperial *clementia* was an ambiguous construct, allowing Nero to exercise mercy to those he judged sufficiently worthy of moral reform, while simultaneously reinforcing his tyranny through the unpredictability of his pardon to individuals. By

---

69. Fitzmyer (*Romans*, 566) writes that YHWH "might have manifested his distributive justice against the Hebrews in punishing them, but revealed instead that his mercy was utterly free."

70. For discussion, see Harrison, "Paul, Theologian of Electing Grace," 77–108, here 92–101.

71. Schreiner, *Romans*, 507. As Fitzmyer observes (*Romans*, 567), Paul cites "words, addressed originally to Moses . . . in order to underscore Yahweh's freedom of merciful activity."

72. Schreiner, *Romans*, 507.

73. Dunn, *Romans 9–16*, 570. Hultgren (*Paul's Letter to the Roman*, 367) insightfully writes, "Above all, God reserves to himself the freedom of election, and election is a result of divine love, not divine justice."

contrast, according to Paul, divine mercy was extended to the entirely unworthy, who, as Jews and Gentiles, were equally incapable of moral reform (Rom 3:9–20, 23), but, remarkably, the compassionate God, moved to pity over their hopeless plight, had decided to intervene. For the Stoic, however, true justice could not be upheld by a God who might compromise his righteous standards due to the fickleness of his emotions. Little wonder, then, that the Gentile gods primarily dispensed favor in response to correct cultic ritual and judgment in response to human hubris or incorrect ritual: the very unpredictability of divine pity as an emotion meant that mercy was "not their primary trait."[74]

But, for Paul, it was solely on the basis of the "mercies of God" (Rom 12:1: διὰ τῶν οἰκτιρμῶν τοῦ θεοῦ)—understood here as the divine grace and love enunciated in Romans 1–11[75]—that believers could present their bodies as living sacrifices in spiritual worship of God. Paul is keen to emphasize God's providential ordering of history so that the catastrophic disobedience of Israel becomes an opportunity for God to extend mercy to the equally disobedient Gentiles from every nation, which, in turn, provokes "remnant" Jews in the present to receive mercy from God (Rom 11:28, 30–32 [: 4x]; cf. 11:1–10). Whereas the gods associated with local cities prospered their various empires, the vision promulgated by their rulers was nevertheless ethnocentric, subjugating the other nations to the rule and customs of the dominant polis. By contrast Paul's vision of mercy has a surprising universalism about it.[76]

Divine Mercy in Romans: Its Messianic Dimension

How does Romans 15:9 function in the rich *florigelium* of LXX texts in Romans 15:9–12, each of which illustrates the leitmotif of God's mercy to the Gentiles (15:9a: τὰ δὲ ἔθνη ὑπὲρ ἐλέους δοξάσαι τὸν θέον) in Romans 15:9–12? Paul's typological use of LXX texts in Romans 15:3 (LXX Ps 68:10a; ET 69:9a), 15:9 (LXX Ps 17:50; ET 18:49; cf. 2 Sam 22:50), 15:10 (LXX/ET Deut 32:43) and 15:11 (LXX Ps 116:1; ET 117:1) is a pivotal part of his rhetorical strategy in persuading his Roman auditors regarding God's *messianic* grace in Christ toward the Gentile nations. The paean of praise serves as the conclusion to Paul's critique of hubristic attitudes within the Roman house and tenement churches, positing instead that mutual welcome should characterize relations between Jew and Gentile in the body of Christ (Rom 15:7–13). These negative attitudes include ethnic superiority on the part of Roman believers toward their Jewish brothers-in-Christ (Rom 11:17–18a), social elitism in relationships (12:16b: "associate with the lowly"), and the insensitivity of the strong toward the weak over calendrical and food issues (14:1–15:13).

---

74. Konstan, *Pity Transformed*, 124.
75. Jewett, *Romans*, 1–11.
76. For a philosophical approach to the issue, see Badiou, *Saint Paul*.

PART D—SEEKING THE WELFARE OF THE CITY

In the wider pericope of Romans 15:1–13, it is clear from the link between Romans 15:3a and 15:3b that the Messiah is the speaker in the LXX text cited in v. 3b.[77] The motif of messianic summons is also present in the LXX texts cited in vv. 9, 10 and 11. The Messiah, as Paul depicts him, addresses the Gentile nations in vv. 9–11 in a winsome and celebratory manner: the Son of David praises God before the Gentiles for his salvation and Davidic descendants (v. 9), invites the Gentiles to rejoice in God's salvation from their enemies (v. 10), and encourages them to praise God for his steadfast love and faithfulness (v. 11). A messianic proof-text from Isaiah (LXX Isa 11:10) brings Paul's typological use of the LXX to a resounding conclusion in v. 12. There the risen and reigning Messiah brings the nations under his personal rule and affirms their present incorporation into the body of Christ through the summons of divine grace.

What role does "mercy" play in LXX Ps 17:50 (ET 18:49)? How is the LXX text theologically adapted in Romans 15:9 in order to illustrate God's mercy? The Psalm commences with David's praise to YHWH, his protector and deliverer (ET 18:2), for his salvation from the king's enemies and from the hands of Saul (superscription, Ps 18). In response to David's cry for rescue from death (18:5–6), YHWH, as a divine warrior,[78] graciously answers him with a dramatic theophany from heaven (18:7–15). YHWH delivers David by empowering him for battle so that he can pursue and destroy his enemies (18:29–42). Consequently, because of YHWH's mercy, David, as the anointed Son, now rules many terrified nations (18:46–50), emboldening David's praise of YHWH among the nations (18:49).

As noted, Paul reconfigures Ps 18:49 (Rom 15:9) within a messianic framework of prophecy and fulfillment, applying it to the summons of the risen and reigning Christ, the son of David (Rom 1:3), who invokes the Gentile nations to praise the God of Israel. However, this Gentile act of submission is not to be performed in fear, as was the case in Ps 18:46–50. Rather, because of the incorporation of the Gentiles by Christ's cruciform grace into the vine of Israel (Rom 11:17–24), they can now voice their praise of God with exuberant joy for his overflowing mercy to them. Roman readers familiar Psalm 18 would also have realized that the victory of Davidic king of Israel over the nations extended to "his descendants forever" (Ps 19:50b). Thus Roman believers, as Abraham's adopted progeny along with the other Gentile nations by means of justifying faith (Rom 4:9–17; 8:12–17), would perpetually participate in Christ's messianic victory over sin and death (5:12–21). The ephemeral reign of Julio-Claudian grace had been supplanted by the vastly superior reign of Christ's grace.[79] Finally, given that the gods of antiquity rarely extended pity or mercy without prior cultic supplication (cf. Rom 1:21–23), reflective Roman Gentile readers, the addresses

---

77. Seifrid, "Romans," 607–94, here 689.

78. On the intensively studied "divine warrior" motif, see Longman and Reid, *God Is a Warrior*; Neufeld, *"Put on the Armour of God."*

79. See Harrison, *Paul's Language of Grace*, 214–34.

of the epistle (1:13; 11:13; 15:15–16), would have been genuinely surprised by Paul's paean of the unsolicited mercy of the God of Israel.

Living Mercifully amid Nero's Spiral of Violence at Rome

We have already highlighted the increasing atmosphere of anxiety that Roman believers faced as the spiral of Nero's violence widened in its social impact at Rome. When would it be eventually unleashed against believers? Paul hints that the imperial sword could eventually be turned against believers at Rome (ἡ μάχαιρα: Rom 8:35b; 13:4a) if they did not live astutely. Consequently, Paul highlights the importance of rendering honor and obedience to the Roman ruler in order to win his praise (Rom 13:3b–6, 7a, 7b). More generally, believers were likely to be persecuted (Rom 12:14) by undefined enemies and have evil inflicted upon them (12:17a). In the face of such provocation (including injury and insult?), they were to adopt not only a culture of non-retaliation (Rom 12:17: "evil for evil" [Matt 5:38–41]) but also, unexpectedly in Roman context, a culture of blessing their enemies as opposed to cursing them (Rom 12:14: "bless and do not curse" [Matt 5:44; Luke 6:27–28]). As far as humanly possible, believers were to live at peace with all (Rom 12:18 [Mark 9:50; Matt 5:9]). There is little doubt that in all these cases Paul is demonstrating his intimate familiarity with Jesus' dominical teaching. Summing up the sweep of his teaching, Paul concludes that evil was to be overcome by good (Rom 12:21; cf. vv. 9, 14, 17, 18, 19). The apostle, therefore, is unpacking with practical examples what authentic love without hypocrisy means for the believer at Rome (Rom 12:9), first with the family of faith (12:10–13), and then beyond the body of Christ (12:14–21).[80]

However, once again in a familiar rhetorical strategy, Paul undermines the Roman right to retaliation and personal revenge by means of the authoritative citation of LXX texts (Deut 32:35 [Rom 12:19]; Prov 25:21–22 [Rom 12:20]). First, in the case of Deuteronomy 32:35,[81] the text represents God's climactic call of obedience (32:46) to the faithless and faltering nation of Israel at the edge of her entry into the promised land. Moses has already outlined in all its idolatrous shame the litany of sins which has characterized Israel in her wilderness wanderings (Deut 32:1–33), notwithstanding YHWH's continuous acts of soteriological deliverance throughout (32:4, 6–14). Although God will repay the sins of his people (Deut 32:35) and of his enemies (32:40–42), he will nonetheless have compassion upon his servants (32:36), heal those whom he has wounded (32:39), and make atonement for his land and people (32:43b). Strikingly, the Gentile nations are summoned to rejoice with his people over God's vengeance upon Israel's enemies and his extension of atoning forgiveness to her (32:43a). No reason is given why the nations should do this, other than the cryptic promise that God will make Israel "envious by those who are not a people" and

---

80. Osborne, *Romans*, 340–41.
81. See the extended discussion of Middendorf, *Romans 9–16*, 1272–74.

"angry by a nation that has no understanding" (Deut 32:21). The same text is cited by Paul in Romans 10:19 to confirm the extension of the life-transforming gospel to the unbelieving Gentile nations (10:19–20), as opposed to disobedient and faltering Israel (10:21). Thus Roman believers in Romans 12:15–20 [cf. v. 19 [Deut 32:35]) are called to be similarly patient with those who currently oppose them, as God historically was with backsliding Israel in the wilderness wanderings, with a view to God also extending to their enemies the same mercy they had recently experienced as Jews and Gentiles in Christ.

Second, to unveil the radical dimension of overcoming "evil with good" (Rom 12:21), Paul cites LXX Proverbs 25:21–22 (Rom 12:26), with Proverbs 25:21 effectively underscoring the importance of extending the beneficence of food and water to one's enemies. Proverbs 25:22 is more puzzling, however, in its instance that "in doing this, you will heap burning coals on his head." Since there is no context for the saying provided in the disparate collection of wisdom logia in Proverbs 25, the theological implication of the text is difficult to discern. Is the author of Proverbs and Paul simply upending the ancient politics of vengeance by exacerbating the frustration and resentment felt by the enemy through the strategy of unexpected kindness? Or is the imagery metaphorically pointing to the possibility of repentance being elicited by the unexpected gift of mercy?[82] In view of the fact that LXX Deut 32:35 (Rom 12:19), in its Old Testament context, underscores God's continuing patience with Israel, it is perhaps more likely that LXX Proverbs 25:21–22 (Rom 12:26) has the eventual repentance of the enemy in mind. Either way, the social context of countercultural *praxis* toward the enemy is eminently clear on Paul's part.[83]

Paul's Social Understanding of Divine Mercy: Undermining Roman Plutocratic Values by Exalting the Poor in the Body of Christ

Roman society was divided into three orders according to the criterion of wealth,[84] underscoring that at its heart Roman rule was a plutocracy. The fact that Augustus in

---

82. Klassen, "Coals of Fire." Thomas R. Schreiner points to the Old Testament metaphorical context of judgment and especially the intertestamental text of 2 Esd 16:53: "God will burn coals of fire on the head of everyone who says, 'I have not sinned before God and his glory.'" Schreiner (*Romans*, 675) posits that it is psychologically probable that "the promise of God's judgement would free believers to do good to their opponents." For the interpretation of the coals metaphorically causing a person to feel shame and experience remorse, see Middendorf, *Romans 9–16*, 1274–78.

83. Keck (*Romans*, 310) writes, "In terms of 'ethics,' Paul's command is not prudential but deontological—that is, verse 20 is not a wise strategy to change the opponent; it is simply one's obligation" (cf. Rom 13:8–10).

84. Roman society was organized around an "'estate' system of classification with legal distinctions between statuses" (Reinhold, "Usurpation of Status and Status Symbols," 279): namely, the senatorial order (1 million sesterces as a property qualification); the equestrian order (400,000 sesterces as a property qualification); the decurion order (the top 100 men of each city).

Res Gestae 15–24 outlines in massive detail the benefactions issuing from his personal largesse reinforces the point. But, in a world of elite benefaction and the routine allocation of the imperial grain dole in the capital, the Roman elite authors rarely evince interest in the poor of Neronian Rome.[85] Furthermore, given the thorny issue of the identification of the "poor" at Rome from the city epitaphs and the slipperiness of the terminology of "poverty" in the Roman writers covering the Neronian era,[86] Roman definitions of the "poor" were so muddied by elite perspectives that the truly destitute passed by without any epigraphic commemoration or attention in the historical literature.[87] Discerning whether the poverty spoken about was idealized or genuine was often a difficult decision. What interest did the apostle show in the fate of the poor as far as the ministry of the Roman churches? And how is the language of mercy brought into play in this regard (ὁ ἐλεῶν ἐν ἱλαρότητι: Rom 12:8d)? Several important perspectives on the issue are enunciated in Romans 12.

In Romans 12:8 there are at least two charisms—with the possibility that there are actually three[88]—which had direct relevance to the beneficence of the Roman house and tenement churches. One charism mentioned by Paul is ὁ μεταδιδοὺς ἐν ἁπλότητι (Rom 12:8b: "the one who contributes who contributes with generosity"). Another charism refers to ὁ ἐλεῶν ἐν ἱλαρότητι (Rom 12:8d: "the one who shows mercy in cheerfulness"). Whether there is a third "welfare" charism, implied by the mediating phrase ὁ προϊστάμενος ἐν σπουδῇ (Romans 12:8c: "the one who governs in diligence" [NRSV]; alternatively, "the one who provides resources in ready concern" [trans. B. Byrne]), is a moot point. If there are indeed three welfare charisms, we have a remarkable explosion of exhortations to beneficence and almsgiving of various kinds, with the subtleties of nuance between 12:8b, 8c, and 8d increasingly difficult to detect.[89]

85. There is reference to Nero depriving Romans of the "free dole of grain" in AD 64 (Cassius Dio 62.18.5). On the "merciless lengths" that some Roman officials went to against the poor in right of sale during the Neronian age, see Tacitus, *Ann.* 13.30. No other references to the genuinely poor of Neronian Rome occur in Suetonius, Tacitus and Cassius Dio.

86. On the difficulty of identifying the "poor" in the epitaphs of Rome, see Harrison, "Reading Romans with Roman Eyes," ch. 3. Examples of the slipperiness of elite discourse about "poverty" can found in Tacitus' account of Nero's reign. For example, the honor of the noble family of Messala, coconsul of Nero in AD 58, received an imperial "increment in a yearly subsidy of *five hundred thousand sesterces*, on which Messala might support *an honest poverty*" (*Ann.* 13.34: emphasis mine). However, some nobility did genuinely fear impoverishment: e.g., Marcellus, grandson of the Asinius Pollio (cos. 40 BC), "regarded poverty as the greatest evil" (*Ann.* 14.40). As another example, Seneca, in response to his maligners (AD 62), orders that his estates be managed by the procurators. However, no reduction to genuine poverty is envisaged: "Not that by my own action I shall reduce myself to poverty: rather, I shall resign the glitter of wealth which dazzles me, and recall to the service of the mind those hours which are now set apart to the care of my gardens or my villas" (Tacitus, *Ann.* 14.54).

87. Martial observes that in Rome the *vespillones* (corpse-bearers) could be seen carrying the body of an anonymous pauper "like a thousand that the pauper's pyre receives" (Martial, *Ep.* 8.75). On the plight of the poor and finding accommodation in Rome and Ostia, see Van den Bergh, "Plight of the Poor Urban Tenant."

88. So Dunn (*Romans 9–16*, 730–32) and Byrne (*Romans*, 373–74) argue.

89. Middendorf (*Romans 9–16*, 1236) correctly notes regarding Rom 12:8b, 8c, and 8d that

B. Byrne, for example, sees in Romans 12:8b a clear cultural allusion to the well-off Roman *patronus* acting on behalf of the less-advantaged,[90] as opposed to the majority view of Romans commentators that προϊστάμενος means "one who presides," denoting instead an authoritative leadership role. If Byrne and Dunn are correct, we have a remarkable exhortation (cf. Rom 12:8a: "the one who encourages in encouragement" [ὁ παρακαλῶν ἐν τῇ παρακλήσει]), repeated three times in various configurations, regarding the practical care for the poor and needy at Rome. It totally severed the early Christian understanding of beneficence from the Greco-Roman reciprocity system, in which the benefactor calculated in advance the moral and social worth of the recipients and then assessed their ability to mount an appropriate return before extending beneficence.

However, if we take ὁ προϊστάμενος ἐν σπουδῇ in Romans 12:8c as a reference to an appointment to a leadership role in a house or tenement church at Rome,[91] then we have to ask why the phrase is "wedged" between two differently phrased exhortations to beneficence (Rom 12:8b, 8d), and why the *three* consecutive phrases (12:8b, 8c, 8d) are prefaced by the charism of encouragement (12:8a). To commence with the charism of encouragement prefacing the three other charisms, the answer lies in the importance of the continuous encouragement of believers to good works, including beneficence (Rom 12:8b, 8d) and leadership (12:8c), within the house and tenement churches.[92] The charism of encouragement in the body of Christ was inaugurated by the mercies of God (Rom 12:1: παρακαλῶ) and empowered by the indwelling Spirit of the risen Christ (15:30: παρακαλῶ), as opposed to the viewers of posterity being motivated to ethical behavior by means of the commemorative exempla found in the Roman elite epitaphs.[93] But does the reformulation of the charism of beneficence in 12:8b qualify, expand, or narrow the charism of beneficence in 12:8d? Is it just a rhetorical strategy on Paul's part designed to reinforce his point or is something new being said?

The charism ὁ μεταδιδοὺς ἐν ἁπλότητι (Rom 12:8b) has aroused intense debate among commentators regarding the distributor of the beneficence: is the beneficence offered by an individual benefactor from his own resources, or is the beneficence corporate and delivered by an administrator?[94] But this dilemma is not the primary focus of the apostle. In contrast to the almsgiving focus of Romans 12:8d, it would seem that *general* expressions of beneficence in the body of Christ are envisaged here, irrespective of whether they are individually or collectively conceived. This beneficence

---

"establishing specific definitions for Paul's terminology becomes especially problematic with the final three participles."

90. Byrne, *Romans*, 373.

91. Jewett, *Romans*, 753.

92. Cranfield (*Epistle to the Romans*, 2:623) states, "The immediate purpose of exhortation was to help Christians live out their obedience to the gospel."

93. On the Scipionic elogia and the imitation of the great man, see Harrison, "Imitation of the Great Man in Antiquity," 213–54, here 223–25, 228–33, 237–38.

94. See, for example, the discussion of Middendorf, *Romans 9–16*, 1236–37.

includes the needs of the poor, but it ranges more widely across the various ministries of the church. So the benefactor "who contributes with generosity," whether collectively or individually conceived, could provide long-term accommodation and hospitality for visiting dignitaries at Rome (e.g., Phoebe: Rom 16:1–2), fund Paul's mission to Spain (15:24) or other (unknown to us) missions into the Italian peninsula, offset the costs of rents or structural repairs in a tenement church/churches, provide the money for the scribal copying of Paul's Letter to the Romans on a new papyrus and expedite its delivery to the churches in the Greek East (cf. 16:22), fund the costs of food at the love feasts of believers, pay for the funeral costs for the destitute among its members (Aristides, *Apol.* 15),[95] to cite a few pertinent examples.

By contrast, the category of beneficence envisaged by ὁ ἐλεῶν ἐν ἱλαρότητι (Rom 12:8d) is specifically almsgiving to the poor. This is signalled by Second Temple Judaism language of mercy (ἐλεημοποιός, ἐλεημοσύνη) which speaks specifically of almsgiving responsibilities.[96] Dunn has also correctly noted the unusualness of Paul's language of "mercy" here, stating that this is the one place in the Pauline corpus where the apostle speaks of human beings showing mercy to human beings, impelled by their response to divine mercy (Rom 9:15–16, 18; 11:30–32).[97] However, this unexpected emphasis on mercy is perhaps more easily answered from a Roman perspective. Paul's emphasis was providentially prescient in a context where Nero had been encouraged by the philosopher Seneca to dispense mercy to the "weak members" in the body politic, which Seneca identified as Nero himself, but, significantly, this mercy was only to be shown to those weak reprobate citizens who showed sufficient indication that they would worthily respond to his grace (*Clem* 1.4.1–1.5.2).[98] For Paul, mercy to the poor should be unconditionally exercised no matter their social worth. Moreover, we are confronting here a social novelty in the Neronian context because the language of "mercy" was never used for beneficence to the poor—which was a highly unusual scenario anyway, apart from the imperial provision of the corn dole. Furthermore, as we have seen above, the language of "mercy" was avoided by Nero in his liberation of Achaia in AD 67 due to its connotation of emotional instability, preferring instead the traditional benefaction language of "good will."

But why, then, did Paul place the charism of authoritative leadership (Rom 12:8c: ὁ προϊστάμενος ἐν σπουδῇ) between the two differently conceived, so I have argued, charisms of beneficence (12:8b, 8d)? The phrase, I believe, does "double duty," showing the necessity of leadership and administration in the house and tenement

---

95. Aristides, *Apol.* 15: ". . . but when one of their poor passes away from the world, and any of them sees him, then he provides for his burial according to his ability."

96. See Dunn, *Romans 9–16*, 732, referring to Tobit (1:3, 16; 4:7–8; 9:6) and Sirach (7:10).

97. Dunn, *Romans 9–16*, 731.

98. For discussion, see Harrison, *Paul and the Imperial Authorities*, 292–99.

churches in order to orchestrate wide-ranging forms of beneficence (Rom 12:8b) and also to deliver alms-giving for the poor (12:8d).[99]

Last, in Romans 12:13, Paul focuses on the importance of extending beneficence to insiders and outsiders of the church, including, contextually, the enemies of believers (12:15, 19–21, esp. vv. 19–20 [LXX Deut 32:35; Prov 25:21–22a]). In this counter-cultural teaching,[100] we observe the intersection of two traditions: the LXX tradition[101] and the dominical teaching and exemplum of Christ (Matt 5:44a; Luke 6:27–28b; 23:34a).[102] But, above all, the death of Christ for his enemies and his soteriological transfer of benefits to them (Rom 5:6–8) redefines social relations toward outsiders in this instance.

Conclusion

We have argued that Paul's understanding of "mercy" (ἔλεος), the equivalent of the despised Stoic emotion of *misericordia* ("pity"), is distinctive in its Roman context. The idea of the God of Israel relentlessly seeking to incorporate elect Gentiles into his covenant people through the reconciliation proffered in Christ, with no prior worthy response required on their part, undermined not only Jewish ethnocentrism but also ancient understandings of those very rare occasions when the gods offered mercy to suppliants independently of any prior cultic appeasement. The initial expressions of *clementia* at the outset of Nero's reign grew increasingly infrequent as a culture of violence and revenge progressively consumed the ruler. Paul's summons to believers to exercise mercy and beneficence toward their enemies and persecutors would have marked out the social relations of Roman believers as distinctive as Nero's rule increasingly slid toward tyranny. Unlike the Stoic, believers were forbidden to retreat into a Senecan imperturbability in the face of injury and insult. Instead they were summoned to bless their persecutors rather than curse them (Rom 12:17b) and to live in peace with everyone as far as their personal circumstances allowed (12:19b). Undeniably Paul's teaching draws upon the dominical teaching of the historical Jesus in this instance, even if the apostle cites Proverbs 25:21–22 (Rom 12:20) as extra arsenal for his case. Furthermore, the extension of mercy through beneficence toward the poor, inside and outside of the body of Christ, without any expectation of reciprocity or prior evaluation of their worthiness, represented a social novelty at Rome. Mercy, it seems, had triumphed over judgment and, in contrast to Julio-Claudian *clementia*, it extended its concern to the economically destitute rather than just to ostracised opponents, as was the case with Nero.

---

99. See the possible understandings of administration in Cranfield, *Epistle to the Romans*, 2:626–27.

100. See Klassen, *Love of Enemies*.

101. See Dunn, *Romans 9–16*, 749–52, and Jewett, *Romans*, 774–78. On the understanding of the difficult text of LXX Prov 25:21–22a (Rom 12:20), see Middendorf, *Romans 9–16*, 1274–78.

102. Thompson, *Clothed with Christ*, 96–105; Harrison, "Jesus and the Grace of the Cross."

Two questions remain. First, did Paul intentionally pivot his teaching on mercy against its Neronian counterpart in writing to the Romans? The extent to which Seneca's private teaching on *clementia* to his young charge was known to Roman believers is a moot point, even if *De clementia* was written at roughly the same time as Paul's composition of Romans. It is possible that believers in the *familia Caesaris* at Rome (Phil 4:22) were well aware that Seneca had counselled Nero from the time of his accession to power about the importance of *clementia* for the ruler. But it seems unlikely that Paul would have access to this specialist "insider" information at Corinth, the place in which he was composing Romans. More likely, Roman believers were familiar at a general level with the imperial understanding of *clementia*, a recurring social motif in the Julio-Claudian propaganda from the dictatorship of Julius Caesar to the reign of Claudius. I suspect that Paul struck out in an independent direction, taking his cue from imperial culture in the eastern provinces and from Roman colonies such as Corinth and Philippi. The apostle established an alternative set of social relations for the body of Christ in Rome, in order to differentiate its behavior toward Jews and Gentiles, internally and externally, from the corrupt values, violence, and behavioral excesses of the Neronian body of state. This would enable believers, who were increasingly being placed under pressure because of their social distinctiveness, to meet the animus of their persecutors with loving resolve. Although the full depths of Nero's savagery would only be revealed later in AD 64, Paul does not idly warn believers about the ever present danger of the ruler's sword in mid-fifties Rome. For Paul, divine mercy was the socially transformative dynamic operative in the body of Christ that would enable believers to meet the challenges of living in Rome with equanimity.

Second, how did Paul reconcile the competing demands of justice and mercy in articulating how believers should live before God and the residents of Rome? As noted, in *De clementia*, Seneca argued that Nero should not put at risk Roman justice by letting his clemency degenerate into unstable pity. But Seneca did not relate his discussion in any way to the Roman gods: they were routinely propitiated for human impiety and reciprocated for their beneficence by the state's meticulous attention to the cult. Nor did the gods evince any interest in the operations of social relations in the city. But Paul argues that God had put forward Jesus as the ἱλαστήριον ("propitiation," "mercy seat": Rom 3:25a) in order to satisfy the full demands of his rightful wrath against sin (3:325b–26; cf. Rom 1:17–31). If those commentators who argue that Paul, in employing ἱλαστήριον, was referring to the "mercy seat" of Leviticus 16 are correct,[103] then justice and mercy seamlessly intersect in the soteriological work of the crucified Christ. When God sovereignly exercised his overflowing mercy in Christ, the full demands of his justice were satisfied. Conversely, in addressing the immutable demands of his justice, God's mercy was never overwhelmed or diminished. Because of this paradoxical meeting of justice and mercy in the Roman cross of Christ, the

---

103. E.g., Schreiner, *Romans*, 191–94, for a sensitive evaluation of all the issues.

social outworking of imperial values was radically upended in the body of Christ, with the result that the mores of classical culture would face increasing challenge.

Bibliography

Adam, T. *Clementia Principis: Der Einfluß hellenistischer Fürstenspiegel auf den Versuch einer rechtlichen Fundierung des Principats durch Seneca*. Stuttgart: Ernst Klett, 1970.

Alexander, P. H. *The SBL Handbook of Style*. 2nd ed. Atlanta: SBL, 2014.

Armstrong, D. "Stylistics and the Date of Calpurnius Siculus." *Philologus* 130 (1986) 113–36.

Arnim, H. F. A. von. *Stoicorum Veterum Fragmenta*. 4 vols. Stuttgart: Teubner, 1903–5.

Badiou, Alain. *Saint Paul: The Foundation of Universalism*. Translated by Ray Brassier. Stanford: Stanford University Press, 2003.

Barrett, A. *Agrippina: Sex, Power, and Politics in the Early Empire*. New Haven: Yale University Press, 1999.

Basore, J. W. *Seneca: Moral Essays*. Vol. 1. London: W. Heinemann, 1963.

Bergh, R. Van den. "The Plight of the Poor Urban Tenant." *Revue international des droits de l'antiquité* 50 (2003) 443–77.

Bird, H. W. *Aurelius Victor: De Caesaribus*. Liverpool: Liverpool University Press, 1994.

Braund, Susanna. *Seneca: De Clementia*. Oxford: Oxford University Press, 2009.

Breytenbach, C. "'Charis' and 'Eleos' in Paul's Letter to the Romans." In *The Epistle to the Romans*, edited by Udo Schnelle, 247–77. Leuven: Leuven University Press, 2009.

Burgess, J. F. "Statius' Altar of Mercy." *Classical Quarterly* 22 (1972) 339–49.

Champlin, Edward. "The Life and Times of Calpurnius Siculus." *Journal of Roman Studies* 68 (1978) 95–110.

———. *Nero*. Cambridge: Belknap Press of Harvard University Press, 2003.

Cranfield, C. E. B. *The Epistle to the Romans*. Vol. 2, *IX–XVI*. Edinburgh: T. & T. Clark, 1979.

Danker, F. W. *Benefactor: Epigraphic Study of a Graeco-Roman and New Testament Semantic Field*. St. Louis: Clayton, 1982.

Davis, P. J. *Seneca: Thyestes*. London: Duckworth, 2003.

Dowling, Melissa Barden. "The Anger of Tyrants and the Forgiveness of Kings." In *Ancient Forgiveness: Classical, Judaic, and Christian*, edited by Charles L. Griswold and David Konstan, 79–96. Cambridge: Cambridge University Press, 2012.

———. *Clemency and Cruelty in the Roman World*. Ann Arbor: University of Michigan Press, 2006.

Dunn, James D. G. *Romans 9–16*. Dallas: Word, 1988.

Earl, D. C. *The Moral and Political Tradition of Rome*. London: Thames and Hudson, 1967.

Fears, J. R. "Nero as the Vicegerent of the Gods in Seneca's 'De Clementia.'" *Hermes* 103 (1975) 486–96.

Fitzmyer, Joseph A. *Romans: A New Translation with Introduction and Commentary*. London: Geoffrey Chapman, 1992.

Girard, René. *Violence and the Sacred*. Baltimore: John Hopkins University Press, 1977.

Griffin, Miriam T. "*Clementia* after Caesar: From Politics to Philosophy." In *Caesar against Liberty? Perspectives on His Autocracy*, edited by Francis Cairns and Elaine Frantham, 157–82. Papers of the Langford Latin Seminar 11. Cambridge: Cairns, 2003.

———. *Nero: The End of a Dynasty*. New Haven: Yale University Press, 1984.

———. *Seneca: A Philosopher in Politics*. Oxford: Oxford University Press, 1976.

Harrison, James R. "The Apostle Paul and the Spiral of Roman Violence." In *Bridges in New Testament Interpretation*, edited by Neil Elliott and Werner H. Kelber, 119–47. Minneapolis: Fortress, 2018.

———. "The Imitation of the Great Man in Antiquity: Paul's Inversion of a Cultural Icon." In *Christian Origins and Classical Culture: Social and Literary Contexts for the New Testament*, edited by Stanley E. Porter and Andrew W. Pitts, 213–54. Leiden: Brill, 2013.

———. "Jesus and the Grace of the Cross: Luke 23:34a and the Politics of 'Forgiveness' in Antiquity." *Journal for the Gospels and Acts Research* 1 (2017) 42–67.

———. *Paul and the Imperial Authorities at Thessalonica and Rome: A Study in the Conflict of Ideology*. Tübingen: Mohr Siebeck, 2011.

———. "Paul and the Social Relations of Death at Rome (Rom 5:14, 17, 21)." In *Paul and His Social Relations*, edited by Stanley E. Porter and Christopher D. Land, 85–123. Pauline Studies 7. Leiden: Brill, 2012.

———. "Paul, Theologian of Electing Grace." In *Paul and His Theology*, edited by Stanley E. Porter, 77–108. Pauline Studies 3. Leiden: Brill, 2006.

———. *Paul's Language of Grace in Its Graeco-Roman Context*. 2003. Reprint, Eugene: Wipf & Stock, 2017.

———. "The Persecution of the Christians from Nero to Hadrian." In *Into All the World: Emergent Christianity in Its Jewish and Greco-Roman Context*, edited by M. Harding and A. Nobbs, 266–300. Grand Rapids: Eerdmans, 2017.

———. "Reading Romans with Roman Eyes: Studies on the Social Perspective of Romans." Minneapolis: Lexington / Fortress Academic, forthcoming.

Harsh, Philip Whaley. *A Handbook of Classical Drama*. Stanford: Stanford University Press, 1944.

Hultgren, Arland J. *Paul's Letter to the Roman: A Commentary*. Grand Rapids: Eerdmans, 2011.

Inwood, B., and L. G. Pearson. *Hellenistic Philosophy: Introductory Readings*. 2nd ed. Indianapolis: Hackett, 1997.

Jacob, Edmund. *Theology of the Old Testament*. London: Hodder and Stoughton, 1958.

Jewett, Robert. *Romans*. Minneapolis: Fortress, 2007.

Karakasis, Evangelos. *T. Calpurnius Siculus: A Pastoral Poet in Neronian Rome*. Berlin: de Gruyter, 2016.

Keck, L. E. *Romans*. Nashville: Abingdon, 2005.

Klassen, William. "Coals of Fire: Sign of Repentance or Revenge?" *New Testament Studies* 9 (1963) 337–50.

———. *Love of Enemies: The Way to Peace*. Philadelphia: Fortress, 1984.

Konstan, David. *Pity Transformed*. London: Duckworth, 2001.

Lefèvre, E. "Die Philosophische Bedeutung der Seneca-Tragödie am Beispiel des 'Thyestes.'" *Aufstieg und Niedergang der römischen Welt* 2.32.2 (1985) 1263–83.

Levick, Barbra M. "Nero's Quinquennium." In vol. 3 of *Studies in Latin History and Literature*, edited by C. Deroux, 211–25. Brussels: Latomus, 1983.

Long, A. A., and D. N. Sedley. *The Hellenistic Philosophers*. Vol. 1, *Translations of the Principal Sources, with Philosophical Commentary*. Cambridge: Cambridge University Press, 1987.

Longman, Tremper, and Daniel G. Reid. *God Is a Warrior*. Grand Rapids: Zondervan 1995.

Malitz, Jürgen. *Nero*. Oxford: Blackwell, 2005.

Mehl, R. *Roman Historiography: An Introduction to Its Basic Aspects and Development*. Malden, MA: Wiley-Blackwell, 2011.

Middendorf, Michael P. *Romans 9–16*. St. Louis: Concordia, 2016.

Mortureux, B. "Les idéaux stoïciens et les premières responsabilités politiques: le 'De Clementia.'" *Aufstieg und Niedergang der römischen Welt* 2.36.3 (1989) 1639–85.

Neufeld, Thomas Yoder. *"Put on the Armour of God": The Divine Warrior from Isaiah to Ephesians*. Sheffield: Sheffield Academic, 1999.

Nisbet, R. G. M. "The Dating of Seneca's Tragedies, with Special Reference to Thyestes." *Papers of the Leeds International Latin Seminar* 6 (1990) 95–114.

Nussbaum, Martha. "Equity and Mercy." *Philosophy and Public Affairs* 22 (1993) 83–125.

———. *Love's Knowledge: Essays on Philosophy and Literature*. Oxford: Oxford University Press, 1990.

Olberding, A. "'A Little Throat Cutting in the Meantime': Seneca's Violent Imagery." *Philosophy and Literature* 32 (2008) 130–44.

Osborne, Grant R. *Romans*. Downers Grove: InterVarsity, 2004.

Parrott, R. L. "Paul's Political Thought: Rom 13:1–7 in the Light of Hellenistic Political Thought." PhD diss., Claremont Graduate School, 1980.

Reinhold, M. "Usurpation of Status and Status Symbols in the Roman Empire." *Historia* 20 (1971) 275–302.

Rist, J. M. "Equity and Mercy." *Philosophy and Public Affairs* 22 (1993) 83–125.

———. "Seneca and Stoic Orthodoxy." *Aufstieg und Niedergang der römischen Welt* 2.36.3 (1989) 1993–2012.

Rodewyk, B. "'Dismemberment' in Neronian Literature." *Pegasos: The Journal of the Department of Classics and Ancient History in the University of Exeter*. http://www.blogs.exeter.ac.uk/pegasus/benni-rodewyk-dismemberment-in-neronian-literature.

Scheid, J. *Commentarii Fratrum Arvalium Qui Supersunt: Les copies épigraphiques des protocols annuels de la Confrérie Arvale (21 AV.–31 AP. J.-C)*. Rome: École Française de Rome, 1998.

Schreiner, Thomas R. *Romans*. Grand Rapids: Baker, 1998.

Seifrid, Mark A. "Romans." In *Commentary on the New Testament Use of the Old Testament*, edited by G. K. Beale and D. A. Carson, 607–94. Grand Rapids: Baker Academic, 2007.

Shotter, David. *Nero Caesar Augustus: Emperor of Rome*. Edinburgh: Pearson Longman, 2008.

Sideri-Tolia, A. "Seneca's *Thyestes*: Might and Perspective." *Velleia* 21 (2004) 175–82.

Smallwood, E. Mary. *Documents Illustrating the Principates of Gaius, Claudius, and Nero*. Cambridge: Cambridge University Press, 1967.

Smith, R. R. R. *The Marble Reliefs from the Julio-Claudian Sebasteion*. Aphrodisias 6. Darmstadt, Germany: Philipp von Zabern, 2013.

Smolenaars, J. J. L. "The Vergilian Background of Seneca's *Thyestes*." *Vergilius* 44 (1998) 641–82.

Sutherland, C. H. V. "Two Virtues of Tiberius: A Numismatic Contribution to the History of His Reign." *Journal of Roman Studies* 28 (1938) 129–40.

Syme, R. *Emperors and Biography: Studies in the* Historia Augusta. Oxford: Clarendon, 1971.

Thompson, M. *Clothed with Christ: The Example and Teaching of Jesus in Romans 12:1—15:15*. Sheffield: Sheffield Academic, 1991.

Victor, William Michael. "Giving, Leading, Caring: A Socio-exegetical Examination of Romans 12:8." PhD diss., Southwestern Baptist Theological Seminary, 2003.

Walker, B. *The Annals of Tacitus: A Study in the Writing of History*. Manchester: Manchester University Press, 1960.

Warmington, B. H. *Nero: Reality and Legend*. London: Chatto and Windus, 1969.

Wiseman, T. P. "Calpurnius Siculus and the Claudian Civil War." *Journal of Roman Studies* 72 (1982) 57–67.

PART E

Well-Being and Aboriginal Australians
Justice, Mercy, and Hope

11

Aboriginal Interpretations of Radical Hope
Noel Pearson's Radical Hope and Warwick Thornton's Samson and Delilah

Neil Holm

Introduction

DESPITE its title, Noel Pearson's essay "Radical Hope: Education and Equality in Australia" dealt with cautious hope rather than radical hope.[1] Warwick Thornton's film *Samson and Delilah*, although not specifically about radical hope, came much closer to the concept but differed from it.[2] Rather than radical hope, living hope best describes Thornton's view of hope.

The term radical hope came from Jonathan Lear's book *Radical Hope: Ethics in the Face of Cultural Devastation*.[3] This chapter begins by reviewing Lear's concept of radical hope. In his context, radical hope arose out of a time of great uncertainty when the future was unimaginable. Involving a shift in perspective, radical hope was an intuition or inner certainty that the future was characterized by goodness while at the same time acknowledging that contemporary understandings were unable to comprehend the nature of this goodness. In some way, future goodness was linked to a new understanding of courage and to some aspect of the past. In a time of great discontinuity, there would be a small element of continuity.

While Lear believed courage was essential to living in radical hope, Pearson associated radical hope with seriousness. Eschewing wishful thinking, a serious person

1. Pearson, "Radical Hope."
2. Thornton, *Samson and Delilah* (2009).
3. Lear, *Radical Hope*.

was realistic and inclined to rationality. Seriousness required determination and discipline. Pearson concluded that, for contemporary Aboriginal people, hope was dependent on education and on their degree of seriousness about the education of their people. I found this conclusion surprising and disappointing because it lacked the cultural power and foundation for which he had been arguing. For Pearson, direct instruction and the separation of school "class" activities from "cultural education" were central to Aboriginal education. Pearson's approach was based on caution, limitation of scope, narrow focus on direct instruction, separation of "Class" and "Culture," and avoiding risks associated with translating deep values into the foundation for practical vision. He held a cautious hope, a risk-free hope, rather than radical hope.

Pearson drew extensively on the work of eminent anthropologist W. E. H. Stanner. Although Pearson drew a different conclusion, Stanner held views on Aboriginal people that pointed to a form of radical hope that was somewhat different to Lear. Stanner believed that Aboriginal people were not captured by the past but were adaptive and capable of creating their own new reality. Pearson believed that for Aboriginal people to create a new reality they needed self-regard (self-interest), direct instruction, and the Enlightenment. He pointed to eight self-regard characteristics that did not cohere into a vision of radical hope. His emphasis on direct instruction reflected an approach to curriculum involving "strong classification" and "strong framing" that are not conducive to radical hope. In his discussion of the Enlightenment, Pearson tried to make room for religion. This is a difficult case to make when secularism is a central aspect of the Enlightenment.

The second half of the chapter examines Warwick Thornton's film, *Samson and Delilah*. Religion was important to Thornton and it formed an underlying theme of the film. The religious theme revealed that Delilah, the central character, was influenced by the Christian faith of her grandmother. The film showed a people whose culture was disintegrating and whose future looked bleak. Delilah's behavior approached radical hope but differed from it in the same way that Stanner's vision of radical hope differed from Lear's. Although Aboriginal and Christian values and morality lay behind Delilah's behavior, they were implicit and tacit. The film paid close attention to Delilah but did not present her as making conscious, deliberate decisions. She was shown to be wise but her wisdom came from sources other than the rational application of the mind. Aware of the disintegrating, collapsing world around her, Delilah moved forward into the future without a process of careful discernment of her options. Rather than exhibiting radical hope, Delilah exhibited living hope of the kind outlined in the First Letter of Peter. Rather than a conscious, rational process, Delilah's behavior was guided in a subconscious way where "the eyes of her heart" guided her way home.

Returning to Pearson's concerns about education, the chapter ends with a few speculations on a model of education consistent with and expressive of radical hope.

Radical Hope

"Radical Hope," Pearson's essay title, was also the title of a significant book by Jonathan Lear, Distinguished Service Professor at the University of Chicago. In his book of philosophical anthropology, Lear analyzed the life story of the last great chief of the Crow nation, Plenty Coups. In Montana in the 1920s, Plenty Coups told his story to Frank B. Linderman, trapper, hunter, cowboy, and author of western novels. Plenty Coups recounted the story of his early life and the later collapse of his Crow civilization. Unlike some of his fellow Crows, of conservative disposition, who fought staunchly but futilely to hold on to the past traditions and way of life, Plenty Coups responded to the disintegration of Crow worldview and way of life by drawing on the vision he received during his vision quest when he was nine years old.

Unlike Freudian dream interpretation that sees the dream as significant and meaningful for the dreamer, the Crow visions had significance for the whole community and were subject to community interpretation. Returning from their vision quests, the young recounted their dreams and visions to the elders who interpreted these dreams. The elders teased out the significance of the dreams and visions. They derived communal meanings and communal significance from these dreams and visions. Most significant dreams or visions guided decision making like when to engage battle. Plenty Coups' vision, however, was of a different order. This vision predicted a change in the world order. The traditional way of life would end and yet the Crow would survive. Life as the Crow knew it would obtain no longer. Past and contemporary guides to meaning and purpose would not help in a world that was yet to exist. Crow civilization would collapse but somehow, in some way, the Crow as a people would adapt to the changes in circumstances. They would not only survive but they would flourish in this new world while at the same time growing into a new Crow identity.

Plenty Coups' vision became the foundation of Lear's concept of radical hope. The Crow had no idea of what the future might look like. They had no parameters by which to judge the future. The future was unimaginable but the vision assured them that something good would emerge. This future good would be different to goodness in their known world. On this basis, radical hope could be described as a feeling, intuition, understanding, or inner certainty that the future is characterized by goodness while at the same time acknowledging that contemporary understandings are unable to comprehend the nature of this goodness. In some way, the future goodness was linked to a new understanding of courage and to some aspect of the past. In a time of great discontinuity, there was a small element of continuity.[4] Perhaps it is better to describe radical hope as a practice, a way of living, perhaps a spiritual discipline built on flexibility, openness, and imaginative excellence.[5] Radical hope enabled the Crow to

---

4. Lear, *Radical Hope*, 103.
5. Lear, *Radical Hope*, 117.

feel sure that the future would be good. However, the relevant concepts to understand the nature of the future or the future good were yet beyond their experience.

Despite the uncertain future, the Crow knew how to live during the times of transition and turmoil. The interpretation of Plenty Coups' vision revealed that this vision "had a divine sanction" and that a successful future lay in listening.[6] The main message in the vision was that, above all else, they should listen like the Chickadee-person; they should follow the wisdom of the Chickadee-person. The Chickadee-person was not physically powerful but was powerful in mind. Like the Chickadee-person, the Crow should become good listeners who were willing to work for wisdom. Wisdom lay not in the past but by application of the mind, by careful discernment of each future event keeping in mind the basic ontological question, "How ought we to live with this possibility of collapse?"[7] They should learn from the successes and failures of others. They should see the future not as pre-ordained but as something in which they had a part in creating and being created by.[8]

Lear used "radical" as a modifier of hope that intensified the meaning of hope. Radical hope was hope in its "essential form," hope at its root or source, "quite precisely the thing itself," that which was necessary for hope to have any vitality. Radical hope was *the* radical, the square root of behavior that was purposeful, conscious, or intentional; the root term out of which good, purposeful, and meaningful life might emerge.[9] Radical hope involved a shift in "perspective, not just in degree but in principle" because it set aside previously accepted perspectives and adopted a new way of seeing the world, a new form of life-orientation.[10] For the Crow, radical hope meant a shift in perspective. The new way of seeing the world came from adopting the Chickadee perspective.

Having outlined the meaning of radical hope, Lear examined the seemingly overwhelming challenge of maintaining radical hope in the face of loss of telos. How can we live when our history has exhausted itself?[11] What is necessary for a person or community to go forward in radical hope? What the essential characteristic is required to live with radical hope in the face of cultural collapse? What is psychologically necessary to respond to foreseen devastation? What distinguishes radical hope from mere optimism? Lear argued that Plenty Coups and the Crow adapted to the anxiety and uncertainty of the new world by courageously following the vision of the Chickadee. Radical hope was sustained only when accompanied by courage. For the Crow a new understanding of courage was required. The traditional understanding of courage was expressed in avoiding shame by always standing firm, never retreating,

6. Lear, *Radical Hope*, 135.
7. Lear, *Radical Hope*, 9.
8. Lear, *Radical Hope*, 70–71.
9. Lummis, *Radical Democracy*, 25, 26.
10. Dalferth, *Radical Theology*, 175.
11. Lear, *Radical Hope*, 3.

and the amassing of large numbers of "kills" in battle. With the knowledge of the foreseen future, this form of courage was futile. New appreciations of shame and courage were required.

To elaborate on the new form of courage exhibited by Plenty Coups and the Crow, Lear drew on Aristotle's five "hallmarks of courage."[12] Courage was now understood to be following the genuine wisdom of others, overcoming despair, and welcoming changes that expressed the new vision. Courage involved living for something that was admirable, worthwhile, valuable, and virtuous. In the case of the Crow, this meant living for the "future flourishing of traditional tribal values, customs, and memories in a new context."[13] Courage involved exercising good judgment and acting in ways that were consistent with that reasoning. For Plenty Coups this meant following the advice of the Chickadee to observe, listen, and discern. Courage involved the acceptance of risk. For the Crow, risk was no longer risking death in battle but following the new vision, the new narrative of what the good life entailed in a changed world. Finally, courage was not based on blind optimism. The Crow did not "hope against hope." They did not hold to a strong hope that something would happen, that things would turn out well, while deep in their hearts they knew it was not likely to happen. They adopted a radical hope that based on a vision of a way of life that they believed was likely, although by no means assured.

Pearson's Use of Radical Hope

Pearson recognized that Australian Aboriginal people, like the Crow, faced or were facing a cultural abyss. The best response that some could make was to ensure, a little like Plenty Coups, that their knowledge was preserved in the ethnographic writings of anthropologists.[14] Preservation became the goal of these knowledgeable people. In Lear's terms, these people were in some way the Australian equivalents of Sitting Bull who was harshly critical of Plenty Coups. Sitting Bull held strongly to traditional understandings of courage and strongly resisted Plenty Coups' vision.

Like Plenty Coups, Pearson sought to draw on ideals and values of Aboriginal tradition. He sought to draw on the principle that "all pre-modern peoples carried within their cultures some institutional essence of what made and maintained them as peoples."[15] According to Lear, courage was essential to living in radical hope. For Pearson, radical hope was associated with seriousness. Eschewing wishful thinking, a serious person was realistic and inclined to rationality. Seriousness required determination and discipline. Drawing on Stanner's description of an iconic Nangiomeri man called Durmugam who died almost 60 years ago, he associated Aboriginal seriousness

12. Lear, *Radical Hope*, 109.
13. Lear, *Radical Hope*, 145.
14. Pearson, "Radical Hope," 10.
15. Pearson, "Radical Hope," 9.

with "classical High Culture."[16] He compared it with the seriousness that St. Paul refers to in 1 Corinthians 13:11 when St. Paul said that children speak like children, think like children, and reason like children. Paul implied that when adults reach maturity they discuss, think, and reason like adults. Children were not serious but adults were. For Pearson, serious people were orthodox people. Serious people adhered to an idea, belief, practice or way of thinking that was accepted as true or correct by most people. Built around language, tradition, and knowledge, classical High Culture once expressed Aboriginal orthodoxy. However,

> Aboriginal High Culture that has survived to the present is fatally compromised by the assumption that the Law which underpins this High Culture does not have anything to say about the European vices [that are] fundamentally destructive of the very things that are supposed to be the purpose [of the ancient rites].[17]

Pearson concluded that for contemporary Aboriginal people "hope is dependent on education" and on their degree of seriousness about the education of their people.[18] I found this conclusion surprising and disappointing. He had laid a strong foundation for radical hope. He showed that radical hope was necessary for those times when their history had exhausted itself. He had shown that radical hope depended on finding some element of tradition that was capable of reinterpretation in ways that made sense and provided a paradigm for living into the unknown future. He had shown that radical hope was unrelated to wishful thinking. The jump to education as hope lacked the cultural power and foundation for which he had been arguing. This jump seemed like wishful thinking, especially when his discussion in the next few sections focused on the *schooling* of Aboriginal children rather than the *education* of Aboriginal children or the vastly more important education of Aboriginal communities. Why start with the renewal of Crow communities through the visionary leadership of adults seeking to transform their communities for survival into the future if you were going to limit your vision of renewal to the schooling of children? How does the orthodoxy of serious Aboriginal adults fit into the future that Pearson paints? Despite pointing to seriousness as an important concept, Pearson did not use the concept (at least explicitly) to develop his argument for Aboriginal education. To some extent, the concept (accompanied by determination and discipline) was embedded implicitly in the list of nostrums that guided their approach to educational reform.[19] Educational progress was essential and "no excuses" were acceptable. The nostrums were built around responsibility as an integral aspect of Aboriginal culture with adults, children, and teachers accepting responsibility for educational progress.

16. Pearson, "Radical Hope," 6.
17. Pearson, "Radical Hope," 11.
18. Pearson, "Radical Hope," 11.
19. Pearson, "Radical Hope," 20–21.

Direct instruction was the means by which Pearson hoped to achieve a major part of his educational goals for Cape York schools. This prescriptive instructional program "provides teachers and schools with packaged, programmed instructional models" that assist "teachers follow a step-by-step, lesson-by-lesson approach to teaching that has already been written for them."[20] The other part of Pearson's approach was to assist children to "achieve a complete bi-cultural capacity. That is, for young Cape York people to be completely fluent in their own culture and the wider culture—and to move with facility and capacity between the two worlds."[21] Although Pearson was aware of, and quoted from, Stanner's account of Durmugam, he did not appear to recognize Durmugam as an example of an Aboriginal man whose life came close to exemplifying the bicultural ideal. Stanner described Durmugam's bi-culturalism:

> He was deeply moved to live by the rules of his tradition as he understood it. He wanted to live a blackfellow's life, having the rights of a man and following up the Dreaming. He venerated his culture; when he grew older, he even found it intellectually interesting. . . . He came to good terms with Europeanism, but found it saltless. . . . But it never attracted him emotionally, it did not interest him intellectually, and it aroused only his material desires. . . . He might perhaps be looked on as a study in benign dissociation. At the conscious level he had found a way of living with duality, an oafish Europeanism and an Aboriginal idealism. I sometimes thought that his slowness, which was certainly not a retardation, might be the measure of the difficulties of transition, for two scales must always be consulted. [He could pass, in the same breath from European details to the equivalent depth of detail and actuality in the Aboriginal realm.] It was not that one was conscious and the other para-conscious: they were coconscious. Yet, paradoxical and contradictory as it may seem, he could dissociate and not merely separate the two.[22]

Although he favored bicultural education, Pearson was opposed to the term "culturally appropriate education." He recognized that its "intention was to ensure respect and recognition of Aboriginal culture and to make education sensitive and relevant" but he believed that the term was mainly used to defend poor educational standards and it led to "disastrous policies and programs."[23] This is a significant comment to understand Pearson's position. His positive attribution was very limited and his negative attribution was very strong. His negativity led to his endorsement of direct instruction and a "no excuses" approach. His positivity revealed a limited appreciation of culturally appropriate education. He maintained a separation between culture and modern school-based education. In practical terms, this meant that Cape York schools operated in two domains. One domain was "Class" when direct instruction

20. Luke, "Direct Instruction Is Not a Solution."
21. Pearson, "Radical Hope," 57.
22. Stanner, *White Man Got No Dreaming*, 97–78, 101–72.
23. Pearson, "Radical Hope," 59.

occurred in mornings and early afternoons. The other domain morning was "Culture" when children became literate in their own culture and language (presumably in the remainder of the day).

A highly positive and, in my opinion, much more defensible view of culturally appropriate education is based on a far greater degree of interplay between the two:

> Culturally appropriate education focuses on educational competence needed in a global world and respect for different world views of learners and teachers from different cultural contexts. The relationship between gene, brain, and culture is complex and dynamical. Cultural experience and learning sculpts the anatomy and function of the human brain and shapes human behavior. This neuroplasticity is the basis of educability in human beings. Education reform should reflect cultural diversity and embed teaching practices into the cultural history of a nation and should promote positive inclusion of minority and indigenous history so as to maximize successful adoption by teachers and parents. This tenet is at the core of the concept of "culturally appropriate education."[24]

Radical Hope or Cautious Hope?

Pearson took a cautious approach to education. He limited the scope of culturally appropriate education. He advocated direct instruction and a separation of "Class" from "Culture." He developed interesting concepts like seriousness, determination, and discipline that drew on deeper values embedded within Aboriginal culture but did not translate them into his practical vision for the Cape York schools. These five factors (caution, limitation of scope, narrow focus on direct instruction, separation of "Class" and "Culture, and avoiding risks associated with translating deep values into the foundation for practical vision) point to a cautious hope, a risk-free hope, rather than a radical hope. His position appears to be the kind of radical hope explored by Lear. Pearson's hope *could not* be described as a feeling, intuition, understanding, or inner certainty that the future is characterized by goodness while at the same time acknowledging that contemporary understandings are unable to comprehend the nature of this goodness.[25] Nor could his understanding of hope be characterized as a practice, a way of living, perhaps a spiritual discipline built on flexibility, openness, and imaginative excellence.[26]

Vaclav Havel, celebrated Czech playwright, defender of human rights, and president of Czechoslovakia, offered a view of hope that was similar to Lear's radical hope. Havel's vision of hope was built on notions of transcendence combined with working

---

24. Zhou and Fischer, "Culturally Appropriate Education."
25. Lear, *Radical Hope*, 103.
26. Lear, *Radical Hope*, 117.

for the good even when it seemed impractical; a sense that it will turn out well; and a willingness to risk and try new things for the sake of the future:

> [Hope] is a state of mind, not a state of the world. Either we have hope within us or we don't; it is a dimension of the soul. . . . It is an orientation of the spirit, an orientation of the heart; it transcends the world that is immediately experienced, and is anchored somewhere beyond its horizons. I don't think you can explain it as a mere derivative of something here, of some movement, or of some favorable signs in the world. I feel that its deepest roots are in the transcendental. . . . Hope, in this deep and powerful sense, is not the same as joy that things are going well, or willingness to invest in enterprises that are obviously headed for early success, but, rather, an ability to work for something because it is good, not just because it stands a chance to succeed. The more unpropitious the situation in which we demonstrate hope, the deeper that hope is. Hope is definitely not the same thing as optimism. It is not the conviction that something will turn out well, but the certainty that something makes sense, regardless of how it turns out. In short, I think that the deepest and most important form of hope, the only one that can keep us above water and urge us to good works, and the only true source of the breathtaking dimension of the human spirit and its efforts, is something we get, as it were, from "elsewhere." It is also this hope, above all, which gives us the strength to live and continually to try new things, even in conditions that seem as hopeless as ours do, here and now.[27]

According to Havel, hope's deepest roots were transcendental. Transcendence takes many forms. It may involve cosmic consciousness, a sense of the numinous, or an ecstatic experience. It includes an affective (rather than cognitive) recognition of something ultimate. "It consists in discovering afresh, as if taken by surprise, an uncanny dimension of reality, an uncircumscribed realm to which one feels open. It is an awareness of being in contact with something that lies beyond one's normal control, power, and understanding."[28]

A particular circumstance (seeing a beautiful flower), situation (becoming aware of the passing parade), or incident (sunshine on the chalice) may evoke a transcendence. A spiritual or physical discipline may also lead to a transcendence. These experiences may occur suddenly and without notice, may vary in intensity, and are usually accompanied by affective states associated with awe, love, beauty, and fecundity. They may reoccur throughout a person's life. Most often, these experiences are relatively short but for some are more enduring and accompanied by longer-lasting states of serenity and equanimity. Depending on a person's past experience and their metaphysical or philosophical bent, these experiences may have divine or other religious

---

27. Havel, *Disturbing the Peace*, 181–82.
28. Roy, *Transcendent Experiences*, 3. Compare this definition of transcendence with that of Husserl in Holm, "Educating the Net Generation."

association. Alternatively, they may have associations of being in harmony or unity with the universe, creation, or all living things.

This reflection on transcendence is included because it is an aspect of Havel's description of hope. Furthermore, transcendence was (is?) a significant aspect of Aboriginal ontology and was "central to Stanner's thinking on Aboriginal religion."[29] Transcendence carries within it openness to the unknown and awareness that reality can take an unexpected form. Stanner's appreciation of transcendence provided his hope for the future. As we will see later, there may have been a transcendent dimension to Delilah's decision making.

Stanner's Version of Radical Hope

Under the sub-heading "Stanner Redux," the epilogue to Pearson's essay sought to revive Stanner's work in the twenty-first century.[30] He began by quoting a passage from Stanner's "Aboriginal people in the Affluent Society" to show that the issues addressed by Stanner were "essentially the same matters unresolved in Australia today." Stanner wrote the quoted piece in 1973. He described two views that split discussion on the solution for Aboriginal problems. One view, "a rather heady and facile optimism," was held by "utopian visionaries" while the pessimists or "realists" held to "a settled pessimism."[31] Despite "being of realistic turn of mind," he tended to side with the visionaries: "we are always free to try to make a new reality." He saw many problems but he believed in a good outcome. In his opinion, the visions of the optimists could be "a powerful instrument of social struggle; a hard working tool to re-shape the very situation in which the impulse to reform arises; and a brightly-lit goal for the will."[32] The possibility of a new future, a new reality, was equally relevant to Aboriginal people themselves, policy makers, and social activists.

Stanner's transcendent views were driven by his fieldwork. He saw people like Durmugam who were not trapped by the past, not trapped by tradition, who were capable and open to change, who were already "exploring new paths," and who were working "out terms of life they know how to handle."[33] Radical hope presupposes that people are neither trapped by the past nor defeated by the present. Radical hope implies working toward something that is good. Aboriginal people are open to change

29. Eller, review of *An Appreciation of Difference*.
30. Pearson, "Radical Hope," 103.
31. Stanner, *White Man*, 381.
32. Stanner, *White Man*, 381.
33. Stanner, *White Man*, 60, 62, 380, 381. More recent research, cited in Griffiths, *Art of Time Travel*, supports this view. Karskens reported that in late 1790 the Eora acted as if they owned Sydney. They knew everyone and forged new lives among the invaders in ways "compatible with their customary habits and laws" (Griffiths, *Art of Time Travel*, 296). In response to modernity, Kimber reported acceptance, questioning, adjustment, and openness to change in Pintupi men (Griffiths, *Art of Time Travel*, 312).

but like Plenty Coups' vision, radical hope maintains elements of continuity. Stanner argued that

> none of the many hundreds of Aborigines I have studied at first hand impress me as already or likely to be "incorporated," or "absorbed," or "assimilated" into the surrounding system of Europeanism. The very contrary is true. Various European things—our authority, our customs, or ideas and goods—are data, facts of life, which the Aborigines take into account in working out their altered system. But I have seen little sign of it going much beyond that. Those Aborigines I know seem to me to be still fundamentally in struggle with us. The struggle is for a different set of things, differently arranged, from those which most European interests want them to receive.[34]

Stanner's vision accorded with radical hope. Although he drew attention to their "oppressive sense of involuntary dependence," he was convinced Aboriginal people had the "capacity for voluntary, positive and intelligent response."[35] He believed they were working toward their understanding of a good future by drawing on aspects of their past and taking them forward as principles to shape the creation of a new future that was currently beyond their conceptual frameworks. This is baffling for those of us who stand outside this process. For Aboriginal people, the aspects of the past were not codified, explicit, or structured. Aboriginal life was guided by implicit rather than explicit traditions and tacit presuppositions:

> What life is, how it should be lived, what it can and cannot become, what things in it are significant, what is their relative place, what their value: all these may be so well known, so unproblematic, that they do not have to be formulated in any clear way.[36]

This notion that things of significance in Aboriginal culture were not formulated in a clear way but were implicit or tacit understandings may mean that the vision of radical hope embedded in Stanner's work, although similar to, was of a different category to Lear's understanding of radical hope. The Crow tradition seemed much more explicit.

So what are the characteristics of this good future? Where will their implicit traditions and tacit presuppositions drive Aboriginal people? Stanner had confidence in the adaptive capacity and the aesthetic cultural values of Aboriginal people: "There is no one amongst us with, as I said, the 'privileged knowledge, the natural insight, the inborn wisdom or the secret doctrine' that allows him credibly to say that the Aboriginal people are wasting their time in an effort to make a new reality."[37] Alter-

---

34. Stanner, *White Man*, 42. The original wording, "Aborigines," has been retained in the quote, as opposed to "Aboriginal people," throughout the chapter.
35. Stanner, *White Man*, 379.
36. Stanner, *White Man*, 64.
37. Stanner, *White Man*, 38.

natively, Pearson had confidence in a threefold response involving self-regard, direct instruction, and the Enlightenment.

Pearson: Self-Regard, Direct Instruction, and the Enlightenment

For Aboriginal people to make a new reality, to engage in social change, Pearson believed that, in contrast to "other regard," they must look to self-interest. He believed that social change was effected by a vast amount of individual change prompted by self-interest. Self-interest or self-regard was promoted in eight ways that included actively taking opportunities to get out of poverty; economic independence; the exercise of responsibility; eschewing victimhood; working toward communal law and order; speaking English and Aboriginal languages fluently and comprehensively; valuing quality education; and rejection of drug abuse. The new reality embedded in the eight characteristics may be prophetic but he did not provide any insights into the implicit traditions and tacit presuppositions that underlie this vision of the good life. To what extent does an *indigenous* philosophy or theology underlie this vision of how life should be lived, what it can and cannot become, and what things in it are significant? The characteristics do not form a coherent whole that in some way encapsulates a vision that might be described as *radical* hope.

In a similar way, Pearson's emphasis on direct instruction pointed to an instructional approach and curriculum materials but not a curriculum. This is not to deny that direct instruction is an effective instructional approach. It can be a useful element in whatever curriculum is adopted but it is not a curriculum in its own right. However, it does express a particular philosophical or sociological perspective that may run counter to radical hope. The understanding of radical hope developed in this chapter and based on Lear's analysis of the Crow and Stanner's anthropological insights suggests that an Aboriginal curriculum be framed in a way that allows Aboriginal learners to express their capacity for voluntary, positive and intelligent response in any learning context. The learning context should provide for independence and avoid processes that continue to encourage dependent behavior and subordination of learners. It should allow learners the opportunity to consider the future while recognizing that learners' futures are not dependent on the past and that current learning must engage their community background knowledge, cultural experiences, and prior knowledge schemata.[38]

At best, direct instructional processes will achieve very few of these outcomes. This is because direct instruction, in the concepts developed by Basil Bernstein, features "strong classification" and "strong framing." This means that in the instructional process teachers exercise power over learners and exercise strong control over what

---

38. Luke, "On Explicit and Direct Instruction."

is learnt, how it is learnt, the extent to which it integrates with other school learning and other communal learning. Strong regulation of learners and what is learnt leads to reproduction of the values, ideals, ideology, and understandings of the dominant teachers. The knowledge and cultural systems of the teachers prevail. Weak regulation creates possibilities for transformation and the integration of all forms of knowledge. Radical hope is more likely to emerge from weak classification and framing because it allows greater scope for learners to reflect on their indigenous knowledge and cultural systems to form relationships with the classroom knowledge and cultural systems. Radical hope emerges from this integration. Weak regulation allows learners to develop behaviors that in some way reflect Durmugam: on good terms with Europeanism but continuing to be influenced by Aboriginal idealism.

So far, I have argued that Pearson's proposals of self-regard and direct instruction are disconnected to the emergence of radical hope. His third proposal, the Enlightenment, was a more comprehensive proposal. His final paragraph included:

> Radical hope for the future of Aboriginal Australia, which honours the inchoate dreams of Stanner and Durmugam—if not in the way that they imagined it (nor perhaps in the way we imagine it)—will require the bringing together of the Enlightenment and Aboriginal culture. . . . The education of our children, at the highest level of effort, ambition, and excellence that we can muster, is, I have no doubt, fundamental to this hope.[39]

At last, in this final paragraph, Pearson addressed radical hope at its deep level. However, this was the end. The essay ended one sentence later: "If our hopes are for our children, then we must take charge of their education." This statement about radical hope is open to interpretation but at first glance, words like "highest level of effort, ambition, and excellence" seem to imply the strong classification and strong framing argued against in the preceding paragraph. Surely, this was the place to start.

Pearson believed that an appropriation of the ideas and ideals of the Enlightenment would provide that hope for Aboriginal communities. He did not define the Enlightenment. However, several characteristics provide an understanding. They include: the significance of individuals and of developing individual potential; the scientific revolution with its emphasis on rationality and the scientific method; secular views based on reason or human understanding that deny religion because religion depends on faith rather than reason; and reason as the basis for progress and beneficial changes affecting every area of life and thought.

Pearson did not go so far as to deny religion completely. He acknowledged a need to leave "space enough for religion" but he was clear that the illumination of the Enlightenment was the main source of hope. Pearson had a strong background in Christianity. He went to a Lutheran primary and secondary school. His father was a lay preacher whose bookshelf was filled with religious tracts, scriptural studies, and

---

39. Pearson, *Radical Hope*, 105.

Lutheran history and theology.[40] Pearson described himself as "an above average God botherer" whose most transformative book was Milton's *Paradise Lost*.[41] In a lecture in 2014 Milton scholar, Nigel Smith, noted that hope was a major theme in *Paradise Lost*. The fallen angels, holding on to a degree of hope, discussed how they might regain hope. After the despair of the Fall, Adam and Eve realized they had hope through repentance. This hope seemed to be "seeded by elements of grace placed in mankind." Interestingly, in terms of Aboriginal people's connection with the land (as we will see later, Delilah's attachment to "country"), Milton connected hope with place and the associated "human (and apparently angelic) need for land possession or belonging."[42]

Pearson was unable to deny the importance of religion but it does not sit comfortably with the Enlightenment. He was unable to deny that religion was a source of hope for fallen angels and for humankind in despair. He was unable to deny that religion was a source of hope for his people. At the same time, he wanted to hold two oppositional forces together to form the basis of radical hope. Conjoining secularism and religion cannot produce radical hope. Will the promotion of individualism provide hope for a people in despair? The values of the Enlightenment may lead to mobility, intellectual freedom, scientific invention, and material progress but they may also lead to destruction of community, worker alienation, contempt for natural world, and economic instability.[43] Are the values and morality embedded in the Enlightenment consonant with the morality and religious and values that Pearson sought for his people? As with self-regard and direct instruction, there is a disjunction between the Enlightenment, religion, and hope.

Hope and the Enlightenment

In variant explorations of hope, other scholars express concern about the relationship between the Enlightenment and hope. In 2000 Jonathan Sacks, Chief Rabbi of the United Hebrew Congregations of the Commonwealth, contrary to Pearson, argued families not education are the foundation for hope. Drawing on a long history in which Jewish people have often found themselves in situations somewhat similar to indigenous people in Australia, he argued that the Judeo-Christian system of morality was a "resource of unparalleled power with which to confront the problems of a new age."[44] The scientific ethic of the Enlightenment largely displaced the tradition upon

---

40. Pearson, *Radical Hope*, 36.

41. ABC-TV, Book Club, series 10, ep. 10, *Books That Transport You*, broadcast 9:50 p.m., Tuesday, July 26, 2016.

42. Notice of event: *Milton and Hope: The Structure of a Feeling in the English Revolution* (http://www.historyofemotions.org.au/events/milton-and-hope-the-structure-of-a-feeling-in-the-english-revolution/).

43. Yeselson, "Avoiding the Lasch of Modernity," 17.

44. Sacks, *Politics of Hope*, 13.

which Judeo-Christian morality was based. Both indigenous society and the Western world at large became demoralized in two senses: a loss of moral meanings and a loss of hope. Both societies increasingly looked to government to meet their hopes. People in both societies had a growing sense of being "not the makers but the made" and this led to despair rather than hope. However, a central theme of the Judeo-Christian tradition was that "individuals are not powerless in the face of the impersonal" because they have the capacity to form social groups "around ideals of love and fellowship and trust" where individuals are valued "for what they are." This vision "locates the source of action within ourselves. It restores the dignity of agency and responsibility."[45]

Sacks' monograph suggested that the Judeo-Christian tradition offered a foundation of hope. Perhaps other religious traditions, perhaps other philosophical traditions, can offer a similar connectedness but the Enlightenment with its emphasis on individual striving and success may work against hope. Furthermore, forgiveness seemed to be an integral feature—connectedness was built and strengthened when people had the ability, will, and motivation to forgive rather than to blame. Such a tradition must be a part of the public square rather than the private sphere. Moreover, morality had become part of the private sphere because the values of the Enlightenment deemed a separation of public and private. What was public must be testable, provable, and empirical and what was not must remain part of the private sphere. Alasdair McIntyre argued that the "enlightenment and the social processes which accompanied it succeeded in destroying the traditions to which the key terms of morality belonged and within which they had lucidity and coherence. The words survived—good, right, duty, obligation, virtue—but they were now severed from the context which gave them sense."[46] These value words belonged to a people shaped by a collective vision rather than an individualistic vision bequeathed by the Enlightenment. Pearson believed that the Enlightenment could be the basis of a system of morality revealed in seriousness, determination, discipline, effort, ambition, and excellence. McIntyre would argue that these values were encompassed by "good, right, duty, obligation, virtue" and consequently Pearson's belief was unfounded.

Samson and Delilah

Pearson offered one view of hope from an Aboriginal perspective. Warwick Thornton expressed another important Aboriginal view of hope in his 2009 film, *Samson and Delilah*. This film won fourteen awards, including the highly esteemed Golden Camera for best first feature at the Cannes Film Festival. Growing up in Alice Springs, Thornton described his experience of Aboriginal spirituality:

---

45. Sacks, *Politics of Hope*, 14, 15.
46. Cited in Sacks, *Politics of Hope*, 32.

> From the day you were born, the spirituality and language and culture is there from day one. And so you learn it, you learn about the creators in a sense and how hills formed and the great kangaroo and all those kind of things are learnt, you learnt from the beginning.[47]

However, he also had a deep immersion in Christian spirituality. By the age of thirteen, Thornton was in danger of becoming a serious social problem so his mother sent him to school at the Benedictine monastery in New Norcia, Western Australia.

> It was almost like I became a monk in a sense. You had schooling. It was agricultural college so there was sheep and wheat and olives and all of that kind of stuff. But it was, all those good things about Christianity came true: that kind of caring and sharing and looking after one another and sort of teachings about morals and protagonists and antagonists and all that. All of that sort of stuff was fantastic. I loved it and I really enjoyed it. I went to mass twice a day and that was part of your schedule, morning mass and afternoon mass. And it kind of, it helped. It helped an awful amount about who I was and what I wanted to do. It helped create a kind of a pillar inside me of goodness, in a sense, and trying to be selfless and helping other people.[48]

Thornton did not see a clash between Aboriginal and Christian spirituality:

> They actually work incredibly well together. If you went up to an old man who's never heard of, a traditional old man who's never heard of anything to do with Jesus or God, and you told him about this guy who was the son of this other bloke and he was the creator and he kind of had special powers that he used but he got half killed by all the jealous people and then he went back to his father who got really angry. He'd go "Oh yeah we've got a whole mob of those." But they're animals not humans in a sense. Or they are humans but they were animals. It was only later, now when I've got older and smarter and I think a little bit harder and I've got a little bit more knowledge that I have much more of a clash of thought.[49]

Thornton's 2011, 3D digital video *Stranded*, graphically expressed this perspective.[50] Thornton described *Stranded* as follows:

> Religion obviously plays a really important part of everybody's life, whoever you are, wherever you come from. You know I really wanted to start looking internally into myself and who I am and where I come from. You know the Stranded piece, it's in 3D. It's me on a cross. Just below the cross is a small

---

47. *Life's Big Questions: Warwick Thornton*, interviewed by Scott Stevens, ABC-TV Compass program, screened November 13, 2011, http://www.abc.net.au/compass/s3338179.htm.

48. Stevens, *Life's Big Questions*.

49. Stevens, *Life's Big Questions*.

50. See a still at http://www.abc.net.au/radionational/programs/awaye/warwick-thornton-stranded/4755640.

water hole. That water hole for Aboriginal people is the life giver. It is the creator in a sense, pre Christianity. It has a story. It has a jukapa. It has songs. It's almost like a bible, and it is the giver of life because it is water.[51]

In some ways, Thornton resembled Durmugam. He understood European ways, took what he wanted but found the old ways more satisfying. *Samson and Delilah* expressed similar perspectives.

In the film, Delilah was about fourteen years old. She lived with her grandmother, her nana. Nana was an artist who painted in the traditional dot-painting style. Delilah helped her and cared for her. Each night, Delilah listened to a cassette of Mexican singer Ana Gabriel who was a devout Catholic, for whom songs were expressions of "communication between myself and God."[52]

Each day she ensured that Nana took her medication and she wheeled Nana to the church where Nana spent time praying or meditating. The church was a corrugated iron shed empty except for the cross on the wall. Samson, a young man about the same age as Delilah, was a petrol sniffer who lived by himself in a nearby house. He was attracted to Delilah. According to Nana, who seemed to approve of him, Samson was in the right relationship, of the correct "skin," to be a husband for her. When Nana died unexpectedly, Delilah mourned in the traditional way by cutting her hair. However, instead of singing culturally-appropriate "sorry" songs, she sang "Little Baby Jesus." (*Little Baby Jesus born in Bethlehem, Little Baby Jesus born to be the Saviour of the world for you and me*). As in *Stranded*, Thornton juxtaposed the two spiritualities by setting Delilah's dot painting with Ana Gabriel and hair cutting with "Little Baby Jesus."

After a fight with his brothers, Samson took his sniffing pot, stole a vehicle and, with Delilah who had been beaten by the women of the community for failing to care for Nana, drove to Alice Springs. In Alice Springs, Samson continued to sniff while they camped under a bridge over the dry bed of the Todd River.[53] They shared the spot with Gonzo, a homeless Aboriginal man who, as his name suggests, was an unconventional, bizarre, or crazy character. Gonzo was hospitable. He not only shared the space, he shared money, food, and empathy. He did not seek to change them but, importantly, he shared something of himself by breaking into song:

> We have survived the white man's world
>
> and the hate and the torment of it all.
>
> We have survived the white man's world
>
> and you know you can't change that.

---

51. Stevens, *Life's Big Questions*.

52. Wikipedia.com, s.v. "Ana Gabriel," https://en.wikipedia.org/wiki/Ana_Gabriel#Bibliography.

53. For a recent summary of some aspects of communal violence and disintegration in Aboriginal society, see Harrison, "Introducing Well-Being," 15–18.

Gonzo's hospitality resembled Nouwen's description of hospitality as "the creation of a free space where the stranger can enter and become a friend instead of an enemy." The free space allows strangers to discover themselves as created free; free to sing their own songs, dance their own dances, and follow their vocations.[54] Although the song appeared to have no impact, Gonzo created a space where they could consider its implications: why have we survived? Thornton continued to explore, gently but persistently, the liminal space between the two worlds. He continued to explore this later in the film when Gonzo was accepted into a Christian rehabilitation center. His announcement that he had a place to stay was accompanied by singing the last verse of Tom Waits' "Jesus Gonna Be Here."[55] The song eloquently captures the intense hope of the singer who manages to persevere in his faith, despite his alcoholism, in the knowledge that Jesus would soon return and usher him into "a better place."

Some white youths abducted and physically and sexually assaulted Delilah when Samson was too intoxicated by fumes to notice. She began to sniff petrol. As the intoxicated pair walked down the street, a car hit her while Samson shuffled on unaware. After her recovery, she entered a church where she gazed at the images of Christ. A young priest stood by silently. The scene is open to interpretation but I like to think that the priest offered her a hospitable space. Nouwen wrote, "If we expect any salvation, redemption, healing and new life, the first thing we need is an open receptive place where something can happen to us."[56] The film segued quickly to a scene in which the now almost unconscious, brain-damaged Samson and the almost fully recovered Delilah, moved to a Kingstrand hut[57] with associated bore in Delilah's "country." Delilah put a cross on the wall and began cleaning and setting up "home." She began to create her own hospitable space.

> In a moment of great tenderness, Delilah bathes Samson in an outside water trough, gently washing his drug-wrecked body. This image of physical intimacy, set against the wide-open blue sky and red sands of the central Australian landscape, takes on transcendent qualities when Samson fully immerses himself in the water, enacting a kind of spiritual cleansing or re-birth. This is a very unusual ending for a teen love story, for, instead of concluding with a youthful romantic union, their true love is represented as a mature sacred love, a love based on responsibility and care for the self and other, a conception of love not normally associated with 14-year-old teens. Taking us then into sacred or ritual time, Samson's rebirth strongly resonates with Christian notions of baptism and redemption.[58]

---

54. Nouwen, *Reaching* Out, 71–72
55. For the lyrics, see tomwaitslibrary.info/lyrics/bonemachine/jesusgonnabehere.html.
56. Nouwen, *Reaching Out*, 76.
57. See http://bit.ly/Kingstrand for an illustration.
58. Davis, "Love and Social Marginality in *Samson and Delilah*."

Finally, Delilah spread out Nana's unfinished dot painting and resumed work on it. Thornton once again juxtaposed (integrated?) Christian faith with a traditional Aboriginal setting where country and Dreamtime representation were salient.

Delilah and Hope

Delilah's decision to create a new and good life back in her "country" was an expression of radical hope. Her hope kept her from drowning in the despair of Alice Springs or the violence of her community. It urged her to good works. It was the source of the majestic dimension of the human spirit exhibited in her decision and actions. It gave her the strength to live and to try something new and radical. As Havel argued, this hope was a dimension of the soul, transcendent; it came from "elsewhere." Delilah was not trapped by the past, not trapped by tradition. She proved herself capable and open to change. She was willing to explore new paths. Radical hope presupposed that people were neither trapped by the past nor defeated by the present.

There was no evidence that Delilah had a clear vision of the future. There was no evidence that she had a conscious strategy. As Stanner concluded, with Aboriginal people aspects of the past are not codified, explicit, or structured. Aboriginal life is guided by implicit rather than explicit traditions and tacit presuppositions. Delilah did not formulate her plans in any clear way but, in some way, her imagination (her soul?) drew together aspects of her past and present in a way that she intuitively knew how to proceed. She may have known in her heart, her soul, her spirit rather than her conscious mind. Her understanding may have been transcendent based on an affective (rather than cognitive) recognition of something ultimate. She may have "seen" the way forward with "the eyes of the heart" (Eph 1:18) rather than with her conscious or rational mind. Lives are changed more by transformed imagination than by ethical urging.[59] Her imagination drew on several things. Intuitively she drew on the Judeo-Christian tradition that she had observed in Nana and recalled in meditating on the images of Christ in the Alice Springs church. As Sacks asserted, this tradition empowered individuals in the face of the impersonal. It did so through the experience of social groups formed around ideals of love, fellowship, and trust where individuals are valued for what they are.

Delilah grew up in the care of Nana who had instilled these ideals of love, fellowship, trust, responsibility, and the dignity of agency. Nana had given Delilah "the rules and virtues, the grammar and semantics, of the language of morality . . . a coherent frame of reference within which to build a life."[60] In addition to the tradition embodied in the dot painting, Nana had passed on a tradition, her own Christianity interpreted in her own terms. Included in the Christian tradition passed on to Delilah was the

---

59. Brueggemann, *Hopeful Imagination*, 25.
60. Sacks, *Politics of Hope*, 19.

notion that "our failures are forgiven as soon as they are acknowledged."[61] This is not the blaming tradition that she and Samson experienced in the community. Rather it is a building tradition—a tradition of edification, of building morale of encouragement, of building not just morale but moral fibre. Delilah inherited this tradition and she lived it. She did not blame Samson for his sniffing or his neglect of her. She had faith in him even when he seemed to have lost faith in himself. She did not disconnect and turn to isolationism but she connected, she joined her individual striving to a larger world of common purpose. Her behavior pointed to a conclusion that "connectedness is part of the logical geography of hope."[62] From the Christian tradition, Delilah knew intuitively that no part of human life is beyond redemption. She learned from Nana that life was good and on this basis, she was unwilling to give Samson up, even when he betrayed her. She knew, above all else, that Samson was capable of redemption where redemption was "liberating what has come to be enslaved," the "remaking of creation, having dealt with the evil that is defacing and distorting it."[63] Delilah dealt with the evil of sniffing and violence by remaking life for herself and Samson. She acted to liberate herself and Samson from the slavery to sniffing and violence.

Delilah's imagination may have been influenced by the experience with Gonzo. He offered hospitality and connectedness to strangers. He invited Samson and Delilah to "live in his house." All he required in return was that they make conversation "(Talk to me! Say something!"). He wanted them to connect at the most basic level. Nana and Gonzo carried the moral thrust of the film. Both spoke, much more than anyone else did and their language was a language of connection, relationship, love, concern, advice, and encouragement. This suggested

> an old-new insight into the nature of morality. We do not learn to behave by private reflection on the basis of experience [as Enlightenment thinkers like Locke would have us believe]. We do so by acquiring socially constituted rules, from our first faltering conversations with our parents, to our ever-widening dialogue with others.[64]

Thornton vs. Pearson

Thornton's film captured the sense of radical hope more comprehensively that Pearson's essay. Pearson's view of hope required a bringing together of the Enlightenment and Aboriginal culture. Although he argued that the Enlightenment and Aboriginal culture are compatible, that the Enlightenment and God are compatible, I have argued that they are not. Even if we concede his argument, this bringing together required

---

61. Sacks, *Politics of Hope*, 26.
62. Sacks, *Politics of Hope*, 27.
63. Wright, *Surprised by Hope*, 107, 108.
64. Sacks, *Politics of Hope*, 218.

the society to split its personality to allow "God, Voltaire, and the abiding spirits of the Ancestors what are theirs."[65] Pearson's program in the Cape York schools maintained a separation between modern school-based education (the Enlightenment) and Aboriginal culture. Pearson wrote that the Enlightenment "forced Europeans to change their societies and cultures in fundamental ways. It forced societies and cultures beyond Europe to make the same change."[66] Pearson's use of "forced" was an interesting choice when other words like "allowed," "enabled," "empowered," or "transformed" might have fitted the context. To some extent, the use of direct instruction became an expression of this sentiment. Conjoining the Enlightenment and Aboriginal culture seemed unlikely to create a hospitable place. It seemed more like a space where the Enlightenment will force itself on the host. Unlike Lear's vision of radical hope, Pearson did not explore how some aspect of the past, some aspect of tradition, might be reinterpreted in a way that allowed the expression of a feeling, intuition, understanding, or inner certainty that the future was characterized by goodness while at the same time acknowledging that contemporary understandings were unable to comprehend the nature of this goodness.

In what seemed an unconscious or tacit process, Delilah brought Christian faith and hospitality together with Aboriginal understandings of land and religion as expressed through return to country and iconography. This radical hope encompassed Christian hope. In *Hopeful Imagination*, Brueggemann explored the hope embodied in Jeremiah, Ezekiel, and Isaiah following exile after 587 BCE. Tom Wright explores Christian hope in *Surprised by Hope*. However, to conclude I will explore the New Testament book of 1 Peter for its vision of Christian hope.

Hope in 1 Peter

Like Samson and Delilah, the readers of 1 Peter were exiled Christians who may have been guest workers in communities subject to abuse without citizenship or power. They may have been exiles in the sense that they were "home" but they were a slandered minority separated and alienated from the culture that surrounded them. Alternatively, they may have been metaphorical exiles whose citizenship was in heaven but who lived on this earth with no lasting home. They were Gentiles rejected by their pagan neighbors because they had chosen to follow Christ. Despite their treatment, 1 Peter was "sectarian without being countercultural"—it did not condemn the world around them.[67] First Peter offered encouragement in their trials, reminding them that in God's mercy they were chosen by God and sanctified by the Spirit. God's Spirit was actively engaged in the lives of the exiles and in the life of Delilah, setting them apart to a very different kind of life and drawing them away from the temptations and

---

65. Pearson, "Radical Hope," 105.
66. Pearson, "Radical Hope," 104.
67. Bartlett, "First Letter of Peter," 310.

troubles of their circumstances.[68] God provided "new birth" and "living hope" (1 Peter 1:3). Faith in Jesus gave living hope, hope that was living in the now, not hope for a better future but hope for the present, hope in the midst of trials. Living hope was the platform for life now.[69]

In this living hope, the exiles and Delilah were ransomed from the ways of the world. By loving one another and building community, they were to live out their call by not conforming to their former desires (1 Pet 1:13–15, 22). These people were now "a people," once disconnected individuals, now connected into a family-like mutuality (1 Pet 2:10). In living hope, they celebrated together and encouraged one another. In the present, suffering and joy combine but when Christ's glory is revealed there will be only joy. They followed the path of Christ who suffered and was raised in glory; they suffered knowing that when Christ returned they will share that glory. Their living hope came from the presence of the Holy Spirit. As sanctified people, the Spirit of glory rested upon them.[70]

In John 14:15–21, Jesus told his disciples that they would receive the Holy Spirit, the Advocate, the Helper, who gives the truth, the right way to do things at all times even in a world that seems alien and ruled by the brutal father of all lies. Even in such a chaotic and troubled times, like that of the exiles and Delilah, where all around was disintegrating, God's people were not alone. They might know peace with untroubled hearts. The Advocate-Helper, will teach all that they need to know in all circumstances. In the company of this Advocate-Helper, God's people, knowing all they needed to know, were able to rise and be on their way. This Advocate-helper may have directed Delilah's "the eyes of the heart" and imagination. Delilah's return to her "country" was directed by the Spirit.

Conclusion

I have argued that despite the title of his essay, Pearson's description of hope fell short of Lear's kind of radical hope. Like Stanner, Thornton's version of radical hope also differed from Lear. Based on the Crow listening to and acting on the voice of the Chickadee, Lear's vision of radical hope was too intentional to apply to the Aboriginal context. I have argued that Delilah held a tacit understanding of Aboriginal culture that was bound up with country but she also had a tacit understanding of the Christian faith as observed through Nana. When disaster struck, she responded with "eyes of the heart," through the inner work of the Holy Spirit, in "living hope" to build community, to become "a people" experiencing family-like mutuality, celebrating together and encouraging one another. In a sense, the Holy Spirit performed the work

---

68. Mounce, *Living Hope*, 10.
69. Parker, "Eschatology of 1 Peter," 27–32.
70. Bartlett, "First Letter of Peter," 310.

of the Chickadee but in a much more subtle, tender, unobtrusive, hidden way, joining Delilah and Samson in the perichoretic dance of the Trinity.

The Thornton vision may provide a model of education. There is no space to explore it here and I am uncertain of what it would look like. However, ideally its characteristics would include the following: an Aboriginal led, Holy Spirit inspired, emergent model that is loose, unstructured, based on tacit understanding. This model may incorporate *dadirri*, an inner deep listening and quiet, still awareness—entering silence, watching, listening, waiting, and then acting.[71] It may incorporate a process of paying attention similar to that described by Simone Weil:

> Attention consists of suspending our thought, leaving it detached, empty and ready to be penetrated by the object, it means holding in our minds, within reach of this thought, but on a lower level and not in contact with it, the diverse knowledge we have acquired which we are forced to make use of.[72]

This model may include a process practiced in some Aboriginal communities. In northeast Arnhem Land, Yirrkala School used a creation story as a cultural foundation for teaching Western concepts. The school believed that "it is much easier for children to think into the western world if they've got their own way of thinking first."[73] This process may be similar to that used to teach theological concepts in Warlpiri communities in other parts of the Northern Territory. The Warlpiri process was "perhaps the most striking use of Aboriginal cultural expression in the Christian context."[74] The striking features were the use of Christian corroborees, Christian iconographs, indigenous music, including the use of the old "law song" as a medium for creedal statements.

Finally, this process may require a setting aside of preoccupation. Much discussion about education in general, including Aboriginal education, is preoccupied with testing, administration, risk management, materialism, success, and progress. Perhaps greater attention should be paid, as Delilah did, to the words of Jesus (Matt 6:31–34):

> Therefore do not worry, saying, "What will we eat?" or "What will we drink?" or "What will we wear?" For it is the Gentiles who strive for all these things; and indeed your heavenly Father knows that you need all these things. But strive first for the kingdom of God and his righteousness, and all these things will be given to you as well. So do not worry about tomorrow, for tomorrow will bring worries of its own. Today's trouble is enough for today.

---

71. Newall, "Whose Values, Which Ethics?"
72. Weil, *Waiting on God*, 56.
73. Dias, "Arnhem Land Community Finds Success."
74. Harris, *One Blood*, 863, cited in Jordan, *Their Way*, 1.

Bibliography

Bartlett, David. "The First Letter of Peter." In *The New Interpreter's Bible*, edited by Leander Keck et al., 12:227–319. Nashville: Abington, 1998.

Brueggemann, Walter. *Hopeful Imagination: Prophetic Voices in Exile*. Philadelphia: Fortress, 1986.

Davis, Therese. "Love and Social Marginality in *Samson and Delilah*." *Senses of Cinema* 51 (2009). http://sensesofcinema.com/2009/feature-articles/samson-and-delilah/.

Dias, Avani. "Arnhem Land Community Finds Success Blending Aboriginal Culture with Modern Education." *Abc.net*, May 24, 2017. http://www.abc.net.au/news/2017-05-25/indigenous-education-in-a-modern-world/8555368.

Eller, Jack David. Review of *An Appreciation of Difference: W. E. H. Stanner and Aboriginal Australia*, edited by Melinda Hinkson and Jeremy Beckett. *Anthropology Review Database*, September 8, 2014.

Griffiths, Tom. *The Art of Time Travel: Historians and Their Craft*. Carlton, Australia: Black, 2016.

Harris, John. *One Blood: Two Hundred Years of Aboriginal Encounter with Christianity; A Story of Hope*. Sutherland, Australia: Albatross, 1990.

Harrison, James R. "Introducing Well-Being, Personal Wholeness and the Australian Social Fabric: Ancient and Modern Perspectives." In *Well-Being, Personal Wholeness and the Social Fabric*, edited by Doru Costache, Darren Cronshaw, and James R. Harrison, 2–30. Newcastle upon Tyne: Cambridge Scholars, 2017.

Havel, Vaclav. *Disturbing the Peace*. New York: Knopf, 1990.

Holm, Neil. "Educating the Net Generation for Transformation and Transcendence." *Journal of Christian Education* 54 (2011) 5–18.

Jordan, Ivan. *Their Way: Towards an Indigenous Warlpiri Christianity*. Darwin, Australia: Charles Darwin University Press, 2003.

Lear, Jonathan. *Radical Hope: Ethics in the Face of Cultural Devastation*. Cambridge: Harvard University Press, 2006.

Luke, Allan. "Direct Instruction Is Not a Solution for Australian Schools." *EduResearch Matters* (blog), July 7, 2014. http://www.aare.edu.au/blog/?p=439.

———. "On Explicit and Direct Instruction." ALEA "Hot Topic," May 2014. https://www.alea.edu.au/documents/item/861:2.

Lummis, Douglas C. *Radical Democracy*. Ithaca, NY: Cornell University Press, 1996.

Mounce, Robert H. *A Living Hope: A Commentary on 1 and 2 Peter*. 1982. Reprint, Eugene, OR: Wipf & Stock, 2005.

Newall, C. "Whose Values, Which Ethics? Science Education and the Civil Society." *Australian Science Teachers Journal* 49 (2003) 6–11.

Nouwen, Henri *Reaching Out*. New York: Doubleday, 1975.

Pearson, Noel. "Radical Hope: Education and Equality in Australia." *Quarterly Essay* 35 (2009) 1–105.

Parker, David C. "The Eschatology of 1 Peter." *Biblical Theology Bulletin* 24.1 (1994) 27–32.

Roy, Louis. *Transcendent Experiences: Phenomenology and Critique*. Toronto: University of Toronto Press, 2001.

Sacks, Jonathan. *The Politics of Hope*. London: Vintage, 2000.

Stanner, W. E. H. *White Man Got No Dreaming: Essays 1938–1973*. Canberra: Australia National University Press, 1979.

Thornton, Warwick, writer. *Samson and Delilah*. Film. Produced by K. Shelper. Australia: Footprint Films, with Transmission Films and Paramount Pictures, Australia, 2009.

Weil, Simone. *Waiting on God*. London: Routledge and Kegan Paul, 1951.

Wright, Tom. *Surprised by Hope: Rethinking Heaven, the Resurrection, and the Mission of the Church*. New York: HarperOne, 2008.

Yeselson, Rich. "Avoiding the Lasch of Modernity." In *What Are Intellectuals Good For? A Crooked Timber Seminar on George Scialabba's Book*, edited by Henry Farrell, 15–22. N.p., 2009.

Zhou, J., and K. W. Fischer. "Culturally Appropriate Education: Insights from Educational Neuroscience." *Mind, Brain, and Education* 7 (2013) 225–31.

PART F

Healthcare, Memory Loss, and Well-Being
Ancient and Modern Perspectives

12

Late Antique Healthcare and the Early Christian Reinterpretation of Sickness and Disease

Adam G. Cooper

In an interview with the Jesuit magazine *Civiltà Cattolica* during his first year in office, Pope Francis proposed his ideal vision of the church as "a field hospital after a battle."[1] This metaphor has proved its veracity countless times in the experience of those involved in pastoral service, especially to the sick and dying. There are numerous facets to it, but in my own experience of ministry among those living within the trauma of illness or impending death, I recall being struck most by a consciousness of treading on holy ground. I recall how deeply such pressing, liminal circumstances brought to light my own helplessness and vulnerability, my own shared dependence with the sick upon the divine healer and the holy communion of co-healing agents. And I would always come away from such encounters—often in the dead of night, humbled and silenced by all I had been part of—with a keen sense of how much the world of the hospital embodies and illumines some deeply ecclesial reality, and concurrently how much the church must always, like a hospital, remain enfolded within the wounds of Christ and signed by the shadow of his cross, if it is to be true to its inner meaning and salvific mission in history.

But of course this motif of the church as a hospital also has a long and well established history in Christian tradition. One of its most famous early protagonists was St. John Chrysostom. A renowned preacher and bishop, Chrysostom was personally involved in setting up and overseeing a range of highly organized, large-scale charitable works. Among these were included a hospital for the poor (χενοδοχεῖον) in Antioch

---

1. Pope Francis, interview by Antonio Spadaro, August 19, 2013.

and hospices for the sick (νοσοκομεία) in Constantinople.² With these institutions playing an essential role in the welfare activities of the late fourth-century church, and featuring prominently in his appeals to the rich in the hope of their providing material support, Chrysostom was inspired to speak analogously of the church itself as a kind of hospital, "an admirable surgery, a surgery not for bodies, but for souls."³ Just as the sick find free refuge, mercy, and healing in a hospital, so people who have sinned and gone astray should be urged to "enter into the Church and repent, because the Church is a hospital, not a court of justice."⁴

Christ as Physician

This ancient metaphor or analogy of the church as a hospital went hand in hand with the even older notion of Christ as a physician or doctor. In a pioneering and detailed historical study on the subject, Adolph von Harnack argued that this *Christus medicus* motif was from the very beginning Christianity's most central characteristic. Early Christianity, he proposed, was above all a religion of healing.⁵ There is much in the New Testament writings that seems to support this view. Healing was not just peripheral to Jesus' ministry, but formed an essential component of his redemptive mission and that of his earliest followers (Isa 53:5; Matt 8:16–17; 10:8; 25:36; James 5:14). Jesus' healing ministry was understood as a sign confirming the advent of the messianic kingdom (Isa 58:8; Jer 33:6; Mal 4:2; Matt 4:23–25; Mark 1:34; Acts 10:38). His acts of healing commonly had a holistic impact—anthropologically, socially, and theologically—being more or less explicitly or implicitly linked to faith and forgiveness, restoration and salvation (Matt 9:22; Luke 8:48; 13:14–17; 18:42; 1 Pet 2:24; John 7:23). Through the healing ministry of Jesus we learn that the category "the sick" designates the privileged recipients of the divine mission: "It is not the healthy who need a doctor," he teaches, "but the sick" (Luke 5:31; cf. Matt 8:3). The category "the sick" however must be interpreted to include much more than those with purely physical maladies. "I have come to call not the righteous, but sinners to repentance." In the New Testament physical and mental illnesses are regarded as symbolic of the disruptive impact of sin, which objectively isolates persons from community and threatens their inner sense of integrity and well-being. Yet Jesus challenged the commonly held idea of direct cause and effect relation between sin and suffering (John 9:1–3). The righteous also suffer illness. Sickness and death are therefore to be viewed through

2. See Miller, "From Poorhouse to Hospital."

3. *Homily against Publishing the Errors of the Brethren* (ed. Schaff, *Nicene and Post-Nicene Fathers* [NPNF], 235–42).

4. *Homilies on Repentance and Almsgiving* 3.4.19 (trans. Christo, *Fathers of the Church*, 39).

5. Harnack, *Die Mission und Ausbreitung des Christentums in den ersten drie Jahrhundertern*; ET: *The Mission and Expansion of Christianity in the First Three Centuries*, published online at: http://www.ccel.org/ccel/harnack/mission.pdf. See also Dumeige, "(Christ) Médecin"; Larchet, "Le Christ Médecin."

the eyes of faith as opportunities for the manifestation of God's redemptive power and glory (John 9:3; 11:4).

Something similar is expressed in Paul's theology of the cross. According to the rationale of the cross, that which in the scale of normal human values is considered weak, ignoble, or humanly unfit becomes a special locus for the embodied manifestation and enactment of divine power and wisdom (1 Cor 1:18–31). If it is true that "healers mediate culture,"[6] then Jesus' healing ministry can be interpreted as inaugurating an entirely new culture of life. In sending out his followers to continue his healing works, and to do even "greater things" than his own miracles, Jesus establishes the conditions for the creative cultivation and ongoing spread of this new culture in history. We might call this the healing culture of the new creation.

Already by the time of Ignatius of Antioch (d. ca. 115), belief in Jesus Christ as the divine physician appears to be a crucial christological motif, set in contrast with the rival healing cult of Asclepius.[7] But it was Origen of Alexandria who depicted Jesus' function as physician "more frequently and fully than anyone else."[8] Many of Origen's statements on the theme were elaborated in his treatise against the cultured philosopher Celsus (fl. ca. 170–180). Celsus had criticized Christianity for what seemed to him to be its ostensible tolerance of morally dubious types. "Let us hear what sort of people these Christians invite. Everyone, they say, who is a sinner, who is devoid of understanding, who is a child, and, to speak generally, whoever is unfortunate, him will the kingdom of God receive."[9] In answer, Origen affirmed Christianity's welcome extended especially to sinners, but pointed out that it is with a view toward their healing and restoration that the invitation is given. A thief invites other thieves into his fellowship in order to help him steal. A Christian, on the other hand,

> even though he invites those whom the robber invites, invites them to a very different vocation, namely, to bind up his wounds by the word [of Christ], and to apply to his soul, festering amid evils, the medicines obtained from the word, and which are analogous to the wine and oil, and bandages, and other healing applications which belong to the art of medicine.[10]

The analogy between the art of medicine and the ministry of Christian healing only goes so far, however, for Christ the Saviour is the "true physician" not just

---

6. Pilch, *Healing in the New Testament*, 15.

7. See Ignatius' *Letter to the Ephesians* 7, 2. Scholarship is divided on the extent to which there existed a Christ-Asclepius rivalry in early Christianity. See *inter alia* Heyne, "Were Second-Century Christians 'Preoccupied'"; Porterfield, *Healing in the History of Christianity*; Dinkler, *Christus und Asklepios*.

8. *Mission and Expansion*, online version, 103n37. Harnack writes: "Deliberately and consciously it assumed the form of 'the religion of salvation or healing,' or 'the medicine of soul and body,' and at the same time it recognized that one of its chief duties was to care assiduously for the sick in body." *Mission and Expansion*, online version, 101–2.

9. *Contra Celsum* 3, 59 (ed. Borret, Sources Chrétiennes, vol. 136, 136–38).

10. *Contra Celsum* 3, 61 (Sources Chrétiennes, vol. 136, 142).

of bodies, but also of souls.[11] Indeed, Origen calls Jesus not just *iatros*, a doctor, but the *archiatros* or chief-physician.[12] Probably the only other patristic author who comes close to Origen's enthusiasm in exploiting the *Christus medicus* motif to this extent is Augustine, who, echoing Origen, calls Christ the "complete physician" (*totus medicus*),[13] the "doctor of all" (*medicus omnium*),[14] the only one able to heal all our wounds of body and soul. Indeed, he is both the doctor and the medicine itself (*ipsa medicus, ipsa medicina*).[15]

Given Origen's creative mind, and the opportunity afforded by his contest with the cultured intellectualism of Celsus, this analogy of Christ as doctor and the Christian as a healed sinner seemed an open invitation to extend the metaphor even further into something like the church as hospital theme. But only once, as far as I can tell, does Origen include an ecclesiological dimension: "Come now to Jesus," he says in his *Homilies on Leviticus*, "come to the heavenly physician. Enter into this medical clinic, his Church. See lying there a multitude of feeble ones."[16] But the problem faced by Origen at this point lies in the fact that hospitals as we understand them were in Origen's lifetime virtually non-existent. Although systematic forms of Christian care for the poor and sick had apparently been operative right from the beginning, and although there were medical clinics operated by a few professional doctors for paying customers, and by the Roman military for soldiers and slaves, the hospitals that would come to function as suitable analogates for the church were an institutional development unique to the fourth century, and without them, there were only limited material or institutional realities to serve as raw material for metaphorical reflection and theological development.

The First Hospitals

The history of the Christian establishment of the first public hospitals has been well documented, and there is no need to rehearse all the details here. While there was a developed tradition of medical practice before and outside of Christianity, and there were many practising Christian physicians, it is widely acknowledged in the history of medicine that the modern hospital has its origin in organized Christian care for the sick and needy.[17] Among the more famous Christian doctors we may mention the twin

11. *Hom. in Lev.* 7.1 (*Patrologia Graeca* [PG] 12, 476B).

12. *Hom. in Kings* (PG 12, 1021).

13. *In Joh. Evang. Tract.* 3.2 (*Patrologia Latina* [PL] 35, 1396).

14. *In Ep. Joh. ad Parthos Tract.* 2.1 (PL 35, 1989).

15. *Teaching Christianity* (*De Doctrina Christiana*) 1.14.13, 111–12. This theme is found also in Jerome and Ephrem. See Arbesmann, "Concept of *Christus Medicus*."

16. *Hom. in Lev.* 8 (PG 12, 492D): "Veni nunc ad Iesum coelestum medicum, intra ad hanc stationem medicinae ejus ecclesiam, vide ibi languentium jacere multitudinem."

17. See *inter alia* Horden, "Earliest Hospitals"; Holman, *Hungry Are Dying*; Miller, *Birth of the Hospital*. Miller argues that these early Christian hospitals "represent not only the first public institutions

brothers and celebrated martyrs St. Cosmas and St. Damian (d. ca. 287), and another partnership, that of St. Cyrus of Alexandria and St. John of Arabia (d. ca. 304).[18]

The earliest hospitals arose from the soil of the monastic culture of Egypt in the fourth century. These early Christian hospitals were not just simple almshouses or hospices. They were carefully managed medical healthcare institutions. In the Latin West, even though there were resident monastic doctors, there was apparently nothing quite comparable until the thirteenth century.[19] Before these first hospitals several bishops had already established large philanthropic hostels and refugee centers—called *ptochotropheia*—from the 340s to attend to the needs of the poor. Particularly in times of plague or famine, "bishops provided energetic leadership in organizing the clergy to direct relief efforts" to the poor, suffering and sick.[20] It was just a little before this time (from the 320s) that the Christian monastic movement arose with thousands of Christian ascetics flocking to the deserts of Egypt and Palestine to live in monastic communities (both eremitic and coenobitic). Removed from the usual context in which healthcare would have been given, namely the family and household, the early monks had to organize their own healthcare, and, according to the research of Andrew Crislip, did so through two main outlets: "inpatient care in an infirmary and outpatient care provided in individual [monastic] cells."[21]

The monastic infirmaries seem to have been modelled on the Roman military infirmaries (*valetudinaria*).[22] Around 324 Abbot Pachomius, widely regarded as one of the founding fathers of coenobitic monasticism, and who had himself served in the military, was said to have "appointed another house of stewards to give comfort to all the sick brothers with attentive care according to their rules, and over them a housemaster and a second in the same way."[23]

In many monastic communities (especially the *laura* type)[24] the church (or a room built off the side) served as the infirmary (Gr. *nosokomeion*). Bigger communities, such as the 5000 strong *laura* community of Nitria (just south of Alexandria), were

---

to offer medical services to the sick, but also the main current in the development of hospitals throughout the Middle Ages, and out of which the Latin West and Muslim East were equally inspired for their own medical structures" (*Birth of the Hospital*, 4).

18. See Matthews, "SS. Cosmas and Damian"; Constantelos, "Physician-Priests."

19. Miller, "Byzantine Hospitals," 54. Of course Jerome famously referred to the wealthy widow Fabiola who in the late fourth century "was the first to establish a hospital" in Rome (*Ep.* 73.6), apparently by converting part of a villa. Horden ("Earliest Hospitals," 377) regards Fabiola's institution more as a "sub-hospital"; Jerome's description of its patients suggest it was more like an early *leprosarium*.

20. Ferngren, *Medicine and Health Care*, 118.

21. Crislip, *From Monastery to Hospital*, 9.

22. See Chitty, *Desert a City*, 22.

23. From the Greek *Life of Pachomius*, quoted by Crislip, *From Monastery to Hospital*, 11.

24. Gr. *laura* = street. The *laura* (or *lavra*) communities were fashioned like small villages or towns, with cells scattered over a wide area. "Lavra monasticism . . . developed as a natural outgrowth of anchoritic monasticism, as a way of accommodating the burgeoning monastic population of Egypt." Crislip, *From Monastery to Hospital*, 4.

served by a number of monastic doctors. Crislip argues that "the monastic doctors possessed the full breadth of medical skills, ranging from dietary therapy to hygiene, to the application of pharmaceuticals, to complicated surgery. While these physicians still practised their craft and continued to identify themselves as physicians, they lived alongside of and in the same manner as all other monastics, contributing to their services as part of the monastic system of mutual aid."[25]

In Shenoute's monastery (mid-4th-century Egypt) there were both male and female doctors. Apparently "the presence of both male and female physicians would not have been unfamiliar in Greco-Roman and Egyptian medical traditions."[26] The presence of monastic doctors became commonplace in both Eastern and Western monasticism. In the fourth century we also witness the emergence of a trained corps of nursing staff, distinct from both the doctors and the regular fellow-monastic caregivers. According to Crislip, in Pachomius's monastic system,

> the nurses were a rotating component of those monastics appointed to look after the "bodily" needs of the monastery. The caretakers of bodily needs were divided into three unit. . . . One corps cooked for and served the healthy monastics. The second, with an administrative hierarchy parallel to the first, provided for the sick monastics. The third cooked and cared for nonmonastics at the gatehouse, whether they were paupers, visitors, or catechumens.

Members of the nursing corps were expected "to master a special set of knowledge." They were "not apprentices to the doctors but were responsible for their own realm of specialized services."[27]

The Case of Basil's *Basileia*

The monastic communities of Pachomius and Shenoute were the first to establish an organized system of medical healthcare, but such hospitals cared mainly for monks within the communities, not for the public, and were initially confined to isolated regions of Egypt. In the early 370s however, in response to the widespread social crisis caused by the famine of 369, the great Cappadocian Bishop, Basil of Caesarea, besides founding a number of almshouses and hospices, extended the tradition of the monastic hospital to Asia Minor by having a hospital built in suburban Caesarea with paid and dedicated medical staff.[28] Basil seems to have modelled his hospital on the basis of his experiences during an extensive personal tour of the Egyptian and Palestinian monasteries in 357. This hospital, which was charitably funded, and built on land

---

25. Crislip, *From Monastery to Hospital*, 14.
26. Crislip, *From Monastery to Hospital*, 14.
27. Crislip, *From Monastery to Hospital*, 15–16.
28. On the chronology of Basil's social welfare enterprises, culminating in the Basileias, see Silvas, "Emergence of Basil's Social Doctrine."

donated by Emperor Valens, was devoted to providing public healthcare for those who could not afford professional treatment.[29] It became known as the *Basileias* (or *ptochotropheion*), and "offered a comprehensive range of hospital services, much more than simple medical or hospice care."[30] Its architectural complex was so extensive that it was soon labelled "the new city."[31]

Basil's hospital marks the inauguration of a tradition of hospital building in the East. Near the end of the fourth century John Chrysostom likewise opened similar institutions in Constantinople, the capital of the empire. Deacon Ephraim the Syrian (306–73) is famous for "setting up [during a plague in Edessa in 373] some three hundred beds in public porticoes for the treatment of the ill . . . Ephraim's reputation stood so high that he was the only person in the city to whom the rich would entrust their gifts to meet the emergency."[32] Later in the fifth century (ca. 479) Patriarch Theodosius of Syria established three hospitals in Palestine, one for monastics, one for the poor, and a third for paying clients. "By the turn of the fifth century, the establishment of hospitals had become a common vocation of ecclesiastical and ascetic leaders, following the lead of Basil of Caesarea, who founded his hospital shortly after being elevated to bishop of Caesarea."[33]

The Christian Reinterpretation of Disease

Besides building the first hospital, Basil contributed more than anyone before him to developing deeper theological foundations for organized and systematic social healthcare, and for likening the ministry of the gospel to the healing profession. For Basil was not only a studied philosopher and theologian, he had also studied medicine in Athens and he constantly envisaged his spiritual vocation as bishop in the terms provided by the medical arts.[34] Apparently his initial interest in learning medicine

29. See Silvas, "Emergence of Basil's Social Doctrine," 104.

30. Silvas, "Emergence of Basil's Social Doctrine," 104.

31. The phrase is from Gregory Nazianzen's panegyric for Basil after the latter's death. See *Or.* 43.63 (NPNF 7:416).

32. Ferngren, *Medicine and Healthcare*, 118.

33. Crislip, *From Monastery to Hospital*, 102–3.

34. I am indebted to Anna Silvas for the following clarifications via personal correspondence: "Basil never practised as a physician. He, and others in his family acquired an intimate practical knowledge of it (to some extent as part of options of the higher curriculum), but not professionally. It could be that the unnamed grandfather, i.e., the husband of Macrina the Elder, had been a physician. Still, the 'medical art' was so important to Basil that it informed all of his approach to soul-doctoring. There was, however, another Basil a generation earlier who *was* a bishop and had been a professional physician, namely Basil of Ancyra. He was sort of in the homoiousian theological stream. Our Basil and Gregory of Nyssa heard Basil of Ancyra discourse in Constantinople in the scarifying Anomoian council of that year. Basil of Ancyra had much to say about the four temperaments and how they affected a life of virginity for the Lord, and of course, he wrote a treatise on Virginity. There is some back reference to this by Gregory of Nyssa in his own treatise on virginity. I also have a hunch that St. Methodius of Olympus (or whatever his surname is now), who died a martyr in ca. 313, was also a physician and a bishop."

arose from concern about his own health problems, and by his profound empathy for the sick. "From these beginnings he attained to a mastery of the art, not only in its empirical and practical branches, but also in its theory and principles."[35]

Basil's program for Christian healthcare was marked by four main features.[36]

a. the destigmatization of illness;

b. the (re-)interpretation of disease in light of Christian anthropology and the doctrine of redemption;

c. the defence of the valid use of Hippocratic and Galenic medicine;

d. the acknowledgment of the limits of medicine.

In short, Basil provided both the theoretical and practical basis for a program of permanent and systematic healthcare as part and parcel of a Christian culture. Before long his hospital "became the standard by which other institutions were judged, the model upon which hospitals were founded across the Mediterranean, in Constantinople, Antioch, Jerusalem, and elsewhere."[37] Herein lie the material foundations for the subsequent development of the church as hospital motif.

But there is a yet a further feature in Basil's program for Christian healthcare, which leads us to another way of construing the church as hospital motif. It has to do with his interpretation of healthcare as a participation with Christ in the activity of divine love for human beings. Recalling the New Testament reference in Titus 3:4 to the Saviour's incarnate *philanthropia* toward the unrighteous, Basil writes to the physician Eustathius to affirm that "all of you who practice medicine are also called to be philanthropists."[38] In other words, doctors and healthcare staff are co-agents with Christ, extending through their work his incarnate healing ministry to the sick.

This point becomes even more poignant in a brief passage in Gregory Nazianzen's eulogy to Basil published a couple of years after the latter's death in 379. This is the oration in which Gregory refers to Basil's hospital complex outside Caesarea as "the new city," more magnificent than the pyramids of Egypt, more splendid than the towering Walls of Babylon, more majestic than any of the other wonders of the ancient world, a city where "disease is regarded in a religious light, and disaster is thought a blessing, and sympathy is put to the test."[39] In just these words we have the basis for our claim that Basil's program for healthcare effected the de-stigmatization of illness and the reinterpretation of disease in the light of the *logos* of the cross and its reversal of worldly values.[40]

35. Greg.Naz. *Or.* 43, 23 (NPNF 7:403).

36. Crislip, *From Monastery to Hospital*, 118–20.

37. Crislip, *From Monastery to Hospital*, 141–42.

38. Basil, *Ep.* 189, 1 (NPNF 8:228, modified trans.).

39. *Or.* 43, 63 (NPNF 7:416).

40. For a more detailed elaboration of this aspect in patristic theology, see Larchet, *Theology of Illness*.

But Gregory goes even further when he makes the claim that Basil's hospital effectively represents "the short road to salvation, the easiest way up to heaven." What does he mean? Apparently there was a church or chapel at Basil's hospital, and we can assume that there were regular hours of public worship there, along with the celebration of the saving mysteries.[41] But Gregory does not seem to have this more strictly liturgical locus in view. Horden interprets the phrase as implying that, to Gregory's mind at least, Basil's hospital was more like a hospice for palliative care, aimed only at easing death for the chronically or terminally ill rather than at promoting recovery.[42] But this I think would be to misunderstand Gregory's meaning here, which is to praise the way Basil's hospital project had become an easy path to salvation not just for the patients, but above all for the hospital personnel—the patrons, the doctors, the pharmacists, the nursing staff—who in ministering to people suffering outwardly disturbing and repulsive symptoms, were actually serving Christ, and so receiving healing themselves. It is not just through the healthcare staff that Christ performs his healing ministry in the world. It is also through the patients, for through them Christ reaches out to the healthy and calls for their compassion, service and care.

On this view, Basil's hospital had become a stairway to heaven not just for the sick and dying, but for all who had been moved to contribute to its establishment, its activity, and its ongoing charitable operation. On account of the way it extended and incarnated the healing presence of Christ, on account of the way it overturned the pretensions and pride of the powerful and healthy and rich, Basil's hospital is thought of by Gregory as a kind of open door to heaven, an ecclesial microcosm of divine charity, spiritual fellowship, and redemptive healing. In the Christian hospital, it is not just the professional health-carers who incarnate divine healing. Christ the doctor is also present and active through the patients themselves, reaching out and communicating his healing to all who serve him there as a kind of wounded healer, or what Gregory would have termed, the "crucified God."[43]

Two Final Examples

Two concluding examples from later in history indicate how this profound idea was assimilated. In fifth-century Constantinople, we find Bishop John Chrysostom echoing just this theme in his homilies. In one he draws a parallel between the body of the Lord present in the Eucharist and his body suffering in the needy. Just as we rightly honor Christ's body and blood in the sacrament and provide costly vessels for the celebration of the mysteries, so in caring for the sick and poor, we pay homage to the body of Christ who identifies himself with them.[44]

41. Basil, *Ep.* 176 (NPNF 8:220).
42. Horden, "Earliest Hospitals," 384.
43. Greg.Naz. *Or.* 43, 63–64 (NPNF 7:416–17).
44. *Homilies in Matthew*, 50, 3–5 (NPNF 10:312–13, translation altered).

Do you want to honour Christ's body? Then do not neglect him when he is naked. Do not come here to honour him dressed in your silk garments, while you neglect him perishing outside from cold and nakedness. For he who said, "This is my body," and by his word confirmed the fact, also said, "You saw me hungry, yet did not feed me."

Chrysostom wants to chide his hearers for decorating the church at the cost of clothing the poor. It is the latter who are more properly regarded to be a temple of God and so worthy of expensive adornment: "Do not therefore while adorning God's house overlook your brother in distress, for he is more properly a temple than the other." Viewed from this perspective, poverty, sickness and disease can come to be viewed not only as a threat and liability, but as medium through which Christ calls for concrete service, as a humbling and salvific resource for the healing of the world. The hospital, where the poor and sick are present in higher concentration, therefore constitutes a kind of temple, a church, in which the Lord's body is present. Through our veneration and service of his body in them, we in turn we receive salutary healing for our deeper spiritual ills.

The second example arises in the practice of two Palestinian hospitals in the 12th century. One was the Hospital of St. John at Jerusalem, the other the Hospital of St. John at Acre (ancient Ptolemais). The practice consisted of two elements: one was the reverential title formally given to patients at these hospitals: *Seignors malades* ("Our Lords the Sick"). The second was the formal intercessory office bestowed upon these patients, and ritually enacted in the night-time prayers in the hospitals' residential wing. There, instead of the healthy praying for the sick, the sick offered lengthy intercessions for the healthy.[45]

Through these select examples, we see how the wounded were enabled to become healers, and how the hospital became a church. What had begun under the aegis of the church as a healing community, ended up transforming the hospital itself into a community of salvation.

Bibliography

Arbesmann, Rudolph. "The Concept of *Christus Medicus* in St. Augustine." *Traditio* 10 (1954) 1–28.
Augustine. *Teaching Christianity (De Doctrina Christiana)*. Translated by Edmund Hill. Edited by Boniface Ramsey. Works of Saint Augustine I/11. Hyde Park: New City, 1996.
Borret, Marcel, ed. *Contre Celse*. Vol. 4. Sources Chrétiennes 136. Paris: Cerf, 1968.
Chitty, Derwas J. *The Desert a City: An Introduction to the Study of Egyptian and Palestinian Monasticism under the Christian Empire*. Crestwood: St. Vladimir's Seminary Press, 1995.

---

45. The title "Seignors malades" is stipulated in the Rule of Raymond du Puy for the Hospitaller Order, approved by Pope Eugene III around 1153. See King, *Rule, Statutes and Customs*, 26–27, 114. On the night-time prayer, see Sinclair, "French Prayer for the Sick."

Christo, G. G., trans. *St. John Chrysostom: On Repentance and Almsgiving*. Fathers of the Church 96. Washington DC: Catholic University of America Press, 2010.

Constantelos, D. J. "Physician-Priests in the Medieval Greek Church." *Greek Orthodox Theological Review* 14 (1967) 141–53.

Crislip, Andrew T. *From Monastery to Hospital: Christian Monasticism and the Transformation of Healthcare in Late Antiquity*. Ann Arbor: University of Michigan Press, 2005.

Dinkler, Erich. *Christus und Asklepios*. Heidelberg: Carl Winter, 1980.

Dumeige, G. "(Christ) Médecin." In vol. 10 of *Dictionnaire de spiritualité*, cols. 891–901. Paris: Beauchesne, 1980.

Ferngren, Gary B. *Medicine and Health Care in Early Christianity*. Baltimore: Johns Hopkins University Press, 2009.

Harnack, Adolf von. *The Mission and Expansion of Christianity in the First Three Centuries*. 2 vols. Translated by James Moffatt. London: Williams and Norgate, 1904–8.

Heyne, Thomas. "Were Second-Century Christians 'Preoccupied' with Physical Healing and the Asclepian Cult?" In *Studia Patristica*, edited by J. Baun et al., 44:63–69. Leuven: Peeters, 2010.

Holman, Susan R. *The Hungry Are Dying: Beggars and Bishops in Roman Cappadocia*. Oxford: Oxford University Press, 2001.

Horden, Peregrine. "The Earliest Hospitals in Byzantium, Western Europe, and Islam." *Journal of Interdisciplinary History* 35 (2005) 361–89.

King, E. J., ed. and trans. *The Rule, Statutes and Customs of the Hospitallers 1099–1310*. London: Methuen, 1934.

Larchet, Jean-Claude. "Le Christ Médecin." In *Thérapeutique des maladies spirituelles: une introduction à la tradition ascétique de l'Église orthodoxe*, 319–44. Paris: Cerf, 1991.

———. *The Theology of Illness*. Translated by John and Michael Breck. Crestwood: St. Vladimir's Seminary Press, 2002.

Matthews, Leslie G. "SS. Cosmas and Damian—Patron Saints of Medicine and Pharmacy: Their Cult in England." *Medical History* 12 (1968) 281–88.

Miller, Timothy S. *The Birth of the Hospital in the Byzantine Empire*. Baltimore: Johns Hopkins University Press, 1985.

———. "Byzantine Hospitals." *Dumbarton Oaks Papers* 38 (1984) 53–63.

———. "From Poorhouse to Hospital." *Christian History* 101 (2011) 16–23.

Pilch, John J. *Healing in the New Testament: Insights from Medical and Mediterranean Anthropology*. Minneapolis: Fortress, 2000.

Pope Francis. Interview by Antonio Spadaro. *Vatican.va*, August 19, 2013. http://www.vatican.va/content/francesco/en/speeches/2013/september/documents/papa-francesco_20130921_intervista-spadaro.html.

Porterfield, Amanda. *Healing in the History of Christianity*. New York: Oxford University Press, 2005.

Schaff, P. *Nicene and Post-Nicene Fathers*. Vol. 9. Reprint, Grand Rapids: Eerdmans, 1978.

Silvas, Anna M. "The Emergence of Basil's Social Doctrine: A Chronological Enquiry." In *Prayer and Spirituality in the Early Church*, vol. 5, *Poverty and Riches*, edited by Geoffrey Dunn et al., 133–44. Strathfield: St Paul's, 2009.

Sinclair, K. V. "The French Prayer for the Sick in the Hospital of the Knights of Saint John of Jerusalem at Acre." *Medieval Studies* 40 (1978) 484–88.

13

New Every Morning
Spiritual Care in the Context of Memory Loss

Stephen Smith and Catherine Kleemann

The steadfast love of the Lord never ceases;
his mercies never come to an end;
they are new every morning.

—Lam 3:22–23 ESV

As life expectancy in Organisation for Economic Co-operation and Development countries continues to rise, a challenge for twenty-first-century civilization is the growing number of residents in aged care centers who are living with memory loss. This memory loss may be a result of dementia, acquired brain injury or other intellectual challenges.

The largest cause of memory loss in Australia is dementia. Dementia refers to the symptoms of a group of illnesses that cause the progressive degeneration of a person's cognitive and physical abilities. The early signs are usually very subtle and may not be immediately evident. As a person ages, their behavior may change for different reasons; however, dementia is a result of neurological changes that manifest as frequent confusion, withdrawal, personality changes and gradual loss of memory, intellect, social skills and the ability to perform everyday tasks, which can become apparent in behaviors such as wandering, mood swings, aggression, hallucinations and depression. Typically, a person's family will notice dementia symptoms three years prior to a formal diagnosis being made.[1]

In Australia, dementia is the greatest cause of disability in people aged sixty-five years or older.[2] Alzheimer's disease is the most common form of dementia, representing an estimated 50–70 percent of all dementia cases. More than half the residents in government-subsidized aged care facilities in Australia have been diagnosed with dementia.[3] In the United Kingdom, the Alzheimer's Society reports this figure as 64 percent; one United States (US) study has found that 75 percent of nursing home residents experience some form of cognitive impairment.[4] In Australia, approximately one person is diagnosed with dementia every six minutes,[5] with the number of diagnosed cases expected to increase by one-third in fewer than 10 years.

This chapter is written by pastoral practitioners—our context is an organization with a large number of ageing residents and a clinical staff of over 800 carers. In this paper, we share questions and insights that have arisen in our work with chaplains in this environment. The chapter is part of a wider exploration of spirituality as an *integral* part of holistic health (and not merely an *influence* on health);[6] within this context, the issue of dementia raises questions that are both theological and pastoral.

As practitioners, we have found that a chaplain's unique role as a vital, hopeful and spiritual presence should be core to the pursuit of wellness for those with memory loss.

Memory Loss Is Deeply Personal

It is highly likely that every human will encounter memory loss and require memory support over the course of their lifetime, either personally or among their family or friends. This encounter will inevitably change the way an individual experiences the world, determines what is important and shapes how they choose to live.

For each of the authors, a personal experience prompted their initial interest and concern with the effects of memory loss. One author, Catherine Kleemann, shares her personal encounter with memory loss as a child and how it shaped her view of God and the world:

If you were to ask me of my earliest childhood memories, one is playing with my friends Ivan and Robyn. They were much bigger than I was; in fact, they were adults. Ivan lived with an acquired brain injury after a car accident, leaving him with limited

---

1. Phillips et al., *Timely Diagnosis of Dementia*.
2. Deloitte Access Economics, "Keeping Dementia Front of Mind."
3. Australian Institute of Health and Welfare, *Dementia among Aged Care Residents*.
4. Rice et al., "Ethical Issues Relative to Autonomy," 27.
5. Deloitte Access Economics, "Keeping Dementia Front of Mind," 12.
6. Smith, "Savouring Life."

short-term memory and processing difficulties, while Robyn had been born with an intellectual delay and had the functioning level of a primary schooler.

Like all children, I enjoyed playing and competing, and my grown-up friends were great playmates. I was not aware that they were different to other adults—to me, they were just who they were. Then, when I was approximately three years old, my mother sat me down and suggested that it would be kind to let Robyn win the Tupperware blocks game. I had made a race of putting those yellow blocks into the correctly shaped holes in the red Tupperware game. I was good at it. Robyn struggled. That conversation with my mother left a mark on my young soul. That was the moment I realised that Robyn was different. Although she was an adult, I could out-think her—my hands moved faster, I could colour within the lines better and I was learning my letters and numbers quicker than she could. But I didn't feel pity, our household respected Robyn. Instead, I was given a challenge: it was my shared responsibility to help and empower Robyn. This was not a condescending act, she was my friend, she had different abilities and we celebrated and supported her. Because God made her just the way she was. "God never makes mistakes," my mother would say.

My parents ran a group for intellectually delayed young adults at our church—around 30 young people who worked at the sheltered workshop in town. Dad would organise activities, and he and the students would do "Bible Studies" together, which usually amounted to a children's Bible story that I could sit in on. At times, some in the Christian community questioned my parents' "waste of time" trying to teach "poor unfortunates" who could "never be saved." The prevailing view was that cognitive ability was necessary to both understand and embrace the gospel story. Those who were young, had a delayed intellect or lived with memory loss were simply unable to articulate the gospel clearly enough—therefore, it was assumed that they could not understand God, connect with God or indeed be "saved."

My parents held a different view. They believed that God loves us, and saves us, regardless of our mental ability. While they pursued biblical studies with integrity, they saw that our prayers, our connection to the Father, is neither dependent upon our memory nor intellect, but rather on God's passion for us. They taught me that we are accountable for that we can understand.

They believed that all souls are valuable because we are children of God, formed in the likeness of the creator. We are loved, honoured and pursued by the Father. We are equal. God does not love His beautiful children more than His disfigured ones, He does not value His intelligent children (as society measures such things) more than His disabled ones, He does not listen to the prayers of the articulate over the inarticulate, He does not favour riches over poverty or the powerful over the weak. Indeed, in the upside-down kingdom, the less honourable become more honourable.

In our household, the less honourable were shown honour. I learned these lessons on the floor playing games with adults who could forget my name on a regular basis.

This has had a profound influence on my pastoral ministry.

Because Robyn and Ivan and the many others who came through our house loved God with a simple faith.

Their prayers were childlike but genuine.

And they have taught me that you don't need to be able to read to love Jesus. They have taught me that you can have a depth to your spiritual life, a faith that can move mountains, a connection to God even if you can't remember all the details of the text, if you confuse the stories and forget the right words to say. Indeed, those who are most shunned, feared and shut away can experience God's love with a purity that our intellect sometimes stands in the way of.

Eight years ago, I visited my grandmother in care. After another stroke, her dementia had taken a sharp turn and she no longer recognised me or even acknowledged that she had grandchildren. She could not speak clearly; she sat and listened to hymns on a CD and mouthed words we could not understand.

I believe she was praying. As she prayed for each us by name for over 30 years, I believe she still prayed somewhere in her mind.

She calmed when scripture was read.

She was otherwise agitated.

For 90 years, this saint followed Jesus; she served with 100% of her heart, mind and soul. She sacrificed her life for others. With her husband of 60 years, she built a church. She memorised scriptures and prayed for hours. Her Bible sat on her desk in her room, and it was common to see both Nanny and Pop sitting by the fire reading their Bibles together.

Now that she could no longer connect with us in the physical world, could she still connect with Christ in her spirit?

I said, "Pray for me, Nanny" as I left. I believe she did.

Five years ago, in my own ministry context, I began to work with residents in an aged care centre. My husband, a guitarist, is far more useful than I am, especially in the dementia wings. He has a powerful weapon into the soul: music. He plays old hymns and songs and residents sing or move along. They connect to memories somewhere in their past.

"Jesus Loves Me" is a favourite that we play at almost every service.

Are they aware of their surroundings, or are they travelling back to their own childhood as their mothers sang to them? Perhaps they return to happier times, when they sang to their own children? Do they remember days in Sunday school or church services? Do they remember hearing the stories of the prophets, the disciples, of Christmas and Easter? I don't know. And I don't think it matters.

Because these wonderful souls, these saints, are connecting with their God. A limitless God whose understanding of time and space is different to mine—and wherever they are, I trust that the connection is real, that their spiritual souls are not dependent upon their physical minds. And I want to be a part of that connection, because somehow, I find myself there too.

We assert here that people are "soul beings" first and physical beings second; in the experience of their organisational context, we have found that this is a central caring philosophy of Christian chaplains. Care services that ignore the soul risk becoming merely "biological garages where dysfunctional human parts are repaired or replaced."[7]

Memory Loss Is a Clinical Challenge

The literature has now widely linked the speed of a dementia patient's deterioration to the care regime of their environment.[8] In their critical commentary of the literature, Baldwin and Capstick note the negative effect of inexperienced, overworked or overly task-oriented clinical staff on the cognitive decline of people with dementia.[9] Bredin, Kitwood and Wattis have found that significant mental deterioration can be directly related to the organizational culture of nursing staff facing excessive pressures from management.[10] In this case, staff learned to cope with their situation by depersonalizing patients, with the result that some patients showed distress through increased problem behaviors, while others went into an almost complete vegetative withdrawal. Following interviews and observations conducted in Norway, Heggestad, Nortvedt and Slettebø have found that nursing home staff can easily become so busy performing their jobs that they may focus on physical tasks rather than socially and relationally engaging with residents.[11] This could be particularly applicable when resources are scarce, and patients' biomedical or physiological needs are usually prioritized over their psychosocial needs. Heggestad, Nortvedt and Slettebø contrasted this task-centered care with person-centered care, where the whole person is treated with dignity and not as an object.

Memory Loss Is a Theological and Spiritual Challenge

Over the past few decades, a number of studies on dementia and spirituality have been published.[12] Considerable literature supports the concept that both religion and spirituality play a significant role in effective healing and wellness.[13] Religion and spirituality are linked, but not interchangeable. *Spirituality* seems to defy a universally accepted definition,[14] yet is mostly understood experientially as the intangible essence

---

7. Gibbons and Miller, "Image of Contemporary Hospital Chaplaincy," 358.
8. Baldwin and Capstick, *Tom Kitwood on Dementia*, 241.
9. Baldwin and Capstick, *Tom Kitwood on Dementia*, 259.
10. Bredin et al., "Decline in Quality of Life for Patients," 969.
11. Heggestad et al., "Dignity and Care for People with Dementia," 832.
12. Richards, "Meeting the Spiritual Needs of the Cognitively Impaired"; Clayton, "Let There Be Life"; Elliot, "Religion, Spirituality and Dementia."
13. Carr et al., "What's So Big about the 'Little Things'"
14. Cobb et al., *Oxford Textbook of Spirituality in Healthcare*, 213.

of a meaningful connection with God (or a higher being or purpose) in what Snyder and Lopez call "a search for the sacred."[15] *Religion* can usually be understood in terms of a belief system, set of doctrines, shared symbols and rituals[16] associated with forms of organized practice within a religious organization.

Clinically, the memory loss associated with dementia raises challenging questions about an individual's personhood.[17] In Churches of Christ in NSW, we have over twenty chaplains dealing daily with the reality of spiritual care for those with memory loss in the form of dementia, intellectual delay or head trauma. These situations pose questions for ministry practitioners:

- Does the disintegration of cognitive ability lead to a loss of self?
- Who am I when I have forgotten who I am?
- If my unique "personness" relies on my pool of memories, does losing my memory mean that my "self" has disappeared?
- Has dementia disintegrated my soul?
- As someone who is made in the image of God, how does God view me when I have forgotten who God is or who I am?

The follow-up questions, then, are theological in nature:

- What makes us who we are?
- When part of who we are has gone, does that change our relationship with our God?
- Is our relationship with God purely cognitive in the first place?

Despite growing understanding of the nature of dementia, pastoral practitioners are challenged by the realities of effective ministry practice. As Wallace says, "Meeting the spiritual needs of people with dementia is not an optional extra."[18] Chaplains, pastoral workers, ministers, and priests are learning that as created beings, people are always "someone" rather than "something,"[19] and not merely defined by their human psychomotor abilities.

This challenge cuts profoundly to the heart of who we are as a Christian community. As C. S. Lewis noted in *The Problem of Pain*, "kindness without love leads to indifference, even contempt," and we are surely called to something higher than kind tolerance. As Saunders writes, the "gentle neglect of people with dementia is not a worthy strategy for the church—and yet this is often the case in practice."[20]

---

15. Snyder and Lopez, *Positive Psychology*, 261.
16. Geertz, "Religion as a Cultural System," 643.
17. Keck, *Forgetting Whose We Are*; Swinton, *Dementia*.
18. Wallace, "Spiritual Care and the Person with Dementia," 423.
19. Spaemann, *Persons*.
20. Saunders, *Dementia*, 21.

PART F—HEALTHCARE, MEMORY LOSS, AND WELL-BEING

Spirituality Is an Integral Part of Holistic Health

It is now generally accepted that spirituality is an integral part of health and not merely an influence on it,[21] with even the secular World Health Organization defining health as "a dynamic state of complete physical, mental, spiritual and social well-being and not merely the absence of disease or infirmity."[22] This spiritual dimension is now recognized in the field of management theory as making a profound contribution to personal and organizational transformation,[23] a concept also understood in education, nursing and social welfare.[24] Even government agencies such as the US Department of Health's Center for Disease Control and Prevention are now developing ways to "champion a focus on wellness that acknowledges the roles of mental health, spirituality, and complementary and alternative medicine across the lifespan."[25]

People being cared for share deep-seated human emotional and spiritual needs, regardless of whether they are religious. Existential questions such as "Why am I here?" "Why is this happening to me?" and "What happens to me when I die?" seem universal concerns. Care of the soul is thus not a side issue, but central to the well-being of all people.

Spirituality pervades every part of who we are. It is bonded to our well-being in ways that seem incomprehensible. Our soul integrates the interplay of physical, psychological, spiritual and social health, and is an inseparable companion to every breath we take. When we experience suffering, the search for meaning that emanates from our soul is radically sharpened. Spirituality is central to how we cope and thrive when life delivers pain and discomfort.

Through our interviews and interactions with pastoral care workers, we found that chaplains were absolutely vital to the care of those experiencing suffering. Of particular note was the success chaplains were achieving with those suffering memory loss. Chaplains found that in their experience, a patient's soul is still present when their memories are gone, and they can connect with the spiritual through familiar music, ritual, sacraments, readings, photos, prayers and touch. In the context of patients with dementia and other forms of memory loss, the chaplains' work was found to contribute positively to spirituality as an *integral* part of holistic health (and not merely an *influence* on health).

---

21. Fleming and Evans, "Concept of Spirituality."
22. Bok, "Rethinking the WHO Definition of Health."
23. Bolman and Deal, *Leading with Soul*.
24. Hart and Bond, *Action Research for Health and Social Care*.
25. Navarro et al., *Recommendations for Future Efforts in Community Health Promotion*, 2.

Memory Loss Presents an Opportunity for Pastoral Care

The growing numbers of ageing people experiencing memory loss provides ample opportunity for spiritual carers to contribute significantly to the holistic well-being of their clients. Memory loss creates strangers—and the contrast between task-centered care (which depersonalizes) and person-centered care (where the whole person is treated with dignity and not as an object) reveals a vital distinction. While clinical practitioners often *speak* about a patient or client, the literature consistently finds[26] that the nature and pressure of their work often leads them to focus on *task-centered* activities. While clinical theoreticians *talk* about person-centered care, the clinical literature in the field seems to lack depth in understanding personhood in a manner that adequately integrates its spiritual dimensions.

The notion of personhood has raised the extreme question of whether those who are suffering from memory loss are better off dead. Warnock, a British medical ethicist, argues that those who become dependent are often a burden on others and should be able, through a living will, to ask for death as part of their duty to "fall on one's sword."[27]

Consequently, the same "non-person" argument used by some in relation to abortion has been extended to other "non-persons," such as those with a mental impairment. Macadam summarizes the work of Warnock, who advocates the "non-person" view in her interview "A Duty to Die?"

The individual diagnosed with dementia has begun making a transition from being a person to being a non-person. As a non-person she has no right to the kinds of moral respect and protection that a person might be entitled to. That being so, to kill her is considered appropriate: if she kills herself, it's convenient.[28]

This sort of pathogenic approach, with its focus on disease and disorder, cannot look past the deficits that impair full human functioning as the defining elements of life—whereas a shift in emphasis to the salutogenic, with its focus on health and wellness, identifies the soul's presence as providing opportunities for joy and fullness of life that may be separated from our experience as carers.

In sharp contrast is the view that *God's memory* of you defines your personhood, not *your memory*. This is where "pastoral care as a 'ministry of presence' becomes less about one's own presence and more about the presence of the divine."[29] As a result, the chaplain is perfectly equipped, as part of the healthcare team, to be a spiritual companion to those experiencing memory loss, for whom every morning is a new experience.

---

26. MacKinlay and Trevitt, *Finding Meaning in the Experience of Dementia*.
27. Macadam, "Interview with Mary Warnock," 25.
28. Swinton, *Dementia*, 122.
29. Swain, *Trauma and Transformation at Ground Zero*, 20.

While the challenge of memory loss causes us to ask these complex questions, chaplains, as ministry practitioners, must respond in practical ways whether they can grasp the answers to those questions or not. Our interviews with chaplains reveal the following about their beliefs in practice:

- *Effective chaplains believe that the soul is present.*

Paul writes of the renewing of the mind (Rom 12:12), the attitudes of the mind (Eph 4:23) and applying the mind to study (2 Tim 2:15). Indeed, it is a good and necessary thing to apply oneself obsessively to the pursuit of God through scholarly theological and biblical study. This is the privilege and responsibility of those who are so gifted.

However, chaplains who actively and consistently seek God through the mind of their clients also recognize that God is neither limited nor empowered by mere cognitive ability. They recognize that the soul is present even when the physical mind is unable to engage in the physical world.

One trainee chaplain asked, "Why do you pray with them, when they don't understand you anyway?" Yet experienced chaplains understand that we pray to enter into the realm of the spiritual, trusting that God enters the soul of the person living with dementia.

If chaplains believe that the soul is present even when the mind is restrained, they can maintain a pastoral approach. If they do not, there is no longer a pastoral role to be fulfilled. Chaplains must believe that the soul is present.

- *Effective chaplains believe that God is at work.*

Chaplains take the view that God continues to pursue and engage with us even when our memories and minds fail us. They take the view that nothing limits the power of God's spirit and, until their final breath, God continues to actively pursue every individual.

- *Chaplains can then be the channel of God's spirit in pastoral interactions.*

This is no longer empty compassion or condescending kindness—the chaplain's role changes from kindness to one of spiritual guide and facilitator, eagerly looking for ways to assist the connection to the soul. Whether individuals have endured a long journey of faith or commenced a new one, chaplains never stop believing that God is actively at work.

- *Effective chaplains believe that God's mercies are new every morning.*

"Because of the Lord's great love we are not consumed, for his compassions never fail. They are new every morning; great is your faithfulness" (Lam 3:22–23 NIV). Memories build upon memories; this is how we grow and learn. Discoveries of yesterday become the basis for new discoveries today. Short-term memories grow into long-term memories, and this enables us to expand our experiences from day to day. However, for the individual who experiences memory loss, intellectual delays or brain injury, both short and long-term memories can be hampered. Their ability to recall the past—their memories of interactions with family, friends and God—is thus affected.

Yet Scripture reminds us that God's love and compassions are new every day. We do not rely on past experiences of mercy or love, for new and fresh expressions are present each day. For God is good and faithful to us; he, not we, is the initiator of that compassion and faithfulness.

Thus, every morning, the experience of God can be new, even when you cannot remember the last morning, or the morning before that. This implies that God's presence, his grace, his communion, can be a fresh experience for us each day. Pastoral carers believe and embody this, leaving the past behind as they enter the client's room each day ready to embody the new realizations of God's goodness. Did somebody have a difficult day yesterday? That is fine—for God's love awaits a new expression every morning.

Chaplains as a Vital Part of the Healthcare Team

As part of a healthcare team, a chaplain's role is to provide spiritual care that involves companionship and emotional support for those in need. When a patient has exhausted their treatment options or has a chronic issue, this is vitally important. This emphasis on a chaplain giving caring time focused on an individual's social, emotional and spiritual aspects enhances what O'Brien describes as finding "wellbeing in illness."[30]

Dementia does seem to present opportunities for thriving. Carr, Hicks-Moore, and Montgomery have found that dementia can prompt people to explore the deeper meaning of their own existence and take stock of their own lives,[31] and Dunn suggests that spiritual identity may increase at the same time as cognitive functioning decreases.[32]

There is no doubt that general residential care facilities provide the required standard of physical care for those who have dementia. However, nursing and support staff are not equipped to deal with the challenge of spiritual issues.[33] While, in God's eyes, "There is nothing that can occur to an individual that can make him less of a person,"[34] in organizational culture, there is certainly a tendency for depersonalization through task-centered management.[35]

---

30. O'Brien, *Nurse's Handbook of Spiritual Care*, 39.
31. Carr et al., "What's So Big about the 'Little Things.'"
32. Dunn, "Hearing the Story."
33. MacKinlay and Trevitt, *Finding Meaning in the Experience of Dementia*.
34. Swinton, *Dementia*, 157.
35. Baldwin and Capstick, *Tom Kitwood on Dementia*.

Being aware of this tendency has resulted in chaplains in our organization intentionally following practices they find helpful when ministering to those with dementia, acquired brain injury, developmental or mental delay or intellectual challenges:

- *Effective chaplains practice "presence."*

Chaplains must be in the room. Our chaplains make themselves present even when individuals do not fully understand the purpose of their attendance. You cannot provide pastoral care without presence—and in this space, our chaplains are also conduits of the divine presence, so their presence cannot be rushed or driven by task-centered outcomes. Chaplains must advocate for an individual's personhood and for their divine birthright.

- *Effective chaplains practice "reminiscence."*

This involves using music, sights, sounds, readings or conversation to help clients reminisce about a place or experience, especially a spiritually significant space. Reminiscence gives people the chance to discuss or re-experience spiritual events in their lives. Chaplains look for the hymns, the songs, the prayers, the Scripture passages that connect with the individual. While chaplains may never fully know or understand the background to the reminiscences these connections yield, they can identify those moments when a connection is made and build on those connections in future.

- *Effective chaplains practice worship/ritual/liturgy.*

While linked to reminiscence, rituals and liturgy play a particular role in an individual's soul care. The use of well-known prayers such as the Lord's Prayer, songs such as "Amazing Grace" or readings such as Psalm 23 are often able to connect to people's experiences of faith. This is especially true for those who have been regular churchgoers and are now disconnected from that experience because of their physical or mental capabilities. Our chaplains and aged care residents note the sharing of communion as a specific practice often lost in the aged care environment, and one that brings great comfort when the time is put aside for it.

The types of sermons and teaching that are useful when we are younger are likely to be less effective during later-stage dementia. Chaplains can find liturgy helpful in this context, and should remain attentive to how individuals react to various forms of worship ritual.

Having noted the power of liturgy, worship and ritual, the chaplains also acknowledged that this is most beneficial to those with previous experience of faith and church liturgy, as ritual must link to an individual's past experience, where comfort is drawn from experience. In interviews some chaplains expressed the need to prepare for our own potential memory loss by ensuring that we each have rituals, Bible passages, prayers, songs and other expressions that ground our faith experience prior to the early signs of memory loss. Some chaplains spoke of residents preparing memory books noting these items for future carers. Further work could be pursued here on how to prepare for memory loss as a society of faith.

- *Effective chaplains undertake a "shared journey."*

In our interviews, we spoke with a chaplain who performs her personal devotions and prayer by the bedsides of those with high-care dementia. While she could limit her interactions to reading a passage for a patient or reciting a prayer over them, she chose instead to enter into a shared journey, inviting that individual into her world.

This particular chaplain's presence in the room, her reading of scriptures aloud, her praying with those who can no longer verbalize their own prayers but remain aware that God is present and listening to their joint prayers, is another way of recognizing an individual's personhood. The use of prayers and scriptures has proved powerful for chaplains, as this personal sharing of the faith journey further connects them with the humanity of those they serve.

Summary

This chapter briefly articulates our observations and reflections from the interviews we conducted with numerous pastoral care workers and chaplains in local church and welfare ministries, including aged care settings. Of particular focus are the questions and insights chaplains offered based on their experiences working with those facing the daily reality of memory loss as a result of dementia, acquired brain injury or other intellectual challenges. As ministry practitioners, we have found that the chaplain's unique role is to provide a vital, hopeful, spiritual presence that is valuable to pursuing wellness for those with memory loss.

Bibliography

Australian Institute of Health and Welfare. *Dementia among Aged Care Residents: Problems and Preferences*. Canberra: Australian Government, 2011.
Baldwin, C., and A. Capstick, eds. *Tom Kitwood on Dementia: A Reader and Critical Commentary*. Berkshire: Open University Press, 2007.
Bok, S. "Rethinking the WHO Definition of Health." Harvard Center for Population and Development Studies Working Paper Series 14.7. Harvard Pop Center, 2004.
Bolman, L., and T. Deal. *Leading with Soul: An Uncommon Journey of Spirit*. San Francisco: Jossey-Bass, 1995.
Bredin, K., et al. "Decline in Quality of Life for Patients with Severe Dementia following a Ward Merger." *International Journal of Geriatric Psychiatry* 10 (1995) 967–73.
Carr, T. "Mapping the Processes and Qualities of Spiritual Nursing Care." *Qualitative Health Research* 18 (2008) 686–700.
Carr, T., et al. "What's So Big about the 'Little Things': A Phenomenological Inquiry into the Meaning of Spiritual Care in Dementia." *Dementia* 10 (2011) 399–414.

Clayton, J. "Let There Be Life: An Approach to Worship with Alzheimer's Patients and Their Families." *Journal of Pastoral Care* 45 (1991) 177–79.

Cobb, M., et al. *Oxford Textbook of Spirituality in Healthcare*. Oxford: Oxford University Press, 2013.

Deloitte Access Economics. *Keeping Dementia Front of Mind: Incidence and Prevalence 2009-2050*. Report for Alzheimer's Australia. August 2009. https://www.dementia.org.au/sites/default/files/20090800_Nat__AE_FullKeepDemFrontMind.pdf.

Dunn, D. "Hearing the Story: Spiritual Challenges for the Ageing in an Acute Mental Health Unit." In *Ageing, Spirituality and Well-Being*, edited by A. Jewell, 153–60. London: Kingsley, 2004.

Elliot, H. "Religion, Spirituality and Dementia: Pastoring to Sufferers of Alzheimer's Disease and Other Associated Forms of Dementia." *Disability and Rehabilitation* 19 (1997) 435–41.

Fleming, S., and D. Evans. "The Concept of Spirituality: Its Role within Health Promotion Practice in the Republic of Ireland." *Spirituality and Health International* 9 (2008) 79–89.

Geertz, C. "Religion as a Cultural System." In vol. 1 of *The World Year Book of Religion: The Religious Situation*, edited by D. Cutler, 639–88. Boston: Hutchison, 1968.

Gibbons, J., and S. Miller. "An Image of Contemporary Hospital Chaplaincy." *Journal of Pastoral Care* 43 (1989) 355–61.

Hart, E., and M. Bond. *Action Research for Health and Social Care: A Guide to Practice*. Buckingham, UK: Open University Press, 1995.

Heggestad, A., et al. "Dignity and Care for People with Dementia Living in Nursing Homes." *Dementia* 12 (2013) 825–41.

Keck, D. *Forgetting Whose We Are: Alzheimer's Disease and the Love of God*. Nashville: Abingdon, 1996.

Macadam, J. "Interview with Mary Warnock: 'A Duty to Die'?" *Life and Work*, October 2008, 23–25.

MacKinlay, E., and C. Trevitt. *Finding Meaning in the Experience of Dementia*. London: Kingsley, 2012.

Navarro, A., et al. *Recommendations for Future Efforts in Community Health Promotion: Report of the National Expert Panel on Community Health Promotion*. Washington, DC: US Department of Health—Center for Disease Control and Prevention, 2006.

O'Brien, M. *A Nurse's Handbook of Spiritual Care: Standing on Holy Ground*. Sudbury: Jones and Bartlett, 2004.

Phillips, J., et al. *Timely Diagnosis of Dementia: Can We Do Better?* Report for Alzheimer's Australia, Paper 24. Newcastle, Australia: Alzheimer's Australia, 2011.

Rice, V., et al. "Ethical Issues Relative to Autonomy and Personal Control in Independent and Cognitively Impaired Elders." *Nursing Outlook* 45 (1997) 27–34.

Richards, M. "Meeting the Spiritual Needs of the Cognitively Impaired." *Generations* 14 (1990) 63–64.

Saunders, J. *Dementia: Pastoral Theology and Pastoral Care*. Cambridge: Grove, 2002.

Smith, S. "Savouring Life: The Leader's Journey to Health and Effectiveness." In *Beyond Well-Being: Spirituality and Human Flourishing*, edited by M. Miner et al., 151–77. Charlotte, NC: Information Age, 2012.

Snyder, C., and S. Lopez. *Positive Psychology*. London: Sage, 2007.

Spaemann, R. *Persons: The Difference Between "Someone" and "Something."* London: Oxford University Press 2006.

Swain, S. *Trauma and Transformation at Ground Zero: A Pastoral Theology.* Minneapolis: Fortress, 2011.

Swinton, J. *Dementia: Living in the Memories of God.* Grand Rapids: Eerdmans, 2012.

Wallace, D. "Spiritual Care and the Person with Dementia: The Development of Guidelines to Support Staff Working with People with Dementia." *Dementia* 2 (2003) 422–26.

PART G

The Moral Compass of Well-Being

14

Spiritual Care and Well-Being
Contradictions, Complexities, and Contexts

Peter Carblis

Introduction

PASTORAL and spiritual care practitioners, by their very nature, are committed to the well-being of those they serve. The spiritual and moral dimensions of well-being, central to their practice, are increasingly challenged by influential philosophical, sociological, and psychological theories. Pastoral and spiritual care is no longer simply the delivery of the spiritual comforts and consolations of well-established faith traditions to those in need (if it ever was just that). Spiritual care operates within a complexity of contradictory and contested philosophies, theories, and theologies. These challenges dramatically increase when practitioners in multi-faith and no faith environments.

Recent years have seen the burgeoning of literatures about well-being. Particularly significant is the emergence of positive psychology.[1] This has deepened the psychological dimension of the timeless philosophical quest to understand the good life and the more recent sociological quest to understand quality of life.[2] Considerations of morality (addressed as character and virtue) and spirituality arise consistently within these studies.

This chapter will commence with a selective survey illustrating the current philosophical, sociological, and psychological landscape of well-being, followed by a consideration of their relation to virtue and spirituality. Virtue will be considered

---

1. For a comprehensive overview, see Snyder and Shane, *Oxford Handbook of Positive Psychology*.
2. For a review of sociological well-being research, see Veenhoven, "Quality of Life Research."

historically. Spirituality will be considered in a contemporary context. The pluriform, inconsistent, and contested nature of current conceptualizations of both of these terms will be highlighted. Ways forward will be explored that embrace plurality by variously incorporating a return to an eternal perspective of love as related to "the Good that is beyond being," recognize those features of the world religions that open people toward humanity, affirm the value of all human beings, and offer benevolence beyond their faith communities. It is argued that pastoral and spiritual care practitioners must have at least a basic understanding of the topography of these issues. Failure will leave practitioners at risk of holding naïve, incoherent, and even contradictory understandings of the practices of pastoral and spiritual care and hence of becoming impaired in their ability to offer effective comfort and consolation to those who share their faith or beliefs and/or those who do not.

A Brief Survey

A philosophical approach seeks to account for what is fundamentally good or bad. This differs from the more instrumental and utilitarian tendencies of psychology and sociology. Focusing on that which is intrinsically good, philosophers will typically ask, "Which things in and of themselves make someone's life go better or worse?"[3] Consideration of well-being has been an important philosophical and ethical topic throughout history.[4] It is at least as old as the ancient Greeks who paid it much attention. Conflicting opinions about its meaning and significance have consistently been offered. Some suggest the conflicts may be because the subject is not unified and multiple issues have become conflated.[5] It is not surprising then that recent studies have provided diverse categorizations of theories of well-being. These include hedonistic, desire-fulfillment, objective list, perfectionistic, happiness-related, and hybrid theories.[6]

The *Routledge Handbook of Philosophy of Well-Being* provides an anthology of these approaches.[7] Brown describes the Platonic emphasis on wisdom.[8] Kraut outlines Aristotle's theory of *eudaimonia* and its emphasis on virtue.[9] O'Keefe considers ancient Western hedonistic theories.[10] Kim examines Confucianism and its concept of sagehood.[11] Tiwald considers the multilayered nature of Daoism and its objections

---

3. Fletcher, *Routledge Handbook of Philosophy of Well-Being*, 1.
4. For a Western philosophical overview, see Crisp, "Well-Being."
5. Campbell, "Concept of Well-Being."
6. Fletcher, *Philosophy of Well-Being*, 5.
7. Fletcher, *Routledge Handbook of Philosophy of Well-Being*.
8. Brown, "Plato on Well-Being."
9. Kraut, "Aristotle on Well-Being."
10. O'Keefe, "Hedonistic Theories of Well-Being."
11. Kim, "Well-Being and Confucianism."

to desire-fulfillment.[12] Gowans examines perfectionistic aspects of Buddhist thinking and its concept of the "no-self."[13] Lauinger overviews Western Christian positions including Augustine, Aquinas, Calvin and contemporary Christian philosophers and apologists including C. S. Lewis and recent Thomists such as Finnis and McInerney, all of whom advocate objective and perfectionistic views. He also addresses Christian philosophers who advocate desire-fulfillment and hybrid approaches.[14] Finally, Shaver discusses well-being in British normative moralists such as Sidgwick, Moore, Prichard, Ross, Carritt, Broad, and Ewing, who express concepts of well-being incorporating hedonistic, prudential and desire-related considerations[15]

Prominent sociologist of well-being, Ruut Veehnoven, reviewed considerations related to well-being under the rubric of quality of life and related this to a matrix of the liveability of the environment, life-ability of the person, utility of life and enjoyment of life.[16] Consistent with this, he noted that among sociologists the notion of subjective well-being is less prominent than among psychologists. For sociologists, concepts of well-being are more often about collectivities and related to issues external to the individual than they are to considerations of internal individual states or capabilities.

Veenhoven suggested that the disinterest of many sociologists may be for pragmatic, ideological, and theoretical reasons. Pragmatically, because of the problem centered nature of sociological practice which is focused on social "ill being." Ideologically, because sociologists are committed to concepts of objective well-being related to issues of equality and cohesion rather than to individuals. Theoretically because the idea of subjective well-being depends on social comparison and therefore may reflect a "whimsical" state of mind.[17]

Some sociologists, nevertheless, are interested in well-being. For example, Sergio Baltatescu arguing for a sociological theory of subjective well-being, proposes a flexible model of the self which is permeable to social influences. He argues for a model of subjective well-being that considers social influences such as communication, social values, and norms, and the relationships between macro- and micro-social considerations of the evaluation of subjective well-being.[18]

Representative psychologists are Martin Seligman and Ed Diener, both of whom have contributed significantly to the emergence of the terms of *flourishing, positive*

---

12. Tiwald, "Well-Being and Daoism."

13. Gowans, "Buddhist Understandings of Well-Being."

14. Lauinger, "Well-Being in the Christian Tradition." Lauinger uses well-being as a rough correlate of blessedness, happiness, and the chief good as translations of terms such as *felicitas* and *beatitudo* ("Well-Being in the Christian Tradition," 83).

15. Shaver, "Later British Moralists."

16. Veenhoven, "Four Qualities of Life," 6.

17. Veenhoven, "Sociological Theories of Subjective Well-Being," 44–45.

18. Baltatescu, "Towards a Sociological Theory of Subjective Well-Being," 209–12.

psychology and *subjective well-being*. Seligman is often credited with the initiating the current use of the term *positive psychology*.[19] This was based on his extensive work on the psychology of optimism and happiness.[20] Seligman, in collaboration with Diener, has embraced a model of flourishing which incorporates positive emotion, engagement, positive relationships, meaning, and accomplishment (PERMA).[21] Seligman also collaborated with Christopher Peterson in the development of a systematic classification of character strengths and virtues using a methodology based on that used for the identification of psychological disorders.[22] Diener has written prolifically on the concept of *subjective well-being*.[23] In an introduction to the science of well-being, Diener, whose work has often been typified as essentially hedonic, relates his approach to the notions of the good life, virtue, and happiness. In this he observed that questions about the good life have occupied the minds of philosophers since before the time of the ancient Greeks.[24] Noting that throughout history happiness has been considered by philosophers to be the highest good and ultimate motivation for human action, he both decried the neglect of attention to this subject by earlier psychologists and applauded the emergence of recent theoretical and empirical work on this subject.[25]

Categories

Across these disciplines, well-being has often been put into two large, diffuse, overlapping, and ancient categories: the eudaimonic and the hedonic.[26] Aristotle is the type philosopher of the eudaimonic, which associates well-being with virtue and purpose.[27]

19. Lopez and Gallagher note that the term *positive psychology* was first used in 1954 by Maslow and reintroduced more than forty years later by Seligman. Both Maslow and Seligman argue that psychology has been too focussed on the negative aspects of human life. Jeffrey Froh argues that the principal components of positive psychology date back to the work of William James and John Dewey and have been carried forward in the tradition of humanistic psychology. See Lopez and Gallagher, "Case for Positive Psychology," 3. Froh, "History of Positive Psychology," 18.

20. For an overview of the contribution of Martin Seligman, see Seligman, *Authentic Happiness*; Seligman, *Learned Optimism*; Seligman and Gillham, *Science of Optimism and Hope*; Seligman and Csikszentmihalyi, "Positive Psychology."

21. The five elements of this model of well-being, positive emotion, engagement, positive relationships, meaning, and accomplishment, are often represented by the acronym PERMA. See Seligman, *Flourish*, 12.

22. Peterson and Seligman, *Character Strengths and Virtues*.

23. For a representative sample of the work of Diener, see Diener et al., *Science of Well-Being*; Diener, *Culture and Well-Being*; Diener, *Assessing Well-Being*.

24. Diener et al., *Science of Well-Being*, 1.

25. Diener et al., *Science of Well-Being*, 11.

26. Cf. Deci and Ryan, "Hedonia, Eudaimonia, and Well-Being."

27. While Aristotle's philosophy may be considered the "type specimen" for eudaimonic approached to well-being, he is in fact not alone in the ancient world. In the West he may have been preceded by Plato, as urged by Eric Brown. See Brown, "Plato on Well-Being," 9–10. In the East Confucius may have construed happiness, self-interest, good life, and flourishing in terms that mirror

In contrast, Epicurus is the type philosopher of the hedonic seen as associating well-being with pleasure. Many recent studies into well-being, particularly those focused on *subjective well-being*, have been categorized as primarily hedonic.[28]

Critical of the view that well-being is primarily hedonic, several writers have argued for an eudaimonic approach. For example, Wills demonstrated empirical validity for the inclusion of an approach to spirituality in the *Personal Well-Being Index* (an often used measure for *Subjective Well-Being*) and argued for the interpretation of life satisfaction in eudaimonic terms.[29] Deci and Ryan related eudaimonia to living life in a full and deeply satisfying way,[30] They suggested that the hedonic and eudaimonic approaches are founded on different views of human nature,[31] and, in the introduction to a special issue of the *Journal of Happiness Studies*,[32] which was focused on the approaches to well-being, described the eudaimonic approach as a process "of fulfilling one's *daimon* or true nature—that is of fulfilling one's virtuous potentials or living as one was intended to live."[33]

The views expressed in this issue of the *Journal of Happiness Studies* generally align with objective-list and perfectionistic approaches to well-being.

---

the concept of eudaimonia used by the Greek thinkers. See Kim, "Well-Being and Confucianism," 41. Daoism and its variants make little reference to pleasure or pain (and hence be non-hedonistic), resist single values or metrics and may overlap in a multilayered way with a "pluralistic perfectionism." See Tiwald, "Well-Being and Daoism," 60, 66. Buddhism may be seen to be committed to an objective understanding of well-being that resembles a nature-fulfillment or perfectionistic theory: such theories are commonly associated with Aristotle's eudaimonistic virtue ethics. See Gowans, "Buddhist Understandings of Well-Being," 76.

28. Deci and Ryan suggest that this has been the case since the 1999 publication of *Well-Being: The Foundation of Hedonic Psychology*. See Deci and Ryan, "Hedonia, Eudaimonia, and Well-Being," 2; Kahneman, Diener, and Schwarz, *Well-Being*.

29. Wills, "Spirituality and Subjective Well-Being."

30. Deci and Ryan, "Hedonia, Eudaimonia, and Well-Being," 1.

31. Deci and Ryan, "Hedonia, Eudaimonia, and Well-Being," 3. Commenting on the two views of human nature, Deci and Ryan write: "The hedonic approach uses what Tooby and Cosmides (1992) referred to as the standard social science model, which considers the human organism initially to be relatively empty and thus malleable, such that it gains its meaning in accord with social and cultural teachings. In contrast, the eudaimonic approach ascribes content to human nature and works to uncover that content and to understand the conditions that facilitate versus diminish it" ("Hedonia, Eudaimonia, and Well-Being," 3). See also Tooby and Cosmides, "Psychological Foundations of Culture," 29.

32. Deci and Ryan, "Hedonia, Eudaimonia, and Well-Being." See also Waterman et al., "Implications of Two Conceptions of Happiness," 42.

33. This quote contains reference to both spiritual and virtue-related considerations. The concept of the spiritual is contained in the term *daimon*, an elusive term which throughout the history of its usage has been related to spiritual issues and applied to a wide range of meanings that include both something like personality and independent divinities or spiritual beings. The relation of *daimon* here to *true nature* relates to the personality aspect of meaning. Deci and Ryan, "Hedonia, Eudaimonia, and Well-Being," 2. Baril comments on the necessity for well-being of virtue which is seen as a fundamental, direct and intrinsic contributor to it. See Baril, "Virtue and Well-Being," 242.

In a similar manner positive psychological studies frequently provide perfectionistic objective lists of personal attributes and dispositions related to well-being, such as the significant *Oxford Handbook of Positive Psychology* and *Character Strengths and Virtues*.[34] Both point to the significance of virtue and spirituality in well-being. These volumes and other psychological literature on well-being, demonstrate a commitment to develop and validate interventions and therapies that increase the ability to intentionally and competently adopt the objects (dispositions and behaviors) prescribed by these lists with the goal of attaining some sort of mastery of them (perfectionism).

This is not unlike similar efforts among educators. A very significant example of this was seen in the *Definition and Selection of Key Competencies* (DeSeCo) project of the Organisation for Economic Cooperation and Development (OECD) which concluded in 2005. This was aimed at defining an object-list of *key competencies* that could underlie all education globally. The purpose was to specify universally valid competencies that contribute to "a successful life and a well-functioning society."[35] Within the consideration of key competencies related to "value orientation," careful attention was given to the ethics of tolerance and human rights and the personal virtues of integrity, reliability, loyalty, and honesty.[36] It is also worth noting here that the OECD has maintained this interest in the well-being of its citizens.[37]

Both editions of the *Oxford Handbook of Positive Psychology* provide extensive object-lists related to well-being. Many are perfectionistic, with items described in carefully researched detail. Of particular note are chapters on the psychology of virtue- and spirituality-related topics such as hope, compassion, empathy and altruism, forgiveness, gratitude, love, passions, humility, and discovering and conserving the sacred.[38]

Character Strengths and Virtues was written as a "manual of the sanities" with the intention "to reclaim the study of character and virtue as legitimate topics of psychological inquiry and informed societal discourse."[39] Intentionally following the methodology of the diagnostic manuals of the American Psychiatric Association (the *Diagnostic and Statistical Manual of Mental Disorders* [DSM][40]) and the World Health Organization (*International Classification of Diseases* [ICD][41]), *Character Strengths and*

---

34. Snyder and Lopez, *Oxford Handbook of Positive Psychology*; Peterson and Seligman, *Character Strengths and Virtues*.

35. See Rychen, "Key Competencies," 3.

36. Salagnik and Stephens, "Competence Priorities in Policy and Practice."

37. OECD, *OECD Guidelines on Measuring Subjective Well-Being*.

38. Rand and Cheavens, "Hope Theory"; Cassell, "Compassion"; Batson et al., "Empathy and Altruism"; McCullough et al., "Forgiveness"; Emmons and Shelton, "Gratitude and the Science of Positive Psychology"; Watkins et al., "Furthering the Science of Gratitude"; Hendrick and Hendrick, "Love"; Averill, "Emotional Creativity"; Tangey, "Humility."

39. Peterson and Seligman, *Character Strengths and Virtues*, 3.

40. American Psychiatric Association, *Diagnostic and Statistical Manual of Mental Disorder*.

41. World Health Organization, *ICD-10 Classification of Mental and Behavioural Disorders*.

Virtues was designed to propose a classification scheme and approach to assessment that would enable a common vocabulary to be used by practitioners of positive psychology.[42] In this, character was defined in terms of a psychology of traits that are stable and general but capable of change.[43] Three conceptual levels were used in the classification: (1) virtues, core characteristics valued by moral philosophers and religious thinkers; (2) character strengths, the psychological ingredients that define the virtues; and (3) situational themes, specific habits that lead people to manifest given character strengths in given situations.[44]

Six core virtues were defined by thematic analysis of the virtues valorized within and across the traditions of China, South Asia, and the West.[45] These were wisdom and knowledge, courage, humanity, justice, temperance, and transcendence. Using a Linnaean approach to classification,[46] they were used as major category headings or genera. Within this scheme, spirituality (religiousness, faith, and purpose) was identified as a character strength within the genus of transcendence.[47]

Contradiction and Complexity

Considerations of virtue and spirituality may therefore be seen as constant and significant contributors to contemporary conceptions of well-being. Questions that arise are "How is virtue/spirituality defined?" and "What virtues/spirituality(ies) are involved?" and "How do virtue and spirituality contribute to well-being?" Answers are often contradictory, complex and contested. Awareness of these issues and the ability to respond contextually and coherently to these questions is essential for all spiritual care practitioners, especially those who practice in multi-faith environments.

The way the first two of these questions will be answered depends on which theories of virtue and spirituality are considered valid. This will, in turn, determine largely how the third is answered. These answers will have a defining effect on how the "virtuous potential" that fulfils a person's *daimon* or true nature is identified.[48] It will also affect how aspects of character (or virtue) are identified as objects of enquiry or development.[49] Similarly, how these questions are answered will have a defining effect of understanding what a person's *daimon* or true nature might be and hence on the nature, place and significance of spirituality in their well-being.

---

42. Peterson and Seligman, *Character Strengths and Virtues*, 4–5.
43. Peterson and Seligman, *Character Strengths and Virtues*, 10.
44. Peterson and Seligman, *Character Strengths and Virtues*, 13–14.
45. Peterson and Seligman, *Character Strengths and Virtues*, 34.
46. Peterson and Seligman, *Character Strengths and Virtues*, 5, 12.
47. Peterson and Seligman, *Character Strengths and Virtues*, 5, 12.
48. Cf. Deci and Ryan, "Hedonia, Eudaimonia, and Well-Being," 2.
49. Cf. Peterson and Seligman, *Character Strengths and Virtues*, 3.

It is at this point that the hedonic/eudaimonic categorization of well-being breaks down. The general uncritical acceptance in the psychological literature that if an approach to well-being is subjective, then it is hedonic and not concerned with virtue and, if an approach is somehow related to virtue then it is treated as Aristotelian and eudaimonic, needs further development. Critical examination of theories of virtue shows that this approach is inadequate.

In the West non-Aristotelian approaches include Platonic, Epicurean, Stoic, Humean, Kantian, and Foucauldian theories of virtue. These contain diverse, often conflicting, understandings. While some are in broad agreement, several are clearly in opposition to others. Virtues in some schemes may be vices in another: for example, the community (polis) centered Aristotelian related systems of virtue are the very antithesis of the ego-centeredness of virtues in the Nietzschean and Foucauldian systems.

Some divergences are so great that, when virtue is being discussed, the differences may not refer to differing perceptions of the same concept but to different concepts altogether.[50] To what degree does prudence as advocated by Aristotle and Aquinas equate to the same term as advocated by Epicurus? What does the Foucauldian concept of virtue described as "a relation of self to itself in terms of its moral agency"[51] have in common with the cardinal virtues or theological virtues of faith, hope and charity?

The problem of diversity in spirituality is equally contradictory and complex. In illustration of this diversity, the recently published *National Guidelines for Spiritual Care in Aged Care*, observed that there are "many published definitions" and offered three definitions of spirituality that "reflect the overlaps, synergies and subtle differences in what is meant by spirituality."[52] This has been the subject of concern in studies considering the relevance of spirituality and spiritual practice.

In 2005, McCarroll, O'Connor and Meakes, noting the vast literature emerging on the topic and arguing that it is important that clear definitions of spirituality and spiritual care be developed, surveyed definitions of spirituality in the health-care

---

50. Cf. Haybron, *Pursuit of Unhappiness*, 32. Haybron, in a similar structure of reasoning, discussing the difficulties involved in defining happiness observes that scholarly discussions of "happiness" center on two uses of the term to which must be added psychological and common usages. He argues, somewhat hyperbolically, that the differences in use may be as profoundly different as the meanings of the word "bank" applying to a place where money is kept and the edge of a river where frogs dwell. He writes: "The well-being and psychological senses of 'happiness' do not mark different conceptions of happiness, any more than definitions of river 'banks' where frogs live, and the 'banks' in which we keep our money offer differing conceptions of the same phenomenon. They express different *concepts* and concern different subject matters altogether."

51. Robinson, "Foucault, Michel: Ethics," *Internet Encyclopedia of Philosophy*, para. 1. Foucault, Ethics, 300.

52. Meaningful Ageing Australia, *National Guidelines for Spiritual Care in Aged Care*, 8, www.meaningfulageing.org.au. The three definitions offered drew on Puchalski et al., "Improving the Spiritual Dimension of Whole Person Care," 643. MacKinlay, *Spiritual Dimensions of Ageing*, 76; McSherry and Smith, "Spiritual Care," 118.

literature. After accessing sixty-eight of seventy-six systematic reviews they located on this topic between 1975 and 1996 they found that only twenty-seven explicitly expounded a definition of spirituality. They also found very little agreement among these definitions but were able to ascertain eight central themes that emerged from them.[53] These were (1) meaning and purpose, (2) connections and relationships, (3) God/God(s)/transcendent other, (4) transcendent self, (5) vital principle (6) unifying force or integrative energy, (7) personal and private, and (8) hope. The definitions of spirituality adopted in the *National Guidelines for Spiritual Care in Aged Care* largely fit into the first, third and fourth of these categories.

McCarroll et al. concluded that there is "both openness and energy as well as confusion and discrepancy around the topic of spirituality." They concluded that a singular definition of spirituality was neither ethical nor possible.[54]

There have nevertheless been attempts to provide a comprehensive definition of spirituality, such as those in the recent Australian *National Guidelines for Spiritual Care in Aged Care*, which express a generally Tillichian position. Emmons described this as that in which the "essence of religion, in the broadest and most inclusive sense, is *ultimate concern*" (emphasis his).[55] Such definitions tend to restrict spirituality to an intrinsic aspect of humanity, the quest for ultimate meaning,[56] the core of being[57] or something deep and individual.[58]

While admirable in their attempt to provide a generous, overarching and unifying framework, they have succeeded only in contributing to one framework of thinking among many others of equally intended generosity. Their approach may be seen to be at odds or at least uncomfortable with current definitions of spirituality such as:

> Spirituality seeks to understand lived experience as it actually occurs, as it actually transforms its subject toward fullness of life in Christ, that is, toward self-transcending life integration within the Christian community of faith.
>
> Spirituality is characteristically involved in the study of individuals: texts, persons, particular spiritual traditions . . . elements of spiritual experience discernment, interrelations of factors in particular situations such as the mutual relation of prayer and social commitment, concrete processes such as spiritual direction.[59]

And:

---

53. McCarroll et al., "Assessing Plurality in Spirituality Definitions," 44, www.wlupress.wlu.ca.
54. McCarroll et al., "Assessing Plurality in Spirituality Definitions," 43.
55. Emmons, *Psychology of Ultimate Concerns*, 6.
56. Puchalski et al., "Improving the Spiritual Dimension of Whole Person Care," 643.
57. MacKinlay, *Spiritual Dimension of Ageing*, 76.
58. McSherry and Smith, "Spiritual Care," 118.
59. Lescher and Liebert, introduction to *Exploring Christian Spirituality*.

The term spirituality in Islam is . . . not separable from the awareness of God and from a life lived according to His Will. Thus, the principle of Oneness (*al-tawheed*, or unity) should be taken into consideration in any study of spirituality in Islam. In Islam only God stands as the very basis of life; without God nothing can exist and function properly. That's why everything in Islamic civilization, including the health sciences, has come from this fundamental statement.[60]

In response to this diversity, McCarroll et al. proposed a five-part typology as a methodological indicator for further research.[61] This was also seen as demonstrating the inchoate nature of the field. The typology of spirituality may be known practically, phenomenologically, linguistically, and in subjective experience, or it is an unknowable mystery.[62] With respect to this McCarroll et al. noted both positives and negatives. On the positive side they suggested that the five perspectives provide a way for ongoing dialogue and understanding the reasons and necessity for plurality. On the negative side, they observed that the tolerant pluralism implied in them easily leads to relativism and nihilism and to the possibility of spiritualities that are ultimately destructive being invited to persist because they appear to offer some consistency or appear to be part of an integrated meaning-making system.[63]

A similar criticism may be applied to the virtue-related pluralisms already discussed. It does not take much imagination also to see how pluralistic approaches to morality could result in vices that detract from well-being being valorized as virtues. The significance of these problems would vary from practitioner to practitioner and would be greatly influenced by the nature of the faith or ideology they represent.

The Way Forward

The question that now needs to be asked is "How does one go forward in a diversity in which the most generous and well-intentioned definitions and construals of virtue and spirituality are invariably complex, contested and even conflicted?" Two offerings are considered. The first is by McCarroll et al.,[64] the second is by Miroslav Volf.[65]

McCarroll et al. propose an approach informed by George Grant and Simone Weil.[66] This is equally applicable to considerations of virtue. Their proposal is to think

---

60. Isgandarova, "Islamic Spiritual Care in a Health Setting," 88.

61. The methodology adapted for this was the approach to the typology of Christian theology by Hans Frei. See Frei, *Types of Christian Theology*. Frei, *Theology and Narrative*.

62. McCarroll et al., "Assessing Plurality in Spirituality Definitions," 49–53.

63. McCarroll et al., "Assessing Plurality in Spirituality Definitions," 53–54.

64. McCarroll et al., "Assessing Plurality in Spirituality Definitions," 53–54.

65. Volf, *Flourishing*. The roots of this book lie in the *Faith and Globalization Seminar* taught in its early stages (2008–10) by Volf and former British Prime Minister Tony Blair at Yale University.

66. McCarroll et al., "Assessing Plurality in Spirituality Definitions," 54.

about multiplicity within a larger whole of love rather than of tolerance. This was presented as a means to remain open to plurality and resist falling into an "anti-ethical relativism."[67] They argued that the impact of the collapse in the modern West of the horizon of the eternal (the Good, God, love) had resulted in "the manifestation of human freedom as an unbridled will to power, conditioned by nothing outside of itself, except vague notions of supposedly contractual societal values."[68]

Arguing that the ideal of tolerance is premised upon the flawed beliefs that humans are good, the self is the center of the universe, and that all perspectives are equally relevant and true, they argued against the idea that all selves should be allowed to coexist within a contractual agreement based on this ideal. They saw this as impossible. Instead they argued for the conceptual retrieval of the Good that is beyond being, the content of which is love and by which the existence of being is a manifestation of that love and is that for which human beings have been fitted.[69] In summation, they argued that love, thus construed, provides the content of the whole within which plurality can healthily exist. This is an understanding of love within a framework centered on openness, receptivity and attentiveness to "otherness" and opposition to tyranny in all its forms.[70]

Volf argued for the place of the world religions in a globalized world.[71] Concluding that the majority of adherents of the world religions are exclusivists and globalization is not decreasing this,[72] he argued that exclusivism was not incompatible with pluralism.[73] Instead of requiring universalized definitions of virtue and spirituality, which threaten belief systems with dilution and syncretism, he argued that a more realistic approach is to encourage an informed embrace of the benevolence often foundational to those systems.

Volf also argued that world religions share two important features. The first is the view that human flourishing reaches beyond the "natural" desires for health, prosperity, fertility and longevity into unseen orders that transcend mundane realities and have strong motifs "calling people to place their desires and enjoyments into a larger spiritual frame and find true joy primarily in love of God and neighbour."[74] The second is that they open people to transcendence. He argued that world religions also open people toward the whole of humanity, affirm the equal worth of all human beings, and teach that benevolence cannot stop at the boundary of one's in-group but must extend

---

67. McCarroll et al., "Assessing Plurality in Spirituality Definitions," 54.
68. McCarroll et al., "Assessing Plurality in Spirituality Definitions," 54.
69. McCarroll et al., "Assessing Plurality in Spirituality Definitions," 56.
70. McCarroll et al., "Assessing Plurality in Spirituality Definitions," 57.
71. Volf, *Flourishing*, ch. 3.
72. Volf, *Flourishing*, 141–44.
73. Volf, *Flourishing*, 151–55.

74. Volf, *Flourishing*, 169. Volf used the term *religion* in a manner that strongly overlaps with the definitions of *spirituality* in use here. His intention was to highlight the differences between spiritual belief systems and spiritual experiences.

to all human beings, outsiders as well as insiders.[75] It was therefore concluded that individuals and communities with differing views of virtue and spirituality could live together in an atmosphere of mutual good-will.

Conclusion

It is important that pastoral and spiritual care practitioners maintain at least a basic understanding of the emerging and complex issues raised in this paper. In particular, critical and discerning attention must be paid to identifying influences arising the contradictory and contested matrix of current and historical considerations within the psychological, sociological, philosophical, and theological dimensions of well-being and the associated issues of virtue and spirituality.

Practitioners must understand that neither they nor those they serve can or do occupy the whole matrix. This is so whether or not they are representatives or adherents of confessional, traditional, progressive or secular theologies, philosophies or ideologies. All are limited.

Failure to comprehend this risks naïve inclusivisms that may obscure unwitting exclusivisms. Such naivetés may arise from flawed conceptions of tolerance that unwittingly hinder the openness, receptivity and attentiveness needed for a true appreciation of the "otherness" of those they serve. This may then give rise to incoherent and contradictory misunderstandings in the practices of pastoral and spiritual care that impairs the ability of such practitioners to accurately deliver the spiritual comfort and consolations that those they serve may see as essential for their well-being.

Bibliography

American Psychiatric Association. *Diagnostic and Statistical Manual of Mental Disorders (DSM-5)*. Arlington: American Psychiatric Association, 2013.

Averill, James R. "Emotional Creativity toward 'Spiritualizing the Passions.'" In Snyder and Lopez, *Oxford Handbook of Positive Psychology* (1st ed.), 172–85.

Baltatescu, Sergiu. "Towards a Sociological Theory of Subjective Well-Being." Social Science Research Network Scholarly Paper. July 4, 2007. http://papers.ssrn.com/abstract=2196346.

Baril, Anne. "Virtue and Well-Being." In Fletcher, *Routledge Handbook of Philosophy of Well-Being*, 242–58.

Brown, Eric. "Plato on Well-Being." In Fletcher, *Routledge Handbook of Philosophy of Well-Being*, 9–19.

Campbell, Stephen. "The Concept of Well-Being." In Fletcher, *Routledge Handbook of Philosophy of Well-Being*, 402–14.

Cassell, Eric J. "Compassion." In Snyder and Lopez, *Oxford Handbook of Positive Psychology* (2nd ed.), 393–403.

---

75. Volf, *Flourishing*, 170.

Crisp, Roger. "Well-Being." In *Stanford Encyclopaedia of Philosophy*, edited by Edward N. Zalta, n.p. Stanford University, 2005. http://stanford.library.sydney.edu.au/archives/sum2008/entries/well-being/#2.

Deci, Edward L., and Richard M. Ryan. "Hedonia, Eudaimonia, and Well-Being: An Introduction." *Journal of Happiness Studies* 9 (2008) 1–11. doi:10.1007/s10902-006-9018-1.

Diener, Ed, ed. *Assessing Well-Being: The Collected Works of Ed Diener*. Social Indicators Research Series 39. Dordrecht: Springer Netherlands, 2009.

———, ed. *Culture and Well-Being: The Collected Works of Ed Diener*. Social Indicators Research Series 38. Dordrecht: Springer Netherlands, 2009.

Diener, Ed, et al., eds. *The Science of Well-Being: The Collected Works of Ed Diener*. Social Indicators Research Series 37. Dordrecht: Springer Netherlands, 2009.

Emmons, Robert A. *The Psychology of Ultimate Concerns: Motivation and Spirituality in Personality*. New York: Guilford, 1999.

Fletcher, Guy. *The Philosophy of Well-Being: An Introduction*. London: Routledge, 2016.

———, ed. *The Routledge Handbook of Philosophy of Well-Being*. London: Routledge, 2015.

Foucault, Michel. *Ethics: Subjectivity and Truth*. Edited by Paul Rabinow. New York: New Press, 1998.

Frei, Hans W. *Theology and Narrative: Selected Essays*. Edited by George Hunsinger and William Carl Placher. Oxford: Oxford University Press, 1993.

———. *Types of Christian Theology*. Edited by George Hunsinger and William Carl Placher. New Haven: Yale University Press, 1992.

Froh, Jeffrey J. "The History of Positive Psychology: Truth Be Told." *New York State Psychologist* 16 (2004) 18–20.

Gowans, Christopher W. "Buddhist Understandings of Well-Being." In Fletcher, *Routledge Handbook of Philosophy of Well-Being*, 81–94.

Haybron, Daniel M. *The Pursuit of Unhappiness: The Elusive Psychology of Well-Being*. 1st ed. Oxford: Oxford University Press, 2010.

Hendrick, Susan, and Clyde Hendrick. "Love." In Snyder and Lopez, *Oxford Handbook of Positive Psychology* (2nd ed.), 447–54.

Isgandarova, Nazila. "Islamic Spiritual Care in a Health Setting." In *Spirituality and Health: Multidisciplinary Explorations*, edited by Augustine Meier et al., 85–101. Waterloo, ON: Wilfrid Laurier University Press, 2006.

Kahneman, Daniel, et al., eds. *Well-Being: The Foundations of Hedonic Psychology*. New York: Russell Sage Foundation, 1999.

Kim, Richard. "Well-Being and Confucianism." In Fletcher, *Routledge Handbook of Philosophy of Well-Being*, 40–54.

Kraut, Richard. "Aristotle on Well-Being." In Fletcher, *Routledge Handbook of Philosophy of Well-Being*, 20–28.

Lauinger, William. "Well-Being in the Christian Tradition." In Fletcher, *Routledge Handbook of Philosophy of Well-Being*, 81–94.

Lescher, Bruce H., and Elizabeth Liebert. *Exploring Christian Spirituality: Essays in Honor of Sandra M. Schneiders, IHM*. Mahwah: Paulist, 2014.

Lopez, Shane J., and Matthew W. Gallagher. "A Case for Positive Psychology." In Snyder and Lopez, *Oxford Handbook of Positive Psychology* (2nd ed.), 3–6.

MacKinlay, Elizabeth. *The Spiritual Dimension of Ageing*. London: Kingsley, 2001.

Maslow, Abraham Harold. *Motivation and Personality*. New York: Harper, 1954.

McCarroll, Pam, et al. "Assessing Plurality in Spirituality Definitions." In *Spirituality and Health: Multidisciplinary Explorations*, edited by Augustine Meier et al., 44–59. Waterloo, ON: Wilfrid Laurier University Press, 2005.

McCullough, Michael E., et al. "Forgiveness." In Snyder and Lopez, *Oxford Handbook of Positive Psychology* (2nd ed.), 427–36.

McSherry, Wilfred, and Joanna Smith. "Spiritual Care." In *Care in Nursing: Principles, Values and Skills*, edited by Wilfred McSherry et al., 117–34. 1st ed. Oxford: Oxford University Press, 2012.

Meaningful Ageing Australia. *National Guidelines for Spiritual Care in Aged Care*. Melbourne: Meamingful Ageing Australia, 2016.

OECD. *OECD Guidelines on Measuring Subjective Well-Being*. Paris: OECD, 2013.

O'Keefe, Tim. "Hedonistic Theories of Well-Being in Antiquity." In Fletcher, *Routledge Handbook of Philosophy of Well-Being*, 29–39.

Peterson, Christopher, and Martin Seligman. *Character Strengths and Virtues: A Handbook and Classification*. Washington, DC: American Psychological Association / Oxford University Press, 2004.

Puchalski, Christina M., et al. "Improving the Spiritual Dimension of Whole Person Care: Reaching National and International Consensus." *Journal of Palliative Medicine* 17 (2014) 642–56. doi:10.1089/jpm.2014.9427.

Rand, Kevin L., and Jennifer S. Cheavens. "Hope Theory." In Snyder and Lopez, *Oxford Handbook of Positive Psychology* (2nd ed.), 323–34.

Robinson, Bob. "Foucault, Michel: Ethics." *Internet Encyclopedia of Philosophy*. http://www.iep.utm.edu/fouc-eth/.

Rychen, Dominique S. "Key Competencies: Meeting Important Challenges in Life." In *Key Competencies for a Successful Life and a Well-Functioning Society*, edited by Dominique S. Rychen and Laura Hersh Salagnik, 63–108. Cambridge, MA: Hogrefe and Huber, 2003.

Salagnik, Laura Hersh, and Maria Stephens. "Competence Priorities in Policy and Practice." In *Key Competencies for a Successful Life and a Well-Functioning Society*, edited by Dominique S. Rychen and Laura Hersh Salagnik, 13–40. Cambridge, MA: Hogrefe and Huber, 2003.

Seligman, Martin E. P. *Authentic Happiness: Using the New Positive Psychology to Realize Your Potential for Lasting Fulfillment*. New York: Free Press, 2002.

———. *Flourish: A Visionary New Understanding of Happiness and Well-Being*. New York: Free Press, 2012.

———. *Learned Optimism*. Sydney: Random House Australia, 1990.

Seligman, Martin E. P., and Mihaly Csikszentmihalyi. "Positive Psychology: An Introduction." *American Psychologist* 55 (2000) 5–14.

Seligman, Martin E. P., and Jane Gillham. *The Science of Optimism and Hope: Research Essays in Honor of Martin E. P. Seligman*. West Conshohocken: Templeton Foundation, 2000.

Shaver, Robert. "The Later British Moralists." In Fletcher, *Routledge Handbook of Philosophy of Well-Being*, 95–110.

Snyder, C. R., and Shane J. Lopez, eds. *The Oxford Handbook of Positive Psychology*. 1st ed. Oxford: Oxford University Press, 2002.

———. *The Oxford Handbook of Positive Psychology*. 2nd ed. Oxford: Oxford University Press, 2009.

Swanton, Christine. *Virtue Ethics: A Pluralistic View*. Oxford: Oxford University Press, 2005.

Tiwald, Justin. "Well-Being and Daoism." In Fletcher, *Routledge Handbook of Philosophy of Well-Being*, 56–69.

Tooby, John, and Leda Cosmides. "The Psychological Foundations of Culture." In *The Adapted Mind: Evolutionary Psychology and the Generation of Culture*, edited by Jerome H. Barkow et al., 19–136. New York: Oxford University Press, 1992.

Veenhoven, Ruut. "The Four Qualities of Life." *Journal of Happiness Studies* 1 (2000) 1–39.

———. "Quality of Life Research." In *21st Century Sociology: A Reference Handbook*, edited by Clifton D. Bryant and Dennis L. Peck, 254–62. Thousand Oaks: SAGE, 2006.

———. "Sociological Theories of Subjective Well-Being." In *The Science of Subjective Well-Being*, edited by Michael Eid and Randy J. Larsen, 44–61. New York: Guilford, 2008.

Volf, Miroslav. *Flourishing: Why We Need Religion in a Globalized World*. New Haven: Yale University Press, 2015.

Waterman, Alan S., et al. "The Implications of Two Conceptions of Happiness (Hedonic Enjoyment and Eudaimonia) for the Understanding of Intrinsic Motivation." *Journal of Happiness Studies* 9 (2008) 41–79. doi:10.1007/s10902-006-9020-7.

Watkins, Philip C., et al. "Furthering the Science of Gratitude." In Snyder and Lopez, *Oxford Handbook of Positive Psychology* (2nd ed.), 437–46.

Wills, Eduardo. "Spirituality and Subjective Well-Being: Evidences for a New Domain in the Personal Well-Being Index." *Journal of Happiness Studies* 10 (2009) 49–69.

World Health Organization. *The ICD-10 Classification of Mental and Behavioural Disorders: Clinical Descriptions and Diagnostic Guidelines*. Geneva: World Health Organization, 1992.

15

Moral Judgment
Where Christianity and Cognitive Science Intersect

ANTONIOS KALDAS

Introduction

ONE of the things that diminishes our sense of well-being is the feeling that justice is not being served.[1] When we see a flagrant criminal being allowed to commit crimes with impunity, with no one holding him accountable, we feel the world is not right and our peace and contentment are diminished. We believe that ultimately justice must be served, and if the criminal does not suffer consequences for their actions here in this world, they must surely suffer them in the world to come.

This disquiet is nicely depicted in a number of biblical passages, such as the parables of the Prodigal Son (Luke 15:11–32) and that of the Workers in the Vineyard (Matt 20:1–16). Like the older son and the early workers, we are apt to condemn quickly people who seem to us to cheat the system. Yet Christ certainly seemed quite amenable to cheating the system in this way, if these parables are any guide. The standard explanation usually provided for this is that mercy trumps justice, and love trumps all. That makes it sound as though God is being unjust in the name of love and mercy.

---

1. Many thanks to Jeanette Kennett, whose courses on topics of moral philosophy inspired this paper, and Mark Brett, Fr. Daniel Fanous and Samuel Kaldas for valuable feedback, corrections, discussion, and suggestions. Feedback from attendees of the *Mercy, Justice and Wellbeing: Interdisciplinary Perspectives* conference, Sydney College of Divinity, Macquarie Park, Australia, July 22–23, 2016, was also invaluable.

Do not call God just, for His justice is not manifest in the things concerning you. And if David calls Him just and upright, His Son revealed to us that He is good and kind. "He is good," He says, "to the evil and to the impious." How can you call God just when you come across the Scriptural passage on the wage given to the workers? . . . How can a man call God just when he comes across the passage on the prodigal son who wasted his wealth with riotous living, how for the compunction alone which he showed, the father ran and fell upon his neck and gave him authority over all his wealth? Where, then, is God's justice, for "while we are sinners Christ died for us"![2]

But perhaps if we dig a little deeper, we may find that the story is not quite so simple. What a person "deserves" depends a lot on factors like her circumstances, her intentions, and her capabilities. We would judge worthy of condemnation an adult in full command of her faculties who steals food from another, but perhaps we would judge her less harshly if she stole food because she was on the verge of starvation (or, *a fortiori*, her baby was on the verge of starvation). We would further temper our judgment if she were mentally disabled or suffered from schizophrenia or perhaps even severe uncontrollable kleptomania. This question of responsibility in relation to things like circumstances and capacity has been much studied from various angles, but the particular angle I would like to focus on in this paper is the question of how we—mentally healthy, unpressured human beings—make our moral judgments. How much of our moral judgments come from our own conscious and voluntary volition, and how much is imposed upon us by unconscious processes over which we have little or no conscious voluntary control?

There is a growing body of empirical evidence that our judgments generally, including our moral judgments, are heavily influenced by factors beyond our conscious, voluntary control. A few interesting examples: one study found that the adopted children of a parent with a criminal record are up to 4.5 times more likely to end up with criminal record themselves, than adopted children whose parents did not have a criminal record.[3] Another recent study found that judges drop their percentage of favorable judgments from 65 percent at the beginning of a session to zero by the end of a session.[4] After a meal break, the percentage jumps back to 65 percent. Small unconscious and unattended cues can change how you feel about someone, how you evaluate them, mostly without your realizing that they have.[5] For example, women are more likely to be positive toward a stranger if the stranger's face objectively resembles their partner, even when they are not consciously aware of the resemblance.[6]

---

2. St. Isaac of Syria, *Ascetical Homilies*, 51.
3. Beaver, "Genetic Influences."
4. Danziger et al., "Extraneous Factors."
5. Monahan, "I Don't Know It."
6. Günaydin et al., "I Like You."

PART G—THE MORAL COMPASS OF WELL-BEING

One might respond that this is not news. Parents famously worry about who their children hang out with, because they fear negative influences being brought to bear on the children's personality as it develops. And there is a thriving industry in advertising that finds ways to make you change your judgment of a product positively (if they want you to buy it) or negatively (if they want you not to vote for the opposition). And of course, we have all felt sorry for those who have "bad parents," and pitied both their genetic inheritance and their suboptimal upbringing. But all of this raises some profound questions for the concept of moral responsibility.[7] To simplify, there are three central questions I wish to address here:

- How much of my thoughts and behavior is conscious and voluntary, and how much is unconscious and involuntary?
- Am I responsible for my own moral judgments—and the thoughts and behavior that are built upon these judgments—if they are unconscious and involuntary, or even partially so?
- How should *insight* into the foibles of my own moral judgments affect my *practice* of moral judgment of myself or others?

It seems to me to be obvious that the manner in which our minds work (Q1) is substantially relevant to the other two questions. To answer Q1 we need to turn to cognitive science.[8]

---

7. There are some important questions I will *not* be addressing here, in spite of their interest and relevance. The question of whether we should consider our wills to be *just* what is conscious and voluntary, or whether we should include our involuntary inclinations and dispositions as being "my will" is a vexed one, and one I will only touch on superficially here. For my purposes, I will simply assume that one ought to be held culpably responsible for actions (or perhaps thoughts as well) that one consciously and voluntarily chose, and not for those that she did not consciously and voluntarily choose, although there will be some nuance later. Another aspect I will not explore here is the contrast between attributing praise and attributing blame. While there is an interesting literature on some of the differences in how we do these two things, it does not impact much on the gist of my arguments. I will therefore focus mostly on blame, but much that is said may also be applied to praise. Similarly, I will focus mostly on cognitions like moral decisions and moral judgments, although of course the actions that arise from such thoughts are also relevant. I will not be discussing here relative culpability of a person having an evil thought without acting on it as opposed to having the thought and acting on it. The question of moral realism is another one that I will not engage in this paper. I am happy to pin my colors to the mast and say that I am a moral realist (I believe that there are real, objective, mind-independent moral truths, and that moral truths are not merely relative), but I will not here try to justify this position. I will also not delve too deeply into what we mean when we speak of justice, mercy or well-being. Definition of the latter is particularly fraught with difficulties. I will just adopt a relatively simple and naïve definition where well-being consists in things like peace, contentment and flourishing.

8. "Cognitive Science" is an umbrella term for the multidisciplinary project of understanding the mind and brain. It encompasses disciplines including (but not limited to) computer science, linguistics, neurobiology, neurology, neuroscience, philosophy, psychology, and psychiatry. For a brief history, see Bechtel et al. ("Cognitive Science: History") and Simon ("Cognitive Science"). For the role of philosophy in this science, see Bechtel ("True Cognitive Science Discipline").

Libet and Wegner: All Is Unconscious

It is natural to attribute moral responsibility only where there is voluntary personal agency. How we understand this concept of personal volition continues to be a topic of considerable debate, encompassing, among other things, questions of "free will" (in which I will not engage here)—whether or not we have free will, and if we do, how it works. In the 1980s, a famous experiment conducted by Benjamin Libet poured fuel onto this fire.[9] In brief, Libet attached electrodes that measure the electrical activity of the brain to the heads of his subjects. In particular, he was looking for the telltale "readiness potential" (RP), a spike in electrical brain activity that accompanies the brain preparing itself to command the body to perform an action. He asked his subjects perform a simple action—flexing a finger or wrist—at a time of their own choosing. As they did so, they were asked to mark the exact time on a stopwatch at which they formed the conscious intention to make the movement. Perhaps surprisingly, the RP preceded the conscious intention by an average of 350ms. Libet interpreted his results as showing that the brain automatically and unconsciously makes the decision to move, and only after that do we tack on the conscious, voluntary experience of making a decision. If this interpretation is correct, then what we experience as free will might be just an illusion.[10]

If Libet is right, we have to rethink not only our understanding of human free will, but also our attributions of moral responsibility. If our voluntary decisions to act are really nothing more than deterministic brain activity with conscious experience "tacked on" as an optional extra, then I can no more blame a bully who steps on my foot for his actions than I can blame a rock for falling on my foot.

But the significance of these results (which have been replicated with many variations since) continues to be hotly debated, spawning a whole field of "Libet Studies." While some, such as Daniel Wegner, have built on Libet's work and extended his conclusions, many others have criticized these conclusions on a variety of bases, too numerous to go into here.[11] In fact, there appears to be a growing trend toward the

---

9. Libet, "Unconscious Cerebral Initiative."

10. This position is in many ways related to the eliminativism of Daniel Dennett (*Elbow Room*; *Consciousness Explained*) and others, whereby even our conscious experience is itself an illusion.

11. Wegner, "Mind's Best Trick," "Illusion of Conscious Will." The interested reader is referred to the commentaries immediately following Libet's original 1985 paper in *Behavioural and Brain Sciences*, and to recent contributions by Ananthaswamy ("Brain Might Not Stand"), Klemm ("Free Will Debates"), and Swinburne (*Free Will and Modern Science*; *Mind, Brain, and Free Will*). Two examples of recent work are the study by Schultze-Kraft et al. ("Point of No Return") which suggests that whatever the RP might signify, it is not an automatic action accompanied by a late experience of conscious volition, since it turns out that a subject is quite capable of consciously vetoing an action already in progress, and the study by Lush et al. ("Metacognition of Intentions"), which shows that subjects' metacognition about when they form an intention to move is quite variable, and may even be changed by mindfulness training. See also O'Connor's entry on "Free Will" in the online *Stanford Encyclopedia of Philosophy*.

realization that Libet studies do not in fact threaten free will (although it may still be challenged on other grounds, of course).

Hume and Haidt: "Reason Is the Slave of the Passions"

Libet was not the first person to wonder whether we voluntarily choose our own actions. The ancient Greek philosopher Plato, of course, famously argued that the good life consists in reason ruling the passions and desires,[12] and this view was predominant in many ethical worldviews that followed him. But roughly the same time, the Chinese philosopher Mencius (372–289 BCE) proposed that moral judgment was a matter of *feeling* rather than of *reason*.[13] The Apostle Paul struggled with our human inability to do the good that we choose (see below). And nearly three hundred years ago, philosopher David Hume famously argued that "reason is, and ought only to be the slave of the passions."[14] While it has been pointed out that Hume's view is somewhat more nuanced than that pithy phrase might suggest,[15] that idea that our moral judgments about our own actions or those of others stem from our emotions—usually thought of as being involuntary and beyond our conscious, rational voluntary control—is a troubling one.

Hume is classed as a Moral Sentimentalist. The early modern debate between Moral Rationalists on one side, and Moral Sentimentalists on the other,[16] has a counterpart today. In modern psychological discourse, *Moral Rationalism* is roughly the view that we make our moral judgments on the basis of "reason and rationality,"[17] and *Moral Sentimentalism* is an umbrella term for a constellation of views in which "our emotions and desires play a leading role in the anatomy of morality."[18] Rationalism and Sentimentalism do not neatly map onto the predicates "voluntary" and "involuntary" respectively. However, while rational thought processes can underlie subconsciously derived judgments, they tend mostly to be conducted consciously and voluntarily. Likewise, while desires and emotions ("sentiments") can of course be under voluntary control, most would agree that they generally do not *arise* voluntarily, although there always exceptions. The distinction I am interested in here in this chapter is between the conscious and voluntary on the one hand, and the unconscious and involuntary on the other.

12. See Plato, *Phaedrus*, 246a–254e, and *Republic* Book IV, 444c–e.
13. Seok, "Mencius's Vertical Faculties," 54–55.
14. Hume, *Treatise of Human Nature*, II.3.3.
15. Jacobsen, "Social Intuitionism," 220.
16. See the "Anti-Rationalist Arguments" supplement to Kaupinen, "Moral Sentimentalism." There is some controversy as to whether these labels are really accurate or even useful, but I will not engage in this debate here.
17. Nichols, "Psychopaths Threaten Moral Rationalism," 285. Nichols also lists some of the chief proponents of Moral Rationalism in recent times.
18. Kaupinen, "Moral Sentimentalism."

In modern times, since the 1980s in fact, the debate between rationalist and sentimentalist views has been reignited, with active proponents on both sides.[19] One of the most widely discussed models is the *Social Intuitionism* of Jonathan Haidt which he develops as a sentimentalist alternative to the predominant rationalist paradigm of modern psychology.[20] In summary, Haidt's *Social Intuitionist Model* (SIM) holds that our moral judgments do not arise out of moral reasoning, but out of influences both internal and external that lie outside of our conscious voluntary control. The role of moral reasoning is largely *post hoc*: to justify moral judgments to which we have already come by means other than reasoning. The real causes of our moral judgments arise from our automatic, heuristic cognitive processes (which Haidt calls "intuitions"),[21] which in turn are influenced by our social environments and past experiences.

Like Libet studies, this approach threatens our voluntary agency in coming to moral judgments. Unlike Libet studies, the threat comes not from eliminating conscious deliberation altogether, or making it an epiphenomenon that plays no causal role, but from relegating conscious deliberation to the secondary or supporting role of *post hoc* justification—Hume's view of reason as the slave of the passions, rather than their ruler. The complex interplay between reason and sentiment that SIM allows for is also important. Haidt's model includes, for example, influences that can alter one's moral judgments both from feedback reasoning by the subject, and from the reasoned arguments of other people.[22] So, it is important to note that Haidt's nuanced model is not just saying that our moral judgments are irrational. Rather, it is better understood as arguing for the recognition of a greater role for involuntary and unconscious processes in moral judgment, and their primacy—contrary to both contemporary rationalism and folk psychology—over the role of conscious, voluntary reasoning.

SIM has proved both popular and durable because it does indeed explain many things. It fits in quite well with a dual-process model of cognition, where there are System 1 processes that are quick, heuristic, automatic, involuntary and not under conscious control, and System 2 processes that are slow, rational, deliberate, voluntary and under conscious control.[23] While this model is by no means settled, it has proven remarkably fruitful and seems to have a great deal of explanatory power. SIM can be seen as one application of this kind of model to the area of moral cognition.

Increasingly today, a moral philosopher cannot ignore empirical evidence, but must often leave the traditional philosopher's armchair and spend some time in the laboratory. If we wish to know how we come to our moral judgments, we must take into account what we learn from cognitive science. Haidt himself lists a number of

---

19. Haidt and Bjorklund, "Moral Psychology," 185.
20. Haidt, "Emotional Dog"; Haidt and Bjorklund, "Moral Psychology."
21. Note that Haidt's use of the term "intuitions" differs in some important ways to the way it was used in the Early Modern moral debate.
22. Haidt, "Emotional Dog," 815, fig. 2.
23. Kahneman, *Thinking, Fast and Slow*.

studies in support for his SIM.[24] Significant empirical evidence has also been brought to bear in favor of the case for sentimentalism more generally.[25] Cullity reviews the relationship between empirical evidence and five central questions in contemporary moral philosophy where sentimentalism (e.g., SIM) has been applied.[26] He concludes that while caution is needed, by and large the empirical evidence has helped to support and refine aspects of sentimentalist theories.[27]

Complexity

But human beings are incredibly complex creatures, and it is unlikely that so intricate a process as moral judgment can be captured with a model as relatively simple as Haidt's SIM. To illustrate this point, I have created a syncretic model of moral judgment that takes SIM as its starting point, but incorporates many of the other significant ideas that have been discussed in contemporary literature (figure 1). As the reader can see, there are a number of factors that influence the way we are likely to make our moral judgments as we grow and develop (the "Moral Development" box, top). All these factors together provide the foundation for our moral cognition, which is also influenced by more immediate factors such as our intuitions, our reasoning and the interaction with others and the environment (the "Moral Performance" box, bottom). This model was developed some years ago. Today, I would modify it even further, adding in factors like the growing insights from *"4E" cognition* and the highly promising *predictive coding* paradigm. The four E's[28] are that cognition is embedded, embodied, enactive, and extended: our thinking is embedded in an environment and there is mutual influence in both directions; the whole physical body plays a strong role in our cognitions; thinking is intimately tied to action; and we sometimes extend our thinking beyond the brain, e.g., when we store some of our memories on electronic devices. Predictive coding[29] is a more complex model of how our brains think, in which the brain does not directly experience the outside world, but constantly creates an "inner model" of

---

24. Haidt and Bjorklund, "Moral Psychology."
25. E.g., Moll et al., "Morals and the Human Brain"; Young and Michael, "Investigating Emotion."
26. Cullity, "As You Were?"
27. For an interesting counterview, see Craigie ("Thinking and Feeling"), who is suspicious both of simple sentimentalism and of too-rapid dismissals of rationalism. Both authors counsel great caution in how empirical results are used. Newell and Shanks ("Unconscious Influences on Decision Making") argue that methodological errors have led to this emphasis on unconscious processes. And for a recent attempt to ground automatic, intuitive moral judgment in rational thought, see Sauer (*Moral Judgments*).
28. For a concise overview of 4E cognition, see Menary, "4E Cognition."
29. An excellent treatment of cutting-edge thinking on predictive coding is Clark, *Surfing Uncertainty*. A very readable broader overview of the current understanding of cognition overall is Eagleman, *The Brain*.

the world, which predicts what the world should be like, and constantly updates that model on the basis of the stream of incoming information from the senses.

The effect of these "updates" to my model would mostly be to increase the complexity of the model, adding more components and connections. It seems this is going to be the trend as we increase our understanding of cognition. So, while I make no strong claims about the validity of my rather underprepared model, I introduce it here merely to illustrate the point that our moral judgments are the end result of what is an incredibly complex process. Factors and influences are involved that are both immediate and reach back in time; both internal and external; both conscious and unconscious. The point is that a simplistic approach to moral judgment is likely to just get it wrong. Whether in judging our own thoughts and behavior, or in judging those of others, when we come to attribute praise or blame, great caution is in order.

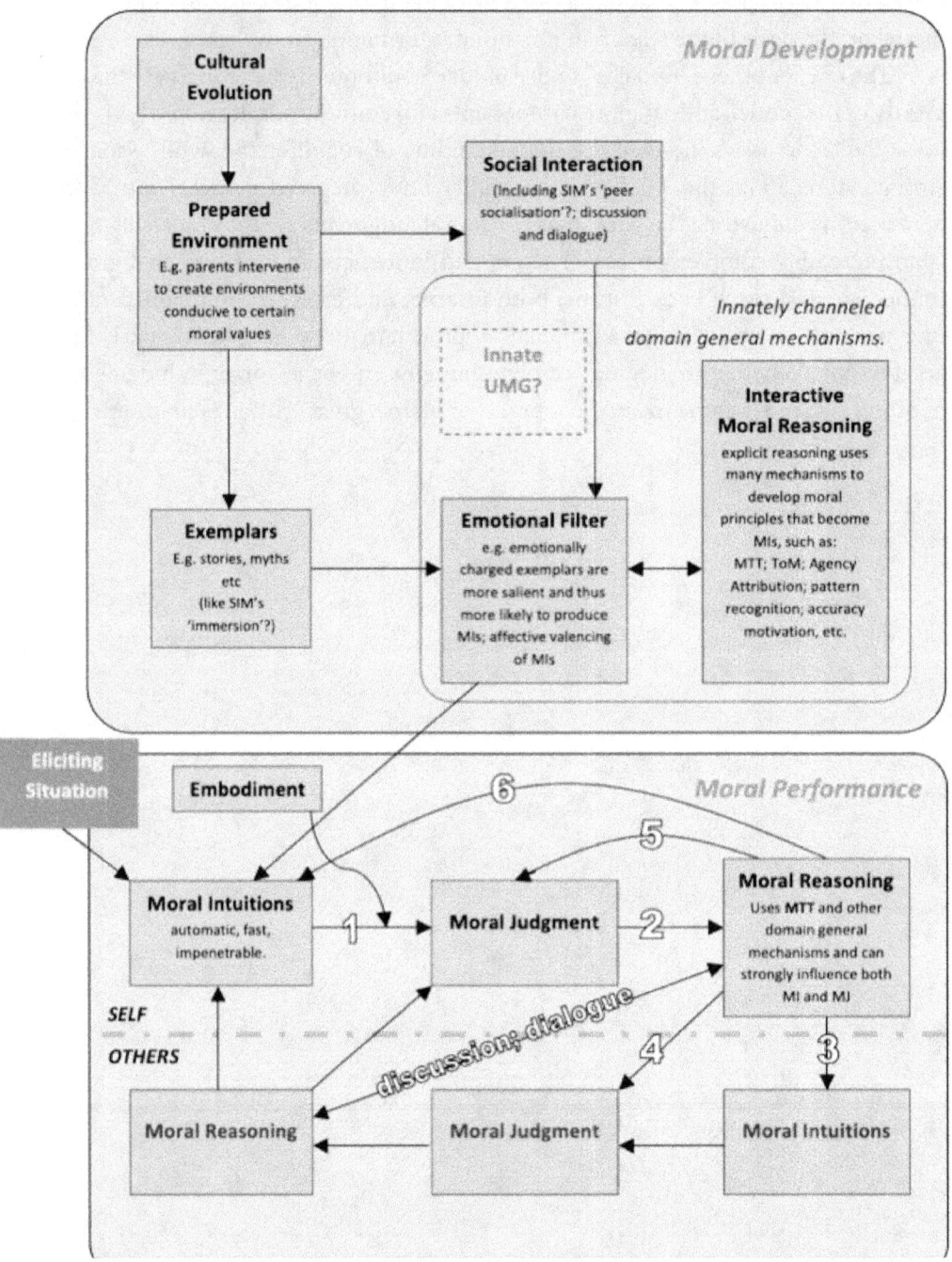

Figure 1. The author's syncretic model of moral judgement, illustrating the complexity of the process. The numbers in the "Moral Performance" box correspond to those in Haidt's SIM model, see Haidt, "The Emotional Dog," 8, figure 2.

Christian Responsibility

My complex syncretic model is mostly made up of factors, processes and influences that lie beyond the individual's voluntary rational control. So, does sentimentalism threaten the Christian concept of moral responsibility? If our moral judgments arise largely out of cognitive processes that lie beyond our conscious control, then how can we hold others truly responsible for their actions? How can we ourselves be held truly responsible for our actions? And how can we be held praiseworthy or blameworthy in the Christian sense?

One response to these kinds of questions is the relatively popular "reasons-responsiveness" approach of Fischer and Ravizza,[30] which bears some similarity to the compatibilist view of free will. Roughly, one acts responsibly just insofar as one's internal cognitive processes are unconstrained by external forces in their responses to moral questions. They distinguish between two kinds of control we can have over our actions: "guidance control" in which the agent performs an act freely; and "regulative control" in which the agent performs an act freely *and* could have done otherwise. They argue that guidance control is sufficient for the attribution of responsibility, even in the absence of regulative control. On this approach, it is still reasonable to attribute responsibility to an agent whose judgments and consequent actions are largely automatic and unconscious, since the unconscious processes are "acting freely," that is, without being constrained by external factors, at least in the moral performance phase, if not so much in the moral development phase. But this approach seems unsatisfactory. To see this, think of a robot vacuum cleaner that is programmed to sweep the floor without human control. If it bumps in to a coffee table and knocks over a cup of hot tea, spoiling an expensive pure white bearskin rug, would you hold it responsible? Would you blame it? Would you punish it? It seems ridiculous to think so, and yet, the vacuum cleaner certainly had "guidance control"—it was acting freely, carrying out its programming.

However, we may not need to try to rescue responsibility from automaticity just yet. A close inspection of models like SIM, or even the studies of Libet, shows that they do not completely excise the role of conscious, voluntary decision. On Haidt's SIM, three of his links represent the influence of one's own reasoning upon one's moral judgment. Link 5 is reasoning influencing one's own judgments directly, while link 6 is reasoning feeding back and influencing one's own intuitions, and link 3 is one's own reasoning influencing the intuitions of others, which in turn feed back to influence one's own intuitions and judgments. This feedback influence of reasoning is even more pronounced in my syncretic model, where the role of rational discussion and dialogue between subjects is also highlighted. At each of these connections, conscious, voluntary reasoning has the opportunity to take charge and direct the overall process of moral judgment in the direction it wills.

Even in Libet-style experiments, there is the possibility of consciously vetoing the action triggered by the RP. It could be argued that this is sufficient for moral responsibility. Regardless of how an impulse arises, it is how one voluntarily responds to that impulse that is relevant to moral responsibility. We did not hold the robot

---

30. Fischer and Ravizza, *Responsibility and Control*.

vacuum cleaner morally responsible for the damage it did to the beautiful rug, but if, hypothetically, the robot was capable of understanding the consequences of its programming, and capable of choosing to terminate that part of it that led to the accident but chose not to do so, we might then plausibly be justified in blaming it. It certainly seems plausible that many of our human impulses arise subconsciously and involuntarily, and that we ought not to be held morally responsible for their so arising. But we are responsible for voluntarily choosing to embrace an evil impulse, and following it through to action. As someone once put it, you are not responsible for a bird landing on your head, but you are responsible for letting it build its nest there.

The picture that emerges, then, is one in which moral judgments arise largely from unconscious, automatic processes, which are nonetheless subject—usually after they arise, but sometimes before—to conscious, voluntary reasoning. However, this reasoning may or may not be successful in taking control of the process. Its success will depend on the strength and resistance of the automatic processes as well as the strength of the reasoning processes. These two forces may of course be in harmony with each other, in which case they will serve only to strengthen each other. But if they are in opposition, then the outcome will be like a balance that can be tipped this way or that.

Well-Being

This idea of a balance of opposing forces within us impacts on our well-being, our ability to flourish and live a good life. I consider two important ways in which does. First, my well-being is compromised if I constantly judge myself to be morally bad. This is likely to happen if the involuntary processes in my mind override my voluntary will, and drive me to think or behave in ways that my voluntary mind rejects. Second, my well-being as a member of a community may be compromised if our involuntary moral judgments are delivering unjust assessments of others (or of myself by others). I consider each in turn.

Judging Myself

The famous passage in Paul's Letter to the Romans strikingly captures the apparently inescapable human cycle of repeatedly falling below even our own expectations of ourselves.[31]

> For we know that the law is spiritual, but I am carnal, sold under sin. For what I am doing, I do not understand. For what I will to do, that I do not practice; but what I hate, that I do. If, then, I do what I will not to do, I agree

---

31. This dilemma can also be found in the ancient Greek philosophical discussions of $ἀκρασία$ (*acrasia*), literally, a lack of command, lack of self-control, so that one acts in ways she does not really want to.

with the law that it is good. But now, it is no longer I who do it, but sin that dwells in me. For I know that in me (that is, in my flesh) nothing good dwells; for to will is present with me, but how to perform what is good I do not find. For the good that I will to do, I do not do; but the evil I will not to do, that I practice. Now if I do what I will not to do, it is no longer I who do it, but sin that dwells in me.

I find then a law, that evil is present with me, the one who wills to do good. For I delight in the law of God according to the inward man. But I see another law in my members, warring against the law of my mind, and bringing me into captivity to the law of sin which is in my members. O wretched man that I am! Who will deliver me from this body of death? I thank God—through Jesus Christ our Lord! So then, with the mind I myself serve the law of God, but with the flesh the law of sin. (Rom 7:14–25 NKJV)

It is not hard to see some of the principles of SIM in Paul's account here. The "other law in my members" sounds very much like the automatic unconscious and involuntary processes that govern much of our cognition and behavior. The conscious voluntary mind is sometimes surprised and even appalled ("Who will deliver me from this body of death?"). It often feels that there is no escape from this horrible thing that's going on inside me ("O wretched man that I am!").

But understanding the mechanisms involved in our moral judgments allows us to better deal with those mechanisms on a personal level. For example, everyone at least sometimes makes bad moral decisions that lead to behavior that is harmful both to the self and to others. If I understand that such judgments are not inevitable, that although they arise out of automatic processes, they are nonetheless susceptible to rational, voluntary conscious feedback and to the influence by my environment, I can voluntarily develop strategies along those lines to change my moral judgments, and therefore my behavior. This is a modern cognitive scientific account of what Christians usually call "repentance." To be clear, I am not here advocating that moral psychology is the only road to heaven, nor that cognitive scientists with an intricate understanding of brain mechanisms are the only people who can attain true repentance. Rather, I am suggesting that a holistic approach, one that synthesizes the spiritual with the scientific, is a more effective approach than one which sees spirituality and psychology as incompatible, perhaps even conflicting domains. If humans are creatures of both brains and souls, inextricably connected together, then any approach that ignores one or the other is less likely to succeed. I would argue that many tried and true traditions of spiritual practice that lead to repentance are based (unknowingly, of course) on the principles we have now uncovered through cognitive science.

An example of this kind of holistic approach is how well (I propose) it fits in with my preferred view of sin and repentance. The ancient Greek word for repentance, μετάνοια (*metanoia*) literally means to change or transform one's mind ("nous"), way of thinking, or one's "inner man." It carries the necessary idea of a change in the very character of one's nature, rather than a superficial change in how one behaves. Josh Glasgow has argued that we can sometimes find an insight into who we really are through these unwilled thoughts and actions.

> You might discover that though you wished you had a desire to be nice to your colleague, every fiber within you actually wants to tell him off for some terrible thing he did. Or you might find yourself feeling romantic towards someone who is not your monogamous partner. Sometimes such unbidden desires reveal hidden aspects of ourselves—that we aren't the pure sweeties we thought we were, or in happier surprises that we are braver or kinder or nobler than we had previously thought.
>
> But other times, unbidden desires, thoughts, motives, and behaviors are not revealing our "deep" or "real" or "true" selves. This seems possible on any plausible story of what the real self is. Such desires and thoughts are alien to us; we are alienated from them. For many of us, this is how implicit biases appear.[32]

Few Christians, I would hope, would believe that healing from physical illness is a matter solely for the grace of God. While most Christians understand that the healing ultimately comes from God's intervention, we also understand that such intervention most often occurs through more mundane or natural means: through the natural history of a disease, or through medical therapies. Only the most fanatical extremist would forego life-saving medication for her diabetic child in favor of fervent prayer! What I propose here is the application of the same principle to diseases of the soul. Prayer and more mundane. On this view, then, repentance goes far beyond merely changing one's outward behavior. It involves a change in the intrinsic disposition or the very character of the person at the deepest of levels, the way one thinks and reacts and sees the world—who you are. Integrating this understanding with the SIM (or my own development of it, above) is thus quite simple. The spiritual process of repentance can be characterized as a process of voluntarily bringing to bear those factors that will produce the required change in one's "nous," one's whole character and way of thinking. That involves changing not *just* the rational mind, but also one's exemplars, emotional patterns, reactions, intuitions, social interactions and even one's environment, to optimize the possibility of change for the good. It now becomes apparent why mere "will power" is insufficient for true repentance, why in Paul's words, "the good that I will to do, I do not do; but the evil I will not to do, that I practice." It is not enough to will to good. So many other things must change if my will is to bear the good fruit that it desires. But this also reinforces the Christian view of free will. While sheer will is often inadequate for true and permanent repentance, the will can nonetheless, when equipped with a better understanding of how our minds work, and

---

32. Glasgow, "What Are We Responsible For?"

together with the grace of God, reorganize those factors that are in its power to induce true and permanent repentance.

Some Christians may object that this leaves an inadequate role for the grace of God, that true and permanent repentance comes only through that grace, and not through our own efforts. But on the view of repentance I have described above, sin is a variety of sickness or disease, albeit illness of the moral sense or soul rather than of the physical body. Varying therapies are not in conflict with each other, but in fact, go hand in hand. Trusting in the love of God leads us to use the brains he gave us to deal with our problems. Understanding the mechanisms of cognition and how to manipulate them only increases our adoration of the One who designed them. This is the venerable Christian principle of συνεργεία (*synergy*): the divine and the human wills working together. The complex model presented here in fact highlights the many avenues open to God to exert his influence upon the life and spiritual and moral development and behavior of an individual.

Judging Others

This understanding can also produce a more compassionate approach to others, especially those we are more liable to judge for their bad actions. If we apply the answer to Q1, i.e., that our thoughts and behaviors are not purely (or even perhaps mostly) the result of conscious, voluntary processes, to Q2, we find that we are more likely to take into account this extenuating circumstance and be more forgiving of those who do wrong. And if we apply the answer to Q1 to Q3, we find that understanding how we ourselves come to our moral judgments puts us in a better position to apply more conscious voluntary control over those moral judgments, and hopefully thereby minimise our unjustified negative judgments.

Does this approach mean we are sacrificing justice in favor of mercy? I don't think so. If we apply it to the parables of the Prodigal Son and the Workers in the Vineyard, mentioned above, it becomes easier to understand that what seem initially to be unjust decisions by the Father / Master are in fact profoundly just. If we understand that humans are not to be held responsible for their actions *simpliciter*, but for their actions *given their circumstances*, we see much to admire in the penitent Prodigal Son who ultimately had the courage to voluntarily overcome his intuitively selfish tendencies and swallow his pride, and return shame-faced to his father. We also see that the workers who were called at the eleventh hour yet worked faithfully in the time allowed to them to work, were just as deserving of their denarius as those who toiled the whole day. An ancient principle of Stoic philosophy comes to mind here: *"it is not what happens to you that matters, but what you do with it."* True justice occurs when we take into account both the voluntary and involuntary factors that led to a behavior, rather than just considering the behavior as an isolated event.

This also makes sense of Christ's words on the cross: "Father, forgive them, for they do not know what they do" (Luke 23:34 NKJV). If SIM is right, and the soldiers and others involved in the tragedy of the Crucifixion were largely being driven by unconscious and involuntary intuitions and social and environmental pressures, then they really didn't know what they were doing. That is not to say they had no voluntary control of their actions, but it does mean that they are significantly less culpable for their crimes than we might at first be tempted to think.

This principle has widespread applications in our own world where the same evil that led to the Crucifixion continues to wreak havoc today. Is it possible to feel compassion for terrorists, rapists and psychopaths? On the one hand, if we understand that much of what they have done was not their own conscious choice, we are more able to adopt a Christ-like attitude of forgiveness. Of course, I am not here absolving such criminals from all responsibility, nor taking a deterministic view of moral responsibility on which no one is truly responsible for any of their actions whatsoever. What I am saying is that the mechanisms of moral judgments (and therefore of the actions that stem from them) are far more complicated than folk psychology would have us believe, and understanding this complexity means understanding how hard it is for any person, even a terrorist, to deal with it, especially without the right kinds of insights and guidance. On the other hand, understanding that our own revulsion and desire for revenge or retribution arise out of our own emotional and automatic intuitions is the first step to controlling those responses and redirecting them in a more loving direction.

What is more, it also helps us adopt more compassionate and loving attitudes toward non-Christians. Consider Paul's assessment of the noble Gentile.

> For when Gentiles, who do not have the law, by nature do the things in the law, these, although not having the law, are a law to themselves, who show the work of the law written in their hearts, their conscience also bearing witness, and between themselves their thoughts accusing or else excusing them) in the day when God will judge the secrets of men by Jesus Christ, according to my gospel. (Rom 2:14–16 NKJV)

This can be read as accepting the involuntary factors in a person's life as an "excuse" for their moral judgments and consequent behavior. For Paul, it is God alone who is aware of all the factors that have led to the Gentile's behavior, and quite justly, God takes all these factors into account in his judgment of that person. This is a highly nuanced approach, one that implicitly rejects simplistic "black and white" views of the human condition. If we care about seeing the world through the eyes of Christ, it behoves us to develop the same tolerance for nuance.

Another interesting consequence that falls out of adopting something like a SIM of moral judgment is that it sheds light on the nature of moral (and other) disagreement. Why is it that people seem so reticent to alter their moral judgments, even in the face of incontrovertible rational evidence that contradicts them? And why is it that peer pressure is so effective in altering moral judgments, even in the absence of rational evidence? SIM explains these phenomena nicely. Impenetrable heuristic automatic intuitions will be little influenced by rational argument, while social pressure brings to bear powerful emotional motivations that influence the moral judgment process from its base. An interesting related application is the field of Christian apologetics. It has been my experience over the years in talking with many atheists, agnostics, Muslims, Buddhists, and Christians with doubts that the vast majority of people do not come to their faith positions through a process of conscious reasoning. Rather, one's faith position can more accurately be traced to their upbringing, social environment, emotional experiences, and so on. However, once arrived at, the faith position is justified by bringing to bear all the reasoning resources available to the subject. Understanding this helps us to understand why reason-based dialogues between people of different faith positions rarely change those positions. On the other hand, it also explains why the Christian evangelistic method of *loving* people into faith (rather than *reasoning* them into faith) works so well. Love works at many levels of the mechanisms of cognition, whereas reason works at relatively few.

On a broader level, a society that has more mutual understanding is one that is kinder and more compassionate, which is conducive to the well-being of all. It is far less likely to fall into lamentable patterns of mass behavior like racism, demonization of minorities, and so on. For example, there is ample evidence for the role of unconscious processes—even basic biological dispositions—in something as apparently completely voluntary as our political views. Subjects who have strong revulsion reactions to disgusting images consistently tend to be more conservative in their political views.[33] While the significance of findings such as these are up for debate, they are strongly suggestive that what we take to be completely free and rational judgments (e.g., political views) may be less under our rational control than we think. Such knowledge ought to make us go back and rethink our political views, and perhaps weed out these unconscious influences and bring them more into line with our consciously affirmed principles. Dare we hope that such an approach might bring about more compassionate attitudes if it were adopted by people who have views that are racist, xenophobic, etc.?

On the topic of crime and punishment, Greene and Cohen have argued that as our understanding of the neuroscience of moral judgment improves,[34] it is likely to lead to a more compassionate society. Rather than intuitively or emotionally reacting to crimes and criminals, and seeking retribution, we should become more sympathetic to the factors beyond their control that led them to become criminals, and seek to heal them rather than punish them. While this approach is susceptible to abuse,[35] so

---

33. Ahn et al., "Nonpolitical Images."
34. Greene and Cohen, "Neuroscience Changes Nothing."
35. C. S. Lewis ("Humanitarian Theory of Punishment," 147) argued that a "humanitarian"

is any approach, given an evil enough will. But abuse aside, it certainly seems far more in harmony with the central Christian paradigm of unbounded love for all humanity, and especially for the worst of humanity.

Conclusion

In summary, then, the advance of knowledge about the automatic, involuntary and unconscious processes involved in cognition generally and in moral judgment specifically does not challenge the concept of free will, mysterious though that concept remains. Neither is it in conflict with the Christian view of moral responsibility, but serves only to enhance it by grounding the love and mercy inherent in the Christian Gospel. As we improve our understanding of human nature, we find ourselves better able to understand ourselves and our fellow human beings, and are led to a more merciful and just approach to both, that can only enhance our well-being.

Bibliography

Ahn, W. Y., et al. "Nonpolitical Images Evoke Neural Predictors of Political Ideology." *Current Biology* 24 (2014) 2693–99. http://doi.org/10.1016/j.cub.2014.09.050.

Ananthaswamy, A. "Brain Might Not Stand in the Way of Free Will." *New Scientist*, August 6, 2012. https://www.newscientist.com/article/dn22144-brain-might-not-stand-in-the-way-of-free-will/.

Beaver, K. M. "Genetic Influences on Being Processed through the Criminal Justice System: Results from a Sample of Adoptees." *Biological Psychiatry* 69 (2011) 282–87. http://doi.org/10.1016/j.biopsych.2010.09.007.

Bechtel, W. "How Can Philosophy Be a True Cognitive Science Discipline?" *Topics in Cognitive Science* 2.3 (2010) 357–66. http://doi.org/10.1111/j.1756-8765.2010.01088.x.

Bechtel, W., et al. "Cognitive Science: History." In *International Encyclopedia of Social & Behavioral Sciences*, edited by N. Smelser and P. Baltes, 2154–58. Amsterdam: Elsevier, 2001.

Clark, A. *Surfing Uncertainty: Prediction, Action and the Embodied Mind*. Oxford: Oxford University Press, 2016.

Craigie, J. "Thinking and Feeling: Moral Deliberation in a Dual-Process Framework." *Philosophical Psychology* 24 (2011) 53–71.

---

approach to justice is disastrous: "The 'humanity' which it claims is a dangerous illusion and disguises the possibility of cruelty and injustice without end. I urge a return to the traditional or Retributive theory not solely, nor even primarily, in the interests of society but in the interests of the criminal." In his fantasy novel *That Hideous Strength*, Lewis depicts this danger of abuse beautifully. When the evil empire takes over British society, they take control of the prisons and introduce a progressive approach that seeks to reform prisoners rather than punish them. But who is to decide when a prisoner is reformed? In effect, they have replaced a finite incarceration for punishment with a potentially endless incarceration for a reform that can always be argued to be incomplete. However, I take this argument to not really be an argument against replacing punishment with reform, but an argument against abusing a system for nefarious purposes.

Cullity, G. "As You Were?" *Philosophical Explorations* 9 (2006) 117–32. http://doi.org/10.1080/13869790500492730.

Danziger, S., et al. "Extraneous Factors in Judicial Decisions." *Proceedings of the National Academy of Sciences* 108 (2011) 6889–92. http://doi.org/10.1073/pnas.1018033108.

Dennett, D. *Consciousness Explained*. Boston: Little, Brown, 1991.

———. *Elbow Room: Varieties of Free Will Worth Wanting*. Cambridge: MIT Press, 1984.

Eagleman, D. M. *The Brain: The Story of You*. Edinburgh: Canongate, 2015.

Fischer, J. M., and M. Ravizza. *Responsibility and Control: A Theory of Moral Responsibility*. Cambridge: Cambridge University Press, 1998.

Glasgow, J. "What Are We Responsible For?" *The Brains Blog*, April 19, 2016. http://philosophyofbrains.com/2016/04/19/what-are-we-responsible-for.aspx.

Greene, J., and J. Cohen. "For the Law, Neuroscience Changes Nothing and Everything." *Philosophical Transactions of the Royal Society of London B* 359 (2004) 1775–85. http://doi.org/10.1098/rstb.2004.1546.

Günaydin, G., et al. "I Like You but I Don't Know Why: Objective Facial Resemblance to Significant Others Influences Snap Judgments." *Journal of Experimental Social Psychology* 48 (2012) 350–53.

Haidt, J. "The Emotional Dog and Its Rational Tail: A Social Intuitionist Approach to Moral Judgment." *Psychological Review* 108 (2001) 814–34.

Haidt, J., and F. Bjorklund. "Social Intuitionists Answer Six Questions about Moral Psychology." In *Moral Psychology*, vol. 2, *The Cognitive Science of Morality: Intuition and Diversity*, edited by W. Sinnott-Armstrong, 181–217. Cambridge: MIT Press, 2008.

Hume, D. *A Treatise of Human Nature*. Edited by E. C. Mossner. London: Penguin, 1985.

Jacobson, D. "Does Social Intuitionism Flatter Morality or Challenge It?" In *Moral Psychology*, vol. 2, *The Cognitive Science of Morality: Intuition and Diversity*, edited by W. Sinnott-Armstrong, 219–32. Cambridge: MIT Press, 2008.

Kahneman, D. *Thinking, Fast and Slow*. New York: Farrar, Straus and Giroux, 2011.

Kauppinen, A. "Moral Sentimentalism." In *Stanford Encyclopedia of Philosophy*, edited by E. N. Zalta. 2016. http://plato.stanford.edu/archives/fall2016/entries/moral-sentimentalism/.

Klemm, W. "Free Will Debates: Simple Experiments Are Not So Simple." *Advances in Cognitive Psychology* 6 (2010) 47–65. http://doi.org/10.2478/v10053-008-0076-2.

Lewis, C. S. "The Humanitarian Theory of Punishment." *AMCAP Journal* 13 (1987) 147–53.

———. *That Hideous Strength*. London: Pan, 1983.

Libet, B. "Unconscious Cerebral Initiative and the Role of Conscious Will in Voluntary Action." *Behavioral and Brain Sciences* 8 (1985) 529–39. http://doi.org/10.1017/S0140525X00044903.

Lush, P., et al. "Metacognition of Intentions in Mindfulness and Hypnosis." *Neuroscience of Consciousness* 1 (2016) 1–10. http://doi.org/10.1093/nc/niw007.

Menary, R. "Introduction to the Special Issue on 4E Cognition." *Phenomenology and the Cognitive Sciences* 9 (2010) 459–63. http://doi.org/10.1007/s11097-010-9187-6.

Moll, J. J., et al. "Morals and the Human Brain: A Working Model." *Neuroreport* 14 (2003) 299–305.

Monahan, J. L. "I Don't Know It but I Like You." *Human Communication Research* 24 (1998) 480–500. http://doi.org/10.1111/j.1468-2958.1998.tb00428.x.

Newell, B. R., and D. R. Shanks. "Unconscious Influences on Decision Making: A Critical Review." *Behavioral and Brain Sciences* 37 (2014) 1–19. http://doi.org/10.1017/S0140525X12003214.

Nichols, S. "How Psychopaths Threaten Moral Rationalism: Is It Irrational to Be Amoral?" *Monist* 85 (2002) 285–303.

O'Connor, T. "Free Will." In *Stanford Encyclopedia of Philosophy*, edited E. N. Zalta. Spring 2013. http://plato.stanford.edu/archives/spr2013/entries/freewill/.

Sauer, H. *Moral Judgments as Educated Intuitions*. Cambridge: MIT Press, 2017.

Schultze-Kraft, M., et al. "The Point of No Return in Vetoing Self-Initiated Movements." *Proceedings of the National Academy of Sciences* 113 (2016) 1080–85. http://doi.org/10.1073/pnas.1513569112.

Seok, B. "Mencius's Vertical Faculties and Moral Nativism." *Asian Philosophy* 18 (2008) 51–68.

Simon, H. A. "Cognitive Science: The Newest Science of the Artificial." *Cognitive Science* 4 (1980) 33–46. http://doi.org/10.1016/S0364-0213(81)80003-1.

Swinburne, R., ed. *Free Will and Modern Science*. Oxford: Oxford University Press, 2012.

———. *Mind, Brain, and Free Will*. Oxford: Oxford University Press, 2013.

Wegner, D. M. "The Mind's Best Trick: How We Experience Conscious Will." *Trends in Cognitive Sciences* 7 (2003) 65–69. http://doi.org/10.1016/S1364-6613(03)00002-0.

———. "Précis of the Illusion of Conscious Will." *Behavioral and Brain Sciences* 27 (2004) 649–59; discussion 659–92. http://www.ncbi.nlm.nih.gov/pubmed/15895616.

Young, L., and K. Michael. "Investigating Emotion in Moral Cognition: A Review of Evidence from Functional Neuroimaging and Neuropsychology." *British Medical Bulletin* 84 (2007) 69–79.

PART H

Well-Being and the Visual Arts

16

Seeing in New Ways
Justice, Mercy, and Social Well-Being through the Arts

Peter Mudge

Introduction: The Art of Mercy

IF I was to ask you (the reader) to associate a work of art with the theme of "mercy," which one would you nominate? Perhaps you might opt for one of the perennial favorites? Picasso's *Weeping Woman*; Rembrandt's *The Return of the Prodigal Son*; Goya's *The Third of May 1808*; Van Gogh's *Self-Portrait with Bandaged Ear*; Sieger Köder's *Home—the invitation poster* (for the Year of Mercy); Caravaggio's *The Seven Works of Mercy* (refer to figure 1 below); or even William Etty's *Mercy Interceding for the Vanquished*.[1] Or possibly you would choose a *different* artwork? All the aforementioned works are paintings. However, I want to devote this article to exploring a range of artworks on mercy and what they can teach us—ranging from paintings to sculpture and other media. This paper focuses on six artworks, each with a specific focus on mercy. In each case I reflect on a number of aspects related to mercy. I then place the artwork in conversation with Scripture, spiritual writers, philosophers, artists and many other sources, to see if any fresh insights emerge from that artwork.

The artworks examined in this paper, each accompanied by a specific "mercy focus," are as follows:

---

1. Websites on which you can view some of these images, all retrieved on 7/3/2016, are as follows: Picasso's *Weeping Woman*, http://www.pablopicasso.org/the-weeping-woman.jsp; Rembrandt's *Prodigal Son*, https://en.wikipedia.org/wiki/The_Return_of_the_Prodigal_Son_(Rembrandt). The reader can find other artworks by Google Image, searching the artist's name or the title of the artwork referred to throughout this chapter.

PART H—WELL-BEING AND THE VISUAL ARTS

1. *Jesus cures the woman with the flow of cash*, by Peter Mudge (2005)

    Focus: Mercy heals through the wound and the "bleeding"

2. Pope Francis—Image from his ministry of mercy (2013ff.)

    Focus: Jesus Christ is the face of the Father's mercy

3. *Come sit awhile*, by Gael O'Leary (2014)

    Focus: An Australian focus on mercy as listening

4. *Fish*, by Thomas Merton (1964)

    Focus: Mercy within mercy within mercy

5. *The Longest Journey*, by Anna Maria Pacheco (1994)

    Focus: Mercy as perilous journey

6. *Memorial for unborn children*, by Martin Hudáček

    Focus: Healing and mercy through the child that never was but still is

Figure 1. Michelangelo Merisi da Caravaggio, *The Seven Works of Mercy* (1607), Pio Monte della Misericordia, Naples. Image in the public domain.

Two Preliminary Issues—Seeing and Worldview

Looking Is Not Seeing

Many of the so-called powers often associated with art are not magical or mystical. They are often associated with privileged insight and "vision" depending in large part on what we see or don't see. The way that we see affects everything. Australian artist

Brett Whiteley has asserted, "The most fundamental reason one paints is in order to see."[2] As John Navone observes about "creation" in a broad sense, and parables in a more specific context,

> We, too, can begin to look on our creation the way Genesis depicts God as looking on all creation. When this begins to occur, delight rather than dissatisfaction becomes the lens through which all is perceived [and so] the spirit of chronic dissatisfaction is replaced by the spirit of the One who first looked on creation and pronounced it "good."[3]

The Purpose of the Parables

Jesus of Nazareth speaks about a related type of seeing and perceiving. In Matthew 13:10–13 he elucidates the purpose of the parables, where the word "art" easily could be easily substituted for "parables." In fact, artworks could be understood as parables embodied in the form of story, symbol, color, texture, movement and so on. In a sense, Jesus is asking us to employ the parables as lenses that facilitate a "seeing with the soul":[4]

> Then the disciples came and asked him, "Why do you speak to them in parables?" He answered, "To you it has been given to know the secrets of the kingdom of heaven, but to them it has not been given. For to those who have, more will be given, and they will have an abundance; but from those who have nothing, even what they have will be taken away. *The reason I speak to them in parables is that 'seeing they do not perceive, and hearing they do not listen, nor do they understand.'"* (NRSV, my emphasis)

In like manner, the French novelist Marcel Proust asserts that "the only true voyage of discovery, the only fountain of Eternal Youth, would be *not* to visit strange lands *but* to possess other eyes, to behold the universe through the eyes of another, of a hundred others, to behold the hundred universes that each of them beholds, that each of them is."[5]

In other words, the ultimate journey is to see differently, to see as another sees, and in the process discern entire new universes. Art, potentially, can invest us with that possibility. To see is actually to wake up, to pay attention, and thus "see" in a new light. Therefore, art is teaching us to see justice, mercy and social well-being in new ways, ways that hopefully are transformative.

---

2. Thomas, "In Dialogue with the Muse of Art History."
3. Navone, "Finding God and Ourselves in Parables," 43.
4. Shepherd, *Seeing with the Soul*.
5. Proust, *In Remembrance of Things Past*, vol. 2, ch. 2, 164.

Worldview

One of the most recent definitions of "worldview" and certainly one of the most useful for the fields of theology, ministry and religious education, has been provided by James W. Sire. Sire allows room in the ensuing quote to accommodate insights from the arts, from stories, and from the "being" part of the word "human being":

> A *worldview* is a commitment [a set of propositions or a web of beliefs], a fundamental orientation of the heart, that can be expressed as a story or in a set of presuppositions (assumptions which may be true or entirely false) which we hold (consciously or subconsciously, consistently or inconsistently) about the basic constitution of reality, and that provides the foundation on which we live and move and have our being.[6]

Sire's definition also echoes a text in Acts 17:27–28, in which Paul recounts how many people throughout history "would search for God and perhaps grope for him and find him—though indeed he is not far from each one of us. For 'In him we live and move and have our being'" (NRSV).

Mercy and art are continually present and interconnected, challenging our worldview. They tap into the fundamental orientation of our hearts. They are linked to stories. Both inform the ways in which we live and move and have our being. In the images and commentaries that follow my aim is to "dwell upon" six different but complementary artworks. I interrogate them in relation to the meanings they might contain and link them at the same time with passages from Scripture, mystical writings, and other texts.

One final caveat. The artworks that we examine below are trying to share their essential nature, insights or "worldview." They are not interested in whether you like them or not. They are trying to say: "Please come over here and have a closer look. I want to show you something that you haven't seen in quite the same way before, and that might transform your view of life." Then each artwork secretly hopes that you will feel, think, imagine and act yourself into a new way of "seeing" and "being."

---

6. Sire, *Naming the Elephant*, 141.

PART H—WELL-BEING AND THE VISUAL ARTS

The Art of Justice, Mercy, and Social Well-Being—Selected Works

Artwork 1: Jesus cures the woman with the flow of cash, by Peter Mudge (2005)

Focus: Mercy heals through the wound and the "bleeding"

Figure 2. Peter Mudge, *Jesus cures the woman with the flow of cash* (2005). Permission to reproduce image from the artist as author.

The first painting to be examined is one of my own. This work is housed in what I refer to as a "domestic gallery," in the possession of the Episcopal parish of Atlanta, Georgia, where it is often used there as an exemplar in its sermons and in other settings.

The woman with the flow of cash (the right-hand side figure) is vulnerable or wounded. The red color indicates that she is accustomed to regular bleeding. The root word behind "vulnerability" is the Latin *vulnus* meaning "wound." To be vulnerable is to leave one's wounds exposed. The wound is the site of both vulnerability and healing.[7]

7. Greenspan, "Vulnerability: The Power of No Protection."

Here are some details that are required in order to deepen your understanding of the painting. The work appropriates some background images and colors from icons such as the mountain to the left behind the figure of Christ, who is a figure taken from a Duccio painting, *The Calling of the Apostles Peter and Andrew* (1308/1311). The image of the woman on the right-hand side has been taken from Jan Vermeer's *Woman Holding a Balance* (or *Woman Weighing Gold*; ca. 1664). The woman also references another biblical woman with a flow of blood or hemorrhage, a pagan and outsider, afterward cured by Jesus (Mark 5:25–34). Jesus (from all ages in an ahistorical sense) is gesturing toward the woman who holds a credit card, stained on its right-hand side with blood as is her inner tunic (refer to figure 3). She is pregnant with avarice and consumption, looking with greater longing at "things" and "consumables" rather than "people."

Figure 3. Close-up detail of hand and credit card from figure 2 above.

Jesus gestures with compassion toward the woman. In some passages where Jesus responds with "compassion," such as in Luke 7:13 (the cure of the widow of Nain's son), where the original Greek verb is *splagchnizomai* (ἐσπλαγχνίσθη),[8] translated as "'have pity, feel sympathy': from the noun *splagchnon*, 'inward parts, entrails,' figuratively, of

---

8. Cognate: 4697 *splagxnízomai*—"from *splanxna*, 'the inward parts,' especially the nobler entrails—the heart, lungs, liver, and kidneys. These gradually came to denote the seat of the affections" (WS, 111). Retrieved on 5/14/2016 from: http://biblehub.com/greek/4697.htm.

the seat of the emotions, or in our common usage 'heart.'"[9] From a Jewish perspective, Louis Jacobs points out that "compassion" refers to feeling for another, for "the emotion of caring concern" with the post-biblical Hebrew word originating from the word *rehem*, "'womb,' originating in the idea of either motherly love or sibling love ... in biblical Hebrew *rehamim*."[10] Abarim Publications *Biblical Hebrew Dictionary* states: "The parent noun of our verb is the masculine רחם (*rhm*; pronounced as *rehem* or *raham*), meaning womb (Gen 49:25; Exod 13:12; Jer 20:17)."[11] Jesus' compassion reflects a key principal dominating the Year of Mercy in the Catholic Church: "The scandal of mercy excludes no one." Indeed, as James Keenan asserts, mercy is scandalous precisely because it excludes no one. Keenan defines mercy as "the willingness to enter into the chaos of another."[12]

Elsewhere in the painting, the woman touches a small table, a feature extracted from Andrei Rublev's *Trinity* also known as *The Hospitality of Abraham* (1411 or 1425–27) which acts as an action threshold. The table is marked by five red wounds referring to the passion of Christ and his *stigmata* (perhaps shared by the woman?). There is a dark shadow on the closer side of the woman's veil that resembles a hand of demonic possession.

I could refer to many other features—but I invite you to read the abovementioned passage from Mark, look at the painting, focus on mercy, and arrive at your own interpretations. I sometimes ask viewers (of all ages) of a particular painting to propose speech bubbles for each aspect of that painting (in this case Jesus, the woman, the card, the table, the mountain, etc.). What do you think Jesus is saying with respect to mercy? How does the woman respond—what type of cure is she requesting of Jesus?

A Hermeneutic of Aesthetics versus Anaesthetics

Like Jesus in this and other narratives of compassionate "encounter" (whether with tax collectors, lepers or prostitutes), the Jesus in this work is trying to open up a person or group to their full potential and reunite them with their family and community, and not close them down, isolate or condemn them.

Using modern parlance, we could say that this image challenges us to become people who champion "*aesthetics*" (the arts) and proscribe "*anaesthetics*" (for example, Brueggemann's lament about the dearth of poetry in a prose-flattened world).[13]

---

9. Source of Greek text insights: BAGD = Bauer et al., *Greek-English Lexicon of the New Testament*, 762–63.

10. Jacobs, "Compassion," 89.

11. *Abarim Biblical Hebrew Dictionary*, "רחם" (sense 1), retrieved on 5/15/2016 from: http://www.abarim-publications.com/Dictionary/r/r-ht-mfin.html#.Vzf3oTV97IU.

12. Keenan, "Scandal of Mercy," 1.

13. Brueggemann, "Poetry in a Prose-Flattened World."

We have the choice between freeing people and opening them up, or closing them down/shutting them out.

Sir Ken Robinson writes elsewhere on the same theme. His context is overuse of prescription drugs among young people in schools but his comments could be applied just as easily to myriad forms of other less detectable "drugs" such as passivity, overloading students with information, inappropriate uses of technology, the disappearance of leisure, an inability to take student experience and narratives seriously, missing connections with the actual world, and lack of praxis applications for topics taught in isolation:

> The arts are victims of this mentality. The arts especially address the idea of *aesthetic experience*. An aesthetic experience is one in which your senses are *operating at their peak*. When you are present in the current moment. When you are resonating with *anaesthetic* is when you *shut your senses off*, and deaden yourself to what is happening.... We are getting our children through education by anaesthetising them. And I think we should be doing the *exact opposite*, we should *not be putting them to sleep*. We should be *waking them up*, to what they have inside of themselves.[14]

The Silence of "Waiting Upon" the Painting

Like many great works by artists such as Vermeer, Caravaggio, Michelangelo, and others, this painting "freezes the action" at a crucial instant, at a time of *Kairos* or momentous decision. There is a silence in this painting, a space, a gap, a caesura. The work issues a demand to wait and pause awhile. It could be called an interval, a threshold, or type of "Sabbath." We need to "wait upon" rather than "wait for." We "wait for" a bus. But we must "wait upon" a person, mercy, forgiveness, or an artwork to reveal itself—perhaps when we least expect it.[15]

In her article "Waiting for Art," Elizabeth Buhe reflects,

> Spending time waiting does not arrest or accelerate perception, but rather *heightens* it. In everyday life, actuality is forever escaping our grasp—once we perceive something it is already past—already an artefact, a history. The same is not true in the museum [or art gallery] where, confronted by static objects [or even moving images], we are the ones with the agency to move. And we do move, until something captivates our gaze, entangles us. We choose to wait. What happens when these [artworks] grab a hold of our attention and keep us there—looking, waiting? These works, which unfold in front of the viewer's

---

14. Sir Ken Robinson, YouTube clip: *Changing the Education Paradigm*. RSA Animate, uploaded October 14, 2010. Clip dialogue taken from 5:50 to 6:32 mins. Retrieved 5/12/2016 from: https://www.youtube.com/watch?v=zDZFcDGpL4U (my emphases).

15. Refer to waiting upon God beyond the silence in Bentz, *Silent God*, 73–88.

eyes, pull the viewer into the object's temporal realm; this is a different conception of time.[16]

This chapter argues that contemplating or "dwelling upon" art in the context of one's life is one significant, yet underdeveloped, way not only of observing the interface between justice, mercy and social well-being but of cultivating each quality within one's life and community. As van Kaam and Muto have noted in relation to the spiritual life, which surely the arts feed into, the contemplative or "dwelling life" is characterized by "quiet, attentive listening to God . . . contemplative dwelling upon the word [leaving time] before God to drink in and savor the experience of his word coming alive in me. The fullness of my being meets the fullness of Divine Reality."[17]

In my view, this painting, as for others discussed throughout this chapter, returns us, not only to lost meanings of "waiting," "dwelling" and Sabbath, but to one of the fundamental meanings of mercy—and one linked to our own ethical behavior as well as the attributes of God. Mercy at its most basic level is that benevolence, mildness or tenderness of heart which disposes a person to overlook injuries. It looks for the very best a person can be and treats them better than they would otherwise be treated. Mercy is tempered by justice, it forgives all (seventy times seven). It is a difficult concept to define but is perhaps nearest in meaning to "grace." It implies all of but more than benevolence, tenderness, mildness, pity, compassion, justice and clemency.[18]

---

16. Buhe, "Waiting for Art," 118.

17. Van Kaam and Muto, *Am I Living a Spiritual Life?*, 44–45.

18. Based on the King James Version Dictionary definition of "mercy." Retrieved on 3/21/2016 from: http://av1611.com/kjbp/kjv-dictionary/merciful.html.

Figure 4. Close-up of hem of Jesus' garment and artist's signature from figure 2 above.

We sometimes believe that our definition of mercy is the best and is beyond dispute. However, this moralistic tactic, referred to in ethics as "the high moral ground," can be a dangerous one. "I am merciful and compassionate . . ." (e.g., toward refugees, substitute your own phrase). Inference—if you disagree with me: "You are not merciful, or at least not as merciful as me. In fact you could be cold hearted."[19] As such, it is an ethical game endeavouring to position superiority over inferiority.

Artwork 2: Pope Francis—Image from a Ministry of Mercy

Focus: Jesus Christ is the face of the Father's mercy

We now move to more contemporary reflections on mercy, this time through photography. Here we will briefly consider a photo of Pope Francis on the theme of

---

19. Refer to a thoughtful article on this topic by Razer, "Refugees Debate," retrieved on 5/15/2016. See also a good description of "high moral ground," retrieved on 5/15/2016 at ChangingMinds.org from: http://changingminds.org/techniques/resisting/high_ground.htm: "Morals define right and wrong. Talking about what is moral, thus is talking about what is right and wrong. *Taking the moral high ground* is to become almost unchallengeable. If you are morally higher than others, then you not only are right, but you can even *define* what is right. . . . When you take the high ground, it puts the other person into a moral double bind: if they argue against you, then they do not recognize what is moral."

mercy and align this with some of his statements on this theme. The image depicts Francis, as he was ending his weekly audience in St. Peter's Square on Wednesday, turning his attention to a man who suffers from neurofibromatosis (refer to figure 5).

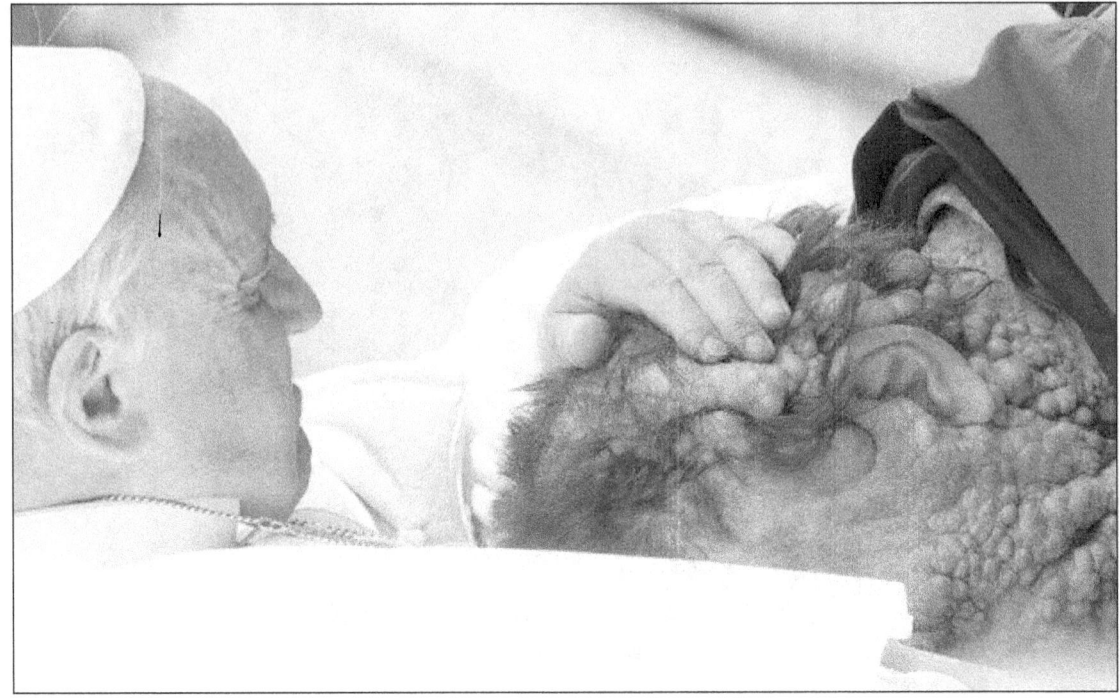

Figure 5. Pope Francis and his ministry of mercy to the marginalized (November 7, 2013). Photo: Claudio Peri. Copyright-free image.

In his *Bull of Indiction of the Jubilee of Mercy* (April 11, 2015), Pope Francis stated,

> Jesus Christ is the face of the Father's mercy. These words might well sum up the mystery of the Christian faith. Mercy has become living and visible in Jesus of Nazareth, reaching its culmination in him. The Father, "rich in mercy" (Eph 2:4), after having revealed his name to Moses as "a God merciful and gracious, slow to anger, and abounding in steadfast love and faithfulness" (Ex 34:6), has never ceased to show, in various ways throughout history, his divine nature.... Whoever sees Jesus sees the Father (cf. Jn 14:9). Jesus of Nazareth, by his words, his actions, and his entire person reveals the mercy of God.[20]

In the ensuing paragraphs he adds,

> The Church is commissioned to announce the mercy of God, the beating heart of the Gospel, which in its own way must penetrate the heart and mind of every person.... Mercy, once again, is revealed as a fundamental aspect of Jesus' mission. This is truly challenging to his hearers, who would draw the line at a

20. Pope Francis, *Misericordiae Vultus*, Bull of Indiction of the Jubilee of Mercy [hereafter MV].

formal respect for the law. Jesus, on the other hand, goes beyond the law; the company he keeps with those the law considers sinners makes us realize the depth of his mercy.[21]

Artwork 3: *Come Sit Awhile*, by Gael O'Leary (2014)

Focus: An Australian focus on mercy as listening

Come Sit Awhile is the title of the bronze sculpture of Catherine McAuley commissioned by the Sisters of Mercy Institute Leadership Team (refer to figure 6).

Figure 6. *Come Sit Awhile*, sculpture by Gael O'Leary (2014).
Used with permission of Sisters of Mercy, Australia and Papua New Guinea.

It was created by sculptress Gael O'Leary for the gardens of the Institute Centre at 33 Myrtle Street, Stanmore, New South Wales, Australia. Completed and installed in

---

21. Pope Francis, MV, 12 and 20.

October 2014, Gael hoped that the sculpture would "be an inspiration and beacon of hope and comfort to all who come to sit beside her."[22]

Here I would like to cite the words of Natalie Acton, currently the Mercy Ethos Educator with the Institute of Sisters of Mercy of Australia and Papua New Guinea, as well as a BBI/TAITE graduate:

> [Catherine McAuley] was a truly fine woman, very down to earth and inspirational. She was not very pious, was very practical, had a great sense of fun and was an astute businesswoman [skills from which] she brought into her religious life. She did not follow convention and ran a very egalitarian and empowering order—unusual for her time. Her spirituality was also very different- it was strongly influenced by Quakerism which meant among other things [that] she had a dexterity with scripture that is years ahead of her time both in terms of her knowledge and capacity to interpret it. She also had a love of silence, and saw God in everyday events and people, so she possessed a unique theological approach for people (let alone women) of her time.
>
> She was known as a very good listener. You will note that she is not in a habit—she did run her ministry as a lay woman for four years until pressure from the church and a desire to secure the future of the project meant that she needed to form a religious order. She didn't become a nun until she was 53 (something which she said that she never intended to do) and only lived to the age of 63 so spent most of her life as a lay woman.[23]

My own interpretation of this sculpture of Catherine is that she challenges some of the more prominent tropes of contemporary culture—including the endless preoccupation with noise, busyness, sport, fashion, social media, cooking and do-it-yourself shows, which in many ways encapsulate the three temptations that Jesus experienced in the desert, and moreover cautioned us to recognize in life: success, status and power (Mark 1:12–13 and parallels).[24]

Artwork 4: *Fish (or Christ Fish)*, by Thomas Merton (January 25, 1964)

Focus: *Mercy within mercy within mercy*

Thomas Merton (1915–68) once sanguinely observed, "Art enables us to find ourselves and lose ourselves at the same time."[25] This is the theme of kataphatic and

---

22. "Image and text used with permission of the Institute of Sisters of Mercy of Australia and Papua New Guinea"; part of email text from Natalie Acton received May 9, 2016.

23. Email sent to me on May 6, 2016. Image courtesy of Natalie Acton; commentary on image with thanks to Sue Manester, Mercy Ethos Administration Assistant, and from the same institute on the same date.

24. Rohr, *Radical Grace*, 294–97. In this series of reflections, Rohr uses the headings of success, righteousness, and control, along with certain synonyms, such as those cited in the text above.

25. Merton, *No Man Is an Island*, 35.

apophatic perception that we will return to several times in this paper. Merton was a writer and Trappist monk at the Abbey of Our Lady of Gethsemani in Kentucky, USA.

He has left us with many artworks, one of which is this image of a fish (refer to figure 7). It could be interpreted as a "Christ-fish," scratched out, blurred, and seemingly trodden upon, disfigured and afterward ignored. As such it could be read as a symbol of mercy, compassion and forgiveness—and thus key signs of God's reign as preached by Jesus.

Figure 7. Thomas Merton, brush drawing, Untitled (1964). Used with permission of the Merton Legacy Trust and the Thomas Merton Center at Bellarmine University.

Roger Lipsey comments that Merton's fish is an unpredictable one that swims against the current, moves into dangerous places, and is on some type of quest:

> Merton could be counted on to produce a lively school of Christian fish, and he does not disappoint. . . . The early work is jaunty and optimistic, slightly awkward, again full of promise. That sort of dynamism—energy large enough to swim against the current—was evident in Merton's art from start to finish.

Lipsey continues:

> As Merton gained mastery of the brush, he continued from time to time to explore the emblem of the fish in ways increasingly impressive. . . . This fish

is not one to cradle in safe places, nibbling dreams. It is a fish on the move, a questing fish.[26]

Biblical scholar Roger S. Boraas has noted: "Sometime in early church life, the figure of a fish took symbolic value as the sign of the Christ. The acrostic [where certain letters stand for longer phrases or words] derived from the Greek letters of the word 'fish' (*ichthys*) were understood to stand for the Greek words for 'Jesus *[i]* Christ *[ch]*, God's *[th]* Son *[y]*, Savior *[s]*' and the use of the symbol persists to this day in Christian iconography."[27]

In 1952 Merton wrote this passage in one of his journals, where he uses the name "Jonas" as God's address of intimacy for him:

> The Voice of God is heard in Paradise: . . .
> What was cruel has become merciful. What is now merciful was never cruel. I have always overshadowed Jonas with my mercy, and cruelty I know not at all. Have you had sight of Me, Jonas, my child? *Mercy within mercy within mercy.* I have forgiven the universe without end, because I have never known sin.[28]

Merton also composed many prayers of mercy, such as this one:

> Lord, have mercy.
> Have mercy on my darkness, my weakness, my confusion. Have mercy on my infidelity, my cowardice, my turning about in circles, my wandering, my evasions.
> I do not ask for anything but such mercy, always, in everything, mercy. . . .
> Lord, have mercy. Guide me, make me want again to be holy, to be a man of God, even though in desperateness and confusion.
> I do not necessarily ask for clarity, a plain way, but only to go according to your love, to follow your mercy, to trust in your mercy . . .[29]

One of Merton's favorite images for God was "a calm sea of mercy" (compare figure 8 below):

> [He] was convinced that the ultimate ground in which we all meet is that "Hidden Ground of Love" we call God. God can be named in many ways, yet God always remains a mystery that no words of ours can ever grasp. For

---

26. Lipsey, *Angelic Mistakes*, 44–45. Cited by Beth Cioffoletti at http://fatherlouie.blogspot.com.au/2007/02/growth.html.

27. Boraas, "Fish," 311.

28. Merton, July 4 reflection, "Mercy within Mercy," 194; originally published in Merton's journals, July 4, 1952, II. 488. The text also occurs in Merton's *Sign of Jonas*, 362. My emphasis.

29. Merton, "A Year with Thomas Merton," 247; originally published in Merton's journals, August 2, 1960, IV.28.

Merton the image of preference [for God] was Mercy. "God," he wrote, "is like a calm sea of mercy."[30]

This leads us into a distinctly maritime artwork of mercy but one, strangely enough, without a physical sea surrounding it.

Artwork 5. *The Longest Journey*, by Anna Maria Pacheco (1994)

Focus: Mercy as perilous journey

Perhaps the first observation you might make about this artwork (refer to full image of the sculpture at http://www.zimbio.com/pictures/0CsdNbmj2HP/32ft+Sculpture+Longest+Journey+Ana+Maria+Pacheco/xmkm4N9WeuX) is that it is a huge boat without a sea. The sea that should be there is only one that can be constructed by your imagination.

God Is a Sea

So, let us create one, a sea that is like God, courtesy of Blessed John of Ruysbroeck, a Flemish mystic who lived between about 1293/94 and 1381. He wrote in the Dutch vernacular, the language of the common people of the Low Countries, rather than in Latin, the language of the church liturgy and official texts, in order to reach a wider audience.

---

30. Shannon, *Thomas Merton*, 52. Other passages on mercy can be found in Shannon and Christine Bochen, *Thomas Merton*, 128, 148, 166, 172, 200, 300.

Figure 8. The ocean at Avoca Beach, Central Coast, NSW, with the Skillion, Terrigal in the background (July 2015). Photo by Peter Mudge.

Ruysbroeck has written a magical passage entitled "God is a sea":

> *This flowing forth of God always demands a flowing back; for God is a Sea that ebbs and flows,* pouring without ceasing into all God's beloved according to the need and the merits of each, and ebbing back again with all those who have been thus endowed both in heaven and on earth, with all that they have and all that they can. And of some God demands more than they are able to bring, for God is revealed as so rich and so generous and so boundlessly good. For God wishes to be loved by us according to the measure of God's nobility, and in this all spirits fail; and therefore their love becomes wayless and without manner, for they know not how they may fulfil it, nor how they may come to it.[31]

---

31. John of Ruysbroeck (Jan Van Ruysbroeck), *Adornment of the Spiritual Marriage*, ch. 40, 103–4.

"The Ship of Death"

Ana Maria Pacheco is a painter, sculptor, and printmaker who was born in Brazil in 1943 and has lived in England since 1973. She is best known for her ensembles of sinister life-size figures in painted wood which comment especially on male cruelty and arrogance. Her work deals with issues of control and the exercise of power, drawing upon the tensions between the old world of Europe and the new world of her Brazilian birth.[32]

Some commentators note that Pacheco's work is based on D. H. Lawrence's 1933 poem "The Ship of Death."[33] "'The Longest Journey' looks both lifelike and otherworldly, so it makes sense when Pacheco states that she is exploring exile[34] and hope, power and inspiration, fear and the unknown in her work."[35] It is an artwork that invites us to dwell upon its details and wrestle with its ethical implications.

Pacheco's sculpture includes a 32-ft. (9.75-m.) life-size polychromed wooden boat. The figures within the boat are bigger than life-sized and include five ethereal figures clothed in creamy white (angels, guardians, threshold figures?) and five ordinary human figures—are they lost passengers in a lifeboat, refugees, escapees from war or persecution? The artist seeks to ask these questions, not necessarily to answer them; or approve of or proscribe certain responses. The artwork is there to make you think, but before that, artists (as Picasso, Tolstoy and many others claim) are more concerned to make you feel.[36] Only one thing seems to be certain—the passengers are traveling on a "Ship of Death."

The artwork also wants you to look at faces, bodily positions, and gestures as a key to the artist's intentions. Why is the young boy standing in the middle (clearly a key position) without any pants. He is higher than the others, perched on a chair, while the man in the back left-hand corner gestures toward him—why? Is this arrangement associated for example with Jesus' words to his disciples in Matthew 18:3: "And [Jesus] said, 'Truly I tell you, unless you change and become like children, you will never enter the kingdom of heaven'" (NRSV).

One could ask many more questions—for art works, like the Jewish Jesus' parables are designed to provoke questions and conversation rather than answers and conversion. For example, is the cluster of white "communion" figures in the middle

---

32. This text retrieved on 4/22/2016 from: http://www.nationalgallery.org.uk/learning/associate-artist-scheme/ana-maria-pacheco. More details can be found in Chilvers, *Oxford Dictionary of Art and Artists*.

33. The full version plus a commentary on "The Ship of Death" was retrieved on 5/15/2016 from https://britlitwiki.wikispaces.com/theshipofdeath.

34. Refer to Fleming and Mudge, "Leaving Home."

35. From "Long Journey for Sculpture," by Anne Morris (May 31, 2012) retrieved on 5/15/2016 from: http://www.salisburyjournal.co.uk/leisure/entertainments/9737019.Long_journey_for_sculpture/.

36. Chloë Ashby, "These Artists Want You to Feel Something" (29.11.13), retrieved on 5/15/2016 from: http://www.thedailybeast.com/articles/2013/11/29/these-young-artists-want-you-to-feel-something.html.

of the boat meant to reference the Holy Trinity? Another angel looks into the depths of the sea while the last looks out across the surface of the sea—do they symbolize respectively the apophatic and kataphatic stances on knowing and spirituality? Many such questions are, in the end, unanswerable and are what educators, such as Gore and Harpaz, would call "problematic knowledge"[37] or an "undermining question"[38]—they have more than one answer, and those answers are often contradictory.

There are many ways to interpret this artwork and to associate it with numerous issues. Perhaps some will respond to this artwork by viewing the occupants as refugees or asylum seekers? One refugee named Qasim stated in the Australian Catholic Bishops' Conference statement of 2008, entitled "A Rich Young Nation":

> I want to feel the responsibility of being part of society . . . I don't want to be a burden on society. I have the ability to be productive, to build and participate. Why don't they give me a chance to use my abilities, and save the country from helping me? Why do they stop me from working, and doing all the other things that make me feel part of the society?[39]

Further on the Bishops ask us to engage in an act of remembering and humanity linked to mercy and justice:

> Imagine arriving in a new country after fleeing persecution and enduring a perilous sea journey and, even though according to United Nations conventions you have the right to seek asylum, you are left languishing for years in a detention centre. That has been the experience of many asylum seekers under Australia's immigration processing arrangements . . .
>
> Australian society as a whole needs to give more consideration to how we welcome the stranger. Many Australians have parents or grandparents who came to this country as strangers, which reminds us of our obligation to people who arrive on our shores, often vulnerable, traumatised and without resources.[40]

---

37. Jenny Gore asserts that "problematic knowledge" is present when "students are required to present or analyze alternative perspectives alternative perspectives; and/or solutions and to demonstrate how the construction of and/or solutions relates to their understanding of the task, . . . moreover this knowledge is not fixed as right/wrong." Courtois, "Quality Teaching Framework of Pedagogy," 13.

38. Harpaz ("Teaching and Learning in a Community of Thinking," 148) defines this as "an undermining question—a question that undermines the basic assumptions and fixed beliefs of the learners; casts doubt on the 'self-evident,' on 'common sense'; uncovers basic conflicts lacking a simple solution; and requires thinking about the roots of things."

39. Australian Catholic Bishops Conference, "Rich Young Nation," in *Building Bridges*, 242 (hereafter ACBC); citing Leach and Mansouri, *Lives in Limbo*, 90–91.

40. ACBC, *Building Bridges*, 242–43.

Artwork 6. Memorial for Unborn Children, Martin Hudáček (2010)

Focus: Healing and mercy through the child that never was but eternally is

As an art student, Martin Hudáček from Slovakia was moved to create a sculpture to draw attention to the devastation abortion can bring to the woman, and to the fact that through the love and mercy of God, reconciliation and healing are possible.

The sculpture shown here[41] reveals a woman (left figure) in great sorrow grieving her abortion. The smaller figure on the right is the aborted child, presented as a young child, who in a very touching, healing way comes to the mother to offer contact, relationship, and forgiveness.

Figure 9. Martin Hudáček, *Memorial for Unborn Children* (2010). Permission granted by artist.

Note that the artwork does not strive to adopt a moral position concerning the abortion—it simply seeks to show the viewer the aftermath of one event from different perspectives: the responses of mother and potential child, and the mercy shown by God through the child to the mother through a gesture of reaching out or even blessing (one of many possible interpretations). The artist appears to leave remnants of red

---

41. The image reproduced here is discussed at the LifeSiteNews.com site, dated April 2, 2012. It can be located at https://www.lifesitenews.com/news/heart-rending-young-slovakian-sculptor-captures-post-abortion-pain-mercy-an.

coloring within both figures, possibly to demonstrate the suffering associated with such a traumatic event and perhaps also to link the entire narrative with the Passion of Christ.

As much seems to be echoed in the artist's own commentary on the work. Martin Hudáček has noted that the sculpture "expresses hope which is given to believers by the One who died on the cross for us, and showed how much He cares about all of us." In like manner, Pope Francis has called the church to be and become an "oasis of mercy" in a wounded and violent world. He prefers to understand "mercy" in its present continuous tense as "mercy-ing"—as an ongoing and active outreach to others.[42] On October 21, 2015, Martin Hudáček gifted to Pope Francis a small replica of *Memorial for Unborn Children*.[43]

Conclusion

What Is the Point of Art? Is It "Useful" and "Effective"?

If someone offered you a set of teaching strategies, or a particular approach to pedagogy, that achieved some or all of the following, would you try to incorporate those into your school work, theological education or ministry? The assortment of claims made about this arts-based approach are:

1. They are languages that all people speak that cut across racial, cultural, social, educational, and economic barriers and enhance cultural appreciation and awareness.

2. They are symbol systems as important as letters and numbers. These pictorial systems teach us to wait and to be suspicious of "the one right answer."

3. They integrate mind, body, and spirit, and provide opportunities for every student to learn by processing materials in their own way.

4. They offer the avenue to "flow states" and peak experiences, but at the same time make students uncomfortable and unsure of any hasty certainties.[44]

5. They develop both independence and collaboration.

6. They help students to tell stories, connect with beauty and wonder, and understand civilization.

---

42. Quotes and ideas from Batlogg and Izuzquiza, "A Merciful Church for a Wounded World," 1.

43. Information about donation of replica to Pope Francis can be found at https://www.catholicnewsagency.com/news/with-a-childs-touch-sculpture-seeks-to-comfort-those-who-mourn-abortion-38799.

44. Note for example the words of UK artist Lucian Freud: "The task of the artist is to make the human being uncomfortable"; retrieved on 5/17/2016 from Donald Kuspit, "Uncensored Flesh," at http://www.artnet.com/Magazine/features/kuspit/kuspit8-19-02.asp.

7. They make it possible to use personal strengths in meaningful ways and to bridge into understanding sometimes difficult abstractions through these strengths.
8. They improve academic achievement—enhancing test scores, attitudes, social skills, critical and creative thinking.
9. They exercise and develop higher order thinking skills including analysis, synthesis, evaluation, imagination, "dwelling upon," and "problem-finding."
10. They are essential components of any alternative assessment program[45]—including an ability to provide balance between kataphatic and apophatic;[46] fast and slow thinking;[47] and a progression from instrumental to emancipatory and on to praxis and wisdom ways of knowing.[48]

This of course is a shorthand and necessarily selective list of a range of responses that the arts can elicit. To return to this section's opening heading: the impact of the arts cannot be understood in terms of economically driven categories such as "usefulness" and "effectiveness." The capacity of the arts to emancipate the human condition and help develop the full potential of the human being, like the values of justice, mercy and social well being themselves, can never be quantified. Perhaps it is only images that can convey the power of art. As the opening reflection on "seeing" and "worldview" argued, art can show us something "up front" but it has hidden and elusive levels that can only be reached through deeper insight and an attitude of "waiting upon." Authors such as Egan have described this dynamic in terms of connected kataphatic and apophatic ways of seeing or knowing.[49]

Kahlil Gibran (1883–1931) is another who has captured this twofold complexity: "Art is a step from what is obvious and well-known toward what is arcane and concealed."[50]

German artist Max Beckmann (1884–1950) notes something similar:

> What I want to show in my work is the idea which hides itself behind so-called reality. I am seeking for the bridge which leads from the visible to the invisible, like the famous cabalist who once said: "If you wish to get hold of the invisible you must penetrate as deeply as possible into the visible."[51]

---

45. The source of these insights is Dee Dickinson, 2012/1993, "Why Are the Arts Important?" (John Hopkins School of Education). Retrieved on 5/13/2016 from http://education.jhu.edu/PD/newhorizons/ strategies/topics/Arts%20in%20Education/dickinson_why_arts.htm; with some insights also from "What Is the Purpose of Art?" Quora.com, retrieved on 5/14/2016 from https://www.quora.com/What-is-the-purpose-of-art.

46. Mudge, "Towards a Reclaimed Framework of 'Knowing.'"

47. Claxton, *Hare Brain, Tortoise Mind*.

48. Mudge, "Four Ways of Knowing," unpublished paper (Baulkham Hills/Pennant Hills, NSW: Transformative Pedagogies/BBI, 2012).

49. Egan, "Christian Apophatic and Kataphatic Mysticisms."

50. Cited in Moss, *Art of Understanding Art*, 37.

51. Beckmann, *On My Painting*, 11–12.

PART H—WELL-BEING AND THE VISUAL ARTS

"The Artists Get There First"

Freud has famously quipped: "The artists get there first"[52]—they "see" reality and reveal "the truth of a situation" most honestly, imaginatively, and accurately, often before others do. This includes not just painting but also music, literature, dance, architecture, and many other forms. The associations between art, justice, mercy, and social well-being discussed in this chapter in relation to just six artworks would appear to support Freud's contention.

Figure 10. Peter Mudge, *Celtic Christ* (May 29, 2006). Permission of the artist.

Finally, as Cardinal Angelo Bagnasco has observed: "Justice and mercy either go hand in hand, each preparing the steps of the other, or they both limp along, groping in the

---

52. Quoted in Garber, *Visions of Vocation*, 69. Originally cited by Sigmund Freud.

fog."⁵³ Without the lens of art, as one important vehicle for revealing the depths of mercy, we too might limp and grope through the fog, instead of walking upright by the light of a Merciful God.

And so, we come full circle with these four key issues of art, justice, mercy and seeing. Without the light of a clear eye, providing the lamp of vision, all remains in darkness. As Jesus states in the Gospel of Matthew: "The eye is the lamp of the body. If your vision is clear, your whole body will be full of light. But if your vision is poor, your whole body will be full of darkness" (Matt 6:22–23 NRSV). If we can respond to justice, mercy and social well-being in this way through the arts, then perhaps we can cultivate the necessary conditions underscored in Psalm 85 for those whom we teach. This is a sacred place where:

> Mercy and truth are met together; righteousness and peace have kissed each other. (Ps 85:10 KJB)

Bibliography

Abarim Biblical Hebrew Dictionary. "סחר" [*rehem/raham*]. http://www.abarim-publications.com/Dictionary/r/r-ht-mfin.html#.Vzf3oTV97IU.

Aquinas, T. *Super Matthaeum.* Translated by Robert Busa. Turin: Marietti, Cap. V, l. 2. 195.

Ashby, C. "These Artists Want You to Feel Something." *Daily Beast*, November 29, 2013. http://www.thedailybeast.com/articles/2013/11/29/these-young-artists-want-you-to-feel-something.html.

Australian Catholic Bishops Conference. *Building Bridges: Social Justice Statements from Australia's Catholic Bishops, 1988 to 2013.* Alexandria, NSW: ACBC, 2014.

Cardinal A. Bagnasco. "Justice and Mercy." *L'Osservatore Romano*, January 14, 2009, 13–15.

Batlogg, A., and D. Izuzquiza. "A Merciful Church for a Wounded World." *Thinking Faith*, December 4, 2015. https://www.thinkingfaith.org/articles/merciful-church-wounded-world.

Bauer, W., et al. *A Greek-English Lexicon of the New Testament and Other Early Christian Literature.* 2nd ed. Chicago: University of Chicago Press, 1979.

Beckmann, M. *On My Painting.* London: Tate, 2003.

Bentz, J. *Silent God.* Kansas City: Beacon Hill, 2007.

Boraas, R. S. "Fish." In *Harper's Bible Dictionary*, edited by Paul J. Achtemeier, 310–11. San Francisco: Harper & Row, 1985.

Brueggemann, W. "Poetry in a Prose-Flattened World." Introduction to *Finally Comes the Poet: Daring Speech for Proclamation*, 1–11. Minneapolis: Fortress, 1989.

Buhe, E. "Waiting for Art: The Experience of Real Time in Sculpture." *Contemporaneity: Historical Presence in Visual Culture* 1 (2011) 117–36.

Chilvers, Ian. *The Oxford Dictionary of Art and Artists.* 5th ed. Oxford: Oxford University Press, 2015.

Claxton, G. *Hare Brain, Tortoise Mind: How Intelligence Increases When You Think Less.* New York: HarperPerennial, 2000.

---

53. Bagnasco, "Justice and Mercy," 13.

Courtois, E. "Introduction to the Quality Teaching Framework of Pedagogy." 2010. https://www.nesacenter.org/uploaded/conferences/SEC/2010/teacher_handouts/EstablishingaProfessionalLearningCulture-1.pdf.

Dickinson, D. "Why Are the Arts Important?" (2012/1993). http://archive.education.jhu.edu/PD/newhorizons/strategies/topics/Arts%20in%20Education/dickinson_why_arts.htm.

Egan, H. D. "Christian Apophatic and Kataphatic Mysticisms." *Theological Studies* 39 (1978) 399–426.

Fleming, D. J., and P. Mudge. "Leaving Home: A Pedagogy for Theological Education." In *Learning and Teaching Theology: Some Ways Ahead*, edited by Les Ball and James R. Harrison, 71–80. Northcote, Australia: Morning Star, 2014.

Francis, Pope. *Misericordiae Vultus, Bull of Indiction of the Jubilee of Mercy*. April 11, 2015. Rome: Holy See, 2015.

Garber, S. *Visions of Vocation: Common Grace for the Common Good*. Downers Grove: InterVarsity, 2010.

Garber, Z. "The Jewish Jesus: Conversation, not Conversion." *Hebrew Studies* 56 (2015) 385–92.

Greenspan, M. *Healing through the Dark Emotions: The Wisdom of Grief, Fear and Despair*. London: Shambhala, 2003.

Harpaz, Y. "Teaching and Learning in a Community of Thinking." *Journal of Curriculum and Supervision* 45 (2005) 136–57.

Jacobs, L. "Compassion." In *The Jewish Religion: A Companion*, edited by Louis Jacob, 89–90. Oxford: Oxford University Press, 2003/1995.

John of Ruysbroeck (Jan Van Ruysbroeck). *The Adornment of the Spiritual Marriage; The Sparkling Stone; The Book of Supreme Truth*. Translated by C. A. Wynschenk. Edited by Evelyn Underhill. London: Watkins, 1951.

Keenan, J. "The Scandal of Mercy Excludes No One." *Thinking Faith*, December 4, 2015. https://www.thinkingfaith.org/articles/scandal-mercy-excludes-no-one.

Lipsey, R. *Angelic Mistakes: The Art of Thomas Merton*. Boston: New Seeds, 2006.

Merton, T. *No Man Is an Island*. Boston: Shambhala, 2005.

———. *A Year with Thomas Merton: Daily Meditations from His Journals*. Edited by Jonathan Montaldo. New York: HarperOne, 2004.

Morris, A. "Long Journey for Sculpture." *Salisbury Journal*, May 31, 2012. http://www.salisburyjournal.co.uk/leisure/entertainments/9737019.Long_journey_for_sculpture/.

Moss, H. *The Art of Understanding Art: A New Perspective*. Illustrated by Peter Suart. London: Profile, 2015.

Mudge, P. "Four Ways of Knowing: Instrumental, Hermeneutical, Emancipatory and Praxis/Wisdom; A Proposed Model for Pedagogy, Teaching/Learning, Knowing, Assessment, Reporting and Evaluation, Abridged Version." Unpublished paper. Baulkham Hills / Pennant Hills, Australia: Transformative Pedagogies / BBI, 2012.

———. "Towards a Reclaimed Framework of 'Knowing' in Spirituality and Education for the Promotion of Holistic Learning and Wellbeing—Kataphatic and Apophatic Ways of Knowing." In *International Handbook of Education for Spirituality, Care and Wellbeing*, edited by M. de Souza et al., 611–29. Dordrecht: Springer, 2009.

Navone, J. "Finding God and Ourselves in Parables." *Human Development* 33 (2012) 43–48.

Proust, M. *Remembrance of Things Past*. Vol. 3, pt. 6, *The Prisoner*. Translated by C. K. S. Moncrieff and F. A. Blossom. New York: Random House, 1923 (French original), 1934 (English translation).

Razer, H. "Refugees Debate: Let's Not Use Compassion as a Self-Serving Device." *Guardian*, August 1, 2013. http://www.theguardian.com/commentisfree/2013/aug/01/australian-immigration-and-asylum-australia.

Robinson, K. *Changing the Education Paradigm*. RSA Animate YouTube clip, uploaded October 14, 2010. https://www.youtube.com/watch?v=zDZFcDGpL4U.

Rohr, R. *Radical Grace: Daily Meditations by Richard Rohr*. Edited by John Feister. Cincinnati: St. Anthony Messenger, 1995.

Shannon, W. H. *Thomas Merton: An Introduction*. Cincinnati: St. Anthony Messenger, 2005.

Shannon, W. H., and C. M. Bochen, eds. *Thomas Merton: A Life in Letters; The Essential Collection*. Oxford: Lion, 2009.

Shepherd, J. B. *Seeing with the Soul: Daily Meditations on the Parables of Jesus in Luke*. Louisville: Westminster John Knox, 2003.

Sire, J. W. *Naming the Elephant: Worldview as a Concept*. Downers Grove: IVP Academic, 2004.

Thomas, T. "In Dialogue with the Muse of Art History: Brett Whiteley." *Escape into Life*, January 15, 2017. http://www.escapeintolife.com/art-reviews/in-dialogue-with-the-muse-of-art-history-brett-whiteley/.

Van Kaam, A., and S. Muto. *Am I Living a Spiritual Life? Questions and Answers on Formative Spirituality*. Denville, NJ: Dimension, 1978.

www.ingramcontent.com/pod-product-compliance
Lightning Source LLC
Chambersburg PA
CBHW080727300426
44114CB00019B/2502